# DISCARDED

Richard Potter

# Richard Potter

## AMERICA'S FIRST BLACK CELEBRITY

## John A. Hodgson

UNIVERSITY OF VIRGINIA PRESS

*Charlottesville and London*

University of Virginia Press
© 2018 by John A. Hodgson
All rights reserved
Printed in the United States of America on acid-free paper

*First published 2018*

1 3 5 7 9 8 6 4 2

Library of Congress Cataloging-in-Publication Data

Names: Hodgson, John A., 1945– author.
Title: Richard Potter : America's first black celebrity / John A. Hodgson.
Description: Charlottesville : University of Virginia Press, 2018. | Includes
bibliographical references and index.
Identifiers: LCCN 2017030696 | ISBN 9780813941042 (cloth : alk. paper) |
ISBN 9780813941059 (e-book)
Subjects: LCSH: Potter, Richard, 1783–1835. | Magicians—United States—
Biography. | African American magicians—United States—Biography. | African
American entertainers—Biography. | Entertainers—United States—Biography. |
Ventriloquists—United States—Biography.
Classification: LCC GV1545.P65 H63 2018 | DDC 793.8092 [B]—dc23
*LC record available at* https://lccn.loc.gov/2017030696

*Cover art:* From Rannie broadside, 1810, "Nefi cos Box" advertisement.
(Courtesy of the New Bedford Whaling Museum)

For Owen, Claire, and Dylan

# Contents

# Illustrations

# Foreword

It's no sleight of hand to say that John Hodgson has written the definitive biography of the pioneering African American ventriloquist Richard Potter (1783–1835). It is a *fact,* whose time—at long last—has come. After all, Richard Potter came of age in the early years of the American republic, when the Founding Fathers walked the earth, and his travels took him to both sides of the Atlantic at a time when the notion of celebrity in the popular imagination was at a formative stage. One of the most captivating personalities in the history of his craft, Potter was, and remains, essential to the longer African American journey, yet his story has too easily been obscured—and misconstrued. With the publication of his pathbreaking book *Richard Potter: America's First Black Celebrity,* John Hodgson has, through painstaking research, helped to set the record straight on his subject's remarkable life and adventures. In doing so, he also treats readers to a fascinating look at the history of ventriloquism in early America.

A few quick, amazing facts about Richard Potter: he was born in Hopkinton, Massachusetts, in 1783, the last year of the American Revolution. Although the Commonwealth of Massachusetts would not officially outlaw the slave trade until 1788, emancipation was in the air and in the courts. The slaves Mum Bett (Elizabeth Freeman) and Quock Walker were suing for freedom under the state's new constitution, which stated, "All men are born free and equal, and have certain natural, essential, and unalienable rights."

Those rights didn't magically appear, and they could be stolen—a reality that Potter's mother, "Black Dinah," may have known firsthand. Dinah Swain was kidnapped during her childhood in Guinea. By her own account, she was poisoned by her captors with a lump of sugar dipped in rum. She was then brought to New England, where she became a slave of Sir Charles Henry Frankland, a tax collector for the Port of Boston. Richard was born to Dinah fifteen years after Frankland died in England, leaving his wife—and, later, son Henry—to manage the family's Massachusetts estate. Richard's father was a local white man named George Stimson, making Potter's surname a mystery.

One of six or possibly seven children, Potter appears to have received some schooling in Hopkinton before the age of ten. Some accounts state that he then sailed to Europe as a cabin boy and arrived in England, where he was enthralled by a Scottish magician and ventriloquist, John Rannie. As Hodgson suggests, Potter traveled to Europe around the age of sixteen, and began his career as an acrobat there, but did not meet John Rannie and his older brother James in Europe.

Potter returned to North America around 1803 and was back in Boston by 1807. In the interim he had begun apprenticing with John and then James Rannie and had acquired expertise as a magician and ventriloquist. The following year he married Sally Harris. They had two sons and a daughter; their first child, Henry, was killed in a wagon accident in 1816. When at home in Boston in those early years, Potter worked briefly for the family of the Rev. Daniel Oliver, and he honed his craft by entertaining the children around the fire. In 1810 James Rannie decided it was time to "hang up his cloak" and retire from public life to tend to the large tract of land he had acquired. When he did, he left his former apprentice with a virtual lock on the U.S. market. Potter wasted little time staking out his claim.

Thankfully, a few broadsides for his engagements were preserved. One of these (circa 1811), adorned with the Masonic symbol and a woodcut of a man communing with birds, previewed the show Potter would perform at a local ballroom. His stated purpose: "to give an Evening's Brush to Sweep away care." The first part of Potter's act would feature his magic, with "100 curious but mysterious experiments with cards, eggs, money, &c." In the second part of the show, the ad stated, "Mr. P. will display his wonderful but laborious powers of Ventriloquism. He throws his voice into many different parts of the room, and into the gentlemen's hats, trunks, &c. Imitates all kinds of Birds and Beasts, so that few or none will be able to distinguish his imitations from the reality. This part of the performance has never failed of exciting the surprise of the learned and well informed, as the conveyance of sounds is allowed to be one of the greatest curiosities of nature." Potter also performed what was known as a "Man Salamander" act for a few years, handling a red-hot bar of iron and immersing his feet in molten lead.

It's a wonder that Potter, throughout his career, seems to have steered clear of white America's fears that black magic lurked behind various slave revolts in their midst. For example, despite fears of a black conspiracy when a black man allegedly set fire to a Boston ship in 1817, Potter remained unscathed. Perhaps aware of his audiences' perceptions of otherness and identity, Potter, early in his career, advertised himself as "West Indian," and he later passed as white when touring in the South. Some accounts identified him as "colored" in the latter part of his career. This is one of the many important revelations in Hodgson's investigative biography.

Wherever Potter was, whatever he appeared to be, he exploited his otherness to add an allure to his fame. In this way, he prefigured such black performers as the fugitive slave Henry "Box" Brown and the great African American ventriloquist of the twentieth century John W. Cooper (1873–1966). Richard Potter died at age fifty-two on 20 September 1835, exactly 145 years before the fictional Harry Potter was born (1980, if you do the math in the Rowling books), and 39 years before that other famous Harry, Houdini, was born in Budapest, Hungary. Potter was buried in Potter Place, New Hampshire, under the headstone transcribed by the nineteenth-century black historian and abolitionist William Cooper Nell: *"In Memory of /* RICHARD POTTER, / The Celebrated VENTRILOQUIST, / *Who died / Sept. 20, 1835, / Aged 52 years."*

Now, in Hodgson's brilliant biography, Potter is brought back to life through the scholarly arts of careful research and reasoned judgment. *Richard Potter: America's First Black Celebrity* is a most wonderful study, and I commend readers to read it as if sitting in the audience of one of Potter's earliest stage shows. The thrill I felt in reading Hodgson's book—and, through it, discovering Richard Potter, the man and his times—was, in a word, *magical.*

*Henry Louis Gates Jr.*

# Preface

I came to Richard Potter quite by chance. I married into a New Hampshire family that had a connection to Andover, New Hampshire, and to one of the town's little village centers, Potter Place (the name, taken from local usage, had been given in the late 1840s by the new Northern Railroad to the small depot it built there). Richard Potter and his wife are buried close by, and Andover has always kept his memory alive. There is even a State of New Hampshire historical marker (number 54) on the nearest highway, noting that Potter Place "takes its name from Richard Potter, noted magician, ventriloquist, and showman," a "19$^{th}$ century master of the Black Arts." Thousands of such roadside markers stand all across the country, of course; Potter was to all appearances just another local-history figure. I soon picked up a little Richard Potter lore.

Over the years, as I devoted my attention to early nineteenth-century English and American literature and cultural history, I gradually came to appreciate, with growing enthusiasm, that a remarkable range of transformative American cultural developments and phenomena came together in Richard Potter's person and life. He was a slave's son who became the most famous and beloved performer in America, a black man who usually passed as white, even in the antebellum Deep South, and the first American ventriloquist. His relevance to the great movements of American life and culture in his era— historical, racial, cultural, performative, even literary (for ventriloquism, especially in the writings of Coleridge and Hazlitt, was becoming an important critical term and concept at this time)—seemed almost blindingly obvious. Richard Potter was a crucial and even seminal figure in American history. And he was almost unknown! So I decided to write a short article about him; I wanted to use him as an entry point for exploring how some of those historical and cultural forces intersected in early nineteenth-century America.

At first—this was back in 1992—I had only a vague, theoretical agenda: I thought that ventriloquism and race and passing and showmanship might reflect interestingly on each other in antebellum American culture, and I was curious to see where an investigation that tried to hold them all together might lead me. (I still remember how I distilled some of those intersections into a single, synoptic sentence: "Richard Potter was a black performer who passed as white by virtue of an act—ventriloquism—that had no color.") But my theoretical ambitions soon foundered on a very fundamental rock. I could theorize about and from Richard Potter all I liked, but I couldn't ground those theoretical arguments on much of anything, for the simple truth was that almost nothing about his life was known and that most of the wonderful, exotic stories told about him and his exploits were suspiciously pat, wildly contradictory, or demonstrably false. If I—or anyone—ever wanted to write anything meaningful that was based on Richard Potter's life, I—or someone—would first need to learn who he really was.

That quest has become my mission. I have sought to discover, as far as I possibly could, the essential facts of Richard Potter's life, the familial and social networks within which he lived, the nature and sources of his professional apprenticeships and training, the characteristics of his domestic life, the influences he exerted on American culture and society. My deepest scholarly obligation is to do this right, and to get it right—and, ideally, to tell Richard Potter's compelling and moving life story in a compelling and engaging way.

It gratifies me beyond words to anticipate that, once my work here is available and the real, historical Richard Potter (not the Richard Potter of credulous or calculating mythmakers) is finally accessible, scholars will be able to connect him to other famous (and not so famous) African American performers, to study how he fits into theories of passing and of playing with racial identities, and to incorporate him into arguments about critical race theory and performance theory, into histories of popular culture and itinerancy. I see this book as enabling all of those subsequent analyses and investigations, and many others.

But those various undertakings are not mine here. Indeed, I think I serve Richard Potter (and scholarship generally) best by maintaining my focus on the facts and story of his life rather than placing that story in the service of a particular critical theory or cultural emphasis. For too long, Richard Potter, despite his one-time fame, has been missing from the larger theater of American cultural and social history in which he figured so importantly. My objective is to correct that omission. I aim to make Richard Potter reappear; I want to give him, at last, a voice.

# Acknowledgments

When I began my research for this book, early nineteenth-century newspapers were accessible only in research libraries (for larger-circulation city newspapers) or local libraries (for town or village newspapers). Some were available on microfilm; others, only on micro-opaque cards; others, only in (typically incomplete) runs of original numbers held in a few libraries' collections. Realistically, the kind of research project I was undertaking would have required several lifetimes then. I was too naïve to realize this initially, however, or too stubborn to admit it; and even while I was beginning to pursue and refine my archival research, the very techniques of such research were evolving dramatically. So while I have visited scores of repositories and reviewed literally millions of documents (a great many of which have still not been digitalized today) in archives and libraries, I have also benefitted immeasurably from the advent of today's digital search systems and databases. I am profoundly indebted both to the archivists and librarians who have preserved and made accessible the documents and artifacts I have been investigating and to the new media projects—the American Newspaper Project, Readex, WorldCat, and other such "digital humanities" initiatives—that have revolutionized the pursuit of research projects such as this one.

Among the many libraries and archives where I have conducted my research, I am particularly grateful to the staffs of the library at Princeton University, my professional home for twenty years, whose Interlibrary Loan staff were invaluable to me; the New Hampshire State Archives, whose former director, Frank Mevers, and current director, Brian Burford, have helped me find early nineteenth-century legal files and records; and the Massachusetts Archives, where Elizabeth Bouvier, Head of Judicial Archives, several times helped me find early legal records for that state. I am also particularly obliged to the staffs at several other institutions—the New Hampshire Historical Society, the Boston Public Library, the Houghton Library and the Harvard Theatre Collection at Harvard University, the Sterling and Beinecke Libraries at Yale University, the Baker and Rauner Libraries at Dartmouth College, the

Manchester, New Hampshire, City Library, the Philadelphia Free Library, the Library of Congress—where I have conducted sustained research.

Some smaller libraries and archives have also proved to be crucial to my research, and I have been most fortunate in the help I received there. At the New Hampshire Antiquarian Society (now operating as the Hopkinton Historical Society), Nancy Jo Chabot has repeatedly provided important research support and even turned up a precious Richard Potter relic. At the Hopkinton, Massachusetts, Public Library, Linda Connelly guided me to Elias Nason's manuscript notes on the history of Hopkinton, which contained unique information about Richard Potter and his family. Also in Hopkinton, Linda Grant, of Faith Community Church (the successor to the First Congregational Church of Hopkinton), gave me access to the originals of the old First Congregational Church records, and Ann Click, Town Clerk, gave me access to originals of Hopkinton vital records. In Andover, New Hampshire, Pat Cutter of the Andover Historical Society pointed me to unpublished accounts of early Andover history that bear importantly on Potter's situation in his hometown. In New London, New Hampshire, Jim Perkins and Nancy Dutton of the New London Town Archives showed me a brief Richard Potter letter (fig. 7) that had never been known to any prior researcher. I offer my sincere thanks to them all.

Because of Richard Potter's involvement with Masonry, I determined that I needed to conduct research in various Masonic archives, too; here, again, I was most fortunate in my contacts. Allan Amman, of St. John's Lodge, Portsmouth, New Hampshire; Marlon Welch, of Triangle Lodge, Portland, Maine; and Jeremy Owen, of Blazing Star Lodge, Concord, New Hampshire, all welcomed me to examine their early Lodge records and educated me in aspects of Masonry pertinent to Richard Potter's life and times. Raymond T. Coleman, Grand Historian of Prince Hall Grand Lodge (PHGL), confirmed some details about Richard Potter's Lodge membership for me. Cynthia Alcorn, Librarian, Grand Lodge of Masons in Massachusetts, gave me guidance on the Prince Hall Grand Lodge archives and access to a microfilm of the PHGL records. In a related quest, Jim Bishop, former president of the St. Andrew's Society of Philadelphia (I had wondered if either of the Rannies might ever have formed a connection there when in Philadelphia), kindly gave me access to his group's early nineteenth-century records and hosted me during my visit.

Many people, too, have graciously poked through far-flung archives and answered queries for me that I could otherwise never have explored. I fear this list is far from complete, but I am grateful to the following for their help: Mark Bowden, Detroit Public Library; Mike Caveney, a distinguished professional magician who checked on the Richard Potter holdings in David Copperfield's International Museum of Magic and the Conjuring Arts for me; Jewell Anderson Dalrymple, Georgia Historical Society; Mary E. Fabliszewski, Peabody Essex Museum; Jim Folts, New York State Archives; Peter M. Griswold, Rhode Island Historical Society Library; Joanne Guggenheim, genealogist, Princeton, New Jersey; Elysia Hamelin, Haverhill Public Library; James L. Hansen, State Historical Society of Wisconsin; Jill Hughes, Albany County (New York) Archives; Ara Kaye, State Historical Society of Missouri; David Kessler, Bancroft Library, University of California, Berkeley; Charles D. King, Kenton County (Kentucky) Public Library; Eileen J. O'Brien, New York State Historical Association; Elizabeth Roscio, the Bostonian Society; Timothy Salls, New England Historic Genealogical Society; Jay Satterfield, University of Chicago Library; Ed Smoak, South Carolina Masonic Research Society; Mariam Touba, Reference Librarian, New York Historical Society.

Both magicians and ventriloquists tend to be interested—often deeply interested—in the histories of their arts and professions; and one of the great pleasures of this project has been the experience of meeting and learning from vibrant members of these artistic communities. I particularly want to thank, and to celebrate, Robert A. Olson, a wonderful magician who, beginning at Old Sturbridge Village in the 1970s, developed a magic act that is a historical reenactment of Richard Potter's, with feats drawn almost entirely from Potter's repertory. For decades, Olson has been re-creating Richard Potter's entertainments for audiences all around New England. Throughout that period, he has done more than anyone else to keep Richard Potter's name and reputation alive. I have also been privileged to swap research discoveries with the late ventriloquist Stanley Burns, author of *Other Voices: Ventriloquism from B.C. to T.V.,* edited by Dan Ritchard (2000) and Stan's gracious wife, Sylvia, and with ventriloquist Dan Ritchard, author of *Ventriloquism for the Total Dummy* (1987). All of these are among Richard Potter's most direct professional heirs.

Several friends and colleagues have given me valuable feedback on portions of this manuscript or on my ideas for it. I particularly thank James Engell and Henry Louis Gates Jr., both of Harvard University; Charles Rzepka, Boston University; and my daughter, Emily H. Anderson, University of Southern California, for their help and interest.

At Princeton University, two Deans of the College, first Nancy Malkiel and then Valerie Smith, annually provided research stipends that covered many of my basic research expenses. I am very grateful for their support and pleased to be able to show them here that it bore fruit.

Richard Potter

# Introduction

I

All his adult life, Richard Potter demonstrated a mastery of misdirection. He was a showman, so first and foremost he needed to call attention to himself: hence the flowing robe, the wig and costumes, the fine carriage and handsome matched horses, the life-sized, carved wooden human figures standing on pillars before his house, the fastidious dress and exemplary manners. But he was especially a magician and a ventriloquist—a sleight-of-hand, sleight-of-voice man—so he also needed to direct attention elsewhere: you were to see or hear what he could do, but you were not to understand how he did it.

He was very, very good at what he did. For many years he was the foremost ventriloquist in America, and the most celebrated magician as well. Indeed, he was the most famous American entertainer of any kind: there was no actor or vocalist or musician in the country who could even come close to Richard Potter's renown. It wasn't just secondhand fame, either, the kind that could be spread by stories from the daily newspapers of the large East Coast cities and republished as entertaining filler in the weeklies of remote little towns, rumors from a wonderful world that the provincial readers were unlikely ever to experience—George Frederick Cooke taking the stage in the role of Iago, the sea serpent again appearing off Cape Ann, the Pig of Knowledge doing arithmetic. While Richard Potter always made his home in New England, his tours took him across the length and breadth of the nation. Wherever you lived in America, even if you had not yourself attended at least one of his exhibitions, you probably knew people, perhaps even many people, who had. When he died, in 1835, he had become a national icon.

Fame comes in various flavors, of course. As a showman, Richard Potter could not expect to achieve the kind of recognition traditionally reserved for prominent politicians, military leaders, or eminent writers. Moreover, even the formal theater at this time still suffered some degree of disrepute across wide swaths of American culture; more populist forms of entertainment, like Potter's, incurred that kind of cultural condescension and disapproval to an even greater degree. Many Americans disapproved of such amusements in and of themselves, associating them with dissipation, frivolity, and "juggling" (knavish trickery), and many others who openly enjoyed them nevertheless felt that their professors were not entirely respectable. But enjoy those entertainments people certainly did; and Richard Potter himself contributed enormously to the long, gradual process of making American showmanship respectable.

Here, for example, is a review of his exhibition—in itself a rare tribute for an itinerant performer—that appeared in the Natchez *Mississippi Republican* in May 1821:

> Last evening, Mr. Potter, who stiles himself the Emperor of all Conjurors, made an exhibition of the astonishing powers he possesses.—His slight of hand tricks were performed with an adroitness superior to any thing of the kind we ever before witnessed. His recitations, songs, and mimicry were executed with taste, and in a natural manner; and he was wholly devoid of the affectation and rant too often used by public performers. We wished to witness some further samples of his powers of Ventriloquism—but what he did exhibit in that line, was excellent.
>
> Mr. Potter is modest, and has much of the gentleman in his deportment and manners.—Although we are far from advising the citizens of Natchez to waste their time and money in idleness and amusement, we in justice cannot refrain from exhibiting to the public our impressions in favor of this ingenious man, and declaring it as our opinion, that those, who can well spare their money, and are fond of amusement, by attending his exhibitions will not only aid in the encouragement of modest merit, but derive much pleasure to themselves.

The first business of this carefully nuanced tribute is to acknowledge Richard Potter's mastery of his profession, the "astonishing powers" of this "ingenious man." There is applause for his decorum and respectability as well:

he has shown himself to be a modest man, with gentlemanly deportment and manners. His "modest merit" is merit conjoined with modesty, the compounding of two virtues; those qualities, too rarely united, make him worthy of patronage.

But "modest merit" can also imply middling merit; and here the familiar note of antitheatrical condescension and social stratification begins to sound. Excellence and preeminence in a highly respectable field of endeavor are highly meritorious; in a less than fully respectable profession, however, their merit can be but modest. Similarly, to have much of the gentleman in one's deportment and manners is to be gentlemanly or gentlemanlike; that is not the same as being a gentleman. Our careful editor, in his own "exhibiti[on] to the public," is not simply attesting to and praising Richard Potter's merits as a performer and recommending Potter's exhibitions to his readers; he is also flattering those readers. Those of more modest means or frivolous inclinations who should not be "wast[ing] their time and money in idleness and amusement" need read no further, for this concluding recommendation is not intended for them; but those of comfortable means and with a taste for respectable and even wonderful entertainment would do well, both for themselves and for the performer, to catch his act.

Does this seem like faint praise? In fact it could hardly have been more favorable for Richard Potter. He wasn't seeking admission into Natchez's finer social circles; he was seeking paying customers. Who among his potential audiences in Natchez would not want to be thought of by his fellow citizens as one of comfortable rather than straitened means, with refined rather than frivolous leanings? Who might care to risk advertising his cramped circumstances, puritanical bent, sour temperament, or commonplace tastes by staying away—especially when the show promised to be highly entertaining, and attending it would confer a touch of *noblesse oblige*? Even the steep prices Richard Potter was charging in Natchez—a full dollar for a ticket (children would be admitted at half price)—would not be an obstacle once the value of admission became defined this way.

But the adroitness and ingenuity—ultimately, the misdirection—of Richard Potter's exhibition in Natchez was beyond even this discriminating editor's ken. Looking beyond the consistently excellent performance to the performer, he had carefully noted Richard Potter's good taste, natural and unaffected manner, and gentlemanly deportment, and had categorized him accordingly: an itinerant showman, yes, but an excellent one, and highly respectable. What he—a sophisticated, reportorial Mississippian, in 1821—had not noticed was that Richard Potter was a black man.

Richard Potter was not only the most famous American entertainer of his time; he was also the most famous black person in America. It was not a designation that he had sought. He was very aware of his racial status and very sensitive to the injustices and denigrations that in America inevitably attended it; he was deeply embedded, furthermore, within the black community of Boston and within a network of its black leaders who were working to bring their community's needs and concerns into the public eye. As an entertainer, however, he needed to keep his public persona apolitical and uncontroversial. He made his living by amusing and entertaining; as he knew full well and had often had occasion to confirm firsthand, he simply could not afford to fret his audiences (the vast majority of whom were white) or lose many of his venues by complicating his appeal with any allusions to his racial identity.

As a mulatto, the son of a black mother (formerly a slave) and a white father, Richard Potter appeared to others to be whatever they already understood him to be or anticipated he would be—a dark-complexioned white man, a light-complexioned black man, or perhaps a West Indian (i.e., Creole) or East Indian (Hindu). His wife's racial status and appearance were much the same (Richard even sported with his last assistant by intimating persuasively that his wife, Sally Potter, was a Penobscot Indian). Because he could be and so readily was taken to be white, then—witness that editor in Natchez—the assertion at the beginning of this section requires a qualification: although certainly Richard Potter at the height of his career was the most famous black person in America, it is also true that most of his audiences were not sure that he was black. They knew him firsthand as an amazing ventriloquist and magician; beyond that, they believed various things about him simply because they had been taught or encouraged to believe them.

Contrast this for a moment with the status of other well-known black Americans in the early years of the nineteenth century. The most famous black American at the opening of the century, Phillis Wheatley, was not even alive then; her youthful *Poems of Various Subjects Religious and Moral,* which had won her such attention and acclaim, had been published long before, in 1773, and she herself had died in 1784. Because of the international attention her book had won, her name was still familiar to many Americans; but her poetry, while still occasionally republished, did not circulate widely now, and it is safe to conclude that very few Americans had read it. Her continuing influence in American society came mostly from her usefulness as an exemplar in abolitionist texts.

The black American who in 1829–30 became for a while perhaps even more famous than Richard Potter was his African Lodge Masonic brother and very possibly his friend David Walker, whose powerful *Appeal to the Coloured Citizens of the World* (1829), a biblically grounded denunciation of slavery, called for blacks to resist it and whites to recognize its immorality. Walker's *Appeal* became an immediate sensation nationwide and provoked alarm and censorship throughout the South. It was widely read, and Walker particularly worked to introduce it surreptitiously into the South, where it might circulate among slaves. From this point on, most black Americans who gained a national reputation, such as Nat Turner, Frederick Douglass, Solomon Northrup, and Harriet Tubman, did so in the context of the struggle against slavery. For all of them, their blackness was an important reason for their fame.

Richard Potter is unique on this list by virtue—and this is a remarkable, even bizarre, fact to note, given his profession—of his very ordinariness. Put simply, he was not controversial; he was not a participant or an instrument in a grand societal argument, save for the old, familiar one about the value and respectability of theatrical entertainments. But more importantly than this, he was always, always associated in people's minds—often at a very impressionable age, for children made up large parts of his audiences—with laughter, mystification, and delight. His lifelong practice was to "sweep away care" for an evening by amusing, astonishing, and thrilling his audiences, making them laugh and wonder and give themselves over to the varied pleasures of his exhibition; he brought the gift of comic catharsis.

A tribute to Richard Potter published nearly forty years after his death (by an editor who firmly believed that Potter was "a native of the East Indies" and insisted that "his complexion had the marked brown tint peculiar to the Indiaman"—so "Black" in the passage that follows should be understood in the first place as evoking "black magic") gives a sense of the audience experience, recalling that "both old and young were wrought up to the greatest pitch of excitement" by Potter's magic tricks: "Among the ignorant the magician was known as '*Black*' Potter, and the most supernatural powers were attributed to him. He was said to be in league with the devil. Superstitious mothers would endeavor to frighten their children into obedience by threatening to give them to 'Black' Potter, but this ruse was robbed of any effect after the little ones once attended an exhibition of the magician, for they invariably came away delighted with the mysteries of the show and in love with the conjuror himself."

"Black" in its racial sense was often still there in the background of Potter's legend, of course, as it is in this 1874 recollection. But that is the point: in the background is just where Richard Potter was careful to keep it. He did not deny his racial identity, but neither did he, in his dealings with the public, foreground it. He did not care to be pinned down about his origins or "found out" by those who did not know him well. Those who persisted in such inquiries would eventually discover how very skillful his misdirecting could be—or, even better, would never even realize they had been fooled.

III

When Richard Potter moved his growing family from Boston to a new home in rural Andover, New Hampshire, in 1815, his personal background was a complete mystery to his new neighbors. He worked to keep it that way; the mystery suited his persona as a magician. Most of the still-continuing confusion and wildly fanciful speculation about his life story can be traced back directly to the bare personal facts he shared there, the vague hints he dropped, and the misconceptions he happily permitted. The resulting farrago of inconsistent and incompatible guesses about his past gave rise to wild theories and claims, untethered to any truth, which soon helpfully embellished the magician's reputation throughout New England.

Some of these rumors may have begun as the merest misunderstandings. For example, Stephen Fellows, who as a young man had served as Richard Potter's assistant during the last years of Potter's life, long afterward assured Silas Ketchum, the president of the New Hampshire Antiquarian Society, "that Potter told him this story in confidence": "that he was the son of a negro woman in Boston, and that Benjamin Franklin was his father. That the mother was a servant in a Boston family, and that, after the birth of his child, Franklin furnished her a home in a back street behind the State House, where Potter lived till he was ten years of age."

The story about Franklin is patently false, of course, as even a callow young man in rural New Hampshire could quickly have discovered: Benjamin Franklin was in France from 1776 until 1785, had not been in Boston since 1764, and was seventy-seven years old at the time of Richard Potter's birth in 1783. Still, there are grains of truth in this story that, in separate bits and pieces, Fellows might well have picked up at various times from Richard Potter. Potter had been born in Hopkinton, near Boston, on the grand estate of Sir Charles Henry Frankland (not Franklin), where his black mother was a servant; Frankland also owned a grand house in Boston itself. The Frankland/Franklin confusion is an easy one: indeed, a genealogist writing to the *New York Times* in 1910, lamenting the "increasing forgetfulness of Sir Harry [Frankland]'s story" in Hopkinton, noted with dismay that locals were now "calling the street where the old house stood Franklin Street instead of Frankland Street." Potter lived on the old Frankland estate until he was ten. And the Boston location "in a back street behind the State House," while quite wrong as a Frankland address, was in fact precisely where Richard Potter had lived in 1827, during a year's absence from New Hampshire, not long before Fellows began working for Potter. Ketchum speculates that Richard Potter might have told this story to Fellows "in one of his fits of humor, to parry enquiries as to his early life," but it seems equally possible that Fellows himself might have cobbled this story together out of several quite separate autobiographical fragments gathered from his employer, a misheard and misunderstood name, and a great leap of fancy.

On the other hand, it is quite clear that every other story Stephen Fellows later related about Richard Potter's early life, without exception, was also utterly false. Thus Potter had told him, Fellows claimed, "that he was at ten years of age, picked up by a sea captain, and carried as a cabin boy to London," where he was "turned adrift upon the city" and "fell in with a travelling circus"; that "when about eighteen years old, he left the circus and set up business for himself as a magician and ventriloquist"; and that his wife "was a full-blooded Penobscot-Indian squaw." All of these are complete fabrications (although the one about the ten-year-old cabin boy turned adrift in London continues to circulate). Perhaps Fellows himself was the fabricator: in the 1870s he was discovering that information about Potter's life was now of interest to historians, and he may simply have spun his own imaginative guesses into good stories. But if, as Ketchum thought, Fellows was not making up these stories but had heard them from Potter and truly believed them ("that Potter had given him a true history, Fellows seems never for a moment to have doubted"), then we can only conclude that Fellows was gullible and that Potter was only too happy to mislead him.

Fellows at least learned that Richard Potter's mother was a black servant in the Boston area. This in itself would not have been surprising in Andover—not by circa 1830, at least, for Potter's nephew Cromwell Potter (usually thought by locals to be Potter's younger brother), who was very obviously black, had moved to Andover by 1827 with his "wife," Phebe, also very obviously black, so Richard Potter's own blackness was no secret at that point. Earlier in Richard Potter's Andover years, however, "the general understanding seems to have been that he was a native of one of the West India Islands." This, too, may well have been partly due to hints from Potter himself, or from his original partner and assistant, an Andover native, for at the very beginning of his career Potter had briefly advertised himself as a "West Indian." Yet the dominant opinion throughout the rest of New England, apart from Boston and Andover, was that Richard Potter was from India—"a native of the East Indies," supposedly the son of an English father and a Hindu mother. To this notion, too, he gave at least some tacit support, not least by costuming himself for his magic exhibitions in "a black silk robe, covered all with emblems" that impressed New Englanders as exotically Eastern. As one historian reports: "When definitely questioned he declined talking or tactfully changed the subject. When rumor decided that he was an East Indian, he took no pains to deny it and that finally became the popular belief." The persistence years and years afterward of these beliefs about Richard Potter's origins says much about the deep conviction with which they were held, and thus about the effectiveness of his misdirections. That effectiveness is reflected as well by contemporaneous signs of local confusion about his race: he and his son were listed in the 1830 census as white, for example, although Cromwell and Phebe Potter, living next door, were listed as colored.

This was all very different from the life that Richard Potter lived in the Boston area, where he had grown up and where he returned to live in his early twenties and again for a while in his mid-forties, and where he was not exotic at all. Boston had a large and modestly thriving black community (Andover had no black community at all), and Richard Potter was part of it. He had been born into the household of one white family and then worked and lived with two others; then, in his mid-twenties, he again lived with and worked for a few white families for briefer periods of time. He had several good friends in white Boston, many comfortable relationships, and a very wide circle of respectable and even prominent connections there. But when he lived on his own in Boston, he lived in the black community and was well known and widely respected within it. In Boston, there were no mysteries about his origins, and thus no mystification about them was necessary. In Boston, Richard Potter was a wonder, but not a mystery.

IV

The wonder of Richard Potter's spectacularly successful career, of the fame and fortune he won as a magician and ventriloquist, is all the more astonishing in view of the limited prospects that lay before him as a youth. In some respects he was very fortunate in his advantages. He had acquired a sound basic schooling in his childhood and then, presumably, a sound practical training in the mercantile business from his new master in his early teens. He was also notably personable, quick-witted, diligent, and nimble. Too, he might well anticipate the sponsorship of his white master, should he ultimately hope to go into some business of his own; and in the meantime he was making many useful contacts within the bustling business world of the Boston waterfront.

Yet even so, to what might he aspire? Even in relatively liberal Boston in the early nineteenth century, few opportunities were available to black men, and very few professions were open to them. One survey of the "Distribution of Occupations in Black Boston, 1826," for example, identifies 273 black Bostonians with a specified occupation (for another 83, no occupation was specified): of these, 191 were unskilled or semi-skilled workers (including 126 laborers, 30 mariners, and 17 bootblacks), 56 were service workers (including 40 barbers and 8 waiters), and 26 were "artisan, entrepreneurial, and professional workers" (including 5 musicians, 2 ministers, 2 tailors, 2 masons, and 2 boardinghouse operators). Even this analysis, drawn from the 1826 *Boston Directory,* was certainly skewed: laborers, for example, had no great need or call to be included in the directory (which was not even close to being complete), and mariners were surely underrepresented in it because of their very transience, so the proportion of black Bostonians who were unskilled or semi-skilled workers was surely rather higher than this survey suggests. For a slightly different perspective from roughly the same time, consider the 36 black Bostonians who were listed in the town's tax valuation books for 1827 as residents of Belknap Street, the racially integrated thoroughfare on Beacon Hill that ran through the middle of Boston's largest black settlement area. Their number included 20 laborers, 6 barbers, 3 tenders (i.e., waiters), 2 men who ran clothing stores, 2 seamen, 1 preacher, 1 coachman, and 1 scavenger (i.e., streetsweeper). (Again, the sample is surely skewed somewhat: there was much cheaper and meaner housing to be found in other parts of Boston, so again unskilled or semi-skilled workers would likely be underrepresented here.) And some twenty-five years earlier, when Richard Potter was beginning to make his own way in life, the realities of gainful employment for black Bostonians were harsher and more constrained still.

Richard Potter finessed these constraints by doing something entirely different, something foreign to the entire society. In his late teens he leaped clear of the usual range of employment situations (leaped quite literally: he began by training as a gymnast and tightrope walker in Europe), and when he returned to America in 1803 at about the age of twenty he soon began apprenticing as a ventriloquist, a profession so novel that it had not even existed in America (for there had never been one in America) until 1801 and that no

American had ever entered. He had solved, brilliantly, the puzzle of what to do for a living. But he still needed to learn how to do it—how, specifically, to do it while black.

It was a tremendously important question, complicated by the fact that, while a ventriloquist per se or even a magician might fall entirely outside the familiar range of social niches, an itinerant performer of any sort would inevitably encounter a certain degree of suspicion and disrespect. Some of Richard Potter's own teachers, moreover, had conducted themselves in ways that would be extremely dangerous for a black man in America: his particular mentor in ventriloquism and magic, James Rannie, for example, on one occasion had brawled (quite successfully) in the main street of a southern town with a contentious spectator who had called him out and had then attempted to horsewhip him (the use of a whip signaling that one's opponent was considered to be beneath one's own status as a gentleman), on another had publicly, on the streets of New York City, accused a ship's captain of the attempted murder of one of his crew, and on yet another, in a Boston inn, had become involved in a drunken, mock-heroic confrontation with the great English actor George Frederick Cooke. Richard Potter's own solution, on the other hand—we cannot call it a strategy, for it seems entirely true to his character—was quite simple: he always behaved like a perfect gentleman.

v

So this was Richard Potter: an itinerant performer, a man of mean birth who somehow acquired the qualities and bearing of a well-born gentleman, a black man of obscure and irregular origins who took measures to misdirect attention from his blackness and origins, and a famous ventriloquist and magician whose exotic stage persona provoked eager and wildly fanciful speculations about his history. It is a wonder that we can learn much about his actual life at all, and no wonder at all that most of the stories told about him are utter nonsense.

Why should we care about his life and its stories? Here, very briefly, are two reasons. First, Richard Potter achieved remarkable success as a free black man at a time in America when such success was unexampled and nearly impossible. There was no pattern for his accomplishment, and he had no peers in it. Thus his story, unique in the annals of African American history, gives new depth and nuance to the picture of the black experience and American race relations in his era.

Second, Richard Potter's success, while it brought him prominence and even preeminence as an entertainer, came in a "popular culture" tradition about which we still know far too little. For too long, popular entertainments received short shrift in cultural histories, dismissed as eddies along the mainstream of serious literature and art. In recent decades that has been changing, and many scholars have begun investigating these traditions. But the challenges of such research are daunting, for the obvious reasons: the performers were transients, the performances were ephemeral and mostly unscripted, and accounts of both performers and performances are typically obscure, fragmentary, and belated. Thus even the best and most durable performers, who could be "celebrated in their own day," typically have become "shadowy figures now." By discovering Richard Potter and his artistry, we gain important new perspectives into American popular culture—into American life—in the era of the early republic.

Beyond these two attractions, both of them compelling in their different ways, there is this: the combining of these two historical narratives into one, into one person's life story, adds something new and strangely powerful to the whole. As a prominent black American and as a prominent magician and ventriloquist, Richard Potter stands out in the early American republic. But as both these figures simultaneously, he embodies a wonderful, rare intersection of forces that were immensely significant in the shaping of America and exemplifies, to an unusual degree, the kind of cultural agency that can tinge an entire society.

As Simon During has strongly argued in *Modern Enchantments: The Cultural Power of Secular Magic,* "magic has helped shape modern culture": "From the moment they were widely tolerated and commercialized, magic shows have helped provide the terms and content of modern culture's understanding and judgment of itself." Magic's "tricks, sleights, and special effects . . . have been pivotal in the development of modern commercialized leisure enterprises," he notes; and once we recognize this, "our sensitivity to the play of puzzlement, fictiveness, and contingency in modernity will be heightened." We have been slow to understand this because secular magic has always been so lightly regarded. "Yet secular magic has become a powerful agent in the formation of modern culture precisely *because* it is trivial": it has disguised its agency behind that appearance. "One reason that there has been almost no academic study of entertainment magic is that magic has been too deceptive for its traps, tricks, and tours to be stored in the archives and recorded as history"; those devices "just vanished from modern culture's stories about, and sense of, itself."

During's analysis has been extended and redirected by a very different kind of cultural critic, Joseph Roach, writing about the phenomenon of "It"—personal magnetism, charisma, celebrity. In Roach's deliberately "paradox-ridden" definition, "'It' is the power of apparently effortless embodiment of contradictory qualities simultaneously: strength *and* vulnerability, innocence *and* experience, and singularity *and* typicality among them. The possessor of It keeps a precarious balance between such mutually exclusive alternatives, suspended at the tipping point like a tightrope dancer on one foot." Roach readily acknowledges what his tightrope-dancer image suggests, that his definition "moves beyond the tautology of innate charm and enters into the realm of theatrical and cinematic technique": he is effectively providing "a definition of It as secular magic." Nodding to During's "historical approach" to the issue of secular magic, he notes that "My goal is similar, but I focus more than he does on the enchanted performer, less on enchanted technology, and I lend more credence than During does to the efficacy of the rites."

Richard Potter's stature in his time as the foremost ventriloquist and one of the finest magicians in America—his place at the very pinnacle of secular magic—prompts an inevitable question here: Did he have "It"? The question is surely too facile in its broadest application: celebrity of the sort that particularly fascinates Roach requires publicity, and mass, nationwide publicity was not a possibility in America at this time, unless your name was something like Jackson or Webster or Lafayette. On a regional or local level, however, the question becomes interesting. When Richard Potter took New York, the nation's biggest city, by storm in 1819, with a modish poet hailing him in witty verses in the press and his exhibitions becoming the "fashionable resort" of the city, he had clearly become a celebrity. Recollections of him some forty years after his death make clear that, within the parameters of northern New England and the last twelve years of his life, when so many of those wild stories began to accrete around him, he had staying power as a regional celebrity, too. And within those stories, as well as in the New York poetry, are hints about the qualities that made him so interesting to others.

Roach proposes that celebrities are "double-bodied persons" who combine "the immortal body of their image" with the vulnerable, perishable natural body, and that they "foreground a peculiar combination of contradictory attributes expressed through outward signs of the union of their imperishable and mortal bodies." The fascinating interaction of these outward signs, "the simultaneous appearance of strength and vulnerability," becomes a "source of public intimacy." Roach cites various examples from English theater history of celebrated, iconic strengths ("Anne Bracegirdle's white teeth, David Garrick's flashing eyes, and Dorothy Jordan's curly hair") and of similarly iconic vulnerabilities ("Elizabeth Barry's asymmetrical face, David Garrick's short stature, and Sarah Siddons's embonpoint"). It is not simply the strength or weakness, but their interplay, which characterizes the celebrity: "As Achilles was a more compelling hero because of his heel, not in spite of it, so Thomas Betterton . . . became a more effective tragedian in part because his increasingly vulnerable body contrasted so poignantly with his growing moral strength."

For Richard Potter, the characterizing strength that shines through so many accounts and recollections was his sheer wizardry. About his corresponding vulnerability there is no doubt: it was his color, his ambiguous, uncertain racial background. The public curiosity about his origins, this is to say, was part and parcel of his celebratory stigma. He was powerfully magical, and simultaneously he was vulnerably dark. As such, he was perfectly poised to strike Americans of his era as altogether *interesting*.

Richard Potter, mulatto son of a woman who had been captured on the Guinea coast, brought to America in a slave ship, and sold in Boston into the household of an English colonial official, grew up to influence and even change American life. He contributed significantly to making popular entertainment popular, and to making it respectable as well. He not only exemplified but effectively defined what "magic" and especially "ventriloquism" meant to an entire generation. He became America's most famous and most widely attended entertainer; and after his death he tinged the country's nostalgia for decades more, as those who as children had delighted in his exhibitions in the 1820s and early 1830s fondly recalled them, and their own childhood innocence, in the decades after the Civil War. He has been almost invisible in American cultural history. He should be so no longer; for he was once the most wonderful man in America.

# 1

## The Hopkinton Years, 1783–1795

I

Richard Potter was born on the Hopkinton, Massachusetts, estate of a master and lady both prominent and storied, and to this circumstance we owe much of our meager knowledge of his origins. His mother, Dinah, had been captured in Guinea and brought to Boston—"Black Dinah, stolen when a child, / And sold on Boston pier," as Oliver Wendell Holmes (who had made meticulous inquiries into this history) later phrased it—where she was purchased by Sir Charles Henry Frankland, an English baronet (and a direct descendant of Oliver Cromwell) who was the collector of the Port of Boston. Frankland owned, in addition to a grand house in Boston, a handsome estate in Hopkinton, and it was here that Dinah was raised in service, along with some twelve to sixteen other slaves. And here she gave birth to at least six children, including four daughters (Julia, Violet, Phebe, and Sidney) and two sons (Robert and Richard), most or all of them by white fathers. Potter was one of her latest-born, probably her last. Dinah's and young Richard's histories were so intimately bound together with those of the Frankland family and the Hopkinton estate that we cannot begin to appreciate the former without the grounding of the latter—all the more so because it was precisely the celebrity of Frankland and his wife and the fame of his estate that led local historians, and authors such as Holmes, to pay attention to Dinah and her fellow servants in the first place.

Frankland, soon after he came to Boston (he was not a baronet then), gained notoriety when he took a fancy to, and soon arranged to become the sponsor of, a beautiful teenaged girl ten years younger than he, Agnes Surriage. He first encountered her in Marblehead, where she, a maid of all work, was scrubbing a tavern floor, barefoot and garbed in a poor dress. She was the fourth of eight children born to a Marblehead fisherman. According to family legend, Frankland was struck by her beauty, engaged her in conversation, and "gave her a crown to buy a pair of shoes." On a later visit to Marblehead he found her again working barefoot and asked why she had not purchased shoes; she replied, "I have indeed sir, with the crown you gave me; but I keep them to wear to meeting." Frankland soon took her to Boston, arranged for her to receive a proper lady's education, and eventually made her his mistress. By this time he had also, upon the death of his uncle (Sir Thomas Frankland, the third baronet), succeeded to the baronetcy of Thirsk.

Neither wealth nor title could shelter Sir Harry and Agnes from the disapprobation of their fellow Bostonians. Frankland's biographer reported that even in 1865 "a few aged persons in Boston can well remember hearing their grand parents speak of the indignant feelings of the school companions of Agnes Surriage, when it was publicly known that an improper intimacy existed between her and the baronet." And in the Royalist circles of King's Chapel, where Frankland was a major benefactor, a vestryman, and a close friend of the rector, "even this and his high position could not reconcile the parish to what came to their knowledge," speculated the church's nineteenth-century historian, noting that Frankland, already a vestryman for six years by 1751, received fewer votes for the office than did any of his fellows. So, seeking a place of "retirement from the annoyance of the busy tongues of Boston," he bought a large tract of land in Hopkinton (where his friend Roger Price, the rector of King's Chapel, had earlier established a residential retreat and a satellite church, St. Paul's) and erected a grand mansion there in 1751–52, where he and Agnes Surriage could live in luxurious rural privacy. (Frankland also had a ward or natural son, Henry Cromwell, born in 1741, whom he brought to Hopkinton at this time.)* When he took her with him to England in 1754, however (he was called there by an important probate case involving his inheritance), he quickly realized how futile his attempts to introduce her into

---

*The presence of Henry Cromwell in Harry Frankland's life rather bedims the Cinderella-like aura traditionally attached to the story of Agnes Surriage. Tradition and most family sources assume that Henry Cromwell was Charles Henry Frankland's natural son. I would suggest, but will not pursue here, the possibility that instead Henry Cromwell was the natural son of Harry Frankland's dashing younger brother Thomas,

his family circle there would be: she was but coldly received and not recognized as a member of the family.

Upon the conclusion of the court case, then, Sir Harry and Agnes left England to tour the continent, and by early 1755 had taken a house in Lisbon. On 1 November of that year, the city was devastated by a great earthquake. Frankland's house was destroyed, its occupants killed; fortunately Agnes was unhurt. Frankland himself was out in his chaise at the time, in his court dress, and he was buried alive by the rubble of collapsed buildings. According to family legend, Agnes set out to find him; somehow managed to do so; immediately engaged nearby survivors, with promise of lavish rewards, to dig him out; "and in the course of an hour or so, succeeds in rescuing him from the horrors of his living tomb." Contemporaneous accounts include no mention of Agnes's role in Harry's rescue but confirm that he had been (in his own words) "buried in the ruins." As an English nun in Lisbon soon reported in a letter to her mother in England, "Sir Henry Franklen [*sic*] . . . was going in his shayz [chaise] and perceived the houses to fall, he jump out an a house fell upon him, he gett out through some little hole . . . he left his shayz in the street broak, his servants and horses Killed." In any event, Sir Harry, taking a heartfelt lesson from his "providential escape"—"We should endeavor to pacify the divine wrath by sorrow for past neglects and a future conscientious discharge of duty to God and our country"—soon thereafter married his paramour.

Thenceforth the now Lady Agnes was welcomed both into Frankland's family in England (they revisited England in 1756) and into the polite society of Boston, whither the Franklands returned that same year. Frankland soon purchased a grand mansion in the town (he retained the estate in Hopkinton), a house famous for its elegance and splendor. Through its center ran a spacious hall, "from which arose a flight of stairs, so broad and easy of ascent that Frankland used to ride his pony up and down with ease and safety." Here Lady Agnes presided socially, and here and also at the Hopkinton estate she and her husband established their now-extended family. Agnes's older, twice-widowed sister, Mary Swain, now resided with them, as did Frankland's ward or natural son, Henry Cromwell, now (in 1756) fifteen, and the two younger

---

who as the captain of a British warship stationed in Providence and patrolling the Eastern Seaboard down to the Caribbean in the early 1740s won great acclaim and recognition for the many prizes (Spanish privateers) he captured at sea.

of Mary's three children by her first marriage, Sally and John McClester (now about sixteen and fourteen, respectively).

But this interval in Boston and Hopkinton was brief. In mid-1757 Frankland was named England's consul general for Portugal, and in early 1758 he and his family sailed to England, then later that year to Portugal. They would not return to Massachusetts until 1763. Their residence there this time was again relatively brief: Sir Harry's health was declining, and they left Hopkinton for Bath, England, and its mineral springs in 1764 (Dinah accompanied them on this trip). Frankland died there in early 1768. Lady Agnes, with Henry Cromwell and their servants (including Dinah), returned to Hopkinton a few months later.

The Hopkinton estate to which Dinah returned, though not so grandiose as the Boston mansion, was nevertheless a place of great beauty and refinement. Frankland's aim had been to create "the show place of the country," and he had attended to its situation and landscaping as well as to its architectural details. Elias Nason (Frankland's future biographer), who knew it intimately, describes it as a mansion "large and strongly built. It stood at some distance from the main road, and was approached by a noble avenue cut through the chestnut forest, and by a flower garden tastefully arranged in front. The spacious hall, sustained by fluted columns, was hung with tapestry, richly ornamented with dark figures on a ground of deepest green, according to the fashion of the times. The chimney pieces were of Italian marble; and cornices of stucco-work and other costly finishing embellished the parlor, anterooms and chambers."

The grounds immediately around the house were terraced and planted with flowers; the walks were bordered with boxwood, lilacs, hawthorns, and roses; orchards of apples, pears, plums, peaches, cherries, apricots, and quinces were set out; elms and other ornamental trees were established. Frankland engaged an estate manager, Jacques Joseph Villiers, who oversaw and maintained the farm, Nason believed, for decades—from "as early as 1757 if not from the first" until long after Frankland's death and possibly even until the property left the family in 1803. But the flowerbeds may have been the particular province of Lady Agnes, who was known for her love of flowers, "many of which she cultivated on the ter[r]aces aroun[d] her Country Hou[se]."

I I

We can catch occasional glimpses of Potter's mother in the patchy records and local lore of these days before the Revolution. Nason devoted a few pages of his Frankland biography to the family's slaves, recording that "Dinah was ... brought from Guinea; her face was jet black and she had been branded with three parallel lines upon the cheek and forehead. She was originally caught in Africa, as she herself used to aver, by means of a lump of sugar soaked in rum which drove her strength and reason out of her." The statement that Dinah had been "brought from Guinea"—this would refer to the Guinea coast, roughly the extensive area between present-day Gambia and the Ivory Coast—should probably be taken seriously. As historians have noted, Americans during the latter part of the eighteenth century were becoming increasingly aware of African ethnology and of ethnic differences among tribes and regions. As Daniel Littlefield summarizes, "colonial Americans had an awareness of the diverse backgrounds of their servile black population." In South Carolina in particular (the focus of his study), "the range of ethnic groups referred to [is] great [and] the precision in their identification is remarkable."

Nason indicates that Dinah was not one of the slaves who accompanied Frankland to Portugal (as we have seen, he was away from Massachusetts, mostly in Portugal, in 1754–56 and again in 1758–63), but another historian reports that, after she was brought to the Hopkinton estate, "She went to England with the Franklands, and returned with Lady Agnes." This would date her arrival at Hopkinton, as a girl, to late 1763 or perhaps early 1764. The brands on her face—"country marks," markers of her African tribal origin—probably also signify that she was at least a young adolescent at the time of her capture and enslavement, since these scars were typically administered during pubertal initiation rites. This suggests a birthdate for her circa 1750.

In her later years Dinah lived with her family (that is, at least some of her children) in Westborough, a town adjacent to Hopkinton, whence comes this bit of local lore:

> She is remembered as short and stout, with snow-white hair and blue eyes, always carrying a cane, and, in the season of them, a bunch of wildflowers. In the later years of her life her mind was gone, and she talked to herself as she wandered around, oftenest about Lady Jane Grey. She was free to go where she pleased, receiving a welcome even in the room where the new baby lay; and being allowed to take it in her arms and clasp it to her bosom, forgetting she was not a young mother herself, and the wee white child her own little one.

These scanty anecdotes—Lady Jane Grey?—point to a world of experience that we would do well to remember. Dinah, it is important to recall, after being enslaved as a child, grew up "in service, petted, spoiled," in the household of a prominent and wealthy English baronet's family, and with a mistress who was particularly remembered for her passionate love of flowers. She had barely been acquired by the Franklands before she left her new Hopkinton environs for Bath, the fashionable spa town that was already a center of English societal life. Bath must have presented a bewilderingly grand scene for her, but her life there, surely, was also often rather sequestered. Sir Harry, already in his late forties an ailing man, had moved to Bath in great part for medical reasons, and would die there four years later at the age of fifty-one. Lady Agnes and young Henry Cromwell sometimes entertained houseguests and certainly received company, and Agnes's older sister Mary Swain and Mary's son John McClester, who had long resided with the Franklands in Massachusetts, stayed with them in Bath for most of their first year there before returning to America. But theirs was a small household—Sir Harry, Lady Agnes, Henry Cromwell, and a few servants (Frankland's journal records a staff comprising a coachman, two footmen, and three maidservants).

For a woman such as Lady Agnes, whose rise in society had been so fantastic, whose education and upbringing had been so calculated by a controlling man to groom her for the foremost social circles, the story of Lady Jane Grey, "the nine days' queen," must have had a particular piquancy. For a man such as Sir Harry, who had so miraculously survived being buried alive in the great Lisbon earthquake, the same story, of great good fortune so quickly reversed and lost, would have had its own resonance. And the story was, at this time, enjoying another of its periodic surges of attention in English culture. Drury Lane had revived Nicholas Rowe's popular *Tragedy of Lady Jane Gray* in 1762. Published in that same year, George Keate's long poem in heroic couplets, "An Epistle from Lady Jane Grey to Lord Guilford Dudley," was still current and popular. An essay in the *Universal Museum* for December 1763 gave Lady Jane Grey sustained attention in "An Historical Account of the Most Celebrated English Beauties." Lady Jane Grey thus was still a topic of polite conversation and popular entertainment in Bath in the 1760s. The dementia into which Dinah descended in her old age—the fondness for flowers and the interest in Lady Jane Grey, no less than the nurturing of newborn babes— was, as dementias so often are, a dream of her youth.

III

Dinah eventually gave birth to six or perhaps seven children. Little is known about their fathers. Elias Nason, who had grown up in Hopkinton and had become the owner of the old Frankland place just before it burned in early

1858, paid particular attention to the histories of everyone connected with the Frankland household, including the servants, as he wrote his biography of Frankland and worked for decades on his never-finished "History of Hopkinton." Nason had known a few of the servants during his childhood, and he first interviewed Dinah's daughter Julia Titus only a few days after the Frankland mansion burned; subsequently he solicited recollections from many other local residents as well. Nason states quite firmly that all of Dinah's children "were born and baptized in the Frankland house," and apparently Julia Titus was his primary authority for this. Unfortunately, Nason, while he assiduously interviewed older Hopkinton inhabitants over the next few decades and preserved much oral history, never got around to examining the records of St. Paul's Church, to which all of the Frankland household were attached. Those records were destroyed when the church building burned to the ground in July 1865.

In the absence of all those baptismal records, only the local lore that Nason accumulated about Dinah's children can give us clues as to their parentage. Some of this came directly from Julia Titus and can be regarded as authoritative. Nason reports, for example, that Julia herself, whom he identifies (or who identified herself) as "mulatto," "was the daughter of Dinah, a slave of Sir Henry Frankland and Jas. Butler his coachman"; and again, "She [Dinah] had Julia by James Butler, Frankland's coachman who went to Eng. with him." Dinah would have known Butler and served in the same household with him since 1764—almost four years together in Bath, then another six or seven years in Hopkinton.

Nason also recounts a story about Potter's surname, which otherwise has never been explained: "He was called 'Potter' from one 'Jupiter Potter', a cooper who lived with Mr. Freeland, a cooper, and was published to Dinah . . . but died before the marriage was solemnized." Since many or all of Dinah's children seem to have taken the Potter surname, we can assume that this connection with Jupiter Potter (whose Christian name clearly identified him as black) dated from sometime between 1768 (when Dinah returned from England) and 1775 (when Julia was born) or soon thereafter.

About the fathers of Dinah's other daughters, Nason offers no information, save that her children "were all mulattoes and very bright." But he has this further to tell about the sons: "Robert used to live with Dr. Stimpson. Said to be the son of Geo Stimson"; and Richard was the "son of Dinah, an African slave with scars upon her face, and Geo Stimpson"; and again, "Geo. Stimpson is father to Dick Potter. So says Julia Titus 1858." Nason thus had this on excellent authority: Julia would have been about eight years old at the time of Richard's birth, plenty old enough to know who was keeping company with her mother.

George Stimson, Richard Potter's father—husbandman and yeoman farmer, sometime trader, occasionally a dealer in real estate as either principal or agent—came from a large, well-established Hopkinton family. (Technically, he lived on the Framingham side of the Sudbury River between the two towns.) His parents moved the family from Ipswich to Hopkinton in 1738, and the last five of their eleven children were born there (George, the eldest, was born in Ipswich in 1726). George married in 1751 and began fathering a large family of his own: his wife bore him ten children between 1751 and 1774. In 1755, he served in the French and Indian War. There are also family stories of his having served early in the Revolutionary War as a Minuteman ("Hearing fighting at Boston was begun, he left his team in the field, where he was plowing, and seizing a pitchfork, rushed to Boston, 30 miles to the fight"), and one very dramatic anecdote of his service then: "He was a bearer of public funds soon afterwards, and on horseback, when was crossing Boston Neck, three ruffians attempted to rob him and in pulling him off his horse he spurred the horse till he rushed from under him, and carried the saddle bags, money and all, swiftly to Boston, and so it reached its destination safely." In any event, he certainly did serve in the Revolutionary War, as did some of his brothers, and certainly he was an early enlistee, despite his age (he was already forty-eight when hostilities broke out).

Stimson was recorded again for a two-week enlistment stint in July–August 1780 as a private in Capt. David Brewer's company, Col. Aimer Perry's regiment, when the company marched from Framingham to Rhode Island "on an alarm." In July 1780, a long-anticipated French fleet landed at Newport, Rhode Island, with six thousand troops under General Rochambeau to support Washington's Continental Army. In response, the British soon began moving their own troops to the east end of Long Island, which did not go unnoticed: "We have advice, that a large body of the enemy's troops have moved, within a few days past, to the East end of Long-Island; and that transports have come thro' Hell-Gate into the Sound, in order, it is supposed to take them on board; where they are bound is uncertain; however, as there can't be a doubt but they are intended for some expedition, it behoves [sic] every man to be ready to meet them at a moment's warning." The Massachusetts militia quickly responded, and in early August a Boston newspaper reported:

> The alertness of our militia in repairing to Rhode-Island, upon an apprehension that the whole collective British force intended an approach to

that place, is one instance, among many, of the happy union between the French and Americans, and the warm disposition of the people of these States to co-operate with our good Allies.... Accounts from Connecticut assure us, that the enemy, which had lately taken post at the east-end of Long-Island, and threatened a descent upon Rhode-Island, have returned to New-York; supposed to be in consequence of Gen. Washington's advance towards Kingsbridge.

The militia then quickly disbanded when the threat dissipated: Stimson and most of his compatriots had enlisted on 28 July, and he and his company were discharged in Rhode Island on 7 August, their fourteen days of service including the three days they would need to return home (seventy miles).

During the period between his 1776 and 1780 enlistments, Stimson was employed in advancing the Revolutionary cause and his town's welfare in other ways, probably as a civilian. In May 1779, the Connecticut Assembly, in one of scores of such actions taken to expedite the movement of goods between and among the colonies for the furtherment of the war effort, voted to "grant liberty to George Stimson, of Old Framingham in the State of the Massachusetts Bay, to purchase in and transport out of this State to said Framingham, for use of sundry families there, fifty-one bushels of wheat, or flour equivalent thereto." This was doubtless related to the activities incidentally recorded in early May 1779 in the diary of the Rev. Ebenezer Parkman, the founding minister of the adjacent town of Westborough, Massachusetts:

Benj. Bancroft of Sutton Stores his Load in my barn. [5 May 1779]

George Stimson was here and carried away from my barn four bushels (as he says) of Indian Corn, which is part of ye load stored there by Benj. Bancroft on last Wednesday. for which he gave me his receipt. He says the load is his, & that he Shall soon take away ye Rest of it. [8 May 1779]

At eve. Mr. George Stimson here about ye Load Stored in my Barn, but took none of it away. [10 May 1779]

All this evidence suggests Stimson's active and sustained involvement in the revolutionary cause.

But Stimson's energetic, forceful personality manifested itself in other, less admirable ways as well. In his dealings with women, for example, he acquired a seamy reputation in the town long before he started paying attention to Dinah. Eventually his behavior made him the object of the Congregational Church's particular opprobrium and thus the talk and scandal of the town.

In early October 1777, "by reasons of a scandalous report being spread abroad concerning our Brother George Stimson, many of the Chh [Church] manifesting so great an uneasiness, as that they could not set down at Communion with him," the congregation voted to defer communion for a week and in the interim schedule a meeting to give Stimson "an opportunity to clear up his character, & to do what might be tho't proper in that affair." Nothing happened at this point (Stimson at the meeting "alledged his Inocency" and no accusers came forward); but soon after, two members of the congregation did advance specific complaints against Stimson "for disorderly walk & behaviour with some Persons in a private & unbecoming way." This was still only a general and vague charge, easily deferred; but the following month it strengthened considerably, as the two church members accused Stimson of "breach of his Christian Covenant by making attempts upon the chastity of several Women." Four women were specifically named, "and others" were referenced as well, so Stimson stood accused of attempts upon at least six.

Stimson was defiant and contentious in his own defense, but the congregation took evidence from the four women and found that "the evidence in support of the complaint was full." Having heard the testimonies of the women, Stimson refused to appear before the church to defend himself, instead submitting a letter arguing that "the whole Chh is become his accusers & consequently cannot be his Judges" and declining to appear until "proper judges" be found. The church then unanimously voted to debar Stimson from all church privileges—not for his offenses against women, as his defense had not been heard yet, but for his contempt of the church's authority.

Stimson threatened a suit against the two fellow congregationalists who had brought the complaints against him and four months later reportedly went so far as to obtain a warrant against them, provoking the congregation into another special meeting in which, again by unanimous vote, the members instructed their pastor to "Remonstrate against any such prosecution" before whatever justice might end up trying the case, on the grounds that the church had a right to deal with its disorderly members and that "it is contrary to the word of God for Brother to go to Law with Brother in matters where the Chh have a right to hear & determine."

Stimson's case against his accusers never went to trial. But the litigious impulse that prompted it was entirely characteristic of the man and illustrated another difficult aspect of his personality. In his dealings with society at large as in his dealings within his church, he was a fundamentally and deeply contentious person. Consequently he went to court quite frequently, several times as a plaintiff and far more often as a defendant—so frequently that this character trait must have become central to his reputation. Further, Stimson was regularly on the losing side of these cases, either defaulting or found to be at fault. These lawsuits ranged over a wide range of financial dealings. Some concerned straightforward promissory notes that Stimson had not made good or bills that he had not paid; some, trading accounts in rum or sugar or flour that Stimson had not settled; and some, defaulted mortgages on tracts of real estate. It is clear that Stimson's personal credit was eventually as suspect within the Middlesex County business community as it was within his church.

The most vexed and consuming of Stimson's legal contestations involved a series of back-and-forth lawsuits with Gilbert Dench, a prominent Hopkinton resident (captain of a company of Middlesex militia during the American Revolution, often a town selectman, sometime member of the Massachusetts House of Representatives, town representative to the Massachusetts constitutional convention) and a neighbor. Clearly there were extensive dealings between the two men and their families, marked by increasing antagonism between the two principals. In late 1771, Dench swore out a writ against Stimson for nonpayment of two notes, dating from spring 1769 and spring 1770; the next day Stimson did the same against Dench, claiming he had not been paid for a number of items and services that been contracted for and rendered from 1766 to 1769, including "Killing & Dressing an ox," wages due his son Jeremy and one of his daughters, use of "my Cart & wheels one Jorney to Boston" and "Damage Dun wheels & Breaking ye Box," "Journey to Framingham to purchase a cow," "Journey to Mr. Jnn. Osburns at your request," "Purchase a Cow for you," and "use of the cow for 10 months & one half of the increase of the cow." The cases were referred by agreement to a committee of three court-appointed referees, and many Hopkinton and Framingham citizens were called in to testify as witnesses. The decisions in these cases, ultimately rendered in the May court term of 1772, were something of a wash, but slightly in favor of Stimson, who recovered his costs of court in both cases and was awarded damages of five shillings eight pence in the second case.

But the vexed dealings, and the bad blood, continued, and ten years later the men were taking each other to court again. Dench now brought three suits (one with a business partner) against Stimson. The first was for nonpayment of two notes dating from the 1770s and also for a delivery by Dench to Stimson of one hogshead (111 gallons, in this case) of rum in 1780 (Stimson had been a trader at that period of his life); the second, for a variety of other debts, including "A Horse sold him" in November 1778 and associated expenses, "Freight of an hd [hogshead] Rum from Seconk [Seekonk] to New-port wharfage & storage," and "Cash paid Joseph Tillinghast for Freightage wharfage & storage of flour." Simultaneously, Dench and a business partner, Lawson Buckminster, brought a third suit against Stimson over a real estate transaction, alleging they had engaged him in 1774 as their agent to sell a parcel of land (almost fifty acres) they owned in Worcester, permitting him to keep anything over twenty-eight shillings per acre, he promising to pay them the twenty-eight shillings per acre when he sold the land. Now, they said, he had sold the land but had not paid them. Stimson in response filed a countersuit against Dench and Buckminster. The judgments this time, while divided, went largely for Stimson, but they were all immediately appealed. The various appeals were merged into one case, and then the case, by mutual consent of the involved parties, was referred to a committee of three individuals for a report. Finally, in the spring of 1785, the committee made its report and the Supreme Judicial Court issued its decision. This time the committee's report and the court's judgment went heavily against Stimson: Dench's and Buckminster's explanations of their financial dealings with Stimson were determined to be valid, and the court found that they should recover more than 250 pounds from Stimson, who was also liable for nearly 40 pounds for the costs of the suit.

By mid-May the county sheriff had been directed to seize Stimson's property toward settlement of this enormous debt. Stimson at this time owned two tracts of land with buildings on opposite sides of the Sudbury River—an eight-acre parcel on the Hopkinton side and a twenty-four-acre parcel, his homestead, just across the river in Framingham. Stimson refused to choose an assessor, so both properties were assessed by the sheriff's appointees; the two parcels, with their buildings, appurtenances, and privileges, were altogether valued at 75 pounds. They were quickly seized and turned over to Lawson Buckminster in partial satisfaction of Stimson's debt. Stimson was still deeply in debt, and now without a home.

The loss of the Dench case, which came on the heels of many other losses in court from 1781 through 1785, led the aggrieved Stimson to make a complete break from his community. He had lived in Hopkinton and Framingham for forty-seven years, since the age of twelve, and was well-established there. His oldest son was a doctor in Hopkinton; two other sons, George and Ephraim, were schoolmasters in Framingham, and three daughters had taken Hopkinton husbands. He still had several children living at home, including three sons who were still minors (the youngest turned eleven in 1785)—not to mention his two young sons by Dinah Potter. He himself was almost sixty years old. Nevertheless, vowing that "he would not live where justice could not be done him," Stimson rather abruptly pulled up stakes and set out to build his life anew in a new territory.

IV

Stimson now engaged himself as an agent and husbandman for Robert Livingston, a wealthy New York landowner and the head of one of the great dynastic families of the Hudson (the third and last lord of Livingston Manor on the east bank of the Hudson River), who with his younger brother John was then initiating ambitious plans to settle and develop his extensive holdings (1 million acres of what had been the Hardenbergh Patent) in the Catskill Mountains on the west side of the Hudson. (John Livingston, it would seem, was simultaneously scheming with a few other wealthy and well-connected men to gain control of and even title to vast tracts of Indian lands in the western part of the state.) In Robert Livingston's service, Stimson in 1786 moved to the eastern Catskills, leaving behind all his family save his young son Henry, a boy of about thirteen, who accompanied his father. The two traveled from Framingham to what is now Windham, New York, in what is now Greene County; at that time it was still raw wilderness, and they were the first and for a while the only settlers. Finding a high, flat-sided, freestanding rock formation there, Stimson decided to build his bark-roofed log cabin up against it, so that the rock "formed one side of the cabin and also a part of the chimney and fireplace." There they lived in isolation through the next winter. (Local history recounts that Stimson at one point during the winter left Henry alone while he traveled to Hudson, thirty-eight miles distant and across the Hudson River, for provisions and was unexpectedly delayed there by a protracted thaw that made the river impassable. He was six weeks away before he was able to rejoin his young son.)

The next year Stimson returned to Framingham to fetch his whole family to the new homestead in New York. His oldest son, Jeremy, now settled in his medical practice and family life, remained in Hopkinton; all his other nine children, his three sons-in-law, and their already growing families left Hopkinton with him *en masse* and became pioneers in the new territory. In a single season, the Stimson family largely disappeared from Hopkinton while emerging as the first settlers of as yet unnamed villages in New York. George Stimson himself, leaving something of a rogue's legacy behind him in Massachusetts, acquired a fresh new local reputation in the Catskills as a founding father and patriarch.

In New York, Stimson was clearly doing more than homesteading and tending cattle. Serving as Robert Livingston's agent, he was apparently working with John Livingston as well. And John Livingston, as a principal partner and ringleader of the newly formed New York Genesee Land Company, was at this time deeply involved in a speculative scheme to gain control and possession of all the lands belonging to the Six Nations of Indians (the confederated Iroquois League). In support of that scheme, a council was held at Kanadesaga, a Seneca settlement, on 30 November 1787, at which forty-six Indian chiefs and sachems signed a 999-year lease on all their lands to the New York Genesee Land Company. There were four non-Indian witnesses present at the treaty; one of them was "George Stimson, Jun." Subsequently, Livingston and his partners, as part of a campaign for approval of their dealings by the New York legislature, arranged for several Indian leaders to appear before a judge of the Inferior Court of Columbia County to sign a memorial of their intent to lease the Indian lands. This time there were two witnesses to the Indian signatories; one of them, again, was "George Stimson, Jr."

John Livingston's undertaking was audacious and highly unethical. As Lewis Cass Aldrich summarizes, "The prime movers of the lease scheme had . . . something more in view than the mere possession of the lands, and it was doubtless their design to form a new State out of the territory of Central and Western New York, and in case of success the long leases would have been declared titles in fee simple." Stimson, working with the Indians on Livingston's behalf, seems to have been in the thick of it—energetic, forceful, and calculating to the end.

Stimson may never have returned to Hopkinton after 1787, when Richard Potter was turning four. It is quite possible, then, that Potter grew up with no memory or even knowledge of his father. Yet there are several reasons to hesitate before drawing such a conclusion.

To begin with, George Stimson already had a direct family connection with the Swain family at the old Frankland estate. On Christmas Eve in 1781, Daniel McClester, the older son of Mary Swain (Lady Agnes's sister, and now the matriarch of the estate) and the only resident adult male in the family, married Sarah Stimson; she was almost certainly George Stimson's sister. Thus George Stimson, as Daniel's new brother-in-law, would have had natural and ready access to the almost entirely female Frankland household and a certain degree of status and influence within it. A servant like Dinah would have been very vulnerable to such a man. A man like George would also have been memorable to such a family. And since Robert Potter (Richard's brother), supposedly also sired by George Stimson, "used to live with Dr. Stimpson" (whose house was adjacent to the Frankland estate)—this was George Stimson's eldest son, Jeremy, the one who remained in Hopkinton when the rest of the family removed to New York State in 1787—it seems likely that Stimson had acknowledged his paternity of the two Potter boys.

After George Stimson and most of his family left Hopkinton in 1787, moreover, the two branches of the family continued to maintain at least occasional contact. A family anecdote from the Hopkinton side, for example, recounts how "in the year 1800, Dr. Jeremy Stimson of Hopkinton took his son, . . . then a freshman at Harvard College, on a trip from Boston to visit his cousins at Wyndham, N.Y. The journey in an open sleigh took six weeks in all, and before they returned the weather had grown so mild that the sleigh was sold at Springfield and a buggy bought instead." With so many other branches of the Stimson, Claflin, and Stone families remaining in the Hopkinton area (Abijah Stone, John Claflin, and Increase Claflin, all originally from Hopkinton, were Stimson's sons-in-law who accompanied him to New York), it is quite likely that other such visits, in both directions, were happening occasionally as well.

To these points we can add the following considerations. When James and John Rannie, the Scottish ventriloquist brothers who would eventually become Richard Potter's mentors, were busily touring through the United States from 1801 to 1811, the towns and settlements along and near the Hudson River north of New York City were simply not of interest to them. James Rannie once, in early November 1802, ventured north from Newark, New Jersey, to Albany, before quickly turning south again and setting off for Charleston, South Carolina. Apart from this one brief visit, however, neither Rannie traveled up the Hudson River valley past the Catskills to Albany, presumably because the opportunities to attract audiences north of New York City were much more promising along the New England routes. Once Richard Potter started touring on his own, however, this was one part of the Rannie touring formula that he significantly changed. From 1810 to 1817, he made nine separate tours that took him to Albany—more than he appeared anywhere else except Boston, and far more than he appeared in seemingly more promising centers (more convenient, too, since during these years he was living in Boston and then New Hampshire) such as Portland, Portsmouth, and Providence. The pattern is quite remarkable, especially since so many of these tours took him to no other major venues. Potter seems to have regarded the Greater Albany area as almost a second home base. Perhaps it was.

It is interesting to note, too, that when Potter's estate was inventoried after his death in 1835, one significant item therein was "2 Shares in the New York State Bank at Albany, supposed to be worth one hundred dollars." Presumably Potter had acquired the stock in Albany years before, and retained it as an investment. Potter's estate included real estate and personal possessions and a few notes due to him on loans to neighbors, but this Albany bank stock, along with shares in another, New Hampshire bank (the Winnipisiogee Bank), represented the entirety of his financial investments.

Finally, after Potter's death, when his prodigal son (Richard junior) first lost the family estate and finally, having mortgaged and then stolen back his father's professional kit, became a fugitive from New Hampshire, he "was last heard of at Lansingburg, N.Y." No one has ever paused to wonder why he went to Lansingburgh, in the Greater Albany area. The answer may well be that it was because he had family there.

V

Dinah's children, whatever their paternity, all were always identified as black. Three of the sisters—Julia, Violet, and Sidney—seem never to have moved far from their birthplace. Julia, born circa 1775, continued to live on the Frankland estate even after it was sold out of the family in 1793, and she remained nearby, living usually in Westborough (a town immediately adjacent to Hopkinton), until the end of her life (she died in 1861). In later years she lived with a succession of local families. Violet, too, remained on the Frankland estate after its sale: she was listed as a servant in the household of Dr. Shepherd, who bought the Frankland estate, in 1794. And Sidney, "a famous maker of wedding-cake in her day," like Julia lived in the adjacent town of Westborough. Earlier, the intention of Reuben Titus of Framingham, Massachusetts, and Sidney to marry was published on 30 November 1797 (and she gave birth to two sons, Cromwell and Charles, in late 1795 and very early 1798), but Reuben was a known slacker and ne'er-do-well, and Sidney was still a Potter, not a Titus, at Charles's birth, so presumably the marriage never took place. Robert Potter, Richard's only brother, seems to have moved to Charlestown, adjacent to Boston. He probably died there in 1816.

Phebe Potter, finally, after going unremarked since her birth, moved to Andover, New Hampshire, and was living there by late 1826 or early 1827 along with her nephew Cromwell (Sidney's older son). (Cromwell himself had already spent some time living in Andover with his uncle in the winter of 1815–16 and perhaps longer, doubtless to help with the labor involved in establishing the new farm; he took IOUs from Richard Potter in December 1815 and April 1816, probably for his wages.) They lived next door to Richard and Sally, to all appearances man and wife (she was consistently recorded in town documents as Mrs. Cromwell Potter), and Phebe consistently gave her age as ten years less than it actually was. While Cromwell acquired a reputation as something of a slacker and drinker, Phebe was by all accounts widely respected. John Eastman, author of the *History of the Town of Andover, New Hampshire 1751–1906,* describes her as "an invaluable member of the community. Honest, industrious, an excellent cook and a competent nurse." He also makes clear how very conscious the residents were of her racial identity: "The colored blood in her veins, and it was very dark, was no bar at any table or fireside in the western end of the town. Twenty-five years ago there were many men and women living whose first toilets were made by the deft hands of Mrs. Potter. She died in the summer of 1860, aged 84. She had solved the race question." Perhaps it would be fairer to say that she had endured and survived it.

VI

The grand Frankland estate in Hopkinton where Potter was born in 1783 was already by that time in notable decline. Even eight years earlier, when Lady Agnes, inevitably suspected of Royalist sympathies, had left it and sailed to England in the troubled spring of 1775 on the very eve of hostilities (while awaiting her departure, she witnessed the Battle of Bunker Hill from her Boston mansion and afterward ministered to the wounded), the estate was becoming a genteel derelict. As the property of a presumed loyalist, it was considered confiscate, liable to sale for the benefit of the state. But the local Committee of Safety, when it arrived in the spring of 1776 to inspect and assess the property, found "many encumbrances"—to wit, "Mrs. Swain, sister of Lady Frankland, and Mrs. Swain's daughter and grandson, and three negro slaves of which one is old and blind." "Mrs. Swain's daughter," a child of her first marriage, was Sally McClester Dupee, herself already a widow; the grandson was Henry Frankland Dupee, the man of the estate, now thirteen or fourteen years old. The three slaves included Robert, an old retainer of Sir Henry's, now blind and sinking into dementia, "a kind of fossilized relict from the other world," who "continued to wear his tarnished livery and to powder his white and crisped locks until his death." Another of these slaves was probably Dinah, Potter's mother, who had given birth to her first child the previous year. These were complications that the Committee was not prepared to address. The Frankland estate remained in Lady Agnes's ownership and Mary Swain's possession.

With its extensive farmland, orchards, and gardens, the Frankland estate would, with some hired labor, have afforded its dependent residents far better than subsistence farming throughout the war; and its French estate manager, Jacques Villiers, would have kept the gardens and orchards productive. By the time of Richard's birth at the end of the war, however, the estate was already becoming a place of faded grandeur, managed almost entirely by women, already a backwater of Hopkinton history, its owner long absent and unlikely ever to return. But soon thereafter several important developments gave prospect of significant changes, whether for good or ill.

In 1783, Lady Agnes Frankland, who had settled in Chichester, England (quite near to Henry Cromwell), since her departure from Massachusetts in 1775 and had recently remarried, died at the age of fifty-seven. Upon her death, the grand Boston house was willed to her sister Mary Swain; the income from the rental of this property surely made a welcome infusion into the economy of the family at Hopkinton. The Hopkinton estate, meanwhile, passed into the possession of Henry Cromwell, who soon enough began trying to sell it. Conditions for a sale were not propitious in the immediate aftermath of the war, but some years later a buyer was found, and the estate was finally sold in 1793.

By this time, inevitably, the resident group in Hopkinton had changed again. Henry Frankland Dupee (Mary Swain's grandson) had come of age and had married, in 1785; his wife came to live on the Frankland estate at first, but by 1790 the couple had moved to Holliston and then to nearby Dedham and had a growing family. At about the same time, Daniel McClester (Mary Swain's first son) and his wife and child apparently moved back to the Frankland estate, for the wife, Sarah Stimson McClester, died there of smallpox in January 1793 and was buried in a solitary grave on the grounds. Then in 1793, when the estate was sold, the Dupees and his mother (Sally McClester Dupee) and grandmother (Mary Swain) all removed to Dedham, much closer to Boston.

But balancing this dispersal there had been other gatherings of the extended family. To begin with, Lady Agnes Frankland's youngest and favorite brother, Isaac Surriage, who had often visited her and Mary in Hopkinton, bought a farm in Hopkinton and settled there with his wife and two children. His daughter, Jane ("Jennie"), already had a long-standing attachment to the Frankland place; she had been "a great favorite of her aunt Frankland, whom she is said to have closely resembled in person, and with whom she spent many of her early days." These would have been very early days indeed, since Lady Frankland left Hopkinton in the spring of 1775, when Jennie was little more than two years old. But it easy to imagine that her resemblance to her famously beautiful aunt became a familial refrain among her other kin, and clearly she continued to stay in close touch with the remaining family on the Frankland estate after Lady Agnes departed. One of Julia Potter's anecdotes of her childhood, in fact, recounts how she and Jennie used to plague old Robert, the blind, antiquated family retainer who continued even after the war to wear livery and to powder his hair, by "powder[ing] his woolly head with Indian meal, ever taking good care to keep out of the reach of his cyclopean arms."

VII

What of young Richard's life during these ten years? He was, to begin with, never a slave, and never treated as one. At the same time, he was always black, and soon enough realized it.

By the time of Richard Potter's birth, slavery had ended in Massachusetts; and even before Dinah had begun bearing children, slavery had ended on the Frankland estate. A widely noted 1769 legal case in Cambridge, brought in the Middlesex County Court of Common Pleas (Hopkinton was in Middlesex County), in which a slave named James had sued his master, Richard Lechmere, for his freedom under the terms of the Massachusetts colonial charter, was a watershed moment for the antislavery movement in Massachusetts. James's lawyer made a strong case for his client, and Lechmere eventually settled out of court, giving James his freedom and paying some recompense for his prior servitude as well. Nason reports that all the Frankland slaves "were set at liberty soon after" this decision.

Other legal decisions soon followed to confirm this *de facto* status with the force of law. In 1780, Massachusetts ratified a new state constitution, and a slave woman in Sheffield, Massachusetts, named Bett (or Mumbet), hearing about its affirmation that "All men are born free and equal, and have certain natural, essential, and unalienable rights; among which may be reckoned the right of enjoying and defending their lives and liberties," sued for her own freedom. Her lawyers argued that the new constitution had effectively made slavery unconstitutional in Massachusetts. The jury agreed, and in 1781 the Berkshire court awarded her and a fellow plaintiff compensation for their slave labor as well as damages. (Bett thereafter took the name Elizabeth

Freeman.) At nearly the same time, in another case brought by another slave (Quock Walker) against his own master in Worcester County, another judge also found that slavery was now unconstitutional in Massachusetts. This case was appealed by the defendant but later dismissed by the Massachusetts Supreme Court. Meanwhile the state's attorney general also brought suit on behalf of Walker in Worcester County and again won Walker's case. With these 1781 decisions, slavery almost completely ended in Massachusetts: there was still no explicit law against it, but whites quickly realized that a slave who walked away from his or her enslavement could not be compelled to return to it. Blacks were still severely disadvantaged in numberless ways, but from now on every black living in Massachusetts was by rights a free person.

All accounts and anecdotes of Richard Potter's early life indicate that he was a favorite of the Frankland household. We can assume that it was Mary Swain, his mistress, who first taught him to read, since we know that she taught his older sister Julia. Nason also says, clearly on Julia's authority, that Potter "attended school" in Hopkinton. This would have been the so-called "District School"; according to a local historian, the children of the Samuel Valentine, Dr. Jeremy Stimson, Dr. Timothy Shepherd, and Gilbert Dench families, "besides several other families," were all educated there. Samuel Valentine and his wife, whose farm was adjacent to the Frankland estate, had twelve children between 1773 and 1797, of whom there were five living children one to ten years older than Richard Potter and five more one to nine years younger; he would have overlapped with from four to six of these in any given school term. Dr. Jeremy Stimson (Potter's much older half brother), whose house was close by, had a son (also Jeremy) Richard's age and four daughters ranging from two years older to six years younger; and presumably Richard Potter's older brother, Robert Potter, who lived with Dr. Stimson's family, attended the school, too. Of Gilbert Dench's many children, three daughters were two to five years older than Potter and one son was two years younger; Potter would have gone to school with all of these, too.

So certainly Richard had many playmates growing up. In addition to his schoolmates and neighbors, there were his older brother and sisters, and a few resident or visiting members of the extended Surriage/Swain family. Jennie Surriage visited regularly, and Polly McClester (daughter of Daniel, Mary Swain's son by her first husband) lived nearby and was about his age; John Dupee, son of Henry Frankland Dupee, lived on the estate or in a nearby town at this time and was two years younger than Potter. It is easy to imagine here a benevolent, female-dominated household with a range of children living comfortably and happily in an idyllic rural retreat.

But darker tones also color this picture, and they are often the tones of race. It is not entirely clear, to begin with, that Potter's mother, Dinah, was always a part of the household. In February 1789, the year that Potter turned six, the marriage intention of Dinah Franklin and "Pompe Allen of Boston" (his name clearly marked him as black) was published in Hopkinton. This could only have been Dinah, taking her last name now from the Franklands rather than from Mary Swain; there were no other Franklins or Franklands in Hopkinton at this time. There is reason to believe, however, that the marriage never actually took place. Richard Potter may have been too young to appreciate the family and racial considerations weighing on this liaison, but his older sister Julia, fourteen at the time, surely was sensitive to them. It was from Julia, moreover, that Nason learned the following anecdotes about Daniel McClester, a sometime resident at the Frankland place and (as she described him) "an inveterate snuff taker — poor — and a common sort of man": Daniel "Undertook to sell some negros — 'Boston' & wife, Jennie, marked on cheek from Africa — but was arrested in the attempt. . . . He bought a Negro of Mr. Lewis, Natick, and carried to H. [Hopkinton] on horse back — Negro's name 'Silvia'–." Boston's wife, Jennie — captured in Africa, branded on her face — could have been Dinah all over again. The man of the Frankland household was again trafficking in blacks. Richard Potter, household favorite though he might have been, would have soon learned and never forgotten that he and his siblings and his mother were not white.

The year 1793, when the property was sold, was a time of significant change at the Frankland estate and for the families intimately connected with it. For Richard Potter and his mother and siblings, it would have been particularly fraught. Julia left Hopkinton for a short time in 1793 to continue in service to Sally Dupee and Mary Swain after they moved to Dedham. But she soon returned to Hopkinton and entered service with the new owner of the Frankland estate, Dr. Timothy Shepherd. Another of Potter's sisters, Violet, also entered service with Dr. Shepherd. Dinah herself remained in Hopkinton, but apparently no longer on the estate; Nason reports that "she used to live in a nail shop below the grist mill." And Richard himself, it appears, soon moved into service with Isaac Surriage's family — already family to him, since Isaac and Jennie had often stayed at the Frankland estate when he was growing up. He was then about ten years old.

Potter remained in Hopkinton with the Surriages for approximately two years. His mother, at least several of his sisters, possibly his brother, and most of Mary Swain's family were still living in Hopkinton or close by, so his world had not changed very dramatically. But Jennie Surriage's world was changing: she was now of a marriageable age, and suitors were calling. What promised to be a major life transition for her proved, in the event, the beginning of a new era for Richard Potter as well.

# 2

# The Boston Years and Europe, 1795–1803

When William C. Nell published his groundbreaking *Colored Patriots of the American Revolution* in 1855, he included several pages about Richard Potter among his supplemental "Sketches of Several Distinguished Colored Persons." Nell was assembling accounts of hundreds of black Americans, both identified and anonymous, and was ready to adapt to the purposes of his book whatever accounts he could find already written. His sketch of Potter is taken nearly completely and nearly verbatim from a column that had appeared in the *Boston American Traveler* a few years earlier, a source that Nell explicitly acknowledges at one point. Yet with a few brief addenda of his own, Nell significantly illumined the next stage of Potter's early life.

Nell's first contribution to Potter's biography was already implicit in his book's arrangement. Nell organized his collection of sketches geographically, by states, and attempted to assign each of his subjects, not to the state of his or her first or greatest fame, but to the state of his or her birth. Thus, for example, he discusses David Walker, a prominent black abolitionist in Boston whose famous *Appeal to the Coloured Citizens of the World* galvanized public opinion throughout the country—and who had been a close neighbor to the Nells, and a familiar antislavery associate of Nell's father, when he wrote and published his *Appeal* in 1829—not in his "Massachusetts" chapter but in "North Carolina," because Walker had been born in Wilmington, North Carolina. Nell is the first historian to declare that Potter was a native of Massachusetts, "born in the town of Hopkinton, Mass." And Nell also offered unique new information about Potter's childhood: "When quite a boy, [he] was prevailed upon to engage himself in the service of Samuel Dillaway, Esq., of Boston—a relative of the family being on a wedding tour to that pleasant town"; he was then "'brought up' by Mr. Dillaway."

Nell's information is highly trustworthy because he was in a position to know such things. He grew up in the heart of Boston's black community on the north side of Beacon Hill and had been a neighbor—and his father, a close acquaintance—of many prominent black Bostonians who knew Potter well, people such as the Rev. Thomas Paul, Cornelius De Randamie, Peter Howard, and David Walker. Moreover, in 1827, when Nell was ten years old, Richard Potter lived for a year or so only a few blocks away from the Nells (and just down the street from Coffin Pitts, another of the senior Nell's close associates), on Beacon Hill in Boston. Nell himself had almost certainly known Potter, then, and had probably been among the children mystified and delighted by Potter's ad hoc sleight-of-hand demonstrations. Whether he got these biographical details firsthand from Potter or not, they were certainly known in Boston's black community, if not so widely in its white one.

With the information Nell provides, we can place the time of Potter's transition from Hopkinton to the Dillaway family in the Boston area quite accurately. As Nell says, Potter connected with Dillaway in Boston when "a relative of the family [was] on a wedding tour to that pleasant town." There is only one family relative, and one wedding, to which this story can possibly apply. In early April 1795, Peletiah Bixby Jr., a young man from a well-established farming family in Hopkinton, and Jennie Surriage, Potter's young mistress, published their intention to marry. The wedding, in Hopkinton, probably took place in May or June. Potter, now about twelve years old, who seems to have become Jennie Surriage's personal servant, would have been in attendance to the newlywed couple as they traveled to Boston.

We cannot be certain exactly how the Dillaways and the Bixbys intersected socially in Boston that season, but there were definitely both Hopkinton and family connections. In particular, two young Boston businessmen from Hopkinton had noteworthy relationships on both sides. Luther Bixby and John Jones Valentine, the two young partners of Bixby & Valentine, a firm dealing in West India goods on the Boston waterfront, would certainly have known Samuel Dillaway and his son as business acquaintances. Bixby & Valentine was based on Gardner's Wharf. Samuel Dillaway was at that time one of the most prominent Boston merchants in the maritime trade, and his own base, on Dillaway's Wharf, was close by, the third wharf to the southwest.

Given the closeness of their ages, moreover, Luther and John might also have known Samuel Dillaway junior as a friend.

Luther Bixby was the younger brother of Peletiah Bixby, Jennie Surriage's new husband, so he was now Jennie Surriage Bixby's brother-in-law. He was also very close in age to Jennie—perhaps nine months older than she—so he probably had been her playmate for years when she visited the Frankland place. John Valentine, not quite three years younger, was Luther Bixby's lifelong friend and now his business partner. John was the second son of Samuel Valentine, who owned a large farm adjacent to the Frankland estate, so he had been Jennie's next-door neighbor whenever she was at the Frankland place, and, two years younger than she, was also close enough in age to have been her playmate. John had grown up in Hopkinton, attending the same school that Richard Potter did (he was eight years older than Potter, so they probably overlapped at the school for only a few years). After his schooling, "he remained with his father a few years, when, becoming restless, his father gave him his time, and he went to Boston, and entered into business, and was long known under the firm of Bixby & Valentine." (Until a son reached his majority at twenty-one and came of legal age, he was legally the property of his father; any wages he might earn were his father's, as were any debts he might contract. If both parties agreed to it, however, a father could "give a son his time" before the son turned twenty-one. Then the son could keep his own wages and enter into contracts in his own right and would also be liable for his own debts.) Assuming that John attended school to about age sixteen, as was typical, it would have been about 1793 that he went to Boston. Luther and John would have been part of the wedding-tour events that took place in Boston.

It is easy to understand how the chance to work for Samuel Dillaway would have come as an inviting opportunity for Potter, an opportunity that the families with whom he had always lived would also have appreciated on his behalf. Hopkinton was a small, rural, agricultural community, with minimal opportunities for advancement in service or trade, whereas Boston was a major commercial and cultural center, bustling and prosperous, already the hub of New England. (Perhaps Potter had personal reasons for welcoming a change, too: Nason reports that the beautiful Jennie Surriage "was ignorant, haughty, and ill-tempered.")

Samuel Dillaway, moreover, was an established and prominent businessman in the city, potentially a very valuable connection. He had come to Boston as a housewright (so he is designated in deeds dating from the early 1780s), then became a lumber merchant, then expanded into the maritime trade more generally. He and a partner, Josiah Knapp, owned one of the many wharves in Boston harbor, Dillaway's Wharf (eventually Dillaway bought out his partner), and this served as the base of his business operations. Dillaway dealt in lumber from Maine for the thriving Boston construction and maritime trades, and flour from Baltimore and Alexandria. He and Knapp also co-owned one of the ships used in this trade, the brig *Neptune* (138 tons). He also traded in other merchandise and served as agent for ships using his wharf, whether for cargo or passengers. As he gained wealth and security, he also increasingly invested in real estate and in mortgages.

Dillaway and his wife had four children. Samuel junior, the oldest, was just turning twenty-one in 1795; he was about nine years older than Potter. He was apparently working for his father at this time but soon enough set up in business for himself, also in the maritime trade: he established a business dealing in ships' supplies and stores (anchors, cordage, rum, chocolate, flour, soaps, and so forth), based at 10 Long Wharf, the longest and busiest wharf in Boston harbor. Eliza, the second child and oldest daughter, was perhaps twenty. Hannah Dillaway, the third child, was about nineteen. She had married in late 1793 and so was no longer living in the Dillaway household and had recently (November 1794) given birth to a son. Her new husband, John Somes, was also a merchant based on Long Wharf (his place of business was 50 Long Wharf); he traded in tobacco, rum, brandy, and wine. The fourth Dillaway child, Mary, was about fifteen and still living at home.

Given the range, complexity, magnitude, and cosmopolitan clientele of Dillaway's businesses, Potter would have had remarkable opportunities for gaining a sound, practical business education. His connections with Samuel junior and perhaps with John Somes would have expanded his contacts and opportunities even further within the mercantile maritime world. He would necessarily have acquired facility with arithmetic and familiarity with book-keeping, accounts, contracts, inventories, and money management. He was now living and working with people who dealt with customers, business partners, professional colleagues, employees, and the general public every business day.

But while Potter's new social and, potentially, professional situation provided a vast change from his life on the quiet, isolated Frankland estate in Hopkinton, his new family, like his former one, was dealing with some serious stresses. Hannah Dillaway, the second daughter, who had left the household before Potter's arrival when she married John Somes in 1793, died in 1796 at the age of twenty, leaving an infant son, who most probably came to live with his mother's family. Another afflicting blow struck the family at about this time when Samuel Dillaway's wife, Mary Lambert Dillaway, died; perhaps her recent or imminent death was even a factor in Dillaway's decision to take Potter into service. There is no record of her death, which probably occurred in 1794 or 1795 (she was certainly still alive in November 1793 because when her husband sold a property then she was recorded as relinquishing her right of dower). She had been born in November 1747, so she was in her late forties at the time of her death. And soon after Potter's arrival, during a period when Samuel junior was courting his future wife, Samuel senior was also courting his second one. The elder Samuel Dillaway married another Mary, Mrs. Mary Minot, a forty-year-old widow, in late June 1797. (The younger Samuel Dillaway married Mary Knapp, the daughter of his father's business partner Josiah Knapp, four months later.)

The father's second marriage seems to have caused significant and lasting tensions and divisions within the Dillaway family. Indeed, the marriage may well have precipitated Samuel junior's decision to go into the mercantile business for himself at this time rather than continue in his father's firm, even though he was Dillaway's only son and his wife was the oldest daughter of Dillaway's longtime business partner. It would seem that most of the Dillaway children did not approve of their father's remarriage and that their father angrily defied their disapprobation. Evidence of this appears starkly and dramatically in the elder Dillaway's will, probated after his death in June 1822, some twenty-five years later. While providing carefully for his widowed sister and for his daughter Eliza (who was still, in her forties, a "Singlewoman"), Dillaway very pointedly left "to my Son Samuel Dillaway, to my Grandson John Somes [the only child of Dillaway's daughter Hannah, who had died in 1796], and to my Son in Law William S. Skinner [the widower of Dillaway's daughter Mary, who had died in 1818], Twenty five cents each. . . . And for reasons which have long influenced my feelings and sense of Justice It is my will that neither of them shall have anything more of my estate." The second Mrs. Dillaway had herself long since died, in 1811. But clearly the rupture provoked by Dillaway's second marriage never healed.

II

In the maritime world in which Potter was now living, a merchant ambitious to cultivate his suppliers and gain new ones, strengthen his trade contacts, and explore new markets would sometimes have cause to go to sea himself. We know that Samuel Dillaway junior did this at least occasionally, because the information surfaces in the shipping news from time to time. Shortly after

Dillaway's October 1797 marriage, for example, the captain of a ship returning to Salem from the Caribbean reported that at Saint-Pierre he had recently encountered the brig *Two Brothers,* Captain Brown, "with Samuel Dillaway, jun. on board" as a passenger (this would have occurred in late March 1798). In mid-May, the *Two Brothers* itself arrived in Boston from Martinique. Years later, in 1816, the younger Dillaway advertised that he would be leaving Boston for the West Indies on 1 November "and offers his services to any of his friends to transact business in the following islands—Barbadoes, Tobago, Grenada, St. Vincents, Martinique, Guadaloupe and St. Bartholomews."

We do not know if Potter accompanied Samuel junior to the Caribbean in 1798. (He may have; he told the publisher Nathan Hale in 1831 that he had been in the West Indies, and this would have been one such window of opportunity for him.) But opportunities for such travel must have arisen occasionally, so it is hardly surprising that he accompanied another family member abroad soon afterward. Nason learned from his Hopkinton sources that Potter "finally went with Mr. Skinner of Roxbury to reside in England." This would have been William Sutton Skinner, the new husband of Mary Dillaway (they married in September 1799). Skinner was another Boston merchant, an agemate of Samuel Dillaway junior. He and his wife and family eventually settled in Dorchester, but in an area that was indeed referred to familiarly as part of Roxbury. With his two brothers, he was part of his father's firm, John Skinner & Sons; they were importers and wholesale merchants of fine goods from England and France, so they were very much part of the business world in which the Dillaways operated. In the mid-1790s, the company's place of business was first on Codman's Wharf, then on Kilby Street (near Long Wharf), and then on Cornhill, a few blocks farther inland. Some of the brothers traveled occasionally to London or Paris on business. By early 1799 William left the family firm and went into business with a new partner as Baker & Skinner, still dealing in fine goods imported from Europe but now selling retail to the general public as well as wholesale. It seems probable that the family maintained connections with England, for later in life William served as agent to the British consul in Boston and, later still, as an agent for Lloyd's of London, the great insurance company.

In traveling to England with William Skinner, then, Potter was traveling with family. Indeed, it is difficult to imagine the arrangement's being countenanced until such a time as Skinner was, at the very least, extremely close to the family—and difficult also to imagine that Skinner could have left Potter behind in Europe without the Dillaways' approval and without Potter's having reached a certain level of education, competence, and maturity. Thus one very reasonable possibility is that this trip, like the one that brought Potter from Hopkinton to Boston, was a wedding tour by a newlywed couple. In that case, Potter would have traveled to England with William and Mary Dillaway Skinner in late 1799; he would then have been about sixteen years old. His young mistress, as well as her new husband, would have been on the scene to give him leave to strike out on his own when that occasion came.

III

There are several very vague and frequently conflicting stories about young Richard Potter's travel to Europe and eventual return to America. The most familiar—and least reliable—of these, recounted by Silas Ketchum in 1878, was that Potter, having been taken as a boy to London,

> was at ten years of age, picked up by a ship-captain, and carried as a cabin-boy to London. Being there turned adrift upon the city, he fell in with a travelling circus, with which, in the capacity of a servant boy, he remained four or five years, visiting all the large towns and cities of England; that the circus then came to America, and was the first that ever exhibited in the United States; then he returned to America with the company, being then past fifteen years of age, and continued in that service two or three years, during which time he acquired from his employers and associates the knowledge and practice of the art he afterwards pursued; and that, when about eighteen years old, he left the circus and set up business for himself as a magician and ventriloquist.

This account was given to Moses Goodwin, a New Hampshire newspaper editor, in the winter of 1875 by Stephen Fellows, who had been Potter's occasional assistant in the 1830s; Fellows was about sixty-eight at the time and was recalling stories from his mid-twenties. Goodwin, acting on Ketchum's behalf, was making inquiries in Andover, New Hampshire (Potter's home for much of his life), to pick up whatever Potter lore could be found.

The unreliability of Fellows's stories about Potter has long been noted, but alternative accounts of Potter's years away from America have been few, tenuous, and obscure. As we have seen, Nason learned from his Hopkinton, Massachusetts, sources simply that Potter "went with Mr. Skinner of Roxbury to reside in England, where he acquired the magical arts." This connection of Potter to a specific person was a unique piece of information, but all else was shadow.

A year or so before Ketchum and Goodwin became interested in learning about Richard Potter's history, however, a brief but very authoritative account of Potter's background was presented in 1874 by Gen. Henry K. Oliver, a prominent Massachusetts public figure. Oliver had known Potter in their younger days, in 1809–10, when Oliver was nine to ten years old and Potter twenty-six to twenty-seven. Potter, "a most worthy and excellent man," had worked as a domestic in the Oliver household in Boston and had fascinated the children (there were several: Oliver had one younger and four older sisters still living at home) with his occasional demonstrations of ventriloquism and legerdemain. About Potter's earlier life Oliver reported simply, "We understood from him that he learned his art from an expert in Italy, while on attendance as a travelling servant with a gentleman there."

Finally, near the end of his life Potter gave a very brief account of his European interlude to the inquisitive editor and publisher of the *Boston Daily Advertiser,* Nathan Hale, who happened to encounter Potter at a hotel while vacationing in the Lake Winnipesaukee region of New Hampshire in 1831 and cornered him to ask about Potter's history. Potter told Hale that "after leaving his relatives and the family of his mistress, he went with a gentleman through various parts of Europe; passed into several services, and finally returned as an assistant to Rennie the ventriloquist."

The last part of Hale's story here is muddled—or, more likely, is simply garbled in the retelling. As we will soon see, Potter certainly gained his ventriloquial training as an assistant to the Rannies. Almost certainly, however, he did not connect with them during his time in Europe, and indeed it was almost impossible that he could have encountered them then, for in the few years before they came to America in 1801 the Rannie brothers were mostly in Scotland and John Rannie was for a while in prison. But Potter did connect with and start working with the Rannies not long after he returned to America; so "returned to become an assistant to Rannie the ventriloquist" would have been a very accurate statement.

But from these accounts a few basic facts are clear. Potter traveled with a gentleman to England, and probably to other European countries as well. And while in Europe, he began his training as an entertainer—very possibly with that "expert in Italy."

As we have already seen, a variety of anecdotal and circumstantial evidence indicates that the gentleman with whom Potter traveled to England was William S. Skinner, Samuel Dillaway's new son-in-law. Skinner's initial destination was almost certainly London, for that city, an obvious attraction in itself, was also the source of almost all his firm's trade. Did he then travel "through various parts of Europe" also? For a honeymoon, he might well have wished to do this; for a merchant seeking to expand his sources of trade, there could be good business reasons for doing so as well. It is perhaps worth noting that while before this time John Skinner & Sons and then Baker & Skinner had imported goods almost exclusively from England (there is one mention of a cargo from France, in 1793), in 1800 one of the ships bringing consignments to Baker & Skinner was calling at Leghorn, Italy, whence it returned via London to Boston; and in 1801, when Skinner first took sole ownership of Baker & Skinner and then, at the end of the year, closed the business and auctioned off his entire stock, he emphasized that this included "Many French and Italian GOODS."

Apart from the information already cited here, there is little solid evidence about Potter's activities and whereabouts from the time he left Massachusetts in 1799 or so until the time he returned to the United States in (I shall argue) 1803. If we look back to these years from hints that surface early in Potter's subsequent American career, however, we can discover a few salient facts that are quite illuminating. With these, we can be quite confident about some turns in his life and make reasonable guesses about others.

One important hint comes from an epithet attached to and adopted by Potter by 1810–11, and what it implies. He was advertised—and, early in his independent career, he even advertised himself—as "the London Little Devil." The title "Little Devil" had very distinctive implications, which would have been clear to all culturally aware Englishmen and Americans: it signified, to begin with, that he was a master performer on the tightrope. The title went back to one Paulo Redigé, who performed as *le Petit Diable,* "the Little Devil." A prominent tightrope dancer in France in the 1780s, Redigé debuted in London with his close friend and fellow tightrope dancer Alexandre Placide at Sadler's Wells in 1781 and set off something of a craze, inspiring many imitators. Redigé returned to England each year from 1781 through 1792, always appearing at Sadler's Wells but making appearances elsewhere in London, too; he also toured widely through England during this period.

For the rest of the century, acrobats in itinerant companies all over England were adapting some version of the "Little Devil" sobriquet to advertise and distinguish themselves. Highfill, Burnim, and Langhans note that "at least three other persons who performed in London during some of the years in which Redigé was there also called themselves 'the Little Devil,' 'the Original Little Devil,' or 'the Real Little Devil,'" identifying them as, "respectively, the equestrians George Smith, Matthew Sully, and Giles Sutton." But that greatly understates the extent of this particular copycat phenomenon. In 1786 alone, for example, Charles Hughes's Royal Circus was advertising

Masters Robinson and Sutton as "the Little Devils" and, later, Master Charini as "a real Little Devil," while Jones's Equestrian Amphitheatre was simultaneously featuring "the Little Little Devil," all of them in direct competition with Redigé's performances at Sadler's Wells.

Once Redigé stopped coming to England after 1792, moreover, several performers who had previously refrained from taking the title upon themselves suddenly adopted it. It was at this point that Astley's Circus began advertising Sutton as "the original LITTLE DEVIL," a claim he had never advanced so long as Redigé had been on the scene. John Smith toured as the Little Devil with Handy's Circus in 1794 and 1795 and may also have been the Mr. Smith who performed with the Royal Equestrians as the Little Devil in 1799; Saxoni, a famous wire dancer from Rome who had been starring in England at least since 1793, toured widely as the Little Devil in 1799 and thereafter (he doubtless could not do so earlier because he frequently appeared with Handy's Circus at times when Handy was already billing Smith as the Little Devil); Mr. West toured as the Little Devil with Astley in 1802. All told, even by the turn of the century there were still typically two to four tightrope dancers or acrobats performing in England as so-called "Little Devils" every year.

Even in America, "the Little Devil" had currency, especially after Redigé joined Placide for a season of ballets and pantomimes (with acrobatics and ropedancing often introduced during the interludes) in New York and Philadelphia in 1792 (Redigé also made a brief solo appearance at Portsmouth, New Hampshire, near the end of that year). In New York, a Mr. Martin tried briefly to capitalize on Redigé's aura by exhibiting as the Little Devil for a short while in 1792 and 1793. In the spring of 1804, again in New York, a Mr. Maginnis (Samuel Jameson Maginnis) from London, presenting a collection of somewhat miniaturized mechanical performers who enacted a variety of dances, dramas, and feats, included in his program (along with such attractions as an "American Tar" who danced a hornpipe and the "Empress of Morocco" performing the "Olympic Castinet Dance") "a small Figure, (in imitation of the celebrated *Little Devil*)" who "will perform all matter of *Ground* and *Lofty Tumbling*, truly astonishing." And early in 1804 an impressive tightrope artist from Europe, Signior Manfredi, a relative newcomer on the American scene, performed in Philadelphia with John Rannie as "the Little Devil from Sadler's Wells."

Redigé, the original "Little Devil," first gained his acclaim as a tightrope dancer but soon added tumbling routines to his exhibitions. Potter seems to have acquired both sets of skills. By late 1810, when he was, as the London

Little Devil, supplementing James Rannie's ventriloquism exhibitions, he was performing a truly remarkable array of feats: "He balances, while on the wire, 100 full wine glasses; will also pass seven times through a small hoop, and, what is still more astonishing, he balances seven common chairs at one time. . . . He balances on his face a common wine glass, on the edge of which is a small sword. He tosses up oranges and eggs, while on the wire, plays on the violin, and goes to his knees." And years later, when Potter's young son (about thirteen years old at the time) began for a while to assist him in his act, young Master Richard was himself featured in acts of balancing: he "will go through many wonderful equilibriums, quite astonishing for a boy of his age." Clearly the father had taught the son.

A second obscure point of great importance about Potter's youthful years in Europe is hinted at in the first part of this same title. Early in his American career, Potter proudly proclaimed in his advertising that he was bringing his act to his audiences "from London"—more specifically, "from Sadler's Wells," London's and England's preeminent venue for ropedancing and acrobatic performances. This was a prestigious claim indeed and could not be made carelessly, for many Americans had taken in a show or two at Sadler's Wells and could at least test another's claim of familiarity with the place. Potter would not have been a featured act, of course; he was still a teenager and would necessarily have been an apprentice in his art. But as an apprentice he would have assisted with his master's feats and performed some of his own in a subordinate role.

Taken together, then, these hints from Potter's early advertising give important information about his history. Clearly he was highly trained and skilled as a ropedancer and acrobat, and he seems indeed to have acquired these skills while he was in Europe. It is worth noting, as well, that both the "Little Devil" and the "Sadler's Wells" allusions point exclusively to a background in tightrope and acrobatic performance, not to legerdemain or ventriloquism. These latter skills he would readily have acquired during his apprenticeship with the Rannies; the former would have been legacies of his earlier, European training. The allusions also lend credence to Henry Oliver's story that Potter had learned from an Italian master: the tightrope, in particular, was generally, although not exclusively, the province of Continental rather than of English artists. In any event, it is clear that, while he was a teenager in Europe, Potter made the initial connection and entered upon the apprenticeship that was to direct his career into a life of performance.

There is one last important assemblage of circumstantial evidence, moreover, that, taken together with these others, strongly suggests the identity of his ropedancing master. For there was one man—an Italian, no less—who connected Sadler's Wells with American stages and theaters, and tightrope dancing and feats of agility with the Rannies' sleights of hand and ventriloquism. We have already encountered him briefly: Signior Manfredi, who performed with John Rannie at the turn of the years 1803–4, when Richard Potter was twenty years old.

To be sure, there were other European ropedancers touring in America at this time, and a handful of other touring performers who claimed Sadler's Wells credentials. It is possible, as well, that Potter returned to America on his own and then later connected with the Rannies independently—although such a scenario would be inconsistent with the various brief stories of his having returned to America as a performer's assistant or as part of a company. But, as we will see, the intersection of Manfredi with the Rannies and their associates was so timely and apt, and Manfredi's own background so consistent with all we can deduce of Potter's apprenticeship, that the circumstantial evidence for their association is quite compelling.

Whether the "expert in Italy" with whom he in his late teens apprenticed as a ropedancer and gymnast was Manfredi or another, we can be fairly confident about what kind of training Potter would have received. That he was physically and temperamentally suited for it there is no doubt: Nathan Hale's source, almost certainly Jennie Surriage Bixby, reported—with racial overtones, surely—that young Richard "was as agile as a squirrel, and as full of trick and mimickry as a monkey." But he was in fact unusually old to be beginning it, for such training typically began in early childhood. As A. H. Saxon has noted, children brought up in circus families "followed a carefully prescribed regimen of increasingly difficult exercises and acts." He instances the training of a young equestrienne: "Beginning with posturing at around five years of age and progressing through balancing, gymnastics, stilt walking, slack wire, tightrope, dancing, combat with broadsword, musical instruments, and riding in entrées—with a variety of exercises in the different steps—the pupil eventually arrived at a single act of horsemanship." For a tightrope dancer in training, the ultimate destination—that special, distinguishing "single act"—would have been different, but the preparatory progression very much the same. Potter's training must have been all the more intense for having been compressed into his later teenage years; some of his fellow troupers would have had a ten years' start on him. Manfredi's own daughters were being featured in solo performances on the tightrope when they were thirteen and fifteen years old, if not earlier.

Most of the acrobats and ropedancers coming to England from abroad came from either France (as had the Little Devil and Placide) or Italy, and Signior Manfredi was Italian. (In 1805 he was even performing with the "Italian Theatre" in New York.) Like many European performers, he raised his entire family in his profession: his wife and his two daughters were also ropedancers and acrobats, and in 1805 he brought them all with him to America, where the family performed regularly for many years. In 1802, however, Manfredi, who had already toured widely across Europe—his advertisements proclaimed that he had performed in Vienna, Madrid, Lisbon, Saint Petersburg, and Constantinople and "the various courts of Europe"—was introducing himself to London audiences, and planning a first, exploratory tour of America, as a solo act. He performed at Sadler's Wells during late 1802 or early 1803. The records of Sadler's Wells from this period are badly incomplete, so we cannot be sure exactly when Manfredi appeared there, but he subsequently advertised himself as "lately from Saddlers Wells" when he was performing in Philadelphia in December 1803–January 1804.

From London, Manfredi and presumably Potter traveled to Paris (this was during a window of uneasy calm, the yearlong Peace of Amiens, between periods of English–French warfare), and performed there. On 6 April, as the peace was threatening to break down, they sailed on the ship *South Carolina* from Le Havre-de-Grace for New York; the ship carried a cargo of dry goods, millstones, and plaster of Paris for merchants in the city, a load of "Casts which have been made from some of the principal statues in Europe" for the recently established American Academy of the Arts, and more than a dozen passengers. The *South Carolina* arrived at New York on 15 May.

Manfredi quickly won wide attention and great praise in New York. On 27 May the manager of the theater announced that, "to give the greatest possible variety and novelty," he had "engaged, for a few nights, a gentleman who has the highest reputation in Europe for performances and grace, agility and skill on the Tight rope and Trampoline, in Ballancing, Pantomime, Artificial Fire, and other Theatric Exhibitions." Signior Manfredi, he added, was "just arrived from Paris, having exhibited at all the courts of Europe." The initial reviews were highly favorable. A critic in the *New York Republican Watch-Tower* reported a few days later that, while he had doubted that Manfredi's exhibition could approach the astonishing claims of the advertisement, he "found the performances really exceed the promise," and declared that "Signor Manfredi is, beyond all comparison, superior to any other performer in his line, we have ever seen." Another, writing in the *New York Herald* the same day, reported that the audience "testified their opinions by repeated and long-continued shouts of applause," and concluded by judging "that in point of agility, grace, and difficulty, neither *Placide* nor *Spinacula* bear any comparison with him."

Manfredi's repertoire was indeed remarkable. While on the tightrope, he would perform various dances (both grotesque and serious) and military maneuvers; "sit in a chair, on the rope, with a table before him, from which he will eat and drink"; "dance with a boy on his shoulders"; "dance with baskets on his feet"; and "do the trick of the Flip Flap on the rope." It is no wonder that he impressed his audiences and his critics.

Evidencing its great success, Manfredi's engagement at the theater stretched out from the initial "few nights" to some five and a half weeks, until the end of the theater season in early July. Then in late July and early August he exhibited for another week and a half at the summer theater in Mount Vernon Garden before leaving New York.

Manfredi's announced destination now was Boston. On his way there he exhibited in several other towns, possibly in Connecticut and certainly in Rhode Island—at the theater in Newport for several nights (a critic there said his "astonishing feats on the Tight Rope far exceed every thing of the kind ever attempted"), at the theater in Providence for several more. But then, surprisingly, he traveled on to Boston only to overshoot it: rather than opening in Boston immediately, he continued on his way north to perform first in Portsmouth, New Hampshire, and then worked his way back to Boston, pausing en route to exhibit in Newburyport for more than a week and in Salem for a week-plus more. He may well not have performed much or at all in other towns along his way: given the nature of his equipment and his feats, he needed a theater or a spacious hall for his exhibitions. A large room at a tavern might do for tumbling and balancing acts, but the height at which Manfredi worked on the tightrope required a much grander venue for that act. Finally, at the very end of October, he moved on to Boston itself.

v

We might pause here to ask why Manfredi contorted his itinerary as he did, bypassing Boston for several weeks to perform instead in much smaller cities and towns first. As it happens, a long-forgotten annotation by a nineteenth-century New Hampshire newspaper editor may give us an important clue, for it hints that Richard Potter, rather than remaining with Manfredi throughout these four months since the latter had arrived in New York from Paris, had hastened ahead back to his New England home and had then established himself temporarily in Portsmouth while awaiting Manfredi's own arrival in New England.

The hint is as follows. In November 1851, the *Boston American Traveller* published perhaps the first sustained reminiscence of Richard Potter (who had died sixteen years before, in 1835). The author was almost certainly one of the newspaper's two editors, Ferdinand Andrews and the Rev. George Punchard; both men had grown up in Salem when Potter was regularly performing there, and both knew Henry K. Oliver (in whose Boston home Potter had worked as a domestic just before beginning his own career), so either man could have had the interest and knowledge to write this article. Eventually a few other newspapers also picked up the article and ran it: it appeared in the *Manchester (NH) Union Democrat* later that same month, and then in the *Portsmouth Journal* in mid-1852. And in the latter reprinting, the *Journal* editor appended a postscript note: "Our old citizens will recollect that Potter, the celebrated ventriloquist, was in his younger days a polite waiter at the old Portsmouth Hotel on Water Street, destroyed by the great fire of 1812."

The author of this note was C. W. Brewster, a famous Portsmouth newspaper editor and local historian who regularly contributed stories about old Portsmouth in a "Rambles about Portsmouth" column to his own newspaper. He returned to this anecdote about Richard Potter years later, in one of his "Rambles" devoted to "Central Portsmouth previous to the Great Fire": "On the west of the Pier edifice and nearly adjoining it, on the north corner of Water street, was the *New Hampshire Hotel*, a large brick building, where ship masters, mates and the public generally, found accommodations. In this hotel the celebrated ventriloquist Potter, whose fame was world-wide in his day, was in his early life a servant." Brewster (b. 1802), too, would have seen Richard Potter in his youth, probably often. And he was famous as an authority on old Portsmouth; his assertion thus is highly trustworthy.

Does this recollection date back to 1803? Potter was twenty years old then—certainly "in his younger days." Indeed, there is really no other time in his life, apart from 1803, when Richard Potter is likely to have been living in Portsmouth for any length of time. It is true that he performed in Portsmouth under his own name as early as 1809, very early in his professional career; but during the 1808–10 period we know he was based in Boston and traveling widely. So it is worth examining seriously the possibility that this brief glimpse of Richard Potter's early life belongs to 1803. And it turns out that various subtle details of Manfredi's advertising strongly suggest that Richard

Potter may well have been serving as something of an advance man for him in Portsmouth at just this time.

When he reached Portsmouth in September 1803 after traveling from Providence via Boston, Signior Manfredi began appearing in one of the largest venues in town, the Assembly Room. Even though Portsmouth then had three weekly newspapers, however, Manfredi did not advertise in any of them. The reason was that he didn't need to: instead, he had arranged to have a special broadside printed advertising his performances and detailing some of the astonishing feats that he would perform.

And what a broadside! These sheets were the most ephemeral of advertising materials, posted in public and usually out-of-doors, so very few of them remain. By great good fortune, one of Signior Manfredi's Portsmouth broadsides has survived (fig. 1). It is one of the most remarkable documents of its type in early American publishing. The text of Manfredi's extensive, tightly structured advertisement for his performance is laid out in careful, dramatic typography across the center of the bill. But what makes the sheet so stunning is that it is framed, top and bottom, by a total of six dramatic woodcuts—three above, three below—each showing, within a near-circular frame about 3.75 inches (9.5 cm) in diameter, Manfredi performing one of his astonishing feats, many of them specifically mentioned in the text. At the lower left, for example, is a woodcut showing Manfredi on the tightrope "danc[ing] with baskets on his feet"; at the lower right, Manfredi is poised upright on the tightrope in a military uniform, aiming a musket—the "Manoeuvre of a Military man"; at the upper left, he and four young assistants present something like "A grand Pyramid, composed of several Children, who will stand on his arms, body and feet, representing several Roman prospects."

A sheerly wonderful material object in itself, this broadside also demonstrates beautifully how a major artist like Manfredi could, at a relatively modest cost, tailor his advertising to his immediate needs and circumstances. The woodcuts, designed and carved by a skilled artisan (in this instance, surely one in New York City), would be the property of the performer, of course, and he would carry them with him on his travels. The performer could then do business with a local printing office even on days when the weekly newspaper was not being printed and could quickly obtain magnificent, eye-catching promotional materials that, when publicly posted, simply could not be ignored. Moreover, this particular broadside is not a fill-in-the-blanks template to be used for various dates and venues; it specifies the time ("This Evening, Friday, Sept. 23") and place ("Portsmouth," "at the ASSEMBLY ROOM") of performance. It would serve well for Manfredi's entire stand in

Portsmouth, since it also gives a schedule of his performances ("every Monday, Wednesday, and Friday"). When he moved to another town, he would need to have another batch of broadsides printed. But that, at least, would afford him the opportunity of designing his broadside anew and varying his use of his woodcuts.

So this particular broadside was carefully crafted for a very specific audience—the citizens of Portsmouth and vicinity in the early autumn of 1803. Thus one more of its promises, which was directly aimed at this particular audience, now speaks suggestively to us as well. It is one of the specific events listed on the program of performances: "A person of This Town will perform a number of feats on the rope, with the ballance pole."

There are no certainties here; we are dealing with probabilities, possibilities, degrees of likelihood. But, that said, and knowing that Richard Potter did live for a while in Portsmouth, it does seem likely that this "person of This Town" is young Richard Potter, appearing on a program (if anonymously) for perhaps the first time in his life; and likely also that Signior Manfredi had traveled directly from Rhode Island to Portsmouth so that he could bring Potter back into his act for at least the remainder of his tour through Newburyport, Salem, and finally Boston.

VI

All the signs now pointed to Manfredi's staging a lengthy engagement in Boston. But something happened: no sooner had he begun to exhibit there than he completely changed his plans. The occasion of this swerve was apparently an encounter and passing collaboration with another foreign, itinerant performer, a journeyman slack-rope dancer, tumbler, and now magician named William Duff. Richard Potter was a mere bystander at this development, but it would completely change his life.

William Duff himself was almost as obscure a figure in the world of entertainment as was Richard Potter. As a slack-rope dancer and balancer, he had never been more than a supporting figure in other performers' exhibitions; later, as a novice magician and as a play-actor, he had remained a shadowy figure, staging very modest exhibitions mostly for remote, provincial audiences. But he had some interesting connections, and this is clearly what captured Manfredi's attention.

Most significantly, Duff was a colleague and associate of two Scottish brothers from Elgin, James and John Rannie, who for more than two years now had been performing widely and very successfully in the United States.

These two brothers would soon change the course of Richard Potter's life, so we need to pause for a moment to learn something of their immediate background.

James Rannie, the older brother, was a highly skilled magician and ventriloquist. He had learned ventriloquism while apprenticing in England, Scotland, and Ireland with Thomas Garbut, one of the earliest English ventriloquists, and had probably learned magic from Sieur Herman Boaz while touring in northern England and southern Scotland. It is also quite likely that he had traveled with a circus for a while, because he had acquired skills in balancing and in slack-wire walking that were not easily attainable any other way. John Rannie, younger by more than four years, had worked as a "Strolling Player" or "Play Actor" before also acquiring skills as a ventriloquist and magician, almost certainly while assisting his brother.

America offered promising new opportunities for Old World performers at the very beginning of the nineteenth century, which of course was why Manfredi himself was now touring there, but the Rannies had particular reasons of their own for coming. John Rannie, indeed, had been on the point of abandoning his itinerant profession and finding stable employment in his hometown of Elgin "in the mercantile line." But these were very hard times in Elgin and across Scotland, and widespread protests were taking place concerning the high price of grain. On two consecutive nights in early February 1800, John had become involved in protests in Elgin which had exploded into mob action, with hundreds of angry people mobbing several farmhouses and mills in parishes near Elgin "for the purpose of procuring Meal." Mob rule obtained; enforcers among the group reportedly threatened hangers-on with violence if they tried or offered to leave it. Many members of the mob had their faces covered with meal or soot in a gesture of disguise.* They forced their way into and searched several houses and buildings for stores of meal and for the suspected hoarders, threatened the occupants, and forcibly confiscated some quantity of meal.

In the aftermath of these particular mobbings, three residents of Elgin, John Rannie among them, were arrested and charged with "Mobbing and

---

*"Mobbing" has workplace connotations today, but it was a well-established form of political and social protest in the eighteenth century. The Boston Tea Party (1773) became America's archetypal instance of mobbing; in that event, the participants disguised themselves as face-painted American Indians rather than smearing their faces with meal or soot as the Elgin mobbers did.

Rioting." Why only these three were identified and charged is not known. Clearly they were not ringleaders, and on the first night the mob was already assembled and in motion when John Rannie (who had been away from Elgin and was just returning to town) happened upon it. But Rannie's involvement, under whatever duress, was incontestable, and surely his plea that he had been forcibly prevented from leaving the mob the first evening lost all of its potential persuasiveness when he ventured out into the riotous crowd again the following night.

The case was tried before the Circuit Court of Judiciary at Inverness at the beginning of May. "After a pretty long trial," the jury found John Rannie guilty of four of the five specific charges made against him; "In consideration of his youth [he was twenty-three years old] and other paliating circumstances [we] recommend him to the mercy of the Court." The court's sentence for Rannie was one month in prison, to begin immediately; after that, he was given a month to leave Scotland and was then banished from Scotland for a period of seven years.

So much for setting up a small mercantile business in Elgin! Suddenly John Rannie's farewell to his itinerant life was thrust back upon him. He had been ready to give over his performing ambitions and pursue a more regular, traditional life at home. Now not only home, but his entire country, were forbidden him, and his skills and experience as a "strolling player" and ventriloquist might be all that he could trade on.

John Rannie would have been out of prison by early June 1800 and out of Scotland by early July. Probably he moved at first to England or Ireland. But soon he began planning a trip to America, where he could make the best of his enforced exile from Scotland; many others from Elgin had already emigrated there during the preceding twenty years of hard times at home. Surely he spent long days and months during this period studying with and assisting his brother James, rehearsing and refining the ventriloquism and sleight-of-hand skills that could bring him success and independence. (At the time of John's trial, James was performing in Aberdeen, sixty-five miles east of Elgin, presumably waiting for news of the verdict. After this there is no further record of his performing anywhere in Great Britain.) And John would have company in his new undertaking; a young Dubliner he had met at some point in his travels, a slack-rope dancer named William Duff, would team up with him and assist him.

John Rannie and William Duff sailed for America in the spring of 1801. In early May they were advertising their exhibition in Philadelphia:

MR. RANNIE,

The celebrated Ventriloquist, from Edinburgh, Glasgow and Aberdeen,
Will display his power in the astonishing natural gift of Ventriloquism, in a
most surprising manner, beyond the power of words to express. . . .
He will also perform a variety of
Magical Deceptions,
and various Imitations
He mimics the notes of various birds in a surprising
Manner—To conclude with
Slack-Wire Dancing and Balancing,
By Mr. Duff, from Dublin.

This exhibition marked the advent of ventriloquism in America.

John's inaugural exhibitions in Philadelphia were a qualified success. A few
critics and audiences were harsh; but he was able to charge good prices for
his tickets, and audiences kept coming as he varied his programs, so that he
continued performing in Philadelphia for a full month. Meanwhile, he was
certainly corresponding with his older brother James, back in Scotland. The
trial run in Philadelphia by his younger brother was proving sufficiently successful to confirm James in his own plans: he would follow John to the New
World, and they would tour the major cities along the seaboard with their
full, combined act. James, accordingly, soon was finalizing arrangements to
sail for Boston. John meanwhile began a leisurely campaign north through
New Jersey to New York City, where he would wait for news of James's arrival
while continuing his own exhibitions with Duff.

James Rannie arrived in Boston in late November and soon took the city
by storm, performing for two months to great acclaim. John, having exhibited six weeks in New York, arrived in Boston in mid-January, and thereafter
the brothers performed together; but the "Messrs. Rannies" joint billing of
the initial evenings soon changed to a celebration of "Mr. Rannie"—that is,
James Rannie—alone, and John Rannie disappeared from his brother's advertising (while remaining part of the program) just as completely as William
Duff had already (while remaining part of both brothers' programs) disappeared from John's. These patterns continued as the Rannies moved from
Boston to New York (for two months) and then Philadelphia (almost two
and a half months). The brothers clearly did not work well together: James
was domineering, and John was resentful. John (probably with Duff) left
James to perform in New York and struck out again on his own, exhibiting in

Baltimore for a week; then the brothers reunited in Philadelphia, only to split up again after about five weeks of performing together again there.

Since mid-1802, the Rannies had been pursuing very separate tours. James, after touring around the Middle Atlantic states for a few months, had headed south to make long stands in Charleston and Savannah, and more recently (summer 1803) had been touring his way back north, performing in North Carolina and Virginia, before veering off for a while into the Caribbean. John, meanwhile, after a bit of exhibiting elsewhere in Pennsylvania subsequent to his departure from Philadelphia, had spent most of the following year touring widely through Maryland, Virginia, and the District of Columbia. (There is a chance the brothers met again in or near Georgetown, D.C., in August 1803, although they did not perform together.) Together and separately, the two brothers had by now widely advertised and firmly established ventriloquism throughout the original thirteen states as a new, exciting performance genre. Their magic was wonderful, and duly celebrated as such, but their ventriloquism was apparently unique and inimitable. It was the attractiveness of this new entertainment power that prompted Signior Manfredi's swerve from Boston in November 1803.

VII

The first hint of this new influence comes just before Manfredi's opening in Boston, during his week in Salem, where, in the midst of an advertisement for his various tightrope and tumbling performances, he inserts the odd and incongruous promise, "He will do various Deceptions never performed here." His advertisement the next week elaborates somewhat on this, for now he announces that his performances on the tightrope will be "followed with a number of new deceptions and feats of legerdemain." The mystery of this new feature on Manfredi's program soon deepens in his first advertisement in Boston, on 9 November. Significantly, this is only secondarily his advertisement; it opens by giving precedence and emphasis instead to a coperformer who, curiously, remains nameless. The anonymous headline exhibitor is "a Gentleman lately from the West-Indies, who, to the astonishment of the spectators, will perform the following feats of Dexterity of Hand." What follows is, first, a list of several of Rannie's tricks, including causing a playing card drawn from a deck to vanish into the pocket of another person across the room, catching a fired bullet on the point of a sword, and breaking and restoring a lady's gold ring. Next, there would be a display of balancing feats, "with pipes, plates, swords, glasses, eggs, keys, tables, chairs, spoons, knives, forks, &c. perpendicular, triangular and horizontal, upon different parts of his face"—again a litany of Rannie's feats and even a borrowing of his descriptions. And finally the anonymous gentleman promises a selection of "Philosophical Experiments" ("the wonderful Flower-Pot," "the transparent bottle"). Only after all this does Manfredi receive mention; his blurb and promises are confined to the latter portion of the lengthy advertisement.

The simple truth is that there was almost certainly no one in America in 1803 apart from the Rannies and Duff who could creditably perform the range of feats that this anonymous gentleman is advertising. But James Rannie was certainly not in Boston at this time. Indeed, he was where this gentleman had just been, in the West Indies: within a week or so of this time he was giving performances in Jamaica, where he continued until mid-February. And John Rannie, most recently in Maryland and eastern Pennsylvania, was now probably already in Philadelphia making preparations for the grand, collaborative exhibition that he would open there in early December. The likeliest explanation, then, is that this gentleman was Duff, who since parting from John Rannie had been performing in New England earlier in 1803 (he had appeared in Newport and Salem that spring), and who was himself now making preparations to reunite with his old collaborator John Rannie in Philadelphia. An encounter with Manfredi in the Boston area would have been natural, almost inevitable: Duff, remember, was a skilled wire dancer himself (although on the slack wire, not the tightrope), as well as a balancing master.

In any event, the upshot was that Manfredi, having barely begun to perform in Boston, almost immediately shut down his exhibitions, decamped, and turned southward to join John Rannie's planned exhibition in Philadelphia. After advertising his second performance in Boston—this time the advertisement was apparently placed by Manfredi rather than by Duff, for it gives all prominence to Manfredi and only secondarily and without attribution alludes to the accompanying performances of his fellow performer on the program—he appeared no more in that city, even though he had just promised that his performance "will be altogether different every evening," indicating that he had indeed anticipated making a longer stand there.

We can begin to derive from all these details a sketchy picture of the networking communications that linked these players to one another. James Rannie was currently touring in the West Indies; William Duff had just arrived in Boston from there and so may have been in touch with James then and very possibly even touring with him for a while; Manfredi would soon enough be planning his own trip to Havana (a decision he made while performing with John Rannie in Philadelphia, although its seed may well have been planted a bit earlier by Duff), where James Rannie would be stopping at the same time on his route back from Jamaica to New York. John Rannie, who had been touring in Virginia, Maryland, and Pennsylvania, now was pointing toward a major engagement in Philadelphia; his old associate William Duff would eventually be joining him there, preceded by Duff's new associate, Manfredi.

These performers were quickly involved in other professional interactions beyond those just mentioned. In Philadelphia, for example, Rannie's exhibitions were sometimes expanded by "Mr. G. Durang," who performed a clown's role and danced a hornpipe. The first initial was an easy misprint; this was certainly Master C. (for Charles) Durang, oldest son of John Durang, a well-known Philadelphia dancer and performer. John Durang and his company (which meant, primarily, his family, just as it did in Manfredi's case) had performed with John Rannie in Lancaster, Pennsylvania, in July 1802. (Durang was a native of Lancaster; he and Rannie had probably met that April, when the Rannie brothers were performing together in Philadelphia while Durang was appearing as a dancer at the theater there.) Now Durang was appearing as a principal dancer with the theater company performing at the New Theatre (the Chestnut Street Theatre). His wife and their two older children (Charles, now barely thirteen, and Ferdinand, about seven or eight) would be engaged as dancers with the same company soon after Rannie's exhibition ended, but for the time being Master Charles was available to clown with Rannie's assemblage. (Such skills were part of the family's repertoire; his father had once played the clown in Rickett's Circus.) This connection, too, led to later collaborations: Manfredi reunited with Durang and his small company for some performances in Baltimore the following August. And years later, when Richard Potter was establishing his own independent career, he found his way to another Durang: Jacob junior, John Durang's younger brother, also in the family business, who sometimes toured with John, had set up in Boston as a dancer and dancing teacher in about 1811, and Potter connected with him and hired his hall as a venue for his performances in May–June 1813.

It was into this new, American network of professional and personal relationships that Manfredi, and with him Potter, now found their way. Richard Potter was now about twenty years old. He was still but an anonymous performer in Manfredi's small troupe, appearing in the "ground and lofty tumbling" that occupied the stage in the intervals between the more prominent acts. There is perhaps a hint of him at the very end of Rannie's, Manfredi's, and

Duff's Philadelphia engagement when one final advertisement announces "famous Tight Rope Dancing by the Little Devil from Sadler's Wells, London," but a simultaneous advertisement in another paper indicates that this sobriquet is suddenly being attached instead to the headliner: "Mr. Manfredi, the Little Devil, from Sadlers Wells, in London, will perform the TIGHT ROPE." Still, the hint should not be dismissed out of hand. Manfredi himself soon enough would hand off this nickname to a new young pupil that he added in America to his own company: the so-called "Little American" ("an *eleve* of Mr. M____'s, not 8 years old") regularly played the role of the "Little Devil" in pantomimes in Manfredi's 1806 and 1807 exhibitions.

So it was that, just as John Rannie's career was cresting in his grand Philadelphia exhibition of late 1803 and early 1804, Richard Potter serendipitously intersected with it and then latched on to it. Probably he had intended to stay in America now in any case and was watching for opportunities, for Manfredi would certainly be returning to Europe soon enough to rejoin his family.* John Rannie, on the other hand, would be staying in America for the foreseeable future and could offer training in entirely new entertainment fields wherein there were few or no competitors. By the beginning of 1804, Richard Potter was apprenticing to a ventriloquist.

*Manfredi remained in America for something over a year, until August 1804. Early the following summer he returned to America, this time with his entire family, and this time to stay; the Manfredis would perform in major cities in the eastern United States and Canada, first on their own and later traveling with a circus, for the next eight years.

# 3

# The Apprentice Years and
# Early Career, 1804–1815

## I

After John Rannie and Signior Manfredi concluded their grand exhibition in Philadelphia in mid-January 1804, their odd assortment of principals and secondaries went their separate ways. William Duff and his wife continued for a while with Rannie, and we can be confident that young Richard Potter accompanied them. They traveled now down the Eastern Shore of Maryland, first to Centreville and then to Easton. In Easton, they divided their acts for the nonce into separate exhibitions: Duff and Rannie placed separate advertisements in a single issue of the local newspaper, the *Republican Star,* according to which Duff would entertain on Tuesday evening with magical deceptions, balancing and slack-wire dancing, and a performance of a brief farce, *The Doctor's Courtship,* while Rannie would present some other deceptions and demonstrate his "Miraculous Powers of VENTRILOQUISM" on the following evening. The division was a prelude to their temporary parting of ways; soon after this, Rannie (and presumably Potter with him) crossed the Chesapeake Bay to perform in Annapolis and then, farther west, in Frederick, while the Duffs remained on the Eastern Shore for another month or so.

Meanwhile, James Rannie had returned from the West Indies in March and by early April was performing to great acclaim in New York. Now the brothers decided to try working together and combining their acts once more. James was preparing to tour next into New England again; John traveled to meet him. Whether the brothers connected in New York and then traveled together thence to Newport, Rhode Island, or instead traveled separately to Newport and met there, we do not know; but in any event James Rannie gave his final New York performance on 24 May, and by 2 June he and his brother were together in Newport. Possibly one or both of them had passed through the town before, but neither had ever performed there—although William Duff had, in early 1803, while John had been in Virginia and James in South Carolina, and Signior Manfredi, possibly with Potter in tow, had exhibited there the preceding August.

Thus it happened that Richard Potter finally came into contact with James Rannie, who would do so much to shape his career, in late May or early June 1804. He came into James Rannie's life just at the time that John Rannie was getting out of it. That week of performances in Newport was probably the only time that the three of them ever all worked together.

II

At this stage of his life Richard Potter was still a deeply obscure, almost invisible person. In the summer of 1804 he was approximately twenty-one years old. He had no settled abode and was listed on the tax rolls of no community. For the past year he had moved about the northeastern coastal towns of America continually, and before that he had been abroad for several years. As an assistant or apprentice, he was nameless in the advertising of his profession, and that advertising itself was highly ephemeral; moreover, his profession was an itinerant one, and its itineraries were themselves irregular and ad hoc.

So while we know from his own testimony and from other supporting evidence that Potter apprenticed with James Rannie, and while clearly such an apprenticeship would require a period of some years, we cannot say with certainty exactly when that apprenticeship began or what interruptions it might have known. Even so, we can confidently date its beginning to this narrow period of time, the late spring of 1804. For, as we will see, there is good evidence placing Potter newly in business, and newly in Boston, in 1804 or so; and Boston was James Rannie's destination now. So from this point forward we can with real confidence trace Richard Potter's career for several years simply by tracing James Rannie's.

For John Rannie, who had frequently worked with his brother before (and as frequently parted company with him, usually in a huff), the Newport reunion with James was a familiar and doubtless a frustrating experience: as always, the older brother was in full control, with the younger relegated to the merest passing mention at the very end of a long and detailed advertisement of the exhibition's wonders ("Mr. Rannie, the younger, will display a variety of surprising imitations"). But what was this experience like for Richard Potter?

The Rannies' acts and skill sets overlapped enormously, but by this time a significant distinction between them was becoming apparent. James, already by wide repute much the better ventriloquist, was placing the greater emphasis on this part of his act and was also becoming more daring and imaginative in his exhibitions of the phenomenon. John typically associated ventriloquism with his imitations and caused a voice to seem to appear from objects in the room at some distance from him (and from his audience as well). But James now had such confidence in his deceptive abilities that he had begun putting the voice right in the midst of his audience. He promised to "cause the voice of a child to appear to speak from the pocket of any lady or gentleman present"; and it was at just this point in his career that he began featuring in his advertisements a set of anecdotes that apparently dated from one of his New York performances in late April 1804: "when the voice [of a child] came from a lady's muff, on a late evening's exhibition, the lady was so impressed with the idea of reality she threw the muff away, with exclamations of terror and astonishment. In like manner the *notes* of a Pig reverberated from a gentleman's pocket, and, on his being asked by Mr. R. to set the pig at liberty, the gentleman said he would do it provided Mr. R. would insure his hand from being bitten." So when Richard Potter observed James Rannie in performance for the first time now, he could easily see that ventriloquism, the rare new form of performance that he was just beginning to study, had entertainment potential beyond his earlier ken and that he could learn much from this potential new mentor.

Richard Potter probably also had strong personal reasons for choosing to work now with James rather than with John. John Rannie was about to undertake a long, multiyear tour through the southwestern territories and states and into the Deep South; James, on the other hand, was en route now to Boston, Potter's home, before beginning a short tour of eastern Canada. It is easy to imagine that both personal and professional considerations guided Potter in his decision to apprentice himself now to James Rannie.

James's itinerary now, after leaving Newport, took him next to Providence and then on to Boston for a long stand there. After two months in Boston, he moved on to Salem, Newburyport, and then Portsmouth. Then he spent the winter of 1804–5 performing in Canada—largely in two major cities, Montreal and Quebec—before returning to Boston and then proceeding to Portland in the spring.

We of course do not see Richard Potter in the records of this itinerary, but it is likely that he shared it. At the very beginning of January 1805 there was an unclaimed letter waiting for him in the Portland post office; this was the city to which James Rannie would be heading after leaving Quebec and where he would soon establish his permanent home, so he may very well have also traveled there from Portsmouth even before heading north into Canada; either way, it was a good place to reach James Rannie by mail at this time and so would have been a good place to reach Richard Potter as well. Too, there are traces of an assistant's presence on the tour itself. Some of James Rannie's deceptions, to begin with, certainly required an assistant: one example would be the trick of cutting off and then restoring a cock's head, so it could "crow and eat again as well as before," which he advertised in Montreal at the end of 1804 (an assistant was needed to hold the cock, as one Rannie woodcut dramatically illustrates; see figure 2, upper left). Again, on the slack wire Rannie would often execute a demanding balancing act of "carrying a table covered with glasses filled with wine in one hand, and a young gentleman in the other"; he performed this in both Boston and Quebec. A glimpse of Richard Potter as this "young gentleman" is the most we can expect to see of him at this stage of his career.

III

While Richard Potter remained quite obscure in his early years as Rannie's apprentice, however, two very reliable contemporaneous stories show that he was back in Boston at this time (circa 1804–5) and already active in his new vocation. The second of the following stories, Joseph Buckingham's narrative of his relationship with Richard Potter, was the anecdote that triggered widespread interest in Potter's biography in the 1870s; the first story, however, has never before been presented.

In 1888, a brief *Boston Journal* mention of a Richard Potter picture on display in the Bostonian Society's new exhibits elicited a few letters to the editor offering recollections of Potter. One of these, from an elderly correspondent who "remember[ed] him well," included information about Potter's whereabouts and activities at the very cusp of his career: "After one of [Potter's] performances, in Quincy, speaking with Mr. Abner Willett with whom I worked, he remarked that when he was a boy he lived in Boston; that young Potter either lived at the same place or nearby (I have forgotten which); that he was well acquainted with him; that Potter, although a boy, was already then performing his sleight-of-hand tricks, much to their amusement and surprise. After that he lost sight of him, as he (Willett) soon left the town, until Potter began to give his public exhibitions."

Abner Willett, who had been born in 1785, was from a large family in Walpole, Massachusetts. He had a much older brother, Joseph, who, probably together with a few other good friends from Walpole, had moved to Boston by 1799 and was beginning to establish himself in business there. By 1803 Joseph Willett had set up a partnership with one of those close friends, Jabez Bullard. The two men were agemates (both born in 1773) and lifelong friends, and now they were also family: Joseph had married Jemima Bullard, Jabez's younger sister, in 1799, just two weeks before Jabez himself had married another Walpole girl. At first Joseph and Jabez worked in Boston as housewrights, but by 1802 they had set up a lumberyard on the South Boston waterfront, and thereafter they were known primarily as lumber merchants or woodwharfingers.

Willett and Bullard began investing in Boston real estate in late 1801, and their first purchases were two adjacent small tracts of land on Atkinson Street, near the midcity waterfront, in 1801 and 1802. Prior to this, Joseph and Jemima Willett had presumably been sharing a dwelling with Jabez and Molly Ballard on Orange Street, near their lumberyard, but now they apparently built their own house on one of the new Atkinson Street parcels. (Jabez and Molly became parents in 1801, which may well have made the need for more living space pressing.) The Willets presumably would have moved to their new Atkinson Street address in 1802 or 1803. Now it would be possible for Joseph to begin housing and employing other members of his own family, perhaps at first even for the construction of his new house, so it would have been now, circa 1803 to 1804 or 1805, when Abner Willett came from Walpole to live in Boston with his older brother and his sister-in-law.

Meanwhile, Willett and Bullard in late 1802 sold a portion—somewhat less than half—of the second, smaller Atkinson Street tract that they had recently bought. The tract already had a dwelling house on it; presumably this was the former home of the William Apthorp family, for it was that estate, purchased in 1793, that was now being subdivided. And the person who bought this property—certainly already a business associate (he was another Boston waterfront woodwharfinger)—was none other than Samuel Dillaway. The Atkinson Street house was very close and convenient to Dillaway's Wharf, so this location was ideal for Samuel.

Thus by 1804, give or take a year, the Samuel Dillaway and the Joseph Willett families were living directly opposite each other in Boston near the waterfront—specifically, catercorner across from each other at the intersection of Atkinson Street and Round Lane. So Abner Willett's story of having lived for a while in Boston close by to Richard Potter rings absolutely true and confirms that, once Potter finally returned to Boston after his years of travel in Europe, he resumed for a while his domestic relationship and employment with Samuel Dillaway. "If my information was correct he was a Boston boy," the *Boston Journal* correspondent had recalled years later, and, since his friend Abner Willett had known Richard Potter as a long-standing member of the Samuel Dillaway household, his information was very good indeed.

Abner Willett's stories not only confirm that by 1804 or so Richard Potter was back in Boston and back with the Dillaways but also make absolutely clear that he had by then already begun his training as a magician and was genially entertaining the local youths with his sleight-of-hand tricks. We have all the more reason to be confident, then, that he had already begun his apprenticeship with the Rannies by this time. Thus it is almost certain that Potter was assisting James Rannie during the latter's Boston performances in the late summer of 1804 and again in the spring of 1805, and accordingly probable that Potter also accompanied Rannie into Canada during the winter of 1804–5.


IV

In 1872 Moses Goodwin, a New Hampshire newspaperman, gave a charming account of an 1848 conversation between two of Potter's erstwhile acquaintances that seems to reveal Potter at the very outset of his independent career. Goodwin's anecdote involved two notable New Englanders, George Nesmith (his source) and Joseph T. Buckingham, who were traveling together on the new Northern Railroad from Franklin, New Hampshire, to White River Junction, Vermont. Buckingham was a prominent Boston newspaper publisher and editor; Nesmith, a New Hampshire lawyer, was also the first president of the Northern Railroad. Their train stopped at the Potter Place station, and Buckingham inquired about the station's name. Nesmith explained that Richard Potter, the famous magician, had lived and died in his house immediately thereby, that he and his wife were buried close beside the tracks there, and that the station had been named in his honor. Buckingham's reaction, forceful and immediate, clearly made a strong impression on Nesmith: "O, is that so? You have given me the name of one of my earliest and long continued friends, as well as one of the noblest and most generous men I have ever known." And he proceeded to tell the story of his first acquaintance with Potter:

When I finished my apprenticeship at Greenfield . . . I went down to Boston a poor printer to start in the world. Some friends helped me to buy a small press and a little type and I started a job business in a small way. I boarded at the old tavern well known to travelers as The Bite, kept in those days by Bradley, near Market Square. One day when I was just starting, a small-sized, sharp-eyed, dark-complexioned man came into dinner, and as he was setting at the table, asked Mr. Bradley where he could find a good, faithful man to do his printing. "There is a young man setting there who has just come here and wants work," was the response of the landlord, pointing to me, . . . and thereupon introduced us; and from that day onward to the day of his death he gave me all his patronage. I did many thousands of dollars worth of printing for him and he always paid him [sic] promptly and gave me more than I charged him. No other man ever gave me more encouragement by patronage, ever helped me more in a pecuniary way than he did.

Buckingham "continued at great length to detail his recollections of this unselfish man expressing the most tender respect for his memory and the highest satisfaction in knowing that the railroad people had given his name a place in their records."

Buckingham's anecdotes are at once marvelously specific and frustratingly slippery. He was reliving them, of course, across a gap of nearly a half century, and Nesmith was then relaying them to Goodwin (both men were prominent citizens of Franklin, New Hampshire, and moved in the same social circles, so the conversation would have occurred quite naturally) across a gap of another twenty-four years. (Buckingham had died in the interim, in 1861.) Clearly, however, the story of that first meeting dates to a time before Buckingham's marriage—before he "married and became a housekeeper," as he elsewhere put it—in July 1805. And in fact we can date it rather precisely to a time not too long before that marriage. For Joseph Bradley operated this tavern and boardinghouse—it was located in Brattle Square, quite close to Market Square (the whole area was indeed known generally as Market Square)—for only two years. Previously it had been Thomas Forbes's business, and then Asa Foote's; Bradley took it over in June 1804. The tavern was a natural watering hole for travelers, for the stage lines to and from Maine, Providence and Newburyport, Dedham and Salem, and Hartford and New Haven and points south all stopped there; Potter thus may himself have visited it several times during his travels with James or John Rannie or Signior Manfredi in the preceding few years. Barely two years after taking over the tavern, however,

Bradley relinquished it in favor of another opportunity, opening a boarding-house, the Province House, on Marlborough Street.

Potter would have been in Boston with James Rannie in July through September 1804, and also in mid-May 1805, when Rannie, just back from his tour to Quebec and Montreal, passed through again en route to Portland. Buckingham's phrase "when I was just starting," applicable to either of these periods, perhaps weakly suggests the former as the likely time of this anecdote: Bradley was then but newly the keeper of the Bite, Buckingham not long in residence there himself (he had left Boston to travel with a theater company during the summer of 1803), and Potter only recently returned to the town after an absence of many years.

There is yet another piece of evidence which further confirms this 1804–5 dating of Buckingham's first meeting with Richard Potter. In the spring of 1804, Buckingham, who had by then worked for the printing business of Thomas & Abraham for several years, contracted with his employers "to carry on their printing business for a term of five years." His contract with them included an attractive condition "by which I was permitted the use of the types and presses to execute printing on my own account"; and he took advantage of this condition in order to increase his income in anticipation of and then reaction to the additional expenses attendant upon his new marriage. Before 1804, then, Buckingham would not have been able to execute printing orders on his own; for the next few years, on the other hand, he would have been not only able but particularly motivated to do so.*

Potter was then about twenty-one years old; Buckingham, about twenty-four. What kind of printing order—handbills, one must assume—Potter was initially seeking to place we cannot say. Probably, indeed, at this time he was not ordering on his own account at all but instead was simply arranging some printing for James Rannie; this seems all the more likely because other first-hand testimony suggests that not until 1809 was Potter preparing to launch his career as an independent performer. But from this initial encounter a relationship developed that was important to both men. It is significant that

*Buckingham's *Personal Memoirs,* completed only a few years after his conversation with Nesmith, say nothing at all about his ever having bought, with the help of friends, "a small press and a little type and . . . started a job business in a small way"; the book is otherwise so full of details about every twist and turn in the early stages of his printing career that we may be confident Nesmith simply misunderstood or misremembered this point.

Buckingham speaks so strongly about Potter not merely as an important customer and a noble and generous man but as a longtime friend. (Nesmith recounted the story of Buckingham's paean to Potter more than once in his later years, and a colleague to whom he recounted it in the 1880s reported his saying that "tears gathered in Buckingham's eyes" as he began to speak of Potter, and that Buckingham spoke of becoming Potter's "life-long printer and friend.") Potter proved to be a major patron of Buckingham's business over the years. There is good reason to think that Buckingham was soon enough able to be of personal and neighborly service to Potter, too.

V

Even such brief, uncertain glimpses as these now suddenly become unavailable; for James Rannie (along with Richard Potter) disappears from all North American records for the period stretching from July 1805 through the spring of 1807. Before and afterward, he gave only vague hints as to where he would be or had been during this time. In the spring of 1804, then "just arrived from the *West-Indies*" (he had just been in Jamaica and Cuba, probably elsewhere in the Caribbean as well), he advertised "that previous to his departure from the United States, for the *East-Indies* [i.e., India], he means to exhibit his performance for a few evenings in this country." In 1809, while he was again performing in America, he began alluding regularly to a ventriloquial trick he had played in Paris (initially he said in Copenhagen rather than in Paris); implicitly he had performed in these cities during the interim. And in 1810 he asserted that "when in the Indies, he has come before upward of 1000 ladies and gentlemen in an evening, when his Tickets were 18 shillings each." "The Indies" could mean either the West Indies (the Caribbean) or the East Indies (India).

Such are the meager hints about this period from James Rannie's history. Are there others from Potter's? Setting aside the foolish local speculations and idle rumors, soon hardening by repetition into accepted truths (perhaps with Potter's encouragement), that he was a native of the West Indies or of India or that he was the son of a Hindu mother and an English father, there are several specific stories about his travels that merit attention here. Most authoritatively, Potter told Nathan Hale circa 1831 that "during the last twenty years he had visited and exhibited in Europe, the West Indies, and most of the large cities of the United States." Hale was an experienced newspaper editor and publisher, had specifically asked Potter for biographical information, and recorded this conversation soon afterward. While "twenty years" probably was only an approximation, we can be confident that Potter himself explicitly told Hale that he had traveled and performed in both Europe and the West Indies.

When Silas Ketchum pursued "minute inquiries" in Andover, New Hampshire, about Potter's biography in 1875, he picked up much misinformation from residents who professed to have acquired it directly from Potter himself or from his wife. Some of this Ketchum himself realized was false; other parts he simply reported as local beliefs. A few claims he declared (without citing his sources) were "certain," and most of these were indeed quite true—that Potter had traveled widely and had become famous before 1820, that he had married and that his children were born before 1820, that his wife had for a while traveled and performed with him. But Ketchum also said this: "It is certain that he had, within that time [i.e., before 1820] visited Europe, for he was for a time with Napoleon; though not as a soldier."

Twenty years later, the *Manchester (NH) Union* sent a staff correspondent to Andover to look into Richard Potter's story. The correspondent interviewed a different group of area residents who remembered Potter, and reported that, after his schooling, Potter "went to England and India, where he acquired the magician's arts." A letter to the editor responding to this article, from an interested reader who had "once looked up [Potter's] life and his home, being within a short distance of Potter Place," affirmed the accuracy of the *Union* report and provided additional details (again, no sources were given), including this: "He went to England on two different occasions, and also extended his journey to India as stated." Some eleven years later, another newspaper feature on Potter, this one in the *Boston Herald,* reported much the same thing. The anonymous writer ("Our Regular Correspondent"), who had pursued at least a few new leads, stated that "Potter made two trips to England, and once went to India in the practice of his profession."

Thus the scanty, hearsay evidence of Richard Potter's biography during these missing years 1805–7 interestingly reinforces the hints from James Rannie's life at the same time—that they had traveled then both to Europe (England, France, perhaps elsewhere) and to India.

To this thin gruel of rumors about the missing years 1805–7 we need now to add one very curious and quite striking piece of evidence. Richard and Sally Potter's only daughter, who died young, was apparently known in Andover as "Jeanette." She was so identified in Eastman's 1910 Andover town history. It turns out, however, that Jeanette was simply a nickname, an easy shortening of her given name. For when she died in 1831, all the newspaper death notices—and there were several, in Maine and Massachusetts as well as New Hampshire, because by then her father was a famous man—carefully recorded the name exactly as Potter or more probably someone very close to him had reported it: "In Andover, Miss Anganet Potter, daughter of Mr. Richard and Mrs. Sally Potter, aged 16 years."

"Ann-jah-net" or "Ahn-jah-net": her "Jeanette" nickname demonstrates that the *g* in Anganet was soft, pronounced like a *j*. The nickname was Anglicized, but the name itself is not English or biblical at all. Anganet is adapted from Hindi: "anjana" means "swarthy" or "dusky" and is also the name of a legendary, beautiful nymph, Anjana or Anjani, cursed at one time to assume a monkey's form, wife of the monkey king, mother of the god Hanuman; and "angana" means "a beautiful woman."

Anganet Potter must have been born in late 1814 or early 1815, just before the Potters took up residence in Andover. Her father gave her a name suitable for a dark-complexioned beauty, a nymph disguised as a monkey. (We might remember here that Jennie Surriage Bixby had fondly described Potter in his youth as having been "as agile as a squirrel, and as full of trick and mimickry as a monkey"; probably the "squirrel" and "monkey" epithets had been applied to him regularly then.) He presumably encountered the name (and perhaps learned about the nymph) during his international travels, and it made an impression on him, even before he was a married man, as a fine name for his daughter, should he ever have one—the daughter of a mulatto ropedancer and acrobat.

So as early as 1815 there was an exotic Anganet living in rural, remote Andover, New Hampshire. Knowing that, it is very easy to believe that Richard Potter, in company with James Rannie, did make it all the way from Europe to India at some point in 1805–7.

In any event, by the late spring of 1807 Rannie and Potter were back in New England, where Rannie set about buying property in Falmouth (he ultimately purchased an island in Casco Bay), arranging to have a house built there for himself and his wife, and becoming a naturalized American citizen. At the very beginning of 1808 Rannie proceeded again to Boston, where he exhibited for a month, afterward touring as far as Norwich, Connecticut, in one direction and Portsmouth in another, then returning to Salem and Newburyport; and at or by this point Richard Potter apparently established his own, independent base in Boston, which was to be his home for the next several years.

Joseph Buckingham and his new wife apparently did not set up housekeeping for themselves until about 1808; the *Boston Directory* editions of this period do not show a residential (as opposed to a business) address for him until 1809. Presumably they initially continued as boarders with Bradley even after Bradley moved from Market Square to open his new boardinghouse on Marlborough Street; this is all the more likely in that the new address would put Buckingham much closer to the offices of Thomas & Andrews, his employer. And at Bradley's boardinghouse at 24 Marlborough Street, the Buckinghams' closest new neighbors included the Rev. Daniel Oliver and his family, at 21 Marlborough. The Olivers, too, were soon to become important in Richard Potter's life, so this new relationship between the Buckinghams and the Olivers was probably crucial.

The Rev. Daniel Oliver and his wife had eight children (another had died in infancy), ranging in age in 1807 from twenty to five. The number and ages are important, because the care and support of this large brood fell largely upon Mrs. Oliver. The Reverend Oliver, at this period of his life (1805–12), was regularly serving as a missionary to the Indians in eastern Maine and Upstate New York. He was thus absent from Boston for long periods of time. According to various annual publications of the Society for Propagating the Gospel among the Indians and Others in North America, the missionary society that sponsored him, Reverend Oliver spent some twenty-three months during 1805–8 on missionary work in Maine (no record for 1809 is available); in 1810–11 he was on missions beyond the Genesee River in New York totaling five months. The synopses of the Society reports give a bare hint of his labors. During his six months of service in 1805, for example, he "travelled about 1200 miles, preached 133 sermons, visited 196 families, and baptized 7 children"; during eight months in 1806, he "rode 2190 miles, visited 298 families, baptized 21 children," and visited a Society-established school; during two months in 1811, "he travelled upwards of 1100 miles; preached 49 times; baptized 2 children; attended 4 conference meetings; visited 5 sick persons; attended 2 funerals; was moderator at 2 church meetings; visited 77 families"; and always he distributed large numbers of Bibles and religious books. Throughout his lengthy absences, his wife, Elizabeth Kemble Oliver, managed their large household on a missionary's meager salary.

Elizabeth Oliver in 1807, when her husband was away for more than half the year, had daughters aged twenty, fifteen, fourteen, twelve, ten, and five and a son aged seven at home; another son, aged seventeen, had recently begun his studies at Harvard. To supplement the family's income—and in truth she may well have provided the better part of it—she began maintaining a boardinghouse at 21 Marlborough Street (the Oliver family first appears there in the 1805 *Boston Directory*). By 1807 she had relocated her establishment to Middle Street, toward the northern end of town; and then by 1810 she had relocated it again, this time to Suffolk Place, a short, blind street with only eight houses, near the Common. At this time, the 1810 census indicates that approximately a dozen men were boarding at her establishment. And at the same time Joseph Buckingham and his young family, who had the previous year taken their first house at Pinckney Street (northwest of the Common, and inconveniently distant from his workplace), also relocated to Suffolk Place.

This co-location was doubtless no accident. The Buckinghams and the Olivers had probably been close neighbors and, at the least, ready acquaintances on Marlborough Street for a year or so. And the proximity and friendship between the Buckinghams and the Olivers provides the easiest and most straightforward explanation for Richard Potter's introduction and recommendation, at around this time, to the Olivers, who were soon to become his employers.

VII

Meanwhile, important changes were occurring in Richard Potter's life. In March 1808, he and Sally Harris, a young black woman from Roxbury, Massachusetts, announced their intention to marry; their marriage took place in Roxbury on 15 September, six months later.

Sally Harris was at this time about twenty-one years old. She was, by all accounts, quite petite, quite graceful, and quite beautiful, qualities that served her well when she began to play small roles in Richard's exhibitions. Apart from these simple dates and descriptive factors, however, we know almost nothing about her—who her parents were and what were their occupations, where she grew up, what education she received, what experiences she had had, how she and Richard met. Still, even the bare details of the couple's engagement and marriage records give us a few hints about Sally's background and provide some additional hints of the social connections that helped Richard thrive in Boston during this time.

It is noteworthy, to begin with, that the marriage ceremony was performed by a prominent divine. The venerable Rev. Dr. Eliphalet Porter (his D.D. had been conferred by Harvard the previous year) was the distinguished pastor of the First Church of Christ in Roxbury and an overseer of Harvard College, and ten years later would be named a member of the Corporation of Harvard. (He and Reverend Oliver were doubtless acquainted, all the more certainly in that both were active in the Society for Propagating the Gospel among the Indians and Others in North America. So Reverend Porter could have provided another recommendation for Richard and Sally when the Olivers subsequently engaged them as domestic employees.) Sally Harris was clearly a member of Porter's Roxbury congregation; he would not have performed the ceremony otherwise. But neither her baptism nor her transfer to the congregation nor any record of her family appears anywhere in the church's archives, so presumably she was in this congregation by virtue of being in service with one of the congregation's established families. (Potter later spoke of her to Hale as one "well acquainted with country business" for whom managing a home would be "a congenial occupation," suggesting that Sally was familiar with country, manorial living.)

At this time Potter's connection with the Dillaways provided him with an important Roxbury connection. Dillaway's son, Samuel junior, was about nine years older than Potter, and the two youths apparently formed a warm relationship during their several years together in the same household. By 1808, the younger Samuel Dillaway was in business in Boston for himself and had established his growing family in Roxbury, where he was now a prominent citizen. Clearly he and Potter had renewed contact with each other after Potter's return to Boston, when Potter was again living with Dillaway senior circa 1804. We can be sure of this because when Potter, by then a well-known and successful performer, sat for his portrait by Ethan Allen Greenwood in September 1815, Samuel junior was having his own portrait painted there at the same time; the two works were completed on consecutive days and were the only ones Greenwood painted that week. Assuredly this was a mutual arrangement, and the two probably alternated sitting times for Greenwood over the course of several days.

So Potter, strongly connected as he was with young Samuel Dillaway, had a ready entry in Roxbury. Moreover, Dillaway and his family were themselves members of the Reverend Porter's congregation. It is easy to guess, then — but this can be only a guess — that Sally herself was in service with the Dillaways, or at least with close acquaintances of theirs, and was already known to them.

What is truly remarkable about the Potter-Harris marriage, however, is that it was mentioned in the matrimonial notices of several Boston newspapers, a recognition almost unheard of, possibly even unprecedented, for blacks in the city at that time.* In 1808 Potter was still a near-complete un-known; he had not yet begun his career as an independent performer. Was this a gesture by Potter himself, or a courtesy by some influential friend? In either case, the publishing of his marriage announcement in these major newspapers was a striking sign of how well established Potter was already be-coming in his home city.

VIII

Within a few months after their marriage, Richard and Sally Potter began working for and living with the Olivers, who had moved from their Marl-borough Street residence to a run a new boardinghouse operation on Middle Street, in North Boston. They continued in service with the Olivers for a year or so. The Olivers' younger son, Henry Kemble Oliver, later to become a prominent Massachusetts public figure (factory manager, congressman, adju-tant general of Massachusetts, mayor of Lawrence and of Salem, educational reformer, music composer), who was about eight years old at the beginning of this period, frequently and vividly recalled the time when Potter "was in 1809 and '10, a domestic in my father's family," with corroborating circumstantial details and anecdotes (including that of his older brother's graduation from Harvard, when "his Commencement festivities were held at this house and Potter assisted in their preparation"; this took place on 30 August 1809) that make the dates quite certain. In 1810, after the Olivers (and also the Bucking-hams) had moved to Suffolk Place, the residents at their boardinghouse— twenty-four individuals in all, including the six Oliver children who were still living at home—included two people listed on the Federal census as simply "Other free [i.e., not white] persons." Probably this indicates that Richard and Sally Potter were still living there at that time. (It also hints that their first child, Henry, had not been born yet; he was probably born a few months later in 1810.)

Henry Oliver's affectionate reminiscences of Potter's appearance and per-sonality, and of his entertainments of the Oliver children, give us a charm-

---

*Announcements of the Potter-Harris wedding appeared in the Boston *Democrat* (21 Sept. 1808), the *Boston Courier* (22 Sept. 1808), the *Boston Gazette* (19 Sept. 1808), and the *Boston Repertory* (20 Sept 1808), as well as in the *Newburyport (MA) Statesman* (22 Sept. 1808). I have not found a marriage announcement for any other black couple in Boston prior to 1819.

ing domestic glimpse of the young magician-ventriloquist early in his career, when "many a winter's evening the children and servants of the family were edified and unspeakably regaled by [his] tricks and pranks":

> While living with us—and he was a most excellent and faithful man in his work, always good-tempered and genial—he occasionally invited us children to the kitchen to see his tricks and hearken to his ventriloquism. He was a light mulatto, of slight figure and very agreeable features, a constant smile seeming to illuminate his face. Many of the tricks named in your article we saw him perform [the article to which Oliver was responding had specifically mentioned that "invisible crying babies and Peters and Jacks were heard under the table and platform, in boxes and corners, and even outside the building, begging to be taken in at the window," and that "[t]hen the performer would draw from his mouth enough parti-colored ribbon to stock a small store with, and after putting tow in its place would blow forth smoke and flame"], and I specially remember the dancing of an egg along and about an old fashioned set of shelves called a "dresser," upon which the kitchen plates, many of them pewter, and other utensils were kept as well as the dropping of eggs into his hat and their coming out as pancakes or flapjacks. So, too, I recall the marvelous voice that came down the chimney in response to his inquiries, rather frightening us at first but vastly amusing us afterward.

The kitchen, of course, would have been one of Potter's many workplaces in the house. The scene reminds us again of how much Potter's shows had always delighted children, and suggests why: he had early learned to pitch his entertainments specifically to them, and the ready, enthusiastic audience of Oliver children, like the earlier audience of the children on Atkinson Street, surely reinforced his sense that this was wise showmanship.


## IX

The 1808 recording in Boston of the marriage intentions of "Richard Potter & Sally Harris of Roxbury, (blacks)" and the 1810 census listing of Richard and Sally as "other free persons" in the Oliver household provide important reminders that, when he began to live again in Boston, where he had grown up, Potter was already widely, if not universally, recognized as being a black man. Henry Kemble Oliver, as we have just seen, later described Potter straightforwardly as "a light mulatto"; and an anonymous commentator writing about Potter in 1851 partly on the basis of conversations with Oliver (but partly also on childhood recollections of Potter's performances) declared that Potter "was a colored man, half way between fair and black, and of the same hue was his wife." Joseph Buckingham, who apparently did not realize at their first meeting that Potter was identified as black, described him afterward as "a small-sized, sharp-eyed, dark-complexioned man." In appearance, then, his racial identity was indeterminate, and at times in his career Potter was not unwilling to exploit this ambiguity. It was not on the basis of his appearance that he was racially categorized in Boston, however, but on the basis of his history. Born in Hopkinton, raised in Boston, he lived in a society where his origins were a matter of record and where his former masters and mistresses and their families and his siblings and cousins were also living. Potter was black in Boston because he was already known to be black.

By 1808, when his intention to marry Sally Harris of Roxbury was published, Potter seems to have settled into residency in Boston—settled, in any event, as much as an itinerant performer can. He continued to live in Boston until 1814 or 1815, when his new home in Andover, New Hampshire, was finally ready; he returned to live in the city again for a while in 1818; and he was once again living in Boston for more than a year in 1826–27. Having spent his earliest years in Hopkinton and then having lived in the Boston area as a boy with the Dillaway family for several years beginning in about 1795, he was very much a familiar of the city and the area, both knowing it and known to it. As we have seen, he had many white friends and guardians and sponsors. But inevitably he was based in Boston's black community.

It would seem, moreover, that he took care to be inconspicuous in his private life. Boston at this time was a center for nascent reform and protest activities affecting blacks, focusing especially on community volunteerism, education, and the antislavery movement. Potter seems never to have played a public role in any of these activities. Although this was first of all simply a function of his frequent lengthy absences from Boston, it was probably a matter of policy on his part as well, for we know both that he was eventually a figure of real prominence in Boston's black community and that he was quite sensitive to the issues of race that so severely defined and confined him. But a public entertainer only loses by alienating any of his potential audience unnecessarily; it behooved him professionally to be ingratiating, apolitical, and uncontroversial.

There was one fraternal organization in Boston, however, in which Potter was significantly engaged. He was a member, eventually a very prominent member, of the African Lodge of Boston, eventually to become known as the Prince Hall Grand Lodge, the first black Masonic lodge in America.

Founded by Prince Hall, a free former slave who had been introduced into Freemasonry by British soldiers in Boston in 1775, African Lodge No. 459 received its charter from the Grand Lodge of England in 1784 and soon became an important black social organization. It fostered sister lodges in Philadelphia and Providence in 1797, and Hall himself became a prominent advocate for black rights and black education, heading a petition to the legislature seeking the establishment of an African school (1787) and another complaining of the kidnapping and enslaving of free blacks (1788). For decades thereafter, the memberships of the African Society (a benevolent group) and the African Lodge and the advocates for African schools in Boston were significantly overlapping groups.

Hall died in late 1807. Potter petitioned the Lodge for membership in early November 1811 and received his first three Masonic degrees in early December 1811. Clearly his involvement with the Lodge could be only irregular over the following years, since he was so infrequently in Boston during 1815–17 and completely absent from late 1818 through mid-1823. But just as clearly it never lapsed, for upon his return to New England in 1823 he soon assumed a position of prominence in Lodge affairs.

The African Lodge was growing in 1811, when Potter joined it, and continued so for a few years, then went into a period of decline until the mid-1820s, when new members and a new sense of mission significantly reinvigorated it. The Lodge's records for this period were often quite scanty and irregular in the first place, and then damaged over the course of time even to the point of frequent illegibility. Despite those limitations, however, these records contain a rich and unique lode of information about social connections among the more prominent members of Boston's growing black community. Lodge membership offered not only social engagement but also a venue for politically inclined activism, for Prince Hall had believed that black Masonry should work to serve the black community, "doing what we can to promote the interest and good of our dear brethren that stand in so much need in such a time as this." Membership also required commitments both of time and of money; the latter effectively meant that only regularly employed and at least modestly established men would be able to pursue it.

Despite the paucity and obscurity of the African Lodge records for the early years of Potter's membership, and the dismaying silence of those records on many points of basic information (for example, the minutes often simply recorded, even for years on end, that officers were reelected without specifying who those officers were, and sometimes did not even say this much), it is possible to derive from them a list of some twenty men who were fairly active in the Lodge at this time (1810–13). It is safe to say that Richard Potter would have known all of these men; and some of them must have been real friends, or else he would never have pursued membership in the first place. These men seem obscure to us today, because their names never featured prominently in the newspapers and books of white Boston and because their race inevitably confined them to a handful of service or unskilled professions (barber or hairdresser, bootblack, laborer, waiter), but they were known and even widely known in their own community.

George Middleton, the Worshipful Master of the African Lodge just a year before Potter joined it, was most certainly widely known. Seventy-six years old in 1811, a Revolutionary War veteran, a close associate of Prince Hall, he was an influential leader and, now, something of an *éminence gris* in the black community. In 1796 he had been one of the founders of the African Society; in 1799 Prince Hall and several others had petitioned to have Middleton licensed as a schoolteacher; in 1800 Middleton and many other blacks petitioned the Boston School Committee to establish an African school, and soon afterward the school opened, first supported by private benefactors but then, from 1812, also supported by the city. With his interest, following Hall's example, in using Masonry to work for the betterment of the larger black community, Middleton set a tone for the African Lodge.

Another widely known African Lodge member, Prince Saunders, had arrived in Boston only recently, in late 1808. Perhaps thirty-six years old in 1811, he had been well educated by his master in Vermont, then taught at a school for African American children for a while, then was sponsored by his master to Moor's Charity School, in Hanover, New Hampshire. During his year or two there he came to the attention of the president of Dartmouth College, John Wheelock, who recommended him as a teacher to the African American school in Boston. He became a Mason in 1809, and by 1811, when Potter joined, he was the Lodge secretary. Like Middleton, he had strong connections with the new African School and with the church that housed and partly sponsored it, the African Baptist Church that had been recently founded by the Rev. Thomas Paul; he was probably already beginning to work with Paul on schemes to resettle American blacks in colonies abroad, especially in Haiti. (Paul, one of the most prominent black leaders in Boston, would become an African Lodge member a few years hence, but he was not one at this time.) Through the school, he also had a connection to the Rev. William Ellery Channing and other prominent Boston citizens who had taken up the cause of the school (it was Channing who had invited him to Boston), and so, like Potter, he had some important contacts in the white community as well as in the black one.

Peter Lew, the Worshipful Master (succeeding Middleton) when Potter joined the African Lodge, was a musician, as were his father and many of his brothers; at least two of those brothers, Eri (at that time the Senior Warden) and Zadock, were also members of the African Lodge. Peter Lew was thirty-two years old at this time, Zadock was forty-three, and Eri was twenty-nine, just a year older than Richard Potter. Given Potter's professional involvement with musicians (he often hired some to perform during intermissions of his shows), it is highly likely that he knew some of these brothers quite well.

Other African Lodge members active with Potter at this time were more humbly or obscurely employed. (As Peter Hinks has noted, "The most prominent figures in black Boston were on remarkably close terms with the more ordinary members of their community.") John Jonah, about forty years old, was a bootblack; he was also a prominent member of the African Society. William Henry, the Deacon (presumably, Senior Deacon) of the African Lodge at this time, was a barber. Elijah Carlton, who joined the African Lodge only a few months after Potter did, was a truckman, or carter. Thomas Carlton, who might have been Elijah's brother and who seems to have entered the Lodge at about the same time, was a trader; given his age (twenty-two in 1811), he was probably in trade on the level of barter rather than merchantry. Samson Moody, who joined the Lodge in 1812 and by 1817 was the Worshipful Master, was a hairdresser. John Brown was either a cook or a bootblack (we don't know which of these John Browns was the Mason). John Williams, the Junior Deacon when Potter joined the lodge, was another bootblack.

Many other of Potter's fellow Masons at this time were even more obscure than these. Some, such as Robert Warr (then about thirty-one years old), seem to have been relatively well known in the community even though we know next to nothing about them today. Others—John Shorten, Caesar Dalton, Arthur Henry, and Brothers Coleman, Martin, Randall, Sumner, many more—are now lost to time.

This was the community that knew Richard Potter back when, and to which he would return when, having left Boston for New Hampshire in 1815, he returned to live there for the better part of a year in 1818 and again for more than a year in 1826–27. In 1808–14 he was just beginning to establish himself in his profession, and he was frequently on the road, away from his home. He moved comfortably among a set of respectable and sometimes well-connected white friends; he also fit comfortably into the black community, in all its variety, and was a friend of many of the most prominent and outspoken members of that community. Many other blacks in Boston could say the same. It is important to note that African Lodge members such as Potter, Middleton, and Saunders were not unusual in having connections to, even friendships with, various white citizens, although Potter was unusual in that his connections to his white friends seem to have been atypically strong. Boston was a broadly integrated city at this time: even the neighborhoods where black citizens were beginning to cluster, notably the north side of Beacon Hill, were still predominantly white, ward by ward and even street by street. All of these black citizens had white neighbors, some had white tenants, some had white housemates, and all of them in service as well as most of them in trade had white customers.

Richard Potter clearly regarded his Masonic affiliation as an important feature of his public persona, and he sometimes invoked it in his publicity. Like many contemporaneous white entertainers who were Masons, he occasionally incorporated Masonic emblems or allusions into his printed advertisements. Masonic iconography appears, in fact, in some of the earliest Potter broadsides that are extant. In one of these (probably dating from circa 1809), headed by a large, bold, and ornate "Mr. POTTER," the gap between "Mr." and "POTTER" is filled with a small woodcut: it depicts a personalized sun and moon looking down on a plank or tabletop on which are assembled a collection of distinctively Masonic items (compass, square, mallet, trowel, Bible) (fig. 4). In another, probably somewhat later (circa 1818), the gap between a large "Mr. and Mrs." and "POTTER" is this time filled by a very large Masonic compass, in the iconic upright pose (fig. 5). These woodcuts served as unmistakable signs to their beholders that this Mr. Potter was a Mason, a person of respectability, and a believer in universal brotherhood.


X


Even while working for and living with the Oliver family in Boston for a year or so, and regularly practicing and refining his ventriloquism and legerdemain on the delighted Oliver children and servants in impromptu kitchen entertainments throughout that time, Richard Potter was already beginning to make his way in the world as an entertainer and performer on his own account. While he probably rejoined James Rannie as an assistant and supporting performer during some of Rannie's farewell performances in 1810–11, for the most part now, and always from 1811 on, he was exhibiting for himself. He did not at first, however, perform alone. Nor did he perform with his wife, although she had talents as a singer and dancer and would soon enough be joining him in his act: she was still relatively untrained in these arts, and in 1810 she was also pregnant with their first child.

Instead, Potter worked with a partner, another man who could contribute to the entertainment program and help with all the necessary arrangements. We know of two men with whom he so worked. One was a Mr. Smith, who brought skills as a slack-wire dancer and a balancer (or perhaps Potter himself gave him some training in these arts). He was surely only a journeyman at best, for there is no other record of his ever performing under his own name anywhere; but "Messrs. POTTER & SMITH" were offering an exhibition of "SLIGHT OF HAND, Slack Wire Dancing, and VENTRILOQUISM" according to what is possibly the earliest surviving Potter broadside (fig. 3). This partnership certainly did not last: it, and Mr. Smith, are known only from this one broadside.

Alternatively, Potter took on a different associate to whom he again gave co-billing, a handsome, forceful, slightly younger man with the personality of a showman. When and where they met, and how long they trained together before they began performing and advertising in larger towns, we cannot say; but in May 1809, advertisements began appearing in Portsmouth, New Hampshire, for "A genteel entertainment of Slight of Hand, Theatrical Performance, and Ventriloquism, By Messrs. Potter and Thompson, Who have performed in the most capital cities in Europe and America." (The following year, they also advertised themselves as "from London.")

His full name was Benjamin Thompson Junior, and he was a rolling stone from the small, agricultural village of Andover, New Hampshire, some twenty-fives miles northwest of Concord, where his father maintained an extensive farm, ran a popular tavern on the new Fourth New Hampshire Turnpike, and established his large family. He appeared as Potter's associate and partner for only a short while before dropping out of the act and the billing (he last appeared in a Potter advertisement in Boston in September 1810) but continued for many years thereafter as Potter's assistant; most importantly, he (and probably his wife) accompanied Richard and Sally Potter around the country during their long North American tour in 1819–23.

Almost nothing is known of Thompson's early life. (While he may have done so, there is no reason to think that he had performed on stage in the capitals of Europe and America, or indeed that he had performed on stage at all, before he connected with Potter circa 1809: these claims were true of Potter and so could appropriately be used in Potter's advertising.) The first commentator to take note of him, an anonymous correspondent for the *Boston Journal* writing in 1874, reported that he was "one of the most celebrated horsemen in that section of the State," and there is evidence that this was quite true, for from 1813 through 1815 he regularly advertised the stud services of one or two prize stallions each year, sometimes providing extensive testimonials. After his years working with Potter, he applied his showman's talents to a new career, setting up a series of large "Botanic Infirmaries" in various cities and towns— first in Boston, then in Concord, New Hampshire, then in several other East Coast venues—and styling himself as "Doctor Benjamin Thompson," a "Botanic Physician." He claimed to have trained with Dr. Samuel Thomson (no relation), who had founded the Thomsonian system of medical practice early in the century, featuring botanical (rather than mineral) medications and steam baths. In Concord, he struck up a strong friendship with the senator and soon-to-be governor Isaac Hill.

As a result of his new prominence in Concord and his notoriety among the established New Hampshire medical community, Thompson drew the attention of local historians who toward the end of the century were preparing a history of Concord's medical profession as a contribution to the new *History of Concord, New Hampshire*. To that research we owe the following sketch of Thompson's appearance and personality, the only one we possess: "He was a handsome man, of prepossessing appearance. He had few school advantages, but was apt in observation, quick to learn, and entirely self-reliant. Possessing a heavy voice and a clear articulation, he was an impressive personage, especially among the ignorant. He had a passion for gaming, and was throughout life a professional gambler, who frequently won large sums of money, which he dispensed with a lavish hand. At other times, he passed a somewhat precarious existence, migrating from place to place with no settled occupation." So they made an oddly matched partnership, Messrs. Potter and Thompson: the quiet, proper, gentle magician-ventriloquist and the loud, flashy, forceful assistant. Potter could easily have had Thompson as well as Rannie in mind when he noted to Nathan Hale that "my profession . . . is exposed to corrupt influences, and seldom leads to anything short of total destruction" and that "few public performers withstood the temptations of dissipation" such as "gambling, drinking, and idleness."

XI

As noted, Thompson performed with Potter for only a short period—less than a year and a half—after Potter's marriage at the very outset of Potter's independent career. They were honing their exhibition on the road in secondary markets, touring for months at a time; their performances included sleight of hand, "theatrical performance" (meaning songs and recitations, and sometimes a brief comic scene), and "feats of activity" (these would have been balancing, tumbling, possibly slack-wire dancing) in addition to Potter's featured ventriloquism. Although we know very little about their itineraries, we have a good sense of their range and duration because Potter and Thompson were performing in York, Upper Canada (now Toronto), in May 1810, and then in Utica, New York, at the end of July. Their itinerary from York to Utica and then on to Boston (where they performed in late September) certainly took them along the main route from Buffalo to Albany (the first of Potter's many known visits to the Greater Albany area, where he had family) and thence across central Massachusetts. Whether they had originally traveled to York along this same general route or instead on the Canadian route north of Lake Ontario (via Montreal and Kingston) we do not know; the latter route is much more likely, for itinerant performers thrived on fresh audiences and rarely took out-and-back routes if circuits were feasible alternatives.

Already, in these early performances with Benjamin Thompson, the general character and tenor of Potter's act was taking shape. While featuring both the sleight of hand and the ventriloquism that he had studied with the Rannies and some of the balancing and gymnastics that he had acquired from Manfredi, he also, with his new emphasis on songs and recitations, was beginning to cast his program as something of a review or olio, a genre already familiar to and popular with contemporaneous audiences. He had probably received some initial guidance along these lines during his brief time with John Rannie, for John and his wife and the Duffs also produced light theatricals as a regular part of their act. The songs on Potter's program, which he regularly varied, were all light; surely the recitations were, too.

By the time he and Thompson returned to Boston in the fall of 1810, Potter had been married for two years. His wife, now about twenty-three years old, was about to bear or had recently borne their first child, a son. With her strikingly beautiful appearance, petite and graceful form, and sweet voice, her gifts and talents meshed well with his desire to create a varied program of "genteel entertainment" and gentle wit. Potter began working with her, not simply to train her as his assistant but to give her a role in their entertainments, and she began receiving co-billing with him in January 1811, the first time Thompson did not.

The change was significant, for immediately Potter's entertainments acquired a distinctive new cast, which would characterize them for the rest of his career. Sally Potter appeared with her husband only occasionally, but his act was ever thereafter one into which she could easily fit, featuring singing, dancing, and sometimes brief theatricals along with his sleight of hand and ventriloquism. Some roles were distinctively hers. She developed a "Dwarf Hornpipe" performance, for example, which was a version of the "Dwarf Dance" that John Durang had long ago perfected, in which he metamorphosed from a three-foot man into a six-foot woman during the course of the dance. (On their bills, Potter sometimes presented this as the "Agreeable Surprise, or the Wonderful Little Giant.") She also played a drag role (Phoebe, disguised as a soldier) in excerpts from George Colman the younger's *The Review, or the Wags of Windsor,* opposite her husband in the role of Caleb Quotem (the wag of the title, a jack-of-all-trades, and a famous comic role).

It was at this time, too, that Potter gave their entertainment a title, one that it would retain throughout his career: "An Evening's Brush to Sweep Away Care; Or, a Medley to Please." The title was not original; rather, it deliberately evoked the famous "Evening Brush" monologues with interspersed songs that the celebrated English actor John Collins performed widely in the latter years of the eighteenth century, most memorably in several long stands in London in 1788 through 1792. Collins had interspersed thematically linked comic theatrical anecdotes with light verses set and sung to popular tunes, a formula that Potter found congenial to his own style. The "Evening Brush" had been brought to America first by Thomas Wade West and John Bignall, English actors who came to America and formed the Virginia Company of actors, who performed it widely in Virginia and Maryland in 1790–92, and then separately by another English actor, Charles Stuart Powell, from the Covent Garden Theatre, when he emigrated to Boston in 1792 (a presentation of Collins's "Evening Brush" was his first performance in Boston); Powell continued to present it occasionally in Boston until 1798. Powell had stressed the inoffensiveness of his stories, and this was a message that Potter, too, always wanted to convey and honor.

Meanwhile, another English actor who had emigrated to America at about the same time that Powell had, William Bates, also started offering occasional reviews that included both the "Evening Brush" and another routine that would later figure largely in Potter's act, the "Dissertation on Noses." Bates, who at various times worked with the theater companies in Philadelphia, Providence, Boston, and finally Albany, seems to have begun presenting his medleys including the "Evening Brush" as early as 1796; in the summer of 1810, he began presenting it again, now in Boston, and here young Richard Potter saw his performance and thought he might succeed with it himself. Bates was aging and was about to leave Boston for good; after Bates concluded his performances in August, he seems to have sold some of his scripts and other accoutrements to Potter.

As Potter refined and developed his exhibition in these early years of his independent career, there was also one element of his earlier advertising that he quietly abandoned. In September 1810, near the end of his partnership with Thompson, he had presented himself in his advertisement as "POTTER, the West Indian." The following summer, while performing on his own in New Brunswick and then Philadelphia, he had repeated the claim. Somehow he had felt the need to address his racial identity, and representing himself as, in effect, Creole was a convenient solution. Clearly, then, his racial status was already a matter of some speculation and, therefore, a matter of concern and even danger to him. There is independent confirmation of this speculation in the passing comment of a correspondent to the *New York Evening Post* in late 1813, who observed that the "cabinet conjurers" of the Jefferson and Madison administrations were "not a whit inferior to the two celebrated itinerant conjurers, Mr. Rannie or Mr. Potter, a colored gentleman." At this time Potter had not yet, to our knowledge, performed independently in New York City, although he had appeared frequently in Albany and other upstate venues; yet both his reputation and his racial identity were already known there.

## XII

There is one additional aspect of Richard Potter's newly evolving exhibition program that merits our further attention. Beginning in early 1812, just as Sally began appearing regularly in his act, and continuing for some four years, Richard occasionally tried out an alternative title or motto for his show. Advertising in Portland in February 1812, he headed his notice, "Laugh when you can, and be happy when you may"; he repeated the formula—"Laugh when you can, be happy when you may"—when advertising his and Sally's performances in Boston in June 1813, and revived it again in a bit of doggerel heading his advertisement for his final performance in Albany in late 1816:

> Laugh while you can, and be happy when you may,
> For this is the last night, I'll invite you to the play.
> To please the public has been my chief delight,
> And if I ever pleased, I'm sure to please to night.
> Look and examine, the less you'll understand,
> The many pleasing instances of Slight of hand.

He most probably used the motto regularly in his posted bills during these years as well.

This motto, like his usual exhibition title ("An Evening's Brush to Sweep Away Care"), was not original (although the Albany doggerel probably was). Like the "Evening's Brush," the phrase "Laugh When You Can" was part of the popular cultural currency of the time and came directly from the theater. *Laugh When You Can*—often advertised on the American stage as *Laugh When You Can; Be Happy When You May*—was the title of a popular comedy by Frederick Reynolds, first staged at London's Covent Garden Theatre and published in 1799, when it also traveled to America. The play was popular in the big-city East Coast theaters for many years, and in particular it enjoyed regular revivals in Boston in 1809, 1810, 1811, and 1812.

At one level, *Laugh When You Can* poses a contest of attitudes between Gossamer, "The Laughing Philosopher," a man determined to have fun in life, with a particular predilection for hoaxes, and Miss Gloomly, "The Crying Philosopher," a sour-tempered, hypocritical, scandal-mongering old maid who is the author of innumerable books of puritanical moral instruction. As she declares early in the play, "All my works are calculated to excite sighs, and tears, and terror, and distress—in short, to make people unhappy—and I hold laughter to be of so low and immoral a tendency, that in the thirty-six volumes I have published, I defy you to produce a single joke" (1.10; citations are to act and page). "Laughter-loving Gossamer," on the other hand, announces to his old college friend Delville in his opening scene, "I leave you and other wiseacres to follow serious, grave pursuits—for me, I'm fool enough to study mirth and merriment; and as long as I'm a man I hope I shall be a boy!" (1.14). Not surprisingly in a comedy, Gossamer gets the play's last words—which he turns and directs to the audience:

> since our smiles are nothing without yours—(*to the audience*)—
> May Gossamer diffuse his joy around—
> Cloud not the sunshine that's so seldom found;
> For if misfortune be the lot of man,
> Laugh when you may—be happy when you can. (5.67)

Gossamer's philosophy thus nicely jibes with the very invitation to and appeal of an evening's amusement that Potter so pleasantly offers his own audiences.

While Gossamer and Miss Gloomly stake out the temperamental poles of *Laugh When You Can*, however, its moral battles are played out even more dramatically by other characters. The play revolves around the attempt of Delville, a decent man with, however, a dangerous weakness for pretty women (as his manservant says, "though your good qualities are beyond naming, yet where women are concerned, you're so thoughtless and so desperate" [1.8]), to seduce or even rape Mrs. Mortimer, the beautiful, virtuous wife of a poor lieutenant. The major obstacle to Delville's scheme is the repeated interference of his devoted manservant, who serves faithfully as his master's conscience (as even Delville realizes: "Plague on the fellow's conscientious language!—he has made me half a coward, and I begin to feel!" [1.6]). To Delville's attendant, his responsibility to and for his master is absolutely clear: "though I know my obedience as a servant, I'll shew him I hav'n't forgot my duty as a man!" (2.25); "as it is my duty to serve my master in a good cause, so it is my duty to oppose him in a bad one!" (4.47).

The name of Delville's servant is Sambo. As both his name and (on stage) his blackface make immediately and unmistakably clear, he is a black man. Sambo, now twenty-one years old, had been captured and enslaved in Africa as a six-year-old child, then educated by his master; "train'd up 'midst all the follies and dissipations of London, though his head has been enlighten'd, his heart remains uncorrupted" (1.6). Sambo has come, over the years, to represent Delville's better half (he even pursues Delville's law studies for him while Delville is instead writing love verses or courting "a certain opera dancer"), and their relationship is one of symbiosis, drawn from its founding fact. When Delville rebukes Sambo for his interferences—"recollect who you are"—Sambo replies, "I do. I am your slave." "No—not my slave—I gave you liberty," Delville demurs. "You did, sir," Sambo agrees; "And that made me your slave. Gratitude has bound me faster to you than all the chains of Africa! 'Tis now fifteen years since you brought me to England; during which time you have fostered me, educated me, and treated me more as a brother than a servant!—and now when I warn you of your danger, you call it impertinence!—Ah, sir!—rather say 'tis selfishness; for my fate is so involv'd with yours, that if your heart bleeds, Sambo's will break, I'm sure" (1.8). As he says again at a later point, "my master's bad conduct makes it more incumbent on me to stay with him—Who else will bear with his follies, and labour to correct them? And spite of all, I know he's still so sound at the core, that I feel I couldn't exist without him!" (4.49). It is Sambo's "African philosophy" (1.6)—really, his Christian morality and decency—that ultimately gives *Laugh When You Can* its ethical foundation, when neither a laughing nor a crying philosophy can adequately serve.

Richard Potter could not have encountered many texts that might reflect his own background, and he must have thought of his mother when he heard and read Sambo's lines, for she, too, had been brought from Africa as a child slave, then raised (if not educated) for a while amid the follies and dissipations of another fashionable English city (Bath, not London). Far more important to him, however, was the larger assertion of the play about the common humanity, and thus the essential brotherhood, of all men and all races—a credo entirely consistent with Potter's Masonic ethos and very close to his heart. *Laugh When You Can* says little about this specifically, leading one recent scholar to express surprise that "Sambo the blackface buffoon" was "construed by some critics as an anti-slavery spokesman." But Sambo is no buffoon: he is virtuous, well-educated, well-spoken, and thoughtful. At two junctures of the play, however, Reynolds does have Sambo momentarily adopt what might seem the pose of a buffoon. Both of these are moments when Sambo's fondest expectations for a fortunate outcome to his schemes (the reformation of his master and a happy reunion for Mrs. and Lieutenant Mortimer) lead him to break out into a song and dance: "Dear Yanko say, and true he say!" The song was not by Reynolds at all; he had taken it from another playwright, Charles Dibden. Although written in what seems at first glance to be a heavy, mocking "negro" dialect, the song is a straightforward celebration of universal humanism:

> Dear Yanko say, and true he say,
> All mankind, one and t'other,
> Negro, Mulatto, and Malay,
> Through all de world be broder.
> In black, in yellow, what disgrace,
> That scandal so he use 'em?
> For dere no virtue in de face,
> De virtue in de bosom.

The song, as Dibden later made clear, is actually an "Indian Song"; the dialect was intended to be Amerindian, not African. Yanko (who himself does not speak in dialect; befitting his nobility, his English is quite good) is an American Indian chieftain who was the protagonist of Dibden's 1780 opera *The Islanders,* and the song would originally have been sung by the Indian maiden who loves him, Orra. Dibden published the song with its musical score separately in 1790, then gave it additional currency by introducing it into his well-received "Sans Souci" medley entertainments in the 1790s, and it became newly popular in that time of increasing antislavery sentiment. It was republished by several American newspapers in the 1790s, when one editor noted that it "was ever very popular, but is become much more so since the recent agitation of the question concerning the SLAVE TRADE, so constantly in every one's mouth; and so forcibly are the generous sentiments it conveys felt and admired, that it is not uncommon to hear Mr. WILBERFORCE called the GENEROUS YANKO." Sambo's joyful outbursts into song were the only songs in *Laugh When You Can,* and would have stood out. They serve to emphasize the broadly humanistic, antislavery sentiments of the entire play.

So "Laugh While You Can," when Richard Potter used it as an invitation to his audiences, was not merely an apt motto for an evening's entertainment. More subtly and more powerfully, it also very specifically evoked the humaneness and nobility of Sambo and, if perhaps only subliminally, put his auditors in mind of Yanko's message: all men are brothers.

Richard Potter would have had a great many opportunities to hear and even read *Laugh When You Can* in Boston in 1809 or 1811. (He might well have known and even seen that it was newly in print; the 1809 Boston edition of the play was printed by his friend Joseph Buckingham, who was living just a few doors away from him on Suffolk Place at the time.) We know that the Boston Theatre staged the play in March, September, and December 1809, May 1810 (but Potter was on the road then, performing in Canada), and February and October 1811 (on the latter occasion, the play opened the Boston theater season); there may have been additional stagings in these seasons as well, and the Boston company also presented it in Providence in August 1811. We might guess that Potter saw it (perhaps not for the first time) in October 1811, since he adapted the title for his own entertainments so soon thereafter.

## XIII

By 1811, as Potter refined and expanded his new suite of entertainments with Sally as his occasional partner, his career began to take off. This is apparent, to some degree, from the duration of his stands and from the venues in which he exhibited. Early in the year, he and Sally performed in Providence for the better part of three weeks. In late July and early August, Richard (traveling without Sally now, apparently) exhibited for more than a week in Philadelphia, initially charging an extremely impressive one dollar for admission. (He reduced this to fifty cents when he shifted to a different venue later in the week.) And in November, he performed for the better part of four weeks at the Columbian Museum in Boston.

Between these major stands in large cities he was also traveling widely and touring hard, as we can tell by the glimpses of him available in the occasional newspaper advertisements that he was now placing. Thus in late April, some two months after he closed in Providence, he was exhibiting in Northampton, Massachusetts; in early June, he was back in Albany. (He teamed up there this time with "Mr. Graham, from the Boston Theatre," who was appearing in Albany at the time as part of a company drawn mostly from the Boston Theatre and headed by the fine actor and manager John Bernard. Potter often stayed at the aptly named Thespian Hotel in Albany, and it is fairly safe to presume that, during the summer tour theater season, he would have been on familiar terms with the actors in town then.) Thence he headed south, appearing in Newburgh, New York (early July), and then in New Brunswick, New Jersey, before his stand in Philadelphia.

These last two were the last places and times, incidentally, that he advertised himself as "West Indian." Why he had done so in Boston initially is perhaps hard to understand, given the city's familiarity with him. In New Jersey and Philadelphia, however, he was on relatively unfamiliar ground, and the local attitudes on matters of race, especially in New Jersey, could be riskier for him. (In New Brunswick, for example, when his advertisement appeared in the *Guardian, or New Brunswick Advertiser,* the advertisement immediately to the right of his own announced "FOR SALE, A NEGRO WOMAN," and the one immediately below his own offered "Forty dollars reward" for "a Negro Man named SAM" who had just run away.)

Meanwhile, James Rannie, Potter's mentor and heretofore the preeminent ventriloquist and magician on the American scene, retired from professional life in mid-1811 after a long series of farewell performances. Rannie had been pointing toward this decision since early 1810, when, during a stand in New York, he began advertising his readiness to reveal to his audiences how he performed some of his deceptions: out of the one hundred he promised to present, "the audience may make choice of six deceptions, the theory of which he will lay open so that any one present may exhibit the same"; and a later letter to the editor of another newspaper indicates that he actually did this. By June he was associating this offer with his announcement that, having "purchased a farm in the country," he was now "just on the point of retiring from public life." After a long stand in Boston from mid-October 1810 to mid-January 1811, Rannie made a few last appearances at Salem, Newport, Providence, and then again for a few nights in Boston, after which he really did withdraw from public life. Richard Potter had probably been with him during at least some of this time (although definitely not all or even most of it): some of Rannie's advertisements in late November 1810 specifically promise feats "by the *Little Devil* as he is called." Rannie was performing wire-walking feats himself during this time and seems to have regularly alluded to himself in the third person as "the Rope-Dancer and Wire-Walker"; but these new, specific, and separate allusions to a "Little Devil" figure probably point to Potter, back for one last set of performances with his longtime mentor.

At this time, or very shortly thereafter, Potter also certainly acquired various legerdemain and advertising items from Rannie, to use henceforth in his own developing career. Most obviously, he gained possession of some of the woodcuts that Rannie had boldly featured in his advertisements and broadsides. We know this because one of these woodcuts, used by Rannie at least since 1804, now took pride of place in some of Potter's new broadsides beginning in 1812. The woodcut shows a man standing at ease under a tree, his arms stretched out asymmetrically; in the tree, a variety of birds have come to perch on the branches immediately above him. The figure illustrates Rannie's skill as an imitator of birds: his calls are so lifelike that the wild birds themselves, this shows us, are deceived and eagerly flock to him.

Rannie had commissioned this woodcut as one of many, all of which illustrated different aspects of his performances. On one of his broadsides, for example, he had arranged five such woodcuts, including this one (fig. 2). One woodcut shows him bloodily decapitating a rooster held by an assistant (he would then restore the head and the bird would be as good as ever); another, presenting a balancing feat, shows him balancing clay pipes upright from his chin and nose and beating a tambourine while standing on a small platform on which is also standing a small table with two lighted candles, the whole platform itself suspended on a pair of slack ropes. These, like the woodcut later used by Potter, are all large illustrations; they would span two columns in a newspaper, which made for difficult printing challenges, so they were used mostly in broadsides. The fourth and fifth woodcuts, both smaller, one-column-width pictures, show Rannie as a ventriloquist, standing beneath a tree, with an idealized figure of his little "Tommy" standing on his outstretched palm, and Rannie as a slack-wire balancer, standing one-legged on the rope while balancing a pole on his chin at the upper end of which a child himself balances upside down on his head. All in all, it was a broadside that no one could ignore.

Potter himself would have been able to make use of many of these woodcuts (and Rannie had several others as well) for his own advertising. But woodcuts were not durable: eventually they would wear down, but usually they—especially the larger ones—would first split under the repeated pressure of the printing press. Perhaps the woodcut Potter later used himself was the only one that was still serviceable. He soon featured it prominently in various broadsides that he had printed for himself (see fig. 5). The bird imitator it pictures now obviously represents Mr. Potter. It is, however, a portrait—doubtless highly stylized—of James Rannie.

Beginning in 1812, the war with England severely depressed the American and especially the New England economy for several years, and entertainers of all stripes drastically cut back on their advertising for the duration. We know little about Potter's work or travels in 1812 through 1814, save for a series of performances in larger cities. He was in Portland in February 1812, so surely he visited with his mentor James Rannie there then (perhaps this was even when he acquired that woodcut from Rannie). Rannie was living with his wife in the home he had built on an island in Portland harbor. He had already made his grand farewell tour a year earlier and had planned to retire to a quiet, manorial life. But rumor now had it that he had blown through all his earnings, and it was certainly true that he would set out on a new tour to the West Indies later in this year; he and Potter, who was looking to establish a manorial retreat of his own someday soon, would have had much to discuss. Potter returned to Portland seven months later, this time with his wife, and would surely have visited again then; Mrs. Rannie was certainly still there, whether her husband was or not.

During these years Potter also performed again in Providence, in Albany (on at least four separate occasions, sometimes with his wife), and in Boston (again, at least sometimes with his wife.) A letter waiting for Richard Potter in the Bennington, Vermont, post office at the end of 1814 probably signals that he traveled through that town then, too: this would have been on the direct route from Albany across Vermont to Brattleboro, and would have offered a good touring loop back to the Boston area—or, possibly, on to Andover, New Hampshire, which would soon be his new home.

XIV

Apart from his trips to Upper Canada in 1810 and through New Jersey to Philadelphia in July 1811, Potter during the first few years when he was establishing his independent career limited his touring to the New England and Upstate New York areas that would always be his primary territory. As we have seen, the major cities in which he performed were Boston (his base), Providence, Portland, and Albany; he was in Albany at least five times between the late summer of 1810 and the winter of 1812–13. During this time he was also casting about for a place where he could establish a home. To judge from the biographical account he later gave to Nathan Hale, he had been carefully focused on this goal from very early in his career:

The surest anchor, I thought, was to have some determinate object always in view, and none appeared to me more decisively powerful, than an independence that would secure me from poverty and public charity, (the common fate of strollers), when advanced age, or youthful competitors drove me from this temporary enjoyment. Having a good wife, well acquainted with country business, I concluded, that instead of carrying her about with me as an assistant, it would be better to have a *home,* which would be to her a congenial occupation, and to me a polar star, towards which I should always set my course.

In view of his very frequent tours to the Greater Albany area in these years, he may well have been scouting that area as well as New Hampshire for this purpose.

Historians have long assumed that, as Eastman summarized, Potter "came to Andover on one of his exhibition trips and gave his first performance in the tavern of Benjamin Thompson, where he made his home when in town. . . . Potter was pleased with the scenery and with the people of that section of the town, and bought the farm, where he built his house in 1814–15." But this is getting matters backward. In fact Potter clearly did not simply stumble upon Andover or upon Benjamin Thompson's tavern, nor is there reason to think that he had begun touring extensively in rural northern New Hampshire in those years; rather, as we have seen, he had already met and formed a personal and professional connection with Benjamin Thompson's son, so he would have been traveling to Andover with Thompson junior—perhaps as early as the spring of 1810, when "Potter and Thompson" might well have passed through New Hampshire to Montreal on their way to York. And it was easy for him to know that the land for his prospective home was available, for it was Benjamin Thompson senior who owned it and sold it to him.

Potter bought this first sixty-acre parcel of Andover land in May 1813, and eighty adjacent acres from another Andover landowner in April the following year. At the time, his wife was already expecting their second child. That year he also began construction of a home there, of his own designing—a hint at another of his significant talents. The home, Potter's "polar star," was designed to be a showpiece; as Potter told Hale in 1831, "I thought I might as well have a genteel, as a mean one. . . . It is the original, as I have been told, from which the government of the State, did me the honor to model the State House. The natural coincidence of professions," he added mischievously, "probably suggested this." While certainly no mansion, the elegantly furnished residence was, as Potter said, most "genteel," with a distinctive facade and impressive grounds. The two-story, side-gabled, center-hall cottage was distinctively Federalist in style, with a blind arch ornamented by a carved festoon of flowers and leaves above the centered front door and blind arches with carved drapery panels above the four symmetrically placed front windows—architectural flourishes that gave the otherwise simple structure a touch of real elegance. These features were certainly not suggested by a local housewright but evoke the artistry of the fashionable architects and craftsmen currently practicing in Boston and Salem. A dormer centered above the front door also let extra light into the upstairs, which was reportedly one single, large room. The first journalist to describe the dwelling (1851) also spoke of it as having "two projecting wings"; and in fact a circa 1869 stereoview of the dwelling shows a small wing set back at the rear of the house on the east side, so presumably there was another on the west side as well (fig. 6). (The architectural awkwardness of the east wing visible in the photograph indicates that the wings almost certainly were later additions to the original cottage and not part of its original, 1814 design, but the inventory of Potter's estate after his death in 1835 strongly suggests that the wings did exist at that time.) Goodwin and Ketchum both stated in the 1870s that there had also been "a house for servants and cooking separate from that of the family"; and there was indeed a second house on the property—probably for Potter's relatives Cromwell and Phebe Potter and some farm laborers—at the time of Potter's death.

The landscaping, too—of the front yard, at least, which stretched down the gentle hillside to the main road—was designed to be attractive in multiple senses of the word. Potter's house stood on a slight rise beside an important road, the Fourth New Hampshire Turnpike, the major artery from Concord across the state to Lebanon on the Connecticut River, which had been completed only a few years before Potter built his home. His house was thus prominently on display to many passersby, and Potter took care that it showed well. "The grounds about his house"—shades of Potter's early years on the Frankland estate in Hopkinton, Massachusetts—"were tastefully laid out, well kept, and ornamented with a great variety and profusion of shrubs and flowers, of which both he and his wife were passionately fond."

Then there were the statues on their plinths—two of them, prominently displayed. As Henry K. Oliver recalled years later, "When I used to pass [the Potter place] in old stage times, on my way to Dartmouth College, where I spent the last two years of my undergraduateship [fall 1816 through summer 1818], there stood on pillars in front of the house two figures, carved in wood, of life size, which once stood with a multitude of others in front of old Lord Timothy Dexter's mansion in Newburyport."

"Lord" Timothy Dexter, a wealthy and notoriously eccentric and egomaniacal Newburyport merchant, had acquired his mansion at the beginning of the century and immediately set about making it an ostentatious showpiece, with towers, minarets, and monumental arches. He commissioned a celebrated woodcarver, Joseph Wilson of Marblehead, to carve dozens of life-sized images for the grounds; he then placed many of these on top of fifteen-foot pillars along the fence bounding his estate, others on pedestals or arches spaced around the grounds, and some (of Washington, Adams, and Jefferson) atop the entrance portico of his mansion. These "handsome carved Images, well painted, designed to represent some of the first characters in the United States of America, and Europe," included (in addition to the first three presidents) American statesmen (Franklin, Hancock, Hamilton, Jay), military figures (Napoleon Bonaparte, Admiral Nelson), the Senecan sachem Cornplanter, and the English minister William Pitt. Dexter also erected a statue of himself (inscribed "I am the first in the East, the first in the West, and the greatest philosopher in the Western World"). There were also one representing the goddess of Fame and at least a few lions. Most authorities estimate that there were approximately forty such statues altogether (Dexter himself once claimed there were thirty-seven). No complete list of them was ever created, and indeed no fixed register was possible, for Dexter sometimes changed their names and had the statues altered accordingly. After Dexter's death in 1806, the statues for the most part remained in place as the property passed through various hands; but a fierce storm in late September 1815 blew most of them down from their pedestals, and at that point they were finally sold at auction. According to a biographer, the images sold at prices ranging from a low of fifty cents to a high of five dollars (the statue of Dexter himself did not find a buyer at any price). This was clearly when Potter, who was performing in the Boston area throughout October 1815, acquired his two figures, for the price of a few tickets to one of his own shows, and promptly installed them on pillars in front of his own house. There was more than a bit of the showman in both men.

Once settled in his new home, Potter began developing his property as a farm. Since he was so frequently absent on his tours for long periods of time, he necessarily left the labor and management of his farming and husbandry operations to others, but he continually strove to improve the property, building barns, sheds, and bridges, establishing a garden, raising crops, developing an orchard, and keeping a number of horses, cattle, swine, and eventually sheep. Over the years, the Potter Place, as it came to be known, became a modest re-creation of the grand Frankland estate where Potter had passed his childhood.

Potter's suggestion that he established his dreamed-of home in a rural location to chime with his wife's inclination for "country business" probably masks another motive. Sally's alcoholism in her later life was well known in Andover, and it has long been assumed that Potter knew of her inclinations from their early years together and sought out a secluded homesite "in order to withdraw her from the allurements besetting her in city life." On the face of it, this might seem an oddly anachronistic, Victorian assumption: alcohol was an inescapable fact of American life in rural no less than urban areas at this period, and Andover itself had more than its share of taverns. In context, however, a different picture emerges. The north slope of Beacon Hill in Boston, the heart of the city's black community, was at the time of Potter's marriage already notorious as a place of dissipation: "*there* is the place where *Satan's seat is*," a missionary minister who spent three months working in the district famously proclaimed in 1817, noting among other, more scabrous details that

> five and twenty or thirty shops are opened on Lord's days from morning to evening, and ardent spirits are retailed without restraint, while hundreds are intoxicated, and spend the holy Sabbath in frolicking and gambling, in fighting and blaspheming; and many in scenes of iniquity and debauchery too dreadful to be named. The street is filled during the day with young and old of all complexions, numbers drunken and sleeping by its sides and corners; and awful noises and confusions are witnessed. . . . Here, week after week, whole nights are spent in drinking and carousing; and as the morning light begins to appear, when others arise from their beds, these close their doors.

To live in black Boston at this time was almost necessarily to live in an at-risk neighborhood. A person or family of sound values could live and thrive there, and a great many did, but it was no place for a young woman whose husband was often away for weeks or even months at a time, especially if she had a weakness for alcohol and if her husband could better provide for her. So, just as the grand Frankland place in the rural Hopkinton of Potter's childhood had had its origins as a place of refuge from the disapprobation and scorn of Boston society, now his own Potter Place began as a hoped-for sanctuary from the ills of another Boston society.

# 4

## Ascent to Fame, 1815–1819

I

With the end of the war with Britain in early 1815, the long-crippled New England economy quickly began to rebound, Americans began to have more discretionary income, and the conditions for Potter's entertainments were vastly improved. So while Potter had just incurred and was still incurring significant expenses as he bought and developed his new homestead, he also was finding greater and more rewarding opportunities to flourish as a showman.

Even so, the requirements of his new homestead and growing family—his son Henry was now about five years old, and his two younger children were both infants—surely placed such demands on his time that his traveling in 1815 was necessarily restricted. He was performing in the Albany area again in April (he had just been exhibiting there barely four months earlier, in December 1814; imaginably this is where he and his family spent the winter, and even where one or two of his children were born). Through the summer we have no record of his performances; perhaps he remained close to home for much of this time, but in truth we have no way of telling, for few towns even had newspapers yet. In mid-August, however, he appeared for a few evenings in Salem, Massachusetts (which did have newspapers), and in mid-September, this time with his wife, for a few evenings in Greenfield, Massachusetts. Then in early October he exhibited again in Boston, for the first time in more than two years, with great success. He was performing in a much larger and much more fashionable venue this time, the Columbian Museum (he had also appeared there in 1811), which housed a large collection of works of art, natural curiosities, wax figures, and interesting artifacts ("Spectators will have the liberty of amusing themselves, in viewing the many curiosities of the Museum, till 7 o'clock, at which time the performance will commence"), and his one-week engagement was so popular that it extended to two weeks, and then to three. His tickets were now pricier, too: in 1813, he had charged 37½ cents for adults, 25 cents for children; now he was charging 50 cents each, "without distinction of age," and was still turning away customers.

It was during this visit to Boston that Potter sat for his portrait, a gesture that bespeaks how comfortable were his circumstances now. The artist was Ethan Allen Greenwood, an increasingly prominent portraitist whose studio was near the Columbian Museum. Greenwood himself took a great interest in the performers who exhibited at the museum—he himself would within a few years become the proprietor and manager of this museum and others—and perhaps he solicited their patronage, too. His portraits at around this time included several exhibitors—a few dwarfs, the Mammoth Boy (Joe Gridley), Mr. and Mrs. [John] Rannie, and Ramo Samee (a juggler from India). Potter may very well have been staying with his old housemate Samuel Dillaway junior at this time, and certainly was in company with him, because Greenwood completed his portrait of "Mr. Dillaway" the following day.

Potter seems to have spent most of 1816 developing his homestead and rehearsing his act—although, again, the absence of newspaper advertisements does not mean that he was not touring locally. He was wise to keep his skills sharp, for competition was coming. Early this year an accomplished magician from Europe, Day Francis, arrived in New York and began a grand tour of the Atlantic states. Styling himself first "Sieur Day Francis—the Great," and soon enough "Emperor of the Conjurors," Francis presented himself as a "necromancer" in the old tradition of Thomas Garbut (who had been James Rannie's mentor in Scotland and England in the 1790s), with exotic Greek appellations for his various kinds of magic; thus he prominently advertised his "Thamaturgic Horologium," "Deceptio Thermopsichia" ("an Omelette Experiment," he translated), and "Cartomantic Deceptions" (card tricks), and promised "many wonderful performances in Rhabdologe, Mathematics, Stegansgraphy, Palegenses, Phylacteria, Papyromance, and many wonderful performances on the BODECAHEDRON." He also demonstrated feats of balancing. While Potter was lying low, relatively speaking, in New England, Francis performed to great acclaim in New York City for two months, then moved to Philadelphia for a week or so, then north by way of Albany to Boston and its environs (Salem, Newburyport, Portsmouth)—he was now very much in Potter's territory—for two more months. (He also sat for his own portrait by Ethan Allen Greenwood in Boston in early September.) He apparently traveled next to the West Indies; but in February 1817 he was back in the United States and exhibiting in Charleston. He also published a book, *Stanislas Outdone, the New Hocus Pocus or the Whole Art of Legerdemain* (Philadelphia, 1818), a compilation of earlier explanations of various feats of legerdemain, that was one of the first such to appear in America. Meanwhile his assistant and then, abruptly, his competitor, a Mr. Handel, broke off in May 1816 to exhibit many of the same acts independently in New York, Washington, Alexandria, Richmond, and possibly Charleston and New Orleans.

These threats to Potter's preeminence, fortunately for him, quickly faded. Francis had the misfortune to die soon thereafter, in early 1818, in Demerara (a recently Dutch and newly British colony in what would eventually become British Guyana, in Caribbean South America). And Francis's ephebe, Handel, who clearly did not possess the skills of his former master, ultimately abandoned the East Coast cities to become a minor performer in Kentucky and Ohio. Even so, Day Francis's advent surely prompted Potter to the dark awareness that he later acknowledged to Hale, that a day would come "when advanced age, or youthful competitors [would drive] me from this temporary enjoyment." It was a lesson to be learned, and remembered.

Many of Day Francis's feats of legerdemain were deceptions that Potter had already mastered—cooking pancakes in a gentleman's hat and restoring it none the worse for wear, making eggs jump from one gentleman's hat to another's, beheading and restoring to life a cock, producing from a deck of cards the precise card that members of the company were holding in mind, and so forth—and Potter remained an unchallenged master of ventriloquism, which Francis did not attempt. But Potter did, directly or indirectly, pick up one important new set of deceptions from Francis that would add a new dimension to his exhibitions for the next several years. This was Francis's "Man Salamander" act (in medieval myth, the salamander was thought to be fireproof). (Francis's protégé Handel later added the epithet "anti-combustible," which Francis himself quickly adopted as well.) As he described it: "Mr. Francis will dance a PAS SEUL on *Red Hot* Iron. He will pass a bar of *Red Hot* Iron over his tongue, draw it through his hands, and afterwards convert it into various shapes with his naked feet. He will immerse his hands into *Molten Lead;* and what is not more astonishing than true, he will pass a large *Body of Fire* over his naked feet and arms, without any injury to himself." Day Francis was the first to perform these feats in the New World.

Perhaps Potter observed Francis's act in Boston in that summer of 1816, although certainly Francis would not have shared the professional secrets of his Man Salamander act with a stranger and potential competitor. But later in the year Potter gained this education straightforwardly from another professional magician with whom he was then collaborating. In November and December, he was on the road again, again to the familiar venue of Albany, and this time he teamed up for a while with some new colleagues—a Miss Dupre or Dupree, who was a slack-wire artist, and Signor Cassania, "the Spanish Magician," who advertised himself as a recent arrival from the theaters of London, Paris, and Naples. (Also joining them to perform a dance at a few performances was "the infant Miss Flint," a young girl who danced occasionally at the Albany Theatre.) Cassania and Dupree had arrived from Europe and opened for an extended and apparently very successful stand in New York in early September. Now Potter, Cassania, and Dupree performed at the theater in Albany for more than two weeks; their exhibition particularly featured Cassania's magic, Potter's ventriloquism and songs and dances, and Dupree's slack-wire artistry, although Potter also performed some magic, Cassania occasionally joined Potter in a dance, and Miss Dupree sometimes sang a song.

At no point during his New York City exhibitions or during his Albany performances with Potter did Cassania advertise any "fireproof" feats, but in December, when Potter, Cassania, and Dupree moved on to Hudson, New York, to perform a few nights more, for their final exhibition Cassania suddenly announced that he would "perform the part of THE ANTI-COMBUSTIBLE Man Salamander," describing his performance in language lifted directly from Day Francis's advertisements: "He will pass a bar of Red Hot Iron over his tongue, and draw it through his hands repeatedly, and afterwards bend it into various shapes with his naked feet, as a Smith would on an Anvil. He will Immerse his Hands and Feet in MOLTEN LEAD, And pass his NAKED Feet and Arms over a large Body of Fire." Cassania, like Day Francis, had clearly learned his anticombustible techniques from some European master; at this time Signora Josephine Girardelli was exhibiting in London as "the Fire-Proof Lady," and Kirby reported that "since her performance in this metropolis, about two years ago [it had been in 1815], several others of this salamander tribe have appeared, and may now be seen travelling from town to town, and from village to village, throughout the kingdom, wherever a fair or great market is held, exhibiting their wonders to the astonished crowd." After that culminating Hudson performance, Cassania appeared no more in America, and presumably returned to Europe (Miss Dupree, however, remained and performed in American circuses for several years). Since he was leaving the continent, he would not have begrudged sharing the secrets of these feats with his new colleague and instructing him in the act. Potter would soon begin performing the same act, and using Cassania's very descriptions of it, in his own exhibitions.

This year was also marked by a personal tragedy. On 5 October 1816, Potter's oldest child, Henry M. Potter, was killed in an accident when he fell under the wheels of a cart loaded with corn. His death was not recorded in the Rev. Josiah Badcock's extensive record of deaths in Andover, nor in Badcock's personal diary, but this was true of a few other children who died in Andover at about this time as well, and so would suggest only that the Potter family was not well known to Badcock then. Henry M. Potter: his first name may have been in honor of Henry K. Oliver—a remarkable tribute, if so, for Oliver was only about ten years old at the time of Henry Potter's birth. We do not even know what name that middle initial stood for; at a guess, Manfredi?—there is no other *M* who figures significantly in Potter's life. Henry was buried along the western edge of the Old Cemetery at Andover Center, and no one was ever buried beyond him, leaving an odd gap, although the cemetery was used for another eighty-five years.

Potter himself had not left for Albany yet (he gave a note of hand to a neighbor in Andover on 16 October), so he was presumably home at the time; certainly he was making extensive preparations for his upcoming tour through the Mid-Atlantic states, which was to continue for several months after his engagements in Albany and Hudson. He would be away from his home in Andover for a lengthy period; this was a devastating way to be leaving it, with the funeral and burial of his six- or seven-year-old heir. With his two other children still infants, his family probably remained behind in Andover; certainly there is no record of "Mr. and Mrs. Potter" appearing together again until the fall of 1817.

Potter's new tour, the most ambitious in his career thus far, took him from Albany and Hudson south to Philadelphia, then on to Baltimore, and then even farther south to the Washington area. In Philadelphia, Potter again teamed up with a new partner, a magician who presented himself as Sieur Breslaw, just arrived from London, "the greatest Necromancer in the Western world"—another journeyman trading on the old Breslaw name. Within a week, Miss Dupree also joined them. (After this collaboration, Breslaw would once, while working in Norfolk with a circus [Miss Dupree was again with him at the time], attempt to "display his wonderful but laborious powers of VENTRILOQUISM" [note his use of Potter's language]. The attempt must have been unsuccessful, because he seems never to have ventured it again.)

Potter and Breslaw performed at Philadelphia's Washington Hall for more than two weeks. Potter then continued alone on to Baltimore for a week of performances there. Then in the Washington area he appeared, first for a week in Alexandria, and then for at least a brief stay at the City Hotel in Washington, on Capitol Hill. His appearances in Alexandria elicited a testimonial from a gratified spectator there: "The novelties were surprising, and excited the wonder and delight of the beholders. The astonishing powers of ventriloquism were displayed, and were only excelled by some particular deceptions, never before attempted in this town." The writer continued, "I understand it is Mr. Potter's intention to introduce many new and singular operations which were not included in the last performance; and should sufficient encouragement offer, he will, I am told, on a future evening, display the extraordinary feat of the *Man Salamander.* In which he is said to excel 'Handel the Great,' and will prove himself the emperor of all conjurers!!" (Day Francis had never made it to Washington, but his rebellious pupil Mr. Handel had performed in both Washington and Alexandria in the summer of 1816.) And indeed Potter did present his new Anti-Combustible Man Salamander act at his next performance.

One feature of this tour is worth noting, although nothing otherwise calls attention to it: his route through Maryland and into the District of Columbia and Virginia marked Potter's first venture into American slave territory. He spent some five weeks south of the Mason-Dixon Line. Perhaps he had Thompson traveling with him? We simply do not know.

At this point Potter finally turned back north, pausing again in Baltimore to give a few additional "solicited" performances there before returning home by the beginning of April. He had been away for five months.

II

Potter now began preparing for another set of extensive tours through his familiar New England territory. This time, however, his preparations had broader consequences: he was moving his entire family away from their Andover home. After making yet another tour back to the Albany area, where he performed for a week (sometimes as Mr. Potter, sometimes as Mr. and Mrs. Potter) in late July and early August, Potter apparently relocated his family back in Boston. He was performing in local venues there (Charlestown and Salem) by the very beginning of the fall.

For the next year and into the late winter of 1818–19, Potter concentrated his performances in eastern Massachusetts and in Rhode Island. He was now a well-known performer, and he could hire and fill major performance halls in large cities and readily attract repeat audiences in smaller towns. During the winter of 1817–18, he alternated major exhibitions between Providence and Boston; throughout the spring and summer of 1818, he performed extensively in Boston. These cities were his major bases, but he performed on occasional tours through smaller towns as well (he was in Newport, Rhode Island, in late December 1817, for example, and in Northampton, Massachusetts, in September 1818; he probably also performed in towns such as Taunton and Worcester, Massachusetts, along the way). His wife continued to assist him and sometimes performed as well, singing "a variety of entertaining Songs."

Potter was continuing to develop and expand his repertory during this time. Indeed, his persistent dedication to his craft was already becoming a noticeable characteristic of his career. He later indicated to Hale that he had regularly used the "pretense of preparation and experiment, for the succeeding exhibition" as an excuse for retiring each night from "the entanglements of company"; "Thus I have avoided gambling, drinking, and idleness." But clearly this was his normal practice, and no mere pretense. Just as he had continually rehearsed and studied his art during the time he had lived with the Olivers in Boston at the outset of his career—"He had several large books filled with directions upon the prestigiatory (?) art, keeping up his study and practice till he went before the public," Oliver reported—so did he throughout his career.

It may have been at about this time that the young Oliver Wendell Holmes (who would later research the Frankland family, including Potter's mother, Dinah, for his poem "Agnes") first beheld one of Potter's performances, and his affectionate synopsis reminds us that the basic sleight-of-hand tricks that Potter had perfected in the Olivers' kitchen years earlier continued to stand him in good stead even as his repertory expanded. (Holmes was a second cousin of Henry K. Oliver and probably had traded stories with him both early and later about Potter's tricks.) As Holmes recalled years afterward:

When "Potter the ventriloquist" . . . went round giving his entertainments, there was something unexplained, uncanny, almost awful, and beyond dispute marvelous, in his performances. Those watches that disappeared and came back to their owners, those endless supplies of treasures from empty hats, and especially those crawling eggs that travelled all over the magician's person, sent many a child home thinking that Mr. Potter must have ghostly assistants, and raised grave doubts in the mind of "professors," that is members of the church, whether they had not compromised their characters by being seen at such an unhallowed exhibition.

But by this time Potter's repertory had expanded far, far beyond these foundational illusions. His dramatic new Man Salamander act was still rare and unmatched in America, and he continued to stage it occasionally, especially in the latter stages of a long stand in a city, when varied exhibitions and new wonders might bring earlier attendees back for second and third visits. Now he also introduced and increasingly featured another new—but also old—entertainment, the "Dissertation on Noses," in which he would "personate the characters of the wearers, with a variety of Songs adapted to each." This particular entertainment became a favorite staple of his exhibitions and was strongly identified with Potter for the rest of his career.

The "Dissertation on Noses" was not new. Influenced by George Alexander Stevens's popular "Lecture on Heads" (1764), it had been written and performed, as a supplement to "A Satyrical Lecture on Hearts," as a dramatic lecture by James Solas Dodd, who presented it very successfully in London in the winter of 1766–67 and then published it in March 1767. It had been brought to America, as we have seen, by two different expatriate English actors, Charles Stuart Powell and William Bates, in the 1790s, but had received little if any attention since then until Bates revived it in 1810. So the "Dissertation" was already vaguely familiar to American audiences, perhaps, but already also wore an air of old-fashioned quaintness. Still, it was genteel and inoffensive, and it gave Potter opportunities to introduce accompanying songs and dances that suited his own developing style very well.

Potter must have acquired a script for the "Dissertation on Noses" from Bates after the latter's final Boston performances in August 1810. He probably acquired some other properties at about the same time, but even before Bates's departure from Boston: Bates had been closing his exhibitions with "a Grand Display of Chinese Brilliancies," and one of these (despite that misleading term "brilliancies," for these were shadow projections, not transparencies) was very likely the "Chinese Umbrose" (always Potter's phrase, although these shows are traditionally called *ombres chinoises*") that Potter soon began featuring in his exhibition, "represent[ing] a prospective view of *Leadenhall-street,* in London, with a view of the River, and country on the opposite side." The shades could be introduced in Potter's act immediately, but the "Dissertation" required developing: Potter had to choose his own songs to accompany the various noses (such as the "hook-nose," which "denotes superstition and gossiping"; the "turning-up nose," that of "the critic"; the toper's "Ruby Nose"; the "sharp nose," "sure sign of a scold"; and so forth) and devise his own dances to accompany them. As noted, he was not ready to introduce the "Dissertation on Noses" into his exhibition until 1817, when he was carefully expanding his repertory.

III

At this time we also catch a private glimpse of Richard Potter and his world and gain some precious hints about his social network and his interests. The occasion was an unpleasant episode that took place in Boston at the very end of January 1818, a time when Potter, recently returned from another tour through Rhode Island, was preparing for an extensive stand in his home city. In brief, what happened was simply that Potter had his pocket picked. He lost twenty-six dollars in bank notes—a significant sum. But he knew when and where the theft had happened, and he was sure he knew the culprit, too—one Samuel Sampson. So he went straight to a justice of the peace to report his loss and have Sampson arrested. He also, according to Sampson, proclaimed his suspicions "in the hearing of many good citizens."

Samuel Sampson was a young (about twenty-six) black Bostonian, a barber and hairdresser (this being one of the few trades open to blacks in Boston at this time) whose business was located at the Exchange Coffee House, a well-known Boston establishment where Potter often performed. Potter obviously knew him somewhat, because the two men had been out for a social evening together. Sampson was not merely defiant in his denial of his guilt but also went on the offensive and filed a retaliatory suit, claiming that Potter, knowing Sampson to be innocent, was nonetheless maliciously contriving to destroy his "good name and reputation" and to "injure him in his trade" and "ruin him in his business." The emphasis in the suit on Sampson's commercial success and Potter's awareness of it—"he had got a considerable profit and gain which the said Potter was well knowing"—probably indicates the threat that Sampson now particularly recognized: Sampson's business depended almost entirely upon the patronage of white customers at the Exchange Coffee House, and Potter's word, especially in that venue, could be very influential among such customers.

It is doubtful, to put it mildly, that Sampson ever made enough money to make Richard Potter or anyone else jealous (Potter was not a jealous man anyway) and easy to suspect that instead he hoped his countersuit might make him some money. (It never did; by September it had been dropped.) Sampson had accumulated enough capital to buy a small house on South Russell Street, an area where many blacks lived, the following year (it cost him $250); he had married earlier that year and probably was seeking a permanent residence for himself and his new wife. But he also had a record of moving his place of business with some frequency—from Devonshire Street to the Exchange Coffee House in 1816, then to Water Street in late 1818 (so perhaps Potter's bad opinion of him really did affect his business at the Exchange Coffee House), then to Congress Street, then to School Street, then to another city, Portland, by early 1823; and when he died in Portland in mid-March 1824, his estate apart from his South Russell Street property was inventoried at only $18, against over $270 in debts. There were other signs of trouble as well: in 1822 he was fined $10 for assault and ordered to recognize $100 to keep peace six months (this is probably at least part of the reason that he moved to Portland); and his death in Portland, at the age of thirty-two, was a suicide.

One final fact from Sampson's brief life story suggests that his situation within Boston's black community might also have been complicated. The woman he married in 1819, Almira Long, another member of that community, had been engaged to another man. In late May 1818, some four months after the pickpocketing incident, James George Barbadoes, a young man who would eventually become a very prominent black Bostonian—a leader in the American Anti-Slavery Society, the Massachusetts General Colored Association, the African Baptist Church, and the African Lodge—published his and Almira Long's intention to marry. But the marriage never took place; instead, she married Samuel Sampson in March 1819. Potter would soon enough be a Masonic associate and even a friend of Barbadoes's, and perhaps already was (it is not clear when Barbadoes was initiated into the African Lodge). These awkwardly shifting relationships would in any event have been well known within the black community.

Against the background of these social currents, it is all the more fascinating, then, to discover what Potter and Sampson were doing together that night in January 1818. Sampson's suit gives an important hint: Potter had asserted on Sunday, 1 February, that his pocket had been picked "'a few nights since at the theatre,' meaning the Boston Theatre." For the entire previous week, the Boston Theatre had been featuring a new musical drama that had never before been staged in Boston—*The Slave.* "This celebrated Drama has been in preparation the whole of the season," the managers announced, and was being presented "with the Original Music, Songs, Glees, Chorusses, &c." and with new scenery, dresses, and decorations.

*The Slave,* by the highly popular playwright Thomas Morton, had premiered at the Covent Garden Theatre in London in late 1816, with the great Macready playing the lead role of Gambia, the slave. In Boston that role was assumed by John Duff, an Irish actor who had recently come to Boston and was the preeminent actor in the company. The play is set in Surinam (thereby invoking Aphra Behn's *Oroonoko*), a formerly Dutch and now newly British colony in South America. Its actions are triggered by the heroic but flawed Captain Clifton's love for the beautiful quadroon slave Zelinda, his mistress and the mother of his young son (also a slave), whom he now seeks to free (but he has gambled away the money with which he could have bought her and their child's freedom) and marry (he finally manages to do this in act 1). The superheroic Gambia, a dominant, noble African slave "of giant strength" (1.1.4), also loves Zelinda but, finally persuaded of her love for Clifton and of Clifton's faithfulness to her, thereafter serves as their steadfast guardian: he soon saves Clifton from death at the hands of a body of rebellious slaves and then repeatedly intercedes to preserve Zelinda, Clifton, and their child from all the threats to their freedom and happiness that Zelinda's lecherous, scheming, and potentially murderous owner (and Clifton's erstwhile gambler adversary), Colonel Lindenburg, can contrive against them, as the play cascades melodramatically from one desperate crisis to another.

While initially Gambia's heroic qualities are most obviously his physical prowess and his nobility of character—with his strong, African passions being presented as a double-edged aspect of his nature, potentially dangerous—he ultimately completes his apotheosis by demonstrating a Christian morality and fortitude, ready to assume the sufferings and endure the assaults of others in order to redeem them. Set free at one point by Clifton (2.1.35), he soon sells himself back into slavery to raise the sum of money needed to free Clifton from a debtor's prison so that Clifton can be restored to Zelinda. Defying and opposing his master, Lindenburg, to prevent him from raping Zelinda, he proclaims himself "So devotedly thy Slave, that I will preserve my master's honour, though the price of duty be my life" (3.2.62). Near the end of the play, having prevented Lindenburg's rape of Zelinda and then given himself over to capture so that Clifton, Zelinda, and their child could escape from Lindenburg's hot pursuit, he wounds Lindenburg in blocking that pursuit but spares his life and then soon after saves his life with a special African herbal remedy and spares even his pride by refusing to reveal the secret of Lindenburg's earlier branding for theft, something Gambia had just discovered during their combat:

L: Slave! I am in thy power—how wilt thou use it?
G: By saving, if I can, my master's life. By inflicting that wound, I preserved the innocent—by healing it, I may preserve the guilty.
    . . .
L: Name thy reward—
G: I never traffic with my humanity.
L: Ah Nature, this is thy work, pure and undefiled!—But my secret—is it revealed?
G: Revealed!—I may destroy, but never can betray—
L: How then to secure it?
G: I am your Slave—here is my breast!
L: (*Falling into his arms*) Receive me in its noble sanctuary!—My wound calls for help—African, thy virtues have subdued me!
G: To be so vanquished, is man's proudest victory! (3.4.68)

The play is full of such grand fustian. The new English governor of Surinam, mouthpiece for a benevolent sovereign, sets the English high moral tone in several public pronouncements:

'Tis not by the thunder of the war, but by the still voice of conscience, that the liberty of mankind will be achieved—yes, slavery must fall before the Christian warrior;—the arena he combats in, is the human mind; Revelation unfolds his banner;—Truth forges his shield;—his armor is rivetted by Reason, and his lance is tempered by Mercy. (2.1.36)

Go, worthy African! And tell the world, that true liberty is the offspring of peace, the nurse of humanity, the parent of benevolence; its home the world; its family mankind; its allegiance, Heaven! (3.5.69–70)

And Morton repeatedly congratulates his English audiences for their country's role in working to dismantle the institution of slavery, as when Gambia prophesies a time "when thro' thy country's zeal the all-searching sun shall dart his rays in vain, to find a slave in Afric" (2.1.36). At the play's conclusion, with Gambia apparently freed by Colonel Lindenburg, the Governor dispatches Captain Clifton to England, and asks Gambia to accompany him, prompting this moment of transport, the concluding speech of the play (smugly characterized by a contemporaneous English critic as "an appropriate panegyric on the efforts of this Country in the cause of Africa"): "England, shall I behold thee? Talk of fabled land, or magic power! But what land, that poet ever sung, or enchanter swayed, can equal that, which, when the Slave's foot touches, he becomes free!—his prisoned soul starts forth, his swelling nerves burst the chain that enthrall'd him, and, in his own strength he stands, as the rock he treads on, majestic and secure" (3.5.71).

Still, the play drives home several fundamental points not merely about the blessings of freedom but about its obligations. Gambia himself acknowledges at the outset that he deserves his enslavement because, "the slave of fierce ambition," he had once sold others into slavery for his own profit, only to be enslaved himself—"just, full retribution." "That freedom I denied to others, is now far from my hopes as hell from heaven" (1.2.4). And the "freedom" to be vicious and tyrannical—in other words, to deny freedom to others—is no freedom at all, but moral corruption; thus Lindenburg (before his final reformation) is rightly denounced by Zelinda as "the slave of passion" (3.2.60). In Gambia's early words again, "There is a state worse than slavery—liberty engendered by treachery, nursed by rapine, and invigorated by cruelty" (1.1.5). These words had resonated on the stage in London, and so did they in Boston, already a center of nascent abolitionist sentiment in the New World.

*The Slave* does not merely celebrate freedom as a blessing that should be the lot of all men; it also—as did Reynolds's *Laugh When You* Can, and the humanistic creed of the African Masonic Lodge to which Potter proudly belonged—sounds more daring notes about the actual brotherhood and shared humanity of blacks and whites. Trivially, we hear this when Zelinda and Clifton's octoroon child is described by the Dutch Mrs. Lindenburg (mother of the colonel), on whose estate they live, as "my little adopted Englishman" (1.2.16). More resoundingly, it rings out in Clifton's recognition of Gambia's nobility when he learns that Gambia has sold himself back into slavery in order to free Clifton from prison: "Oh, I were unworthy the name of man, did I suffer this generous sacrifice! And is that the being with whom the proud European denies fellowship? If we are not brothers, let the white man blush that he is alien to the blood that mantles in that noble breast" (2.3.44).

So this was the play that two free black Bostonians in January 1818 went to attend; this, the white man's heroic, optimistic, abolitionist drama that Richard Potter (himself a "dramatic" performer), ready to enjoy an evening's entertainment celebrating black heroism and morality and perhaps also eager to discover what new currents might be moving in his country's race relations, would forever afterward associate with having his pocket picked, and then his reputation smeared for good measure, by a black acquaintance.*

For most of the following summer of 1818, Potter stayed in Boston and, remarkably, exhibited continuously (sometimes with his wife) for almost two full months, from the very beginning of July into the last week of August. He appeared in at least two venues, first at Association Hall and then in the large room under the Columbian Museum, one of his regular places of performance. One new feature now began to distinguish his advertisements: beginning in late August, as his stand drew toward its close, he encouraged patrons to seize the opportunity to attend his exhibitions now, for "he may never again appear before a Boston audience, as he contemplates leaving the country."

## IV

Potter was forming a career plan; but he was not ready to leave the country just yet. He had had a tremendously successful summer in Boston, and his repertory of sleight-of-hand tricks, dramatic monologues and dialogues, songs, and ventriloquial feats was now enormous, enabling him to vary his program significantly each night for weeks and weeks on end. He had refined his techniques and his personal style through endless practice and, by now, in many hundreds of performances. He had made himself into the most prominent and widely known entertainer in all of New England. Now he was ready to venture into even larger markets.

At the very beginning of February 1819, Potter began advertising in New York City. This was very much a departure from his familiar and even his occasional itineraries. While he had certainly passed through the city on occasion, he had apparently never performed there before, not even as James Rannie's assistant: he had joined up with Rannie only after the conclusion of the latter's New York exhibitions in the spring of 1804 and had left him before Rannie's farewell performances in New York in the early spring of

---

*The only critical response to the play in the Boston newspapers, meanwhile, was a decidedly racist one: "We feel the noble and lofty thoughts of Othello, and can listen with the Venetian Senate to the recital of his valiant deeds. Othello was a Moor, and had 'done some service to the State.' But to hear gorgeous sentiments and nonsense proceeding from the thick lips and flattened nose of a Plantation Negro, puts common patience at defiance" (*Boston Daily Advertiser,* 6 Feb. 1818, 2).

1810. Indeed, Potter had probably not included New York City in any of his itineraries before this because it had never been part of any of the itineraries he had followed with Rannie during his apprentice years. Now, as a seasoned and accomplished master of his arts, he ventured into this great new venue at last.

He began cautiously, advertising in a few newspapers quite modestly and briefly (his posted broadsides and circulated handbills, or course, would have been bolder) and planning to exhibit for a week only. But his success was immediate. His exhibition venue, Washington Hall, located right on Broadway, was very grand ("Washington Hall contained the largest room in the city" and "was a great place for balls for many years") and one of the most fashionable addresses in the city. Very quickly crowds of citizens, including many prominent ones, began patronizing his exhibitions.

Within a week of his opening, unsolicited reviews began appearing in the city's newspapers, and they were unanimously favorable and even enthusiastic. Great stress was placed on the superior qualities of his performances:

> Mr. Potter, whose powers as a ventriloquist place him above the celebrated Rannie, will perform this evening at Washington Hall.—Those who have never witnessed the extraordinary manner with which those who possess this skill of managing their voice to imitate the voices of others, as well as the cries of animals, and the notes of the various feathered throng, must be highly delighted with the exhibition. Mr. Potter, in addition to ventriloquism, astonishes his audience with the most surprising "slight of hand" tricks, and other interesting amusements, which never fail to awaken the most lively feelings, and call forth the warmest applause.
>
> His deceptions are equal, if not superior, to any thing of the kind we have seen in this city. He possesses the rare powers of a ventriloquist; and shews off this extraordinary talent to great advantage.
>
> He is more adroit in "legerdemain" than any other person we have seen in this city. The dissertation on noses, excited much merriment, and his comic songs were well received. His ventriloquism is the most extraordinary and attractive part of the exhibition.... This part of Mr. Potter's performance, gave general satisfaction, and produced three rounds of applause.
>
> In addition to his *slight of hand,* Mr. P. possesses very respectable comic powers—sings well, and obtains the general applause of his visitors.

Figure 1. Manfredi broadside, Portsmouth, 1803. "Signior Manfredi,
ARTIST OF AGILITY, AND ROPE DANCER."
(Courtesy of the American Antiquarian Society)

At *The Newbafra Hotle* HOUSE,
On *Monday Evening April it 1811*

# EVENING,

*WILL BE DISPLAYED THE*

# Neficos Box,

Rope Dancing, Wire Walking, and 100 deceptions: Alfo, *imitations* of all kind of Birds, Ducks, Chickens, Cats, Dogs, and Hogs.

*TO WHICH-WILL BE ADDED,*

## An Imitation of a Bagpiper, and a

### BRITISH OFFICER.

The whole to Conclude with the Surprifing Powers of the

# VENTRILOQUIST,

He poffeffes by *nature* the *power* of caufing a voice to be heard in all Parts of the Room ;---alfo, from the adjoining Rooms and Clofets. HE CAUSES THE VOICE OF A *CHILD* TO BE HEARD IN A TEA-POT, and exclaim, "Let Me Out, Let Me Out, or I Shall Smother ;" the fame Voice will be heard in any Gentleman SNUFF BOX, or in a Ladies' THIMBLE. Mr. R. will throw his Voice into a COD-FISH, which will immediately make a noife like that of a Hog. He will caufe an OYSTER to imitate a number of BIRDS : To give a minute detail of this Exhibition would fill Volumes.

Doors opened at half paft Six, the Performance to begin at Seven o'clock ;---Admittance Fifty Cents.

Figure 2. Rannie broadside, 1810. "Neficos Box" advertisement.
(Courtesy of the New Bedford Whaling Museum)

EXHIBITION,

At _____ on

_____ Evening, _____

A Genteel Entertainment of

# SLIGHT OF HAND,

AND

# VENTRILOQUISM,

By Messrs. POTTER & SMITH,

Who have performed in the moſt Capital Cities in EUROPE and AMERICA.

## Part 1ſt.

# Mr. POTTER will cauſe Money to

leap through a China plate, table, and cloth, paſs and repaſs ; to leap out of one man's hand into that of another ; alſo, a great variety of other tricks with the ſame, too numerous to particularize.

He will let any perſon draw a card from the pack, examine and return it, and after ſhuffling, throw them up, fire a gun, and nail the card which was drawn, to the wall, ſeparate from all the reſt. He will cauſe a card to change its face into different forms ; will find cards in eggs, money, &c. He will cauſe eggs to dance a hornpipe, and leap out of one hat into another, and cards to leap out of the pack.

He will exhibit a wonderful SHEET of PAPER, which will change into above fifty different forms.

He will break a dozen of eggs into a hat and cauſe them to come out pancakes, excellently fried ; will ſwallow a caſe of knives and forks, cauſe ribbons to come out of his mouth, &c. &c.

## Part 2d.

# A Small Figure, in the character of

Tom Thumb, will dance a hornpipe on a table, and put his body in many different forms, which has been the greateſt wonder of any thing yet exhibited.

The Exhibition of the Italian Shades, with the diverting Scene of the broken Bridge, and ſaucy Carpenters will form an intereſting picture, in the ſecond part of the exhibition.

Mr. Potter will exhibit the wonderful curioſity, called the MAGIC WONDERS.——This is truly a ſubject of admiration.

He will place one or two dozen of eggs on the floor and dance a hornpipe blindfolded among them, without breaking any.

## Part 3d.

Mr. POTTER will add to the diverſion of the entertainment in his repreſentation of the Comic Scenes of the Clown, and cloſe with the favorite Song of

## "Giles Scrogging's Ghoſt," with alterations.

Tickets, at _____ may be had at the place of performance. Doors opened

and performance commence preciſely at _____

Printed at the COLUMBIAN Museum.

Figure 3. Potter & Smith broadside. "EXHIBITION, . . . SLIGHT OF HAND, AND VENTRILOQUISM, by MESSRS. POTTER & SMITH." (Courtesy of the J. V. Fletcher Library, Westford, Massachusetts)

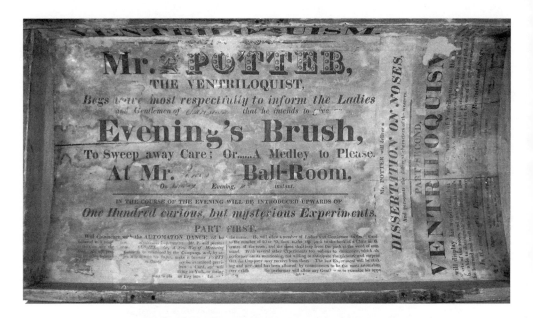

Figure 4. Potter broadside, with detail of Masonic emblem. "VENTRILOQUISM.
Mr. POTTER"; cut and pasted into the lining of a trunk.
(Courtesy of the Robert A. Olson Collection)

# VENTRILOQUISM.

## Mr. & Mrs.  POTTER,

### Beg leave most respectfully to inform the Ladies and Gentlemen of *North~~~~* that they will give

### An Evening's Brush to sweep away Care; Or,
*A MEDLEY TO PLEASE.*

### At Mr. *~~~~* Ball Room, on

## *Wednes* day Evening,

*In the course of the evening will be offered upwards of*

### 100 Curious, but Mysterious Experiments.

**PART FIRST.**

Mr. Potter will commence the Performance with the *Ataratian Dance*, to be followed by a number of Philosophical Experiments, a few of which are here detailed.

Mr. P. will fire from a gun, any lady's or gentleman's ring, and cause... love immediately to appear, in whose bill the ring will be found. He will allow any lady or gentleman to cut their gown or handkerchief and will unite it in such a manner that the most discriminating eye cannot discover the least blemish. He will break a number of gentlemen's Watches with a large hammer and restore them to their regular form again. He will allow any gentleman to

draw a Card, and make the same apparently to have the appearance of life, and move across the room. These are but few of the Experiments that will be offered in the course of the evening.

Mr. P. flatters himself that his Performances have been so well known, in various parts of the Country, as not to require the aid of a pompous advertisement; but will only inform the ladies and gentlemen, that may wish to honor him with their company, that this Bill can give but a faint idea of the Performance.

## A SONG, by Mr. Potter.

**PART SECOND.**

## VENTRILOQUISM.

Mr. P. will display his wonderful but laborious powers of Ventriloquism. He throws his voice into many different parts of the Room, and into Gentlemen's Hats, Trunks, &c. &c. Imitates all kinds of Birds and Beasts, so that few or none will be able to distinguish his Imitations from the reality. This part of the performance has never failed of exciting the surprize of the learned and well informed, as the conveyance of Sounds is allowed to be one of the greatest curiosities in nature. *AFTER WHICH WILL BE SUNG*

**THE FAVORITE SONG** of by Mr. *Potter.*

**PART THIRD.**
*WILL BE PERFORMED THE FOURTH SCENE OF THE REVIEW, OR THE*

## Wag of Windsor,
(WRITTEN BY COLEMAN, Jun.)

Phœbey, or the disguised Captain, with a Song, - - - - Mrs. *Potter.*
Caleb Quotem, with a Day's Work and Song, - - - - Mr. *Potter.*

*TO WHICH WILL BE ADDED THE PANTOMIMICAL PIECE, CALLED THE*

## Agreeable Surprise, *or the Wonderful Little Giant,*
GIANT, - - - - - - - - - Mrs. *Potter.*

Mr. POTTER will add to the diversion of the Entertainment in his representation of the Comic Scenes of the CLOWN, and close with a favorite Song in the Character of TIMOTHY NOKPOT.

Tickets, Cents, to be had at the place of performance. *and at the Lyman~~~* Performance to commence at early candle-light. The public may red assured that the Room will be in ample order for the reception of Visitors, handsomely illuminated, with good music during the Interludes. Ladies or Gentlemen desirous of having seats reserved for them, are requested to send timely notice.

THEN & ROWE, Printers, 76, Main-street, Boston

---

Figure 5. Potter broadside, 1818. "VENTRILOQUISM. Mr. & Mrs. POTTER."
(Courtesy of Historic Northampton, Northampton, Massachusetts)

Figure 6. From a stereoview of Potter estate, Andover, New Hampshire, circa 1869.
(Private collection)

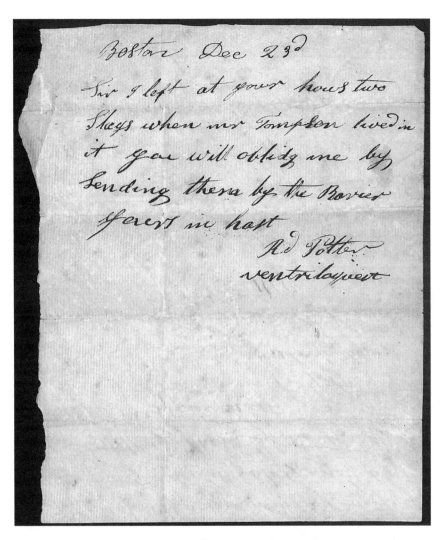

Figure 7. Potter note to Mr. Colby, 23 December 1823. "Boston Dec 23d
Sir I left at your hous two Slays." (Courtesy of the New London
[New Hampshire] Town Archives)

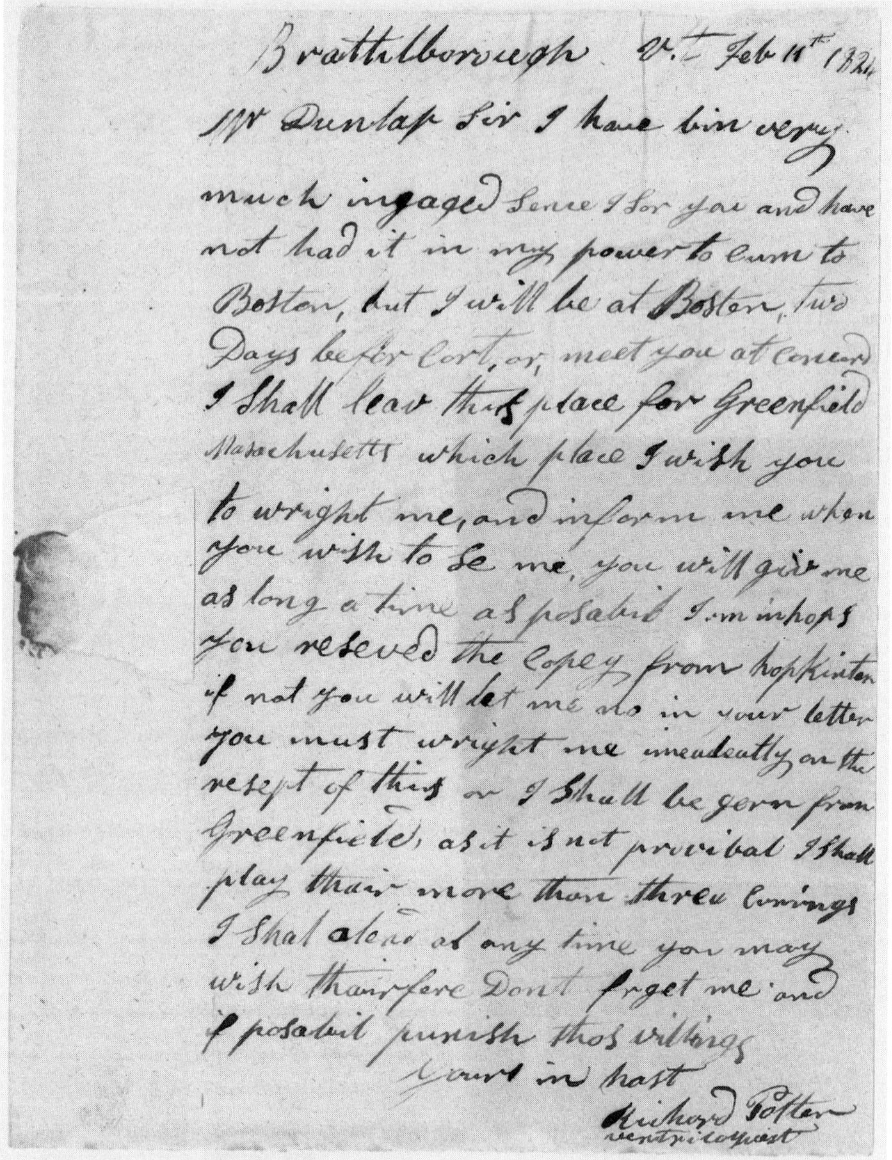

Figure 8. Potter letter to Andrew Dunlap, 11 February 1824. "Brattleborough Vt Feb 11th 1824 Mr Dunlap Sir." (Courtesy of The Phillips Library, Peabody Essex Museum, Salem, Massachusetts)

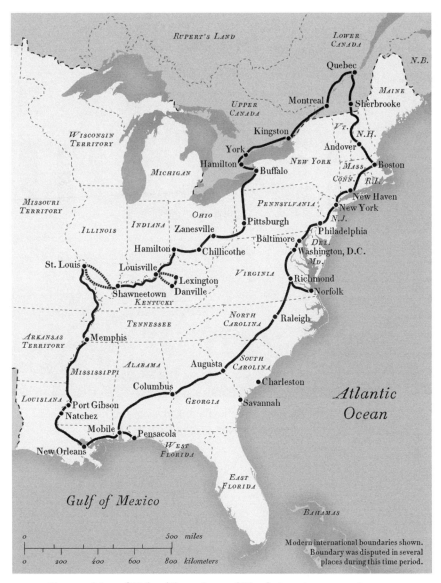

Figure 9. Map of Richard Potter's grand North American tour, 1819–23.
(Map by Nat Case, INCase, LLC)

Figure 10. Richard Potter's gravestone. (Photograph courtesy of Larry Chase, Andover, New Hampshire)

But more than this, there was quickly an emphasis on the numerousness and also the quality of his patrons as he "continue[d] his exhibitions of Legerdemain, ventriloquism, &c. at Washington Hall to overflowing audiences." One of his first reviewers reported:

> On Saturday (his 2d) night the room was extremely crowded. . . . Among the audience, we observed some of the most respectable families in our city. Mr. Potter's exhibition promises to become a fashionable resort.
>
> AN IMPARTIAL OBSERVER

Another, who had attended that same performance, similarly noted:

> The large room was extremely crowded; so much so, as to prevent my seeing the first part of the performance. . . . We were happy to see Mr. P's talents patronized by the presence of the most respectable families in the city. Mr. P. is really deserving: We wish him every success.
>
> JUSTICIA.

And another reviewer noted the following week:

> The general anxiety to witness Mr. P's exhibitions has caused the room to be crowded to excess the last 2 nights. Never has any person in his line attracted more attention, or been more successful in giving complete satisfaction to public expectation.—We understand Mr. P. will cause such arrangements to be made as to prevent his room's being in future uncomfortably crowded.
>
> HONESTUS

(An update in the same newspaper the following day reported that "*Mr. Potter* continues to attract crowded audiences at Washington Hall, and we understand that arrangements have been made so as to accommodate his visitors in a more suitable manner than heretofore.")

Crowds continued to flock to his exhibitions—at the beginning of March, he even advertised that, "in consequence of a great number of persons not being able to gain admittance on Saturday evening," he would repeat that evening's performance on Tuesday—and Potter continued to vary and expand his offerings. In late February he began introducing his Man Salamander act into his program occasionally; in late March, he announced that "he has received lately from Paris, many new and interesting PIECES OF MECHANISM"; one of these, never before seen in America, was "the beautiful MERCARIUS," which could "discover the thought of any lady or gentleman in company; and will likewise tell the number of spots on several cards drawn by the audience, and the color of any lady's or gentleman's clothes, by the wearer asking the question; and the hour of the night by any person's watch; and will, as if by sympathy, communicate the thoughts of one person to another." Other new mechanisms included "the Changeable Ring," "Flora's Basket," and "the Golden Orange Tree, that produces any lady or gentleman's ring, money, or any other metalic substance, previously locked up in another part of the room." (It was not quite true that these had never before been seen in America, for the magician Mr. Stanislas, "having arrived lately from France, with a rich and interesting collection of Philosophical and Mechanical apparatus," had exhibited some of them in New York early the previous year; but Potter may not have known this.) To better accommodate his large audiences, moreover, Potter now—already seven weeks into his New York exhibitions—moved to a new venue, the Columbian Picture Gallery, just off Broadway, "where he will be able to give a more splendid and elegant exhibition than he has hitherto done," "having recently fitted up the room so as to accommodate 600 persons with ease and convenience."

The capstone of Potter's celebrity—and doubtless an important stimulus for those continuing crowds of New Yorkers so eager to attend his performances—came when a timely, witty poem titled and addressed "*To Mr. POTTER, the Ventriloquist*" appeared in the *New York Evening Post* on 13 March. This was a humorous satire on state and local politics by a new, still anonymous voice on the New York scene, someone signing himself "Croaker"; it was only the fifth of his poems to appear (the first had been printed in the same paper only three days earlier), and a great enthusiasm for and excitement about this new, urbane sensibility also transferred easily to the ventriloquist, his latest vehicle. Croaker seized upon a happy conjunction of events: a socially conservative state assemblyman from far Upstate New York was planning to introduce a bill to prohibit "the exhibitions of mountebanks and jugglers" of every sort just at this moment when a very unique juggler, one who could imitate others' voices and make those voices seem to come from other places and people, was captivating New Yorkers. Would poor Mr. Potter now "lose [his] occupation"? (The passing, mock-heroic allusion to "Othello's occupation's gone!" offered a knowing hint about Potter's blackness.)* If

---

*Another subtle allusion to Potter's race may also appear in another highly complimentary notice of this time, although the reviewer's language is so pretentious and convoluted as to leave this uncertain. Day Francis (who advertised himself both as "Day Francis the Great" and "Emperor of the Conjurors"), the magician to whom the writer alludes, had appeared in New York in 1816. "Since the days of Day Francis the Great,

so, then Croaker had an attractive proposition to make to him: Potter could be gotten into the state assembly, where, whenever other politicians seemed about to speak, Potter, with his "ventriloquial powers," could instead surreptitiously speak for them, "stop their speeches in their lungs, / And bring out such as I [Croaker] shall furnish." Rather than the foolishness and incivility so characteristic of petitions and debates in the state legislature, Potter could replace all with "honey," "decent speech," and "common sense." Should Croaker's plan work, then, "As you're to be the only speaker, / We'll make you speaker of the house."

Croaker's witty poem was full of topical allusions to local and state political figures that let his readers share a sense of their city's raucous sophistication. As one critic has noted, "The Croaker poems helped define New York itself": they presented "a well-defined literary voice that expressed the complexities of an emerging metropolis and clearly had an impact on the national imagination." The idea of a ventriloquist's ruling people by controlling debate is an old one, going back to de la Chapelle's *Le ventriloque* and to Charles Brockden Brown's *Memoirs of Carwin, the Biloquist,* and had always seemed a threat. (An article in the *Boston Independent Chronicle* in 1810, widely reprinted, had used Rannie to make the same point.) But this Croaker—the pen name recalls a pessimistic character in a Goldsmith comedy, but more generally "it was slang in England and the US for any kind of naysayer"— turns all such doom-saying upside down, as the comedic Potter bids fair to elevate all public discourse. Croaker, Potter, and the upscale readers of the *New York Evening Post* all are complimented by this reversal.

Croaker carefully shielded his identity for some time (it remained unknown for the duration of Potter's stand), even from the editors who were publishing his sallies, and was soon supplemented in the newspapers by a second, also anonymous, colleague ("Croaker, Jr.") who then became a collabo-

---

who was first crowned by imperishable fame emperor of all the *conjurors,* the public have despaired of a successor of that imperial monarch; yet but a short time has elapsed, and we find that a *Potter* has been seen, who, if as a talisman he boast not of the same composition in a lineal descent of that celebrated prince, still leaves the public at liberty to place the wreath and entwine the laurel upon the brow of living merit." "Not of the same composition in a lineal descent" would seem to be a hint about Potter's race. The writer's conclusion then seems to build on this understanding: "The writer of this article thinks it but justice due to Mr. Potter to observe, that he never puffs; but submits his humble endeavors to the good opinion and to the superior judgment of the public." In other words, Potter is not presumptuous or uppity; he is respectful, and knows his place (*New York Mercantile Advertiser,* 16 Feb. 1819, 2).

rator as well ("Croaker & Co."). This secrecy, of course, made the question of authorship all the more interesting and kept the poems in public conversation even after their journalistic occasions had passed. (Croaker was eventually revealed to be Joseph Rodman Drake; Croaker, Jr., Fitz-Greene Halleck. Both men went on to win poetic renown, although Drake's career was cut quite short when he died of consumption in 1820.) Potter had been most fortunate in his celebrant.

V

After his huge success in New York, Potter continued to Philadelphia, a city where he had exhibited at the very outset of his independent career in 1811. But this time he performed not in a tavern but at Washington Hall, a grand new venue that was now the chief concert and assembly hall in the city. He continued there for four weeks, extending his stand from three weeks due to some inclement weather and "the many applications from respectable families, who have not as yet had an opportunity of witnessing his exhibition." And as in New York, the reception was most enthusiastic, to judge by the review published in the *Franklin Gazette* after Potter had performed there for a week:

> Mr. Potter.
>
> The citizens of Philadelphia have now an opportunity of witnessing one of the most extraordinary powers of nature, that has even [*sic*] been exhibited. We allude to Mr. Potter's *Ventriloquism*. The manner in which he throws his voice at a distance, as though another was speaking, and not himself; and his imitations of several of the animal creation, are done to admiration, and cannot fail to astonish and gratify. Mr. Rannie some years since, exhibited similar performances, but not in so great a degree of perfection as Mr. Potter.
>
> Added to his Ventriloquism, Mr. Potter's *Legerdemain,* also furnishes a pleasing variety for the amusement of his audience, and the whole entertainment is well worthy the attention of the citizens of Philadelphia.

From Philadelphia, finally, Potter turned north toward home. He stopped en route to perform once more, this time in New Haven, another city, like New York, where he is not known to have performed previously. An editor of the *Connecticut Herald* noted his visit, in terms consistent with the enthusiastic reviews from New York and Philadelphia: "Mr. POTTER, the Ventriloquist, whose astonishing powers have been the admiration of the most enlightened and polite audiences in Europe and America, performed in this city, two evenings of last week, to very crowded houses. His experiments on attraction, as well as his imitation of different voices, were surprising. He was honoured by the approbation and applause of our most respected citizens, who attended." And again, as in New York, he became the subject of a poetic address; this one, too, was titled "To Mr. POTTER—*The Ventriloquist.*" Again, too, the occasion was an official threat to Potter's occupation: this time, when Potter had intended to exhibit for a few evenings more, someone had invoked the state's blue laws and complained to the authorities, so the additional exhibitions were cancelled. As the *Connecticut Herald* editor put it, "Some poor, over-zealous soul, whose conscience was disturbed at the idea that other people should be allowed the enjoyment of pleasures from which he was excluded, entered a complaint against Mr. P—; (no doubt) with the expectation of receiving the award allowed in such cases to informers." Potter fortunately got wind of the complaint and left town; had he been caught performing in violation of the blue laws, he stood to lose all his proceeds and perhaps his equipment as well.

The anonymous poem to Potter in the *Connecticut Herald,* a Scots dialect piece by someone calling himself "Rob Dhu" (the name evokes an old Scottish poet), congratulates Potter on escaping the plot of the conspirators who wanted to arrest him and fine him "for making daffin [jesting] / That kept the lads and lasses laffin." He is sure of their motive:

> I ken fu' well it was their meaning,
> To let ye work for many an e'enin,
> > Wi' all your fash [trouble];
> Then tak' your siller [silver] from your pocket,
> And in their money-chests they'd lock it,
> > Wi' ither cash.
> Your fines would be as muckle money
> As you would get from tricks, tho' funnie,
> > Each dainty night:
> Fifty pund Scot, I shrewdly reckon,
> For ilka time they would hae taken–
> > (By law they might.)

He hopes Potter will return to New Haven another summer, after the local laws have changed, for Potter had been a fine entertainer ("Auld farrant Chiel [clever young man], your tricks were pleasing"). And then he closes with a mild mock-complaint, worth our attention now mostly because it gives us a glimpse of part of Potter's performance:

> But still I dinna' like your teasing
> A Scot brither;
> Oh' haen *some* brawsome Scots been present,
> Shelty and you had gab'd mair pleasant
> To ae anither.

We discover from this parting shot that the song "Shelty the Piper," and some mimickry in it of the Rannies' brogue as well, were still a part of Potter's repertory, as they had once been of John Rannie's.

"Rob Dhu" was not the poet to circulate Potter's name or boost his reputation that Croaker had been, but in many respects he was the more prescient commentator. Potter was now a celebrity, but as a black man, a "juggler," and an itinerant he was still vulnerable. The shadows of persecution and discrimination that colored his reception in New Haven would increasingly darken his entire career, despite his increasingly widespread reputation for wondrous entertainments and irreproachable behavior.

By the time Potter returned to Boston in the summer of 1819, he was the preeminent entertainer in all the northeastern United States. He now, with barely a pause, set out to make himself also the most widely familiar entertainer in all of North America. He was already becoming a household name in large areas of the country; now he would take his exhibitions across all of America, so that the rest of his countrymen could enjoy them, too.

# 5

# The Grand North American Tour, 1819–1823

I

When Richard Potter was about to leave Boston in August 1818, he had advertised that "it is probable he may never again appear before a Boston audience, as he contemplates leaving the country." Only after he had completed his triumphal tour through New York and then Philadelphia did his contemplated destination finally become clear: he headed straight to Canada, where he soon appeared in Quebec and then Montreal—so soon that he could barely have paused in Boston if, indeed, he ever went there at all.

This was not Potter's first visit to Canada: he and Benjamin Thompson had performed together in York (present-day Toronto) in 1810, and presumably he had visited Montreal and Kingston as well as they traveled westward toward York along the highway north of Lake Ontario. Both James and John Rannie had traveled and performed in Canada as well. James had performed in Montreal and Quebec in the winter of 1804–5 and then in New Brunswick and Nova Scotia in the winter of 1808–9, while John had traveled widely through Lower Canada (the province of Quebec) in 1811 and 1812 and had probably lived there throughout that period. So Potter could easily have gotten a healthy dose of advice about the customs, audiences, venues, roads, weather, laws, competition, and accommodations that he would be encountering there.

It was quite common for itinerant performers in America to travel into

Canada, just as it was for them to travel into the Caribbean (as James Rannie and Potter had also done). The three areas were part of a single, larger circuit, and theater companies, ropedancers, jugglers, and magicians might circulate among some or all of them. So it was not particularly unusual for Potter to choose to pursue his own tour there now. Nevertheless, the tone of Potter's Boston farewell seems quite final: this is not simply an intention to go abroad, but a suggestion of never returning—not, at least, to New England.

It is very difficult to imagine, however, that Potter was contemplating a permanent move to Canada. While he may have been regularly dismayed and harmed by the racial attitudes of America, he had no reason to think that they were any different in Canada (where slavery was still legal), and indeed the Boston black community was one of the most active in the country in challenging such attitudes, and its white community one of the more open to the debate. More probably Potter's plan was simply much like James Rannie's had apparently been in 1810–11, when, having "purchased a farm in the country, where he is resolved to settle and appropriate his future time in the useful pursuit of Agriculture, &c.," he undertook a last grand, and grandly profitable, tour through all the major northeastern venues as a way of amassing a nest egg.

Potter's new undertaking, however, was more than simply grand. Had any entertainer in America ever pursued such an ambitious tour before? (See fig. 9 for a map of Potter's itinerary 1819–23.) Several had toured widely among the major Eastern Seaboard cities and towns, and a few small theater companies, such as that of Noah Ludlow, had ventured inland to such towns as Cincinnati, Pittsburgh, Lexington, Nashville, St. Louis, and Natchez. But the theater managers tended to follow circuits within certain geographical areas, whereas Potter was literally making the rounds of the entire country. Probably his closest exemplar in this ambitious undertaking was his mentor John Rannie, who had made an impressive tour around the entire United States in 1805–8. But the country had been smaller then, and Rannie, starting in Pennsylvania, had traveled southwest from Ohio through Kentucky and into Tennessee, then had taken the new Natchez Trace southwest to Mississippi and thence on to New Orleans before journeying back east to North Carolina, Charleston, and Savannah. Potter, after his swing north into Canada, would now be traveling also into Indiana, Illinois, Missouri, then down the Mississippi River valley, thereby taking in the Northwest Territory as well as the older states. His was surely by far the most ambitious North American tour that had ever been pursued. By the time he concluded it, he had probably (including places where he had performed in the past but did not include in this tour now, such as

Delaware, Rhode Island, Maine) entertained in every one of the twenty-four states in the Union as of that time (1823), and in two territories (Arkansas and Florida) and several Canadian provinces besides.

II

Although Potter barely paused in either Boston or New Hampshire as he began his grand North American tour with a venture into Canada, we might want to pause here to consider a few basic questions that he would necessarily have dealt with carefully by that point. To begin with: Would his wife accompany him, or not?

For certainly Sally Potter did accompany him, and not only assisted him but occasionally appeared on his program throughout his tour. This was entirely inconsistent with the personal policy that he later described to Nathan Hale: "Having a good wife, well acquainted with country business, I concluded, that instead of carrying her about with me as an assistant, it would be better to have a *home,* which would be to her a congenial occupation, and to me a polar star, towards which I should always set my course." But these were not exactly the conditions that Richard Potter was now facing. To begin with, he had apparently leased his Andover property and had not lived there for the past year and a half, instead renting accommodations elsewhere (probably in Boston) while making several short tours through parts of Massachusetts and Rhode Island. So it was not as if he currently had a country home available for his family anyway. Making this decision all the more difficult now, however, was the inescapable fact that Richard and Sally now had two young children, aged about five and four years old. Who would be taking care of them?

As it happens, a New Hampshire family tradition offers an answer to this question, although it also raises new questions. In 1906 a Concord, New Hampshire, correspondent for the *Boston Sunday Herald* took a fresh look at the Potter legend and, in addition to recycling some of the tales told by earlier reporters, also provided some new information available in Concord; indeed, the new tidbits about Potter very possibly prompted the new article. Mr. and Mrs. Alexander McKee, of South Street, Concord, it was reported, possessed two Potter relics, "an oil portrait of King Philip of Macedon" and an old, round, drop-leaf mahogany table. The *Herald* article offered an account of how the McKees had come by these items: "When travelling about the country with his wife, giving exhibitions, it was Mr. Potter's custom to leave his children at the home of Harrison Colby in Andover, a grand-daughter of whom is Mrs. Alexander McKee. Upon Potter's death the portrait, the table and some other pictures, among which latter was one of Washington, came into Mrs. McKee's possession."

The family tradition that Mrs. McKee—she was Alice C. McClure McKee, and was indeed Harrison Colby's granddaughter—was recounting was garbled in ways that she could not have known but nevertheless is very compelling. While the Potter children may well have stayed with Harrison Colby's family, it was not his household, for he himself was about five or six years younger than they (he was born in 1820). The householders would have been Harrison's parents, Aaron and Edith Colby. And their house was not in Andover, although they later moved to Andover and lived there for many decades: before 1838 the Colby family lived in Bow, New Hampshire, just south of Concord. Aaron Colby, moreover, was the man to whom the Potter estate finally passed when Dick Potter, having finally run through his inheritance and mortgaged the property far beyond his ability to redeem it, sold the farm in 1837, two years after his father's death. This was not likely to have been sheer chance: through long-standing connections with the family, Aaron would have been familiar with the Potter farm and its neighborhood and had possibly even lived there at times while helping care for the Potter children; and Dick, for his part, would have known Aaron intimately and might well, for a competitive offer, have wished to sell the place to one who already had reason to care for it and for him.

Alice McKee was born in 1869, and her great-grandfather Aaron Colby lived until 1877, her grandfather Harrison until 1905; so she had many years to hear their family stories and learn about the family heirlooms, and the surge of interest in Potter in the 1870s may well have prompted particular family reminiscences about him then.

It is worth noting now, too, that, while possibly Sally Potter continued to travel with and assist her husband in his exhibitions in the years after their return from their grand tour, there is no evidence whatever that she did so (she last appears in one of their advertisements in early 1823, in Virginia, while still on that grand tour with him), and many Andover stories agree that she was too incapacitated by intemperance to work with him in those latter years. So the Colby anecdote almost certainly does refer especially to the 1819–24 period, and young Harrison Colby would have grown up with the Potter children for the first several years of his life.

Sally Potter may have had important contributions to make to Potter's act and especially to its family-friendly tone, but, for this long, strenuous tour at least, Potter needed more assistance than she alone could provide. Hence his important decision to engage Benjamin Thompson to accompany him again as his assistant.

Thompson brought many assets. He thoroughly understood the details of Potter's performances and the logistics of his exhibitions and tours, to begin with, for he had already shared and assisted with them himself for several years. And apparently he and Potter got along well as a team: according to a later report, "the two traveled together very pleasantly for many years." Too, he was a fine horseman, and Potter needed a driver highly skilled with horses. And apparently he was also an attractive, forceful, and alert man, qualities that would serve travelers well in iffy situations. (Potter himself was a small man*—"*little Mr. Potter,*" a humorist writing about the wonders and fashions of Boston in 1818 called him—and Sally was diminutive.)

It is possible and even likely, as well, that Thompson had made some of this tour before and so would have had some familiarity with the parts of it of most concern to Potter: there was a Mr. Thompson in William Duff's American Company that was staging plays in New Orleans in the spring of 1811, and this may well have been Benjamin Thompson, back on the road with another Rannie associate after his early partnership days with Potter.

There was one additional, all-important quality about Thompson, moreover, that made him an invaluable assistant for Potter now. He was white.

The importance of this attribute cannot be overestimated. Richard Potter could easily be categorized by strangers as some sort of Creole and had even so advertised himself at the very outset of his career. His manners were impeccable, his behavior decorous and polite, his bearing gracious and almost courtly. But his complexion was dark, as was his wife's, and he was already being identified, in Massachusetts and New York and increasingly across the entire Northeast, as black. To arouse such notions in the slaveholding states

---

*A dancing slipper that Potter wore "when singing the comic song Will Sneer the Critic" (from his "Dissertation on Noses" medley) survives in the collection of the New Hampshire Antiquarian Society, in Hopkinton. Decorated with a flamboyantly oversized silver buckle, it is approximately the size of a modern men's U.S. size 6 or 6.5 slipper. It is not the shoe of a large or tall man.

of the Union, through which he would soon be traveling for what proved to be a full three years, would be both foolish and dangerous. (In Missouri, for example, the new state constitution explicitly enjoined the state's general assembly "to prevent free negroes and mulattos from coming to and settling in this State, under any pretext whatsoever" [Article 3, Section 26].) Thus it was imperative that Potter present, throughout his travels, immediate, unmistakable evidence of his acceptable societal status. Benjamin Thompson was that evidence—a presentable, competent, worldly white man who served comfortably as the great magician's assistant and employee and took direction from him. The employer of such a man could only be white, or perhaps a distinguished foreigner.

There were complicating circumstances in Thompson's personal life at this time, just as there were in Potter's. He had married not long after his first partnership with Potter, but his wife had died a few years later, leaving him with a young son (also a Benjamin). Then in December 1815 he had married again. It proved to be a tempestuous marriage. His new wife, Hannah Colby, from Hopkinton, New Hampshire, was the local belle, described as "self-willed, proud, and handsome." In courting her, Thompson "represented himself as being wealthy, retired, and living in New York," none of which seems to have been true (not only had he been an itinerant showman, but he was also reputedly a professional gambler). After she married him, "the denouement which followed was a terrible blow to her. She was too proud, however, to return to her home and admit her mistake, and after some deliberation, she determined to stake her fortunes with those of her husband. For the next fifteen years, probably no two persons in the country, as husband and wife, ever led such a variegated life. . . . They frequently quarreled, and several times separated."

Did Hannah Colby Thompson, too, travel with her husband and the Potters as they toured around the country in 1819–23? We simply do not know, but it seems highly likely that she did. She would have been a suitable companion for Sally Potter, and her drifter husband's employment by the eminently respectable and now famous and prosperous Richard Potter would have afforded the strongest warranty of Benjamin's own respectability and stability, however itinerant the work, that she could possibly have anticipated. So Hannah, although she may have parted from him at other times (as she did finally for good in the 1830s), would have gone along. Thompson's young son (he would probably have been about six years old in 1819) would be left in the care of Hannah's family back in Hopkinton.

## IV

It would seem that this time Potter traveled north into Canada not along the more usual highway up the Hudson River and Lake Champlain valley to Montreal but instead up the Connecticut River valley at first, probably to Sherbrook, Lower Canada, and then on to Quebec. In any event, his first appearance after New Haven was only five weeks later, in Quebec: by 20 July, "just arrived in this City," he was starting to perform in Malhiot's Hotel, exhibiting his "Ventriloquial, Philosophical and Theatrical Talents." After a week there, he continued to Montreal, where he performed at the Theatre. The editor of the *Canadian Courant* soon celebrated his skills:

Mr. POTTER.

Last evening we witnessed a performance than which none that we have as yet seen in this city has given us greater satisfaction. The dexterity of Mr. Potter is, without exaggeration, surprising, not only to those unaccustomed to such exhibitions, but also to those who have been familiar with similar spectacles. The art of VENTRILOQUISM, in itself of a most curious nature and capable of being exercised in the most humorous manner, has never been more ably professed or practiced. By the aid of it, the Ventriloquist in the market has made the fish or the sheep declare themselves stale or tainted, to the astonishment of the affrighted vender — old maiden aunts have heard masculine voices in the chambers of their nieces — and even loads of hay become vocal. In fine, we have beheld nothing more amusing, or better calculated to exemplify the wonderful ingenuity of man.

An editorial follow-up five days later reaffirmed this judgment:

Mr. POTTER.

This gentleman will perform again on Friday evening. To pronounce an eulogium on the talents displayed in every part of his performance, would be superfluous, as those who have witnessed it bear ample testimony to his merit. We therefore confine ourselves to notice his intended exhibition, as being one of those localities of which it is our duty to make mention to the Public.

At this point, Richard Potter's progress through Canada becomes invisible to us. Very few Canadian towns had newspapers at this time, and even in larger towns and cities Potter was advertising almost exclusively through broadsides and handbills; indeed, it is only through the survival of a single broadside that we know about his appearance in Quebec, for he never placed even the smallest newspaper notice there. Famous though he now was, he left no trace as he passed through the mostly rural and agricultural expanses of Upper Canada, not even in the larger towns of Kingston and York (present-day Toronto), although almost certainly he would have performed there.

We can be fairly confident, even so, that this was Potter's route because his next known appearance was in Pittsburgh, in southwest Pennsylvania. He must have arrived there via Buffalo (where he would have reentered the United States) and then Erie, Meadville, and Franklin. The only alternative, around the other side of Lake Ontario—south from Montreal to Plattsburgh, New York, then west across New York or possibly Pennsylvania—would inevitably have taken him through so many towns where he was already known and so many where his reputation had preceded him that it is extremely unlikely he could have passed undocumented. His purpose, after all, was to entertain and thereby to earn his living and fund his family's future; he was performing and advertising, and there would have been at least some evidence of him in the many local papers, just as there is of his progress beyond Pittsburgh.

Potter would return to Canada in future years, but only to the Maritime provinces; never again did he travel through Lower or Upper Canada. If he had been considering a future move there, that was no longer a consideration. He had much touring to do yet, but he would ultimately be returning to New Hampshire as his home.

V

From Pittsburgh, Potter and his wife turned westward along the old National Road and then southwestward through Ohio. We know several towns where he performed (always for at least several nights)—Zanesville, Chillicothe, Hamilton—so we can also guess intelligently at several others (Washington, Pennsylvania; Wheeling, Virginia; Lancaster, Lebanon, and Cincinnati, Ohio). To judge from his extant advertisements, Potter could profitably give multiple performances in even the smallest towns: he seems, for example, to have performed for a full week or even longer in Chillicothe and another full week in Hamilton. Considering the populations of these towns in 1820—Zanesville, 2,052; Chillicothe, 2,426; Hamilton, 660—it is clear that Potter was drawing audiences from large surrounding areas, and repeat customers at that.

Potter's next move, in the spring of 1820, was south, across the Ohio River, into Kentucky. This brought with it two particular resonances that we need to consider now—one professional, one personal.

Potter's first mentor in ventriloquism, John Rannie, had spent several months touring back and forth across Kentucky in the spring and early summer of 1805, presenting ventriloquism, sleight of hand, and balancing and even staging light comedies. Potter had left John to work instead with James Rannie, John's older brother, shortly before John Rannie began that tour, but it is probable that Richard and John had remained in contact with each other and even seen each other subsequently. Knowledge of the road—inns, performance venues, local laws, audience preferences, and so forth—was a precious, hard-won commodity among itinerants, much worth seeking. Even after the passage of fifteen years, John Rannie could have given Richard Potter valuable information about such matters, both for Kentucky and for later sections of Potter's current itinerary—just as both John and James Rannie could have advised him about his tour stages through Lower and Upper Canada.

The new personal resonance was of quite a different sort. When he crossed the Ohio River, at Cincinnati or perhaps Louisville, Richard Potter was traveling into a state where slavery was still legal. Even with his professional equanimity, his national fame, and his white assistant, Thompson, this must have focused his attention. What impact it might have had on his self-presentation or his performances, we do not know. But perhaps it is worth noting that, while "Mr. and Mrs. Potter" were always on the program throughout Potter's known Ohio exhibitions, his advertisements in Kentucky almost always (with one extant exception) offered "Mr. Potter" only. Perhaps putting both of the couple, both of them dark-complexioned, on stage together as man and wife was a risk that Potter only cautiously and occasionally assumed in the South; better to perform solo with Mr. Thompson as his main assistant. But we dare not put too much weight on this speculation. The evidence is very fragmentary and sparse—extant advertisements from three towns in Ohio over a three-month period, and from three towns in Kentucky over two more months, when Potter surely gave multiple exhibitions in scores of towns in each state. And it is worth noting that later "Mr. and Mrs. Potter" were advertised on the program together in Port Gibson, Mississippi, and in Norfolk, Virginia. It is more accurate simply to say, then, that Potter tended to introduce "Mr. and Mrs. Potter" into the billing only after he had already performed for some time in a town as the single featured performer on his program. What seems a bit unusual is the frequency with which his wife was featured with him in Ohio.

In Kentucky as in Ohio, from our knowledge of several towns where Potter exhibited we can interpolate others along his routes. He appeared in Louisville in mid-May, then in Lexington in mid-June, and in Danville at the end of that month. Almost certainly, then, he performed in Frankfort (between Louisville and Lexington) as well (Rannie, too, had performed there). Where Rannie had continued south into Tennessee and then down the Natchez Trace, however, Potter instead moved farther west. He probably passed through Baird's Town (now Bardstown), Hardensburg, Yellow Banks (now Owensboro), and Henderson, Kentucky, to Shawneetown, Illinois (his name appears on a list of letters remaining in the post office there at the end of September). From there he might have followed the Goshen Road, the main road across Illinois from Shawneetown to Goshen Settlement, near the Mississippi just north of St. Louis; alternatively, he could have taken the newer Kaskaskia Trail to the Mississippi River town of that name, and thence traveled north to Cahokia, directly across the river from St. Louis. By early December he was exhibiting in St. Louis, Missouri Territory. Here he performed for several weeks—long enough to present his Man Salamander act at least twice. He had now traversed the entire United States as it existed at that time, and just beyond.

## VI

As Richard Potter now continued his grand North American tour by following the Mississippi River south to New Orleans, he increasingly disappeared from the view of the wider American public. Even at that time, there was much less of a record of his progress through and exhibitions in the Deep South than there is for his travels in other parts of the country, primarily because there were significantly fewer newspapers there than elsewhere. Too, East Coast newspapers were much less likely to pick up occasional news items and filler stories from southern papers than from others: newspapers traveled by mail, after all, and the mail between the Mississippi valley and the East Coast was slow and irregular. This disparity of coverage has only been compounded by the passage of time, especially because so many southern archives of newspapers and of many other records were subsequently destroyed during the Civil War. Our tracing of Potter's itinerary south and east across the country, then, will necessarily be somewhat uncertain and less particular than it has been heretofore. The specific routes he took are generally still quite clear, but the timeline of his travels is not.

It is clear at least, to begin with, that Richard Potter and his small company spent most or all of 1821 along the Mississippi River. He had been performing in St. Louis in December 1820 and may well have continued there for a good while; he performed in New Orleans in August 1821. During the intervening period, and very possibly after it as well, he was traveling and entertaining in towns and villages all along the river. We know he was traveling both up and down the river because he performed in Natchez in mid-May 1821 and then in Port Gibson, fifty miles north, some two weeks later. (There was a letter waiting for him in the Natchez post office at the end of March, so we can be confident he had not reached that town before then.) Towns such as Ste. Genevieve, Cape Girardeau, and New Madrid, Missouri, would have been on his itinerary in the earlier months of the year, and St. Francisville, Baton Rouge, and Donaldsonville, Louisiana, later on.

We can be sure, moreover, that if Potter had not been bringing in good audiences all this time, he would not have lingered in the area. The purpose of his tour, after all, was to build his nest egg; were his exhibitions not flourishing at any point, he could and would simply have traveled on to fresh venues all the sooner. So the leisurely pace of Potter's journey from Missouri south through Mississippi and Louisiana is a strong sign that he was enjoying much success.

This impression is reinforced by his reception in Natchez, where he entertained for at least two nights, possibly more. Potter charged a dear one dollar per ticket for his exhibitions in both Natchez and Port Gibson (children were half price); this was what he would often charge in a major venue in a large city, but in smaller towns he typically charged fifty cents (with children, again, at half price), sometimes even less. So his sense of his audience already bespoke great confidence in their receptiveness (as well as in Natchez's prosperousness).

That confidence soon proved justified. The *Mississippi Republican* editor reported after Potter's first performance:

> Last evening, Mr. Potter, who stiles himself the Emperor of all Conjurors, made an exhibition of the astonishing powers he possesses.—His slight of hand tricks were performed with an adroitness superior to any thing of the kind we ever before witnessed. His recitations, songs, and mimicry were executed with taste, and in a natural manner; and he was wholly devoid of the affectation and rant too often used by public per-

formers. We wished to witness some further samples of his powers of Ventriloquism—but what he did exhibit in that line, was excellent.

Mr. Potter is modest, and has much of the gentleman in his deportment and manners.—Although we are far from advising the citizens of Natchez to waste their time and money in idleness and amusement, we in justice cannot refrain from exhibiting to the public our impressions in favor of this ingenious man, and declaring it as our opinion, that those, who can well spare their money, and are fond of amusement, by attending his exhibitions will not only aid in the encouragement of modest merit, but derive much pleasure to themselves.

Potter's Mississippi advertising also affords us another charming glimpse into his repertoire and practices, for in Port Gibson he also featured, for the first time of which we have record, one of the little dramatic episodes that he and Sally frequently staged. This one, performed "interspersed with Duets," was offered as an excerpt from "The True Lovers, or Rake Reformed." It was actually from a popular light opera by Thomas Morton, *The Children in the Wood,* which was often staged in major theaters as an afterpiece. In the Potters' excerpt, Richard played both Apathy (the drunken, irresponsible tutor of the eponymous children) and Walter (a carpenter, the hero of the drama), while Sally played Josephine (the children's nurse and protectress, Walter's beloved, the heroine). Their excerpt probably comes from the very beginning of the play, where Apathy appears with Josephine and then Josephine with Walter and she sings a comic song of her love for Walter while Walter sings a comic one about settling his affections on her; but there is also a comic Josephine/Apathy duet at the end of act 1, scene 3 (she talks of her honor, he of his dinner), which the Potters probably presented as well; and of course they could introduce alternative songs to serve their purposes, as sometimes even happened when the play was staged by professional companies in theaters.

*The Children in the Wood* had long been popular in America and was regularly staged in the major East Coast cities, although rarely in smaller or more provincial theaters. Significantly, it had a notable revival in the Boston Theatre in October 1815, when Potter was also performing there at the Columbian Museum nearby. Potter almost certainly saw it then: he would have been particularly eager to scout the theater for musicals that might provide excerpts or songs suitable for his act and especially for his wife, so he would have been a very interested and attentive spectator. (It is noteworthy, too, that both Mr. and Mrs. Bray of the Boston Theatre were performing in secondary roles that night; they certainly were acquaintances and probably friends of Potter's, for he later once featured Mrs. Bray as a vocalist on his own program.) So this little dramatic interlude had been in Potter's repertoire for more than five years. Probably he decided to feature it now because *The Children in the Wood* had recently been staged in St. Louis, in early February 1821, its first appearance in the Mississippi valley; even if Potter had left St. Louis by then, the news of this new production could easily have encouraged him to present his timely excerpt from it in Port Gibson in early June.

Potter's first exhibition in New Orleans, on 4 August, attracted the notice of the Francophone editor of the bilingual *Louisiana Gazette / Gazette de la Louisiane,* who, sometimes stymied by a lack of events to write about, fussed happily that that night he had been faced with an "embaras de richesses," with three to cover: "le ventriloque Potter," a balloon flight with fireworks, and a theater performance. Trying to review them all in the one evening, he could not stay for the entirety of Potter's exhibition, but the glimpses of it that he shared are expressive. Potter, with his hair powdered—"la tète fort blanche," "les cheveaux bien poudre"—was probably wearing a wig (we know that he did this, because years later the wig he sometimes wore in his performances was donated by his last assistant to the New Hampshire Antiquarian Society; and of course he had been familiar with the old-fashioned custom of hair-powdering since his earliest childhood days with the Franklands' aged, blind servant, Robert). The editor enjoyed Potter's act but, not trusting his own good but not fluent grasp of English, sought the opinion of a companion much better versed in "le dialecte Anglais," who assured him that Potter spoke very intelligibly and had *"la bagou de l'etal,"* a marvelous gift of gab. The editor left after the very amusing ("fort plaisante") "Dissertation on Noses" ("scène des nez"); it seemed to him that Potter, in common with the English actors he had seen, had a habit of putting off his audiences until tomorrow ("renvoyer les spectateurs le landemain"—with an implication of "leaving them hanging" or "asking for more"). (Incidentally, "les acteurs anglais" here very likely refers to Duff's American Theatre Company of 1811–12—which may well have included Benjamin Thompson.) So, just as John Rannie had advertised his exhibitions in Francophone newspapers in New Orleans in 1806 (in this same newspaper, in fact) and in Charleston in 1807, and as William Duff had his American Theatre Company in New Orleans in 1811 and 1812, now Richard Potter was demonstrating that his exhibitions—the ventriloquism, sleight of hand, music, and dancing, at least, if not the dramatic repartee—could appeal to French-speaking audiences, too.

In 1821, as he worked his way along the Mississippi River valley, Richard Potter had left little record of his passing. In 1822, as he worked his way east from New Orleans to Georgia and beyond, he became almost invisible. He exhibited for some time that spring in Mobile, Alabama—a remarkable twelve nights, we are told—as he prepared there for the long, arduous journey to the East Coast. Beyond Mobile, he even traveled on to Pensacola. The Floridas had just become possessions of the United States, and Pensacola, in particular, quickly experienced something of a boom, fueled chiefly by land speculation and boosterism; the town also had a reputation as a wealthy community, and a theater had recently been built there. Potter clearly expected the trip—probably a detour for him—would be worth his while: when he performed there he engaged the new theater, and charged a steep seventy-five cents per ticket.

From Pensacola, Potter would have two itinerary options. He could continue east across the Floridas from West into East Florida, through almost entirely unsettled country, to St. Augustine, and thence north to Savannah; or he could return to Mobile, and there pick up the Federal Road northeast into Georgia, a much more established route. We cannot be sure of his path, but it seems very likely that he would have chosen the latter course: it, too, traversed much wilderness, but the road was better and in Georgia it went through several well-established towns. In that case, Potter probably traveled through Macon, Milledgeville, Sparta, and certainly through Augusta, then across northwestern South Carolina through Columbia.

In Mobile, there occurred a few episodes, never reported in Potter's lifetime, that remind us how fundamentally risky his touring could be and how particularly vulnerable he himself always was. These anecdotes came from Goodwin's inquiries about Potter in Andover in 1875 and were reported by Silas Ketchum in his seminal 1878 sketch of Potter: "He was once turned out of a hotel in Mobile, while Thompson of Andover traveled with him, by a landlord who would not entertain a 'nigger.' Potter did not deny the charge, removed to another hotel, performed twelve nights in the town, and carried off $4,800 in silver, in a nail cask, as the net result. Learning that there was danger of being waylaid, he gave out that he was going to a certain place on a certain day, and departed the night previous in the opposite direction." The picaresque qualities of these stories—shrewd, honest protagonist outwits nasty antagonists and profits at their expense—should not blind us to the very real dangers of the threats—racial discrimination and subjugation, highway robbery—that they suggest.

The incidents in Mobile changed nothing for Potter; they simply served to remind him forcefully of concerns that he always needed to keep in mind in any case. But significant change, nonetheless, was already coming, even as he traveled east across Alabama toward the coastal states.

For any itinerant performer hoping to find large and receptive audiences in the South Atlantic states, the cities of Savannah and especially Charleston were the preeminent attractions. Not only were they populous; they were also prosperous, with a growing leisure class, and had long-established traditions of support for theater and tolerance of entertainers at a time when many or most New England communities were still persecuting strollers and enforcing antitheatrical laws. James Rannie, Potter's mentor in ventriloquism, had spent several months in Charleston and Savannah in the winter and spring of 1802–3; and then John Rannie, Potter's first instructor in magic and first American mentor, had spent a full year in and between the two cities in 1807–8. Both men thus knew both cities well and had developed extensive networks of contacts among the theater managers, entertainers, and hoteliers there. Potter's ropedancing mentor, Signior Manfredi, had performed with his family troupe in Charleston for over a month, too, in 1808, and may have shared information about the city as well. So Richard Potter would have been well briefed on both these venues, and they would have beckoned as enormously important destinations for him as he journeyed across the unsettled scrublands of southern Alabama and the Creek Indian territory of southwestern Georgia. Very simply, it is almost inconceivable that Richard Potter, after enduring the long, hard overland slog from New Orleans to the Atlantic Seaboard, would not have planned to perform at least in Charleston and probably in both cities, and for a considerable period of time.

Doubtless such was Potter's intention when he left New Orleans. In the summer of 1822, however, the social climate in Charleston, and indeed throughout the Tidewater region of Georgia, the Carolinas, and Virginia, significantly and even drastically changed. In May of that year, the city fathers of Charleston were stunned and alarmed by reports of a planned slave uprising. They quickly initiated militia patrols, arrests, and secret inquisitions; by the end of June they had arrested more than thirty blacks, both slaves and freemen, and in July they arrested one hundred more. Six of the initial detainees, including the presumed ringleader of the plot, a free black carpenter named Denmark Vesey, were quickly executed, on 2 July. Twenty-nine more were executed later that month or early in August, and another thirty-one were transported.

Initially the Charleston newspapers had almost nothing to say about these events, although brief stories about the sentencing and swift execution of Vesey and several other conspirators (all slaves) for "an attempt to raise an Insurrection in this State" did appear. But wild rumors and intense alarm about the planned uprising spread rapidly and widely, along predictable lines: for example, a letter from a Charleston resident to a friend in New York which was published there in July reported, "It is said that they [the arrested conspirators] have, or that some of them have, acknowledged their object to have been the murder of the white males, the taking of the ladies for their wives, and the plunder of the city." Consequently, on 10 August the governor of South Carolina published and widely distributed a circular about "the Negro Plot." This document, which was republished by many newspapers, acknowledged that, since June, "the public mind was agitated by a variety of rumours calculated to produce great excitement and alarm" concerning "a very extensive conspiracy." It aimed to counter those "gross and idle reports, actively and extensively circulated, and producing general anxiety and alarm" by assuring citizens that the conspiracy had been limited, fully uncovered, and thoroughly stifled—and that it had been in any case doomed from its inception by the incapacity, folly, and "dastardly dispositions" of slaves ("Servility long continued debases the mind, and abstracts it from that energy of character which is fitted to great exploits").

The report went on to make clear that free blacks, such as the ringleader Vesey, were quite dangerous because of their easy and influential interactions with slaves; that blacks who could read and write, such as Vesey and co-conspirator Monday Gell ("He could read and write with facility, and thus attained an extraordinary and dangerous influence over his fellows"), were particularly dangerous; and that one of the main conspirators (a third "principal," along with Vesey and Gell), Gullah Jack, was very dangerous because, as a native Angolan "conjuror and physician," he had great influence over other blacks ("Vesey, who left no art or power unassayed, seems in an early stage of his design, to have turned his eye on this Necromancer, aware of his influence with his own countrymen, who are distinguished both for their credulous superstition and clannish sympathies").

Richard Potter was a free black man, a literate man with a remarkable gift of gab, and a conjuror—the very "Emperor of Conjurors," by his own claim. Were he to present himself publicly, not to mention advertise his particular gifts and abilities, in Charleston, South Carolina, in the fall of 1822, he would certainly have blazoned himself to a great many of its citizens as indisputably the most dangerous man in the city.

The *Augusta (GA) Chronicle* published a long, three-part account of the Charleston slave insurrection in consecutive issues running from 29 August to 5 September 1822, and indications are that Potter reached Augusta (another town where James Rannie had once performed, in April 1803) in early September, so he would have been able to read the story then, although probably he had already been hearing rumors about it along his way. It was now abundantly clear that he would not, after all, be exhibiting in Savannah or Charleston, nor indeed in any other area of the Deep South where slaves were numerous and slave owners agitated. Instead, Potter headed straight to Raleigh, North Carolina (probably on the Fall Line Road, which would have taken him through Columbia, Camden, and Cheraw, South Carolina), and made good time doing it. He probably did not exhibit or even lodge in Columbia: William Garner, one of the main insurrection conspirators, had been traced to and captured near Columbia in late July.

## VIII

Potter next appears in late September, when he finally paused in Raleigh, North Carolina, to exhibit — probably for at least a week, for he rented the Theatre and promised that he would be "opening" on a Thursday evening, which implies that he anticipated giving multiple performances. Obviously he felt much safer now: having passed quite hurriedly through South Carolina and southern North Carolina, he now again slowed the pace of his tour, suggesting not only a longish stay in Raleigh but probably extensive exhibiting through the adjacent areas as well; he may have done the same in Warrenton, to the north, the following month. He finally moved on, not north to Richmond but northeast to Norfolk, and here again he stayed in one area for an extensive time — at least two months.

In Norfolk, we finally find a sustained set of newspaper advertisements from which we can gain a sense of the rhythm and range of Potter's performing patterns within one multitown area. (Unlike the newspapers in smaller towns, one in Norfolk now published daily, six days a week, and another published triweekly.) Potter most frequently exhibited in Norfolk itself but several times advertised performances that he would be giving in Portsmouth, right across the harbor, and once, near the end of his stay, announced a performance in Smithfield, a bit farther up the James River. A few times he canceled and rescheduled a performance because of bad weather; once, in Portsmouth, the Potters "were unable to reach town in time to perform" and so returned for a makeup performance at the end of the week. He began advertising his "last night" as early as late December, but, continuing to attract "an overflowing house," he continued to exhibit, ultimately stretching out his time there to two full months, from mid-December 1822 to mid-February 1823.

After Norfolk, Potter seems not to have advertised in any newspapers for several months and states, although the easy pace of his progress north suggests that he continued to give exhibitions along his way. A "letter remaining in Post Office" notice in Washington indicates that he may well not have passed through that city until early April, which would mean that he had spent another six weeks or so in northern Virginia. He would spend two more months in Maryland, Delaware, Pennsylvania, and New Jersey before finally returning to New York, where he announced that, "after an absence of four years, he has returned to this City and has engaged the large Commodious Room in Tammany Hall, for three nights only."

Potter had indeed been on the road for more than four years now, traveling in his great circuit first through Lower and Upper Canada, then through the Old Northwest, Southwest, and Gulf territories of his country before returning to the Atlantic states. He had found and won vast new audiences and had introduced his sophisticated magical arts, his entertaining dramatical excerpts, songs, dances, and his absolutely novel ventriloquism to many hundreds of communities that had never seen or heard anything like them before. Like the Rannies before him, he had become an American pioneer and popularizer of whole new kinds of entertainment across broad reaches of the country. He had become a truly national figure and touchstone, known far from his home territory in New England not simply as a big-city, East Coast rumor but as an actual, wonderful, fascinating, thoroughly entertaining master performer.

By the same token, however—indeed, the other side of this very token— in taking his exhibitions into the hinterlands and to the outermost reaches of the expanding country, he had not only abandoned his East Coast audiences for more than four years but had completely disappeared from their ken. In the interim, much in the world of popular entertainment had inevitably changed; many new figures were vying for those audiences. After James Rannie had retired from his American exhibitions and then died, and with John Rannie effectively in retirement also, Richard Potter had for many years been not only the preeminent magician but also the only ventriloquist in all of America. That status, so emphatically confirmed by his triumphant New York exhibitions in 1819, was now at serious risk. It was not unusual that other magicians, whether from Europe or homegrown, would occasionally appear on the American scene. But now, for the first time, there was competition from other ventriloquists.

The first of these, Mr. Charles, came to America from Europe in the fall of 1819, several months after Potter had begun his great tour, and finally returned to Europe in the summer of 1821, while Potter was still in Mississippi and Louisiana. He was an experienced ventriloquist but, remarkably for someone who was for several years so prominently in the public eye, very little is known about him. (We do not even know his first name, only an initial: he sometimes presented himself as "Mr. L. Charles.") He was probably French (he occasionally advertised himself as "the Sieur Charles," and a New York critic noted of his ventriloquism that "His first dialogue was delivered in French"), but his professional background seems to have been mostly German: he proclaimed himself to be "Professor of Mechanical Sciences to the King of Prussia" and under the privilege and patronage also of the Duke of Mecklenburg-Schwerin. He boasted of having performed in "Paris, Vienna, Warsaw, Copenhagen, Dublin, Edinburgh, and London." To prevent his "be[ing] confounded with itinerant performers in general," he supposedly offered "recommendations from the King of Bavaria, the Russian Prince Repnin, the Emperor of Austria, the Royal family of Prussia, the Courts of Wirtemberg and other German powers, the Kings of Denmark and Holland, and finally an order of Napoleon Bonaparte that he should perform before him." He had journeyed to London from Berlin in late 1813 and had thereafter performed steadily and widely in various English and Irish cities for the next five and a half years before deciding to test the market for his entertainments in America. (After leaving America in 1821, he returned to England, and scattered records show him in Ireland, Scotland, and England as late as 1829.)

Potter most certainly began hearing anecdotes about Mr. Charles by the time he reached New Orleans, for Charles had preceded him there, by several months, performing at the Orleans Ball Room at the end of January 1821 for just over a week. Afterward, during the latter stages of Potter's tour, he would have found himself on Charles's trail again, for Charles had also preceded him into Georgia (Charles had performed in Savannah in March 1820) and in Norfolk (Charles had been there in late May 1820).

Charles advertised boldly, traveled fast and widely, circulated lots of amusing anecdotes about his ventriloquial exploits, and usually concentrated on larger cities. During his two-year American tour he preceded Potter into a few important venues (Lexington, New Orleans, Norfolk) and followed him into a great many cities and towns where Potter had previously exhibited and would soon enough exhibit again—New York, Philadelphia, and all the major northern New England centers (Portland, Portsmouth, and Concord, New Hampshire; Boston, Newburyport, and Salem, Massachusetts; and Providence and Newport, Rhode Island). In doing so, he inevitably made ventriloquism seem just a bit less unique.

Charles had come from abroad and soon enough returned there. But a second new competitor ventriloquist was a native American and made a prominent point in his advertising of being "the American Ventriloquist." He was a young man (only nineteen when he began exhibiting in 1821) originally from Nantucket, William Nichols, and he took his inspiration from Mr. Charles. According to a widely repeated anecdote about his introduction to ventriloquism that he shared early in his career:

> He did not know, till lately, that he possessed the power of ventriloquism.—About 18 months ago, while a clerk in a counting house at Savannah, he first saw the famous *Charles* exhibit at that place. Charles, in an address to the audience at one of his exhibitions, on the power of ventriloquism, observed, that there were undoubtedly many in the world who possessed the same powers he did, but that they did not know how to call them into action; he said there might be some even in his present audience. Young N. immediately recollected, that while he was a lad he could whistle in his throat, which none of his companions could do, and was determined to try the experiment of ventriloquism as soon as he should arrive at home the same evening; he did so, and found himself perfectly successful.

The story is a bit of utter mystification, of course, but the connection to Charles seems certain, for Charles had performed in Savannah in mid-March 1820, and Nichols's first exhibition was in Charleston in June 1821. The following month, Nichols performed in New York. Thereafter he exhibited regularly up and down the Eastern Seaboard, from Halifax to Savannah, and occasionally in the interior of the country as well, for the next twenty years, when he retired into private life and a career as a dentist (by this time he was still not forty years old).

Charles, although primarily a ventriloquist, presented "Mechanical Games" and "Philosophical Recreations" of legerdemain as well (as befitted a "Professor of Mechanical Sciences to his Majesty the King of Prussia"), but Nichols was exclusively a ventriloquist. His exhibitions typically presented a varied program of ventriloquial dialogues:

1. Mr. Nichols will converse with a person or voice in the Chimney, and with another voice under the floor; the voice passing from one Chimney into another; and from the floor beneath, to different parts of the room.
2. He will hold a Colloquy with an Old Gentleman behind a Screen, upon the profound subject of Logic.
3. He will represent a Person in the street, and talk with him familiarly, upon a variety of topics, near to, and at a distance from, the window; the Ventriloquial Voice distinctly graduating itself on the principles of Sound.
4. He will throw his Voice into the body of any gentleman present, and seemingly hold a conversation with him.
5. He will carry on an amusing *tete a tete* with a Count Piper, behind a Screen; represent *himself* and two Servants at the same time, in the Kitchen below; a musical Old Lady under the floor together with the crying of two Children apparently in great distress; *in all SIX VOICES!*

After which, Mr. *Nichols* will give some IMITATIONS, to show the difference between the Art of Imitating Sounds, and the Power of Ventriloquism.

Although they both performed widely across the same regions of the country for the next fourteen years, there is no evidence that Potter and Nichols ever met. They came very near to doing so in Virginia in the spring of 1823, when Nichols was performing in Fredericksburg just when Potter was traveling north thither from Norfolk; but just at this point Nichols turned west to perform in Kentucky and Ohio, while Potter continued north. A few years later, Nichols performed in Boston in early March 1827, at a time when Potter was again living there, but Potter himself was on the road at the time, performing first in Shrewsbury and then in New Hampshire, and was also spending some time again at his Andover, New Hampshire, home.

Both Nichols and especially Charles, like many ventriloquists before them—Thomas Garbut, Lee Sugg, the Rannies—won widespread publicity for themselves by playing tricks of ventriloquism upon unsuspecting victims in everyday life. Charles was particularly like Sugg in that he seems to have written and circulated the anecdotes himself. Charles took care that some such anecdotes from his European travels should be resuscitated in American newspapers, but he also provided a few fresh episodes for his new audiences. In the most elaborate of these, staged in Albany, he confounded and dismayed a fortune-teller. Here is the story as it appeared in a letter to the editor in the *New York National Advocate:*

Albany, Oct. 3d, 1819.

The following circumstance, of which I was a witness, occurred here last night. Should you deem it worthy of insertion, it is at your service—it will, probably, gratify your readers, and, no doubt, afford entertainment to all lovers of mirth.

In looking over the Albany Directory, at the Eagle Tavern, a gentleman, near me, observed the name, "*Silva Zebere,* fortune teller, no. 8 Chapel-street;" and proposed, if I would accompany him, to pay a visit to this palmister and professor of necromantic art, wishing no better sport. [Silva Zebere, fortune-teller, was indeed listed at that address in the *Albany Directory* for 1819; and her name there was indeed thus italicized, apparently to indicate that she was colored.] We set out, and, after a mile's walk, arrived at this albanic oracle, mounting a broken stoop, and entering the mystic parlour; a black, dirty sybil, nearly fourteen stone weight, made her appearance—requesting us to sit down—took a pack of cards, made a circle, and went through the regular mode of proceeding: "*a journey by water,*" "*severe illness*" "*fortune in marriage,*" "*six or seven children,*" "*great danger*" and "*happy escape*"—when, suddenly, out of the drawer, of which she had taken the cards, a tremendous voice vociferated, "*hold! You d——d old hag—you're telling lies!*"—the voice ceased, and the astonishment depicted on the countenance of poor Silva Zebere, and on that of her assistant, a black girl, can be more easily imagined than described. This silence continued for a few seconds, in some degree recovering herself from her confusion—when again voices assailed her, apparently, under her seat, and out of the chimney: the scene now became truly alarming—both women started—overthrowing table, cards, and the whole apparatus, running out of the room, swearing the devil was in the house—leaving to ourselves to act as we thought best—accordingly, we walked home. The gentleman, who caused all this ludicrous bustle, and made an impression on me that I shall not speedily forget, was Mr. Charles, the celebrated ventriloquist.

Several months later, in another city (Philadelphia), Charles pulled off another such stunt. Again, the butt of his joke was a stereotypically gullible black, and again, the story comes from a set of slightly varying letters to the editors of several of the city's newspapers. The version that appeared in the *Democratic Press* is as follows:

Sir, The following laughable scene of which I was a witness, took place a few days ago, at one of our principal Hotels; should you think it worth while publishing, it is much at your service, and will no doubt amuse some of your numerous readers    MOMUS.

A large Green Turtle was killed last week at one of our hotels in this city, the uncommon size and manner of dispatching this *bon Morceau les gourmans* attracted the attention of many of the boarders of the house. At the moment Mr. Mongo, after commending a good while, the breadth and fatness of his hanging victim with a grinning face, commenced his operations by drawing the carving knife across the throat of the suspended animal. But, lo! at the moment the fatal weapon entered, the Turtle in a most pitiful tone, cried out, "O Mongo, Mongo, Mongo, why doest thou kill me; let me live, and happy will be thy days!" The gaze and amazement of all around and particularly of Mongo, may be now more easily conceived than described, but such was the effect that the knife dropped and Mongo ran screaming, "massa, massa, it be a devil and no turtle, and me no touch him more." The scene was ludicrous in the extreme, and required all the persuasion of those present to convince the frightened cook that it was only a humorous trick of Mr. Charles the ventriloquist, who stood by and caused all this laughable merriment.

Slightly different versions of this anecdote were submitted simultaneously to the editors of the *Franklin Gazette* and *Relf's Philadelphia Gazette*. The incident was soon republished by scores of newspapers across the country.

Readers of these stories would have understood immediately that Mongo (a variant of Mungo) was a black menial: the name, like Guinea and Gambia, was an African place-name, indicating a slave's country or tribe of origin (the Mungo were from the coastal area of what is now Cameroon), and it had become widely familiar from Charles Dibdin's popular short opera *The Padlock* (1768), in which the character Mungo is a clownish, obsequious, conniving black slave. (Only a few years after this, in 1826, the great black American actor Ira Aldridge would start regularly performing the role of Mungo in England, frequently pairing it with his performance of the title role of *Othello,* and giving new depth and pathos to Mungo's character. But that was in another country.) Mungo's blackness is emphasized in the *Democratic Press* version of the anecdote by his dialect ("massa, massa, it be a devil"), and in the *Relf's Philadelphia Gazette* version (which omits most of Mungo's exclamations) it is made explicit (Mungo is called "the black executioner"). Both Mungo and Silva Zebere are easy dupes for the sportive ventriloquist because, as blacks, they are stereotypically gullible and superstitious, quick to detect the devil and quick to run from him.

Such anecdotes are not random; they are symptomatic of a new strain of humor, condescending and racist, that was increasingly permeating American culture in the 1820s. (Mungo, in particular, was an important progenitor of the Jim Crow craze that would saturate American culture in the 1830s.) They do not aim at Richard Potter, of course; but they do not shoot wide of him, either. They say much about the mainstream East Coast culture to which he was obliged to reacclimate himself as he returned to the Northeast in the latter months of 1823.

A third new ventriloquist in America at this time, finally, represented yet another kind of competition. Charles Mathews was one of the most famous comic actors in England and had won particular renown as the master of the one-man show. He was a brilliant vocal mimic and impersonator, and for the preceding several years he had each year introduced a new "Mathews at Home" entertainment involving many different characters (all of whom he presented himself) caught up together comically in a single journey or story, interspersed with recitations and songs—the "Mail Coach Adventures," the "Trip to Paris," "La Diligence" (the return from Paris), the "Country Cousins," the autobiographical "Youthful Days of Mr. Mathews" ("The lectures open with an account of the speaker's birth and adventures till he was an hour and a quarter old," an early London critic reported). In September 1822 he came to America, where he presented his one-man entertainments in the largest northeastern cities—Baltimore, New York, Washington, Boston, Philadelphia—for some half a year.

Mathews was a ventriloquist only occasionally and incidentally and in truth was not considered particularly skilled in many of the technical aspects of the art. But he had exhibited it from time to time since 1802—he was indeed one of the very earliest English practitioners—and the sheer star power and sustained comedic entertainment that he brought to his performances was enough to make them triumphs, while his own indisputable stature in the theater also confirmed for ventriloquism all at once the status that Richard Potter had been slowly winning for it over many years, the cachet of social respectability and highbrow approval.


IX

Potter planned only a short stay in New York this time—three nights, no more. He now began advertising himself for the first time as "the American Ventriloquist," strong evidence that he had become aware of Nichols's advertising. Then he moved on to New Haven to exhibit for a few nights, apparently his last performances before his return, at long last, to Boston.

There is one Richard Potter anecdote preserved in local Andover tradition that concerns an incident said to have occurred in or near New Haven; if that is accurate, it probably dated to this visit. The earliest written record of it is as follows:

> On his arrival, he went to the best hotel, and a little while before dinner, entered the office.
>
> When dinner was served, Mr. Potter started to enter the dining room with the other guests, but the landlord stopped him, saying that his guests would not care to sit at the table with a colored man. Mr. Potter made no reply but went quietly back to the office and seated himself where he could command a good view of the table. At the time it was customary for the landlord to carve. A fine roasted pig was set before him. At the first stroke of the carving knife, a grunt issued from the pig. Everyone started and looked at the pig. At the next incision such a piercing squeal was heard from the pig that some of the ladies became terror stricken, and left the table. The landlord became white in the face, and began to tremble, and shouted in a loud voice, "My goodness, this pig ain't dead!"
>
> After quiet had been restored, a man present, who had met Mr. Potter, said to the landlord, "I think if you should ask that gentleman there to dine with us, you could carve your pig."

As a specimen of a ventriloquist's wit and skill, this anecdote is highly reminiscent of those about Charles and Nichols (such as Charles's "Mongo" story) currently circulating. As a reminder of the particular kind of discrimination Potter regularly endured, however, it is *sui generis* and would never do for his advertising—which is all the more reason to suspect, then, that it actually happened. We know from much other testimony that Potter, like both the Rannies, could do an absolutely first-rate imitation of a stuck pig: as one Rhode Island reporter who had attended Potter's exhibitions as a child (the only shows of magic and ventriloquism he ever saw in his childhood, so surely he did not mistake) fondly recalled, "The squeal of *that* pig when he was punched with a dagger, was more natural than any pig ever gave, and when the tin box was turned to the audience and they saw there was *nary* pig there, the belief in a personal devil reached its climax."

In such mingled triumph and unease, then, did Potter and his small group return finally to Boston, where he marked the conclusion of his long tour "after an absence of five years" (it had indeed been almost that long since he had last performed there) by exhibiting again "for three nights only" in the familiar Columbian Museum. He was home—not yet back to his gentleman's farm in New Hampshire (he would return there within a few months), but home at least to the city and community where he had grown up and where he had again been living during the year before he began his tour. He would occasionally undertake long tours after this, but nothing on a remotely similar scale of duration, distance, or difficulty. It was time now to retrieve his children, provide some stability for his family, and savor and preserve the independence that he had won for them. His mentor James Rannie, at just this point in his career, having accumulated his own nest egg had quickly squandered it, then had set out on one last tour only to die almost two thousand miles from home, in Puerto Rico, leaving his own wife impoverished on his own gentleman's farm back in Maine; he had been almost exactly forty years old, just the age that Richard Potter was now. Potter was acutely aware that "My profession . . . seldom leads to any thing short of total destruction"; he was determined to create a different outcome for himself.

# 6

# Return to New England, 1824–1829

## I

Richard Potter's homecoming should have been a time of restoration and consolidation for him. His grand tour of North America had clearly been a great professional and financial success, and he was now back in his home territory and on his gentleman-farmer estate, with his family together again at last. Now he began to invest in improvements to his farm and to his home as well, even while he and his wife began planning for a new set of domestic arrangements that would have him traveling much shorter tours, while she would be able to help their finances with a new domestic business as she remained home with their children.

Instead, the next several years became something of a continuing, slow-motion disaster for Richard Potter, as racial attitudes grew nastier, financial woes accumulated, and his family's fabric was severely and repeatedly torn. It is unlikely that he saw much of this coming: he had not been in New England, or even seen his growing children, for almost five years, and had not lived in Andover for six.

His problems began accruing as soon as he got home—before he returned to Andover, even. Late in 1823, he was touring at a leisurely pace through Rhode Island, not so very far from his Boston base of earlier years and an area where he had often performed in the years before his national tour. This time, he received three nasty jolts in rather quick succession. At the very beginning of December, he was arrested in Smithfield, a town in the northeast corner of the state, for exhibiting without a license; less than two weeks later, he was banned from performing in Woonsocket (a village within the township of Smithfield), seven miles to the south, on the road to Providence. Then, in Concord, New Hampshire, an attempt was mounted to block or at least cripple his performance.

The Smithfield incident quickly developed into a protracted lawsuit, a significant burden for Richard Potter over the next several years. The Woonsocket and Concord incidents were, to appearances, only minor unpleasantnesses. Yet they echoed across New England nonetheless, and those echoes help us better locate and gauge the earlier incident also.

The Smithfield and Woonsocket incidents were directly related in that, since Potter had just been arrested in Smithfield for exhibiting without a license, he would now presumably have been most scrupulous about seeking a license before exhibiting in Smithfield again—and Woonsocket was part of Smithfield. An anonymous source now publicized the astonishing claim, however, that Potter had instead tried to exhibit again without a license but had been prevented by the concerted actions of indignant, righteous residents. The story appeared as a letter to the editor in one of Providence's major newspapers:

[COMMUNICATED.]

A mulatto juggler, by the name of Potter, who has lately exhibited his deceptive arts in various places, advertised to perform at Nathan Mowry's Inn, in the village of Woonsocket (Smithfield) on the 13th instant. It was, however, determined at a meeting of the citizens of that place, to enforce the law of the State against any person who should attempt to exhibit juggler's tricks, without a license from the Town-Council, as required by the Statute.—In consequence of this determination, Potter prudently left the State.

"A mulatto juggler": this is a loaded opening, for both "mulatto" and "juggler" here are clearly meant to be pejorative. Both as a black and as a practitioner of "deceptive arts," Richard Potter is being stigmatized. Did a group of Woonsocket residents really band together to stop his performance? It seems more likely that they worked to persuade the town council not to license it. That was the council's prerogative: it could, "as [it] shall find expedient, prohibit and suppress theatrical performances, rope and wire-dancing, and all other shows and performances" in the town, although implicitly this was for the purpose of "prevent[ing] riots, and all disorderly behavior." The law was a not atypical New England statute for the regulating of acting companies and showmen; if a significant number of Woonsocket voters opposed permitting this particular exhibition to proceed, it is not surprising that the town council would decline to license it. But why then would Richard Potter have "prudently left the state"—in particular, why "prudently"? He was traveling toward Providence, where he had performed several times before, sometimes for lengthy stands (for that matter, he had advertised his exhibitions in this very newspaper). Just as "mulatto" and "juggler" function in this communication as pejoratives, so "prudently" signals a warning. There had been animosity and at least implicit threat in this encounter.

This animosity quickly followed Richard Potter to Concord, the New Hampshire state capital, only twenty-five miles from his home. Returning "after an absence of five years," he began exhibiting there at the very end of December 1823 and was well received, drawing crowds for two and a half weeks. But early in this stand, a sour note was sounded in the *New Hampshire Repository*, a recently established religious newspaper in Concord. Under the heading "DECEPTION," the paper first reprinted the "mulatto juggler" paragraph of the Woonsocket article from the *Rhode-Island American* quoted above, and then added this commentary:

> It seems that this same Potter, being driven from Rhode-Island, by the wise regulators of that State, is seeking indemnity by drawing upon the resources of New-Hampshire. Believing, from information, that the arts with which he practices are not only *deceptive* but of *immoral* and *irreligious* tendency, we are compelled to raise our voice against them, and can but express surprise that he should be countenanced by civil authority. We would inquire whether it comes within the true meaning of the laws of this State, that license should be granted by selectmen for this kind of exhibitions?

A campaign against Richard Potter was building. Had he indeed been "driven" from Rhode Island? Not by the state authorities, certainly: a refusal to license his exhibition in Woonsocket had no bearing on other towns there. And on what "information" is the *New Hampshire Repository* editor relying? The implication is that what we are reading here is a conservative religious objection to shows and entertainments generally, but of course that "mulatto juggler" tag still prefaces everything.

More concerning than this, however, is the mounting evidence that this campaign was not limited to an occasional querulous letter to the editor. The biggest newspaper in town, the *New-Hampshire Patriot,* after applauding

Richard Potter's exhibitions, took note of the attacks and came to his defense. Near the end of his stand in Concord, it published this notice:

> Mr. POTTER.–The exhibitions of this performer have been each evening attended by a crowded audience. That his talents as a comic actor are of a high class, and that his performances are of a good moral tendency, is admitted by the best judges, and by those men who set the best examples in society. We are sorry to perceive, in this enlightened age, a spirit which has a smattering of the persecution of the darker ages in relation to Mr. Potter—a spirit which savours too much of bigotry and intolerance. Every man in this five [*sic;* fine] country has an undoubted right to enjoy his own opinion unmolested: no man is compelled to attend the exhibitions of Mr. Potter. Why, then, is he molested?
>
> Mr. Potter performs for the last time in this place, this evening.

What antagonistic acts had been occurring? "Intolerance" (like "juggler" in the Rhode Island story) could suggest religiously based antipathy to showmen generally, but "bigotry" (like "mulatto") suggests race as an issue, and "molested" certainly suggests active rather than passive aggression. Perhaps there were disruptions at or outside of his exhibitions? We do not know.

But we do know that other measures were actively taken to interfere with his exhibitions in Concord. Two days after this last story appeared in the *Patriot,* the *Repository* weighed in once more:

> MR. POTTER AGAIN.–A few weeks since, we copied a brief notice of Mr. Potter, the Mulatto juggler, from a Rhode Island paper, by which our readers were informed that he could not be allowed to practice his deceptive arts before the people of that state. We mentioned likewise his arrival in New-Hampshire, and we now add, humiliating as is the fact, that he was so far patronized by the Ladies and Gentlemen in this town at that time, as to warrant him in making an exhibition of his *wonderful* and *miraculous* skill in weaving *ribbons,* frying *pancakes,* dancing *hornpipes,* &c. for the edification of our citizens, and strangers, on a second occasion. We are pleased however to remark, to the honour of the Masonic Fraternity, that the Lodge in this town, on a little reflection, resolved, in a regular meeting, that their HALL could not consistently be perverted to such purposes. The *Gentleman* and his *Auditors* were therefore obliged to put up with other accommodations.

It was true: even though Richard Potter was himself a Mason (albeit of a lodge not then recognized by most of the white lodges in the country), the members of the Blazing Star Lodge in Concord, whose hall Potter had been renting for his exhibitions during the first two weeks of his Concord performances, decided to close it to him forthwith. At the Lodge's 13 January meeting, two brothers proposed an amendment to the bylaws: "Notice that the Agent of Blazing Star Lodge be instructed not to let their Hall to any person who may practice the art of Ledgerdemain [*sic*] or who wishes to make in it any theatrical exhibition and that the Secretary notify him accordingly." The motion to amend the bylaws was passed (this would have required a vote of two-thirds of the members present). For his final performances in Concord, Richard Potter was forced to find a different venue. So while Potter's exhibitions were by all accounts a sustained, well-received success, there was nevertheless social pressure in Concord from certain people who wanted to prevent him from performing there.

Finally, as a sad, painful, yet utterly charming coda to this Concord story, there appeared on the front page of yet another Concord newspaper the following letter to the editor a few days after Richard Potter's last exhibition there:

Mr. Editor,

I fear the Selectmen of the town, some of the heads of families, and those persons who think themselves at the top notch of the circle, are bringing a serious evil on Society, by the encouragement of vice, folly, and extravagance. For several days last week, our village was disturbed by the exhibitions (or impositions) of a little black fellow by the name of *Potter*. It is said that the Selectmen of the town gave him a license to play his tricks of deception, and to gull the people out of as much money as he could in one week; and I am sorry to say that many of the respectable inhabitants, were seen following this retailer of nonsense—encouraged by their example; every apprentice boy, and every child ten years of age, must be furnished with twenty-five cents each to buy a ticket.

Now I am a poor man, have a large family of children, and by hard labour am hardly able to support them from year to year. On entering the house one day last week, four of my children came to me with a hand bill, setting forth all the wonderful *feats* which were to be performed by Mr. Potter; I told them they could not go, that I had not paid my taxes, and had no money to spend in that way—but my wife who differs a little from me in matters and things, took side with the children; she told me I was an old fashioned sort of a fellow, that if I had my way our children would grow up in perfect ignorance and know nothing of the fashionable world, that these exhibitions were encouraged by some of the first people in town, that all the children in the neighbourhood were going and ours should go let it cost what it would. I found it was of no use to remonstrate; for I hate family quarrels above all things, and was about leaving the house in silence, when my wife called to me and said I must give them one dollar to purchase tickets.—Now this was the worst of all, for I was obliged to get out the old purse, and I assure you Mr. *Printer,* I never emptied it with more reluctance in my life. The little change that I had saved from my hard earnings was now reduced to a single 4d, and my taxes are still unpaid.

Now Mr. Printer, these things are intolerable; if our rich folks have money to spend, cannot they spend it in a way that will be more honourable to themselves & more beneficial to society.

It is in the power of the *Selectmen* to prevent these things, and it is to be regretted that they have not the independence, good sense, and sound judgment, to set their faces against such impositions, and prevent the people from being gull'd out of their money by such stale nonsense as that exhibited by Mr. Potter.

HOMESPUN

Here again is the racist sneer ("a little black fellow"), along with more than a touch of class antagonism, dressed up in a high moral tone ("encouragement of vice, folly, and extravagance"). By now it has become quite clear that the mulatto, not simply the juggler, was the target of this antagonism.

And yet, from this same sour source, what a testimonial to the allure of this showman! The "respectable people" are flocking to him, and all the children are wild to see his wonders ("every apprentice boy, and every child ten years of age, must be furnished with twenty-five cents each to buy a ticket"; "all the children in the neighbourhood were going and ours should go let it cost what it would"). Even a poor man's wife, eager to give some of her children a brief taste of fun or fashion or simply belonging, insists that the family spend on Potter's show money that it cannot afford. The chasm between Potter's allure and his stigma, between his celebrity and his victimization, can scarcely be clearer anywhere than it is in this one grim, bad-tempered letter from a poor, struggling laborer.

II

What, then, had happened at Richard Potter's earlier exhibitions in Smithfield? The simple, legal answer is that he was found to have performed there without first obtaining a license from the town, and that he was then fined exactly as Rhode Island law prescribed. He contested this penalty, but a jury and court upheld it. He then appealed the court's decision; ultimately the Superior Court also upheld it, while striking a modest compromise on the penalty. This judicial process dragged on for years: the Superior Court's decision, rendered in mid-December 1828, came almost five full years after the charges had first been filed against Potter.

The case (technically it was two cases, a separate one for each performing-without-a-license offense, first on 29 November and then on 1 December) against Richard Potter seems unassailable. He had not obtained a license to perform in Smithfield; he had nevertheless exhibited there, more than once, and had posted playbills announcing his performances and had charged admission for them. Why, then, had he contested the charges against him so vigorously and persistently?

One obvious answer is that he might have fought them simply because the fine was enormous, almost ruinous, and he would have been clinging desperately to any hope of escaping or reducing it. In this respect, Rhode Island's penalties were unusual, although not unexampled. In New Hampshire at this time, the penalty for exhibiting without a license was "not less than ten dollars, nor more than thirty dollars with costs of prosecution," and this was a typical range; in New York, for example, state law set the penalty at twenty-five dollars per offense. (In 1827, Richard Potter was again charged with exhibiting without a license, this time in Shrewsbury, Massachusetts; his penalty on that occasion was ten dollars.) Many states did not have such regulations at all (Rhode Island itself did not until 1822, a law enacted while Potter was absent from New England on his national tour), although individual cities might. In Rhode Island, however, he now found himself facing a flat fine of four hundred dollars, a punishment that certainly would have driven most performers out of business.

Apart from this "act of desperation" possibility, however, many aspects of the Town of Smithfield's charges against Richard Potter suggest that the case against him was highly contrived. To begin with, the Rhode Island law on regulating theatrical exhibitions generously rewarded informants (this, like the severity of the fine, was atypical but not unheard of; we may recall that, when Potter left New Haven due to a blue laws complaint in 1817, a local editor had speculated that the complaint had been lodged "with the expectation of receiving the award allowed in such cases to informers"). The fine for performing without a license was two hundred dollars per offense; of this sum, the informant was to receive one-half (the town would receive the other half; the sums had to be "sued for and recovered by action of debt, in the name of the town-treasurer of the town in which such offense is committed"). Informing, then, could be extremely profitable, vastly exceeding the performer's gross for an exhibition. And if it were known that a performer had advertised two performances, an informer could wait until the second one was under way before providing his information, or a town treasurer could so wait until acting on that information, thereby doubling their reward. The town treasurer of Smithfield, the person bringing the suit against Richard Potter, was Isaac Wilkinson. The informer in the case was Joseph Wilkinson, also of Smithfield. As the surname suggests, Isaac and Joseph were related: their fathers were brothers, so they were first cousins.

It is easily imaginable, then, that Richard Potter might have felt he had been entrapped when he discovered that the penalty now being assessed him had been doubled through a "per offense" gambit and that the man informing on him was a close relative of the man now assessing him. Whether he realized it at the time or not, moreover, it is also suspicious that no one else in this case was being penalized. As the "mulatto juggler" communication in the *Rhode-Island American* had noted in closing, "Tavernkeepers are reminded that the law imposes a heavy penalty on any person who shall furnish a room for any such exhibition, without a special license from the Town-Council therefor." The law was indeed quite clear on this point: any person or persons allowing an unlicensed exhibition "in any house or room to him or them belonging, or under his or their control" would be fined fifty dollars. But that did not happen in this instance: instead, the tavern owner, David Farnum, was deposed as a witness in the case against Richard Potter, and no charge was brought against him.

While the Smithfield case against Richard Potter may reek of opportunism, it does not necessarily indicate racism: insofar as it might not have been evenhanded justice, financial gain was the obvious motive. The case is important in this narrative, however, for three reasons beyond that of illustrating the hazards of an itinerant profession. First, it helps clarify and quantify the kinds of financial pressures that were now beginning to burden Potter. (In the ultimate resolution of this case, Potter's lawyer won for him the Superior Court's agreement that, if Potter paid in full the fine of one suit [$200] plus the costs of both suits [at this point they amounted to $114.16] by 1 February 1829, the fine in the second suit [another $200] would be waived.) Second, the court documents in this case provide rare glimpses of Richard Potter's touring practices. And third, Potter's dismay and outrage about this predicament prompted him to write the only sustained letter from his hand that has ever been discovered, a document that not only illuminates his feelings at this time but also sheds wonderful light on such topics as his style, his education, and even his accent.

The Providence County case file for *Isaac Wilkinson, T.T. [Town Treasurer] v. Richard Potter* includes a short deposition by David Farnum, the occupant-owner of the tavern where Potter performed, taken (at the request of Joseph Wilkinson, the informant) on 26 April 1826. In this testimony Farnum affirms that "Richard Potter the Ventriloquist performed many curious Experiments called Ventriloquism and other Public Shows, at the House occupied by me in Slatersville, as a Tavern" on 29 November and 1 December 1823. Asked if Potter had posted bills announcing the place and times of his performance and the price of admission, he testified that "He pasted up Bills to inform the Publick the price of Admittance was 25 Cents for grown persons and half price for Children." How many people attended? "I should suppose there was about fifty attended the performance each night." (Do the math: since some of the attendees were likely children, Potter's gross before expenses would have been perhaps ten or eleven dollars each night.) "Was you present during the performance of said Richard Potter?" Potter's lawyer then asked. "I was present at said Potter's performance about half an hour one evening," was the reply (he later clarified that this was 29 November). Did Potter have any assistants? "There was two persons that came with said Potter and assisted him."

Then, oddly, Potter's lawyer, upon asking "Are you positive that Richard Potter did perform?," received a hedging reply: "I should not want to swear that Richard Potter did perform all the time but I have no doubt it was he that did perform all the time." The lawyer soon rephrased his question—"Are you positive that Richard Potter did perform any of the time?"—and received essentially the same answer: "I should not wish to swear . . . but I have no doubt said Richard Potter did perform." Then Joseph Wilkinson asked the obvious question: "Why do you hesitate to swear that Richard Potter did perform all the time?" Farnum's reply: "He did not appear all the time alike[;] he altered his Physiognomy."

Richard Potter's exhibitions in Smithfield included "dancing, singing, juggling and ventriloquism," the court documents tell us. And here, through David Farnum's eyes, we see some of the effects of Potter's costuming—the wig, the old woman's costume, the garish dancing shoes, perhaps the makeup. The man was a Play Actor indeed: the landlord knew full well that that performer before his eyes still had to have been Richard Potter, but he simply couldn't be sure just by looking at him.

## III

Early in 1824, Richard Potter, still reeling and apparently seething from the series of disruptions and indignities he had endured over the past few months, wrote a letter to a Boston lawyer, Andrew Dunlap, whom he had engaged to help him (fig. 8). Almost certainly Potter had initially reached out to Dunlap as soon as he reached Boston in mid-December, immediately after leaving Rhode Island on his way north; he would have paused to take care of this business and doubtless to renew many old friendships after his more than five years' absence, before he traveled on to Concord, New Hampshire, at the end of December to perform there.

Andrew Dunlap was still a young man, not quite thirty at this time, but he was already becoming prominent in Boston. A Harvard graduate, he had moved from Salem to Boston only in 1820 and quickly began making a name for himself both in law and in politics, where he was an ardent Republican and Jacksonian and (unlike many Jacksonians) an outspoken opponent of slavery. The Republicans had distinguished him with an invitation to deliver the Fourth of July oration at Faneuil Hall in 1822, and in a speech celebrating the Founding Fathers and their moral principles his peroration had frankly acknowledged the "single exception" to the "correct political principles" of the present generation:

> Could the voice of our fathers, be heard from the tomb, . . . with their praises would be mingled the accent of complaint, that the crying sin, the heavy curse of slavery, should exist among a people adoring their liberty, and appealing to the Declaration of Independence as the charter of freedom and the record of the rights of man. . . . In Massachusetts the sentiment of the Declaration of Independence, all men are born free and equal, engrafted upon her bill of rights, with a breath, and in a moment enfranchised the slave, and restored that liberty which is the unalienable right of every being who bears the impress of Heaven, the form and the aspect of a man. Until that stain which rests upon our character be removed, we may celebrate our Independence, till the earth and the heavens are filled with our rejoicing. But the sound which is echoed from the tombs of our ancestors, will ever be accompanied with a sigh, till the day shall arrive when every heart shall leap with the consciousness of freedom, when every voice shall sing the joys of liberty, and no spot of our Republic shall be found, on which a slave can be reared.

And in 1823 Dunlap had won an important court case for an ordinary Boston truckman who stood accused, as it happens, of selling without a license: he had been "arrested and charged with hawking his products directly to the public and shopkeepers below retail and established wholesale rates—something he did not have a city license to do." So Dunlap was widely recognized in Boston at this time as a distinguished and skilled attorney with pro-worker and antislavery leanings.

Richard Potter had probably never met Andrew Dunlap before December 1823, because Dunlap had not moved from Salem to Boston until after Potter had left New England in 1819—although of course Dunlap probably already knew who Potter was and may well, as a young law student or neophyte lawyer, have attended some of Potter's exhibitions in Salem in 1815 or 1817. Someone in the Boston area, then, must have referred him to Dunlap or otherwise brought the two men together. (Henry K. Oliver had moved to Salem in June 1819; Dunlap didn't move from Salem to Boston until 1820. Perhaps Oliver was the intermediary responsible for connecting the two men.) It is significant, certainly, that Richard Potter would have found his way to so prominent a lawyer. Yet while Dunlap could certainly give Potter advice, he could not serve as his attorney at court; for his practice was in Massachusetts, and Potter's trial, should matters come to that, would be in Rhode Island. But Dunlap did, as it happened, have good connections with some members of the Rhode Island bar: in particular, he had studied law in Salem under John Pitman, who had moved to Providence in 1821 and soon thereafter had been appointed the United States district attorney for Rhode Island. So Dunlap may well have been able to put Potter in touch with some capable lawyers in Providence.

In any event, Richard Potter found his way to Andrew Dunlap, who accepted him as a client (and who would subsequently serve as Potter's lawyer in a few Boston lawsuits later in the decade). He then continued north to Concord. He had already sent ahead to Benjamin Thompson's father-in-law, Nathaniel Colby, in Hopkinton, New Hampshire, to retrieve the "two Slays" [sleighs] that he had stored there years earlier, at the beginning of his great North American tour; his party would have been traveling in those sleighs now (fig. 7). (Possibly he now traveled also to his home in Andover, although this may well have still been rented out and thus unavailable to him for a while yet). He performed in Concord for those two and a half sometimes difficult weeks. (His children, as we have seen, had probably been living these past five-plus years with the Aaron and Edith Colby family in Bow, a town adjacent to Concord, so the Potter family would finally have been reunited now, at least temporarily.) Soon thereafter, he headed west on a tour toward the Connecticut River valley on the New Hampshire–Vermont border and then down the valley into western Massachusetts. Probably his first stop out of Concord was in Hopkinton, New Hampshire, the next town to the west, because in his letter to Dunlap he spoke of having earlier sent Dunlap "the copey [sic] from Hopkinton," presumably a copy of some legal document he had recently received that bore on his case. Hopkinton was a natural stopping point for him and his party now in any event, because Benjamin Thompson's wife's entire family lived there and Thompson's son would have been living there with them as well.

From Hopkinton, the main road led southwest through Hillsboro and Keene and then crossed the Connecticut River at Brattleboro, Vermont. It was from Brattleboro that Richard Potter finally wrote to Andrew Dunlap. The subject of his letter certainly seems to be a pending court case. Was it the Smithfield case? There is no evidence of any other. Moreover, the date seems to suggest as much. Suffolk County (Boston's court district) had January and April terms in 1824, so the former had already gone by and the latter was not yet urgent. Providence County, Rhode Island, however, did have a February term in 1824. Typically a term began on the fourth Monday of the month; in 1824, this would have been 23 February—leaving enough time for Richard Potter to perform three evenings in Greenfield and still get back to Boston (or Concord, Massachusetts, which Richard Potter had reason to think might be alternatively preferable for Dunlap) to meet with Dunlap well before the court in Providence began to sit.

Brattleborough Vt    Feb 11th 1824

Mr Dunlap Sir I have been very much ingaged sense I sor you and have not had it in my power to cum to Boston, but I will be at Boston two Days before Cort, or, meet you at Concord I shall leav this place for Greenfield Massachusetts which place I wish you to wright me, and inform me when you wish to se me, you will giv me as long a time as posabil I am in hops you reseved the copey from Hopkinton if not you will let me no in your letter you must wright me imeadeatly, on the resept of this or I shall be gorn from Greenfield as it is not provibal I shall play thair more than three evenings I shal attend at any time you may wish thairfore Don't frget me and if posabil punish thos villings
  Yours in hast
  Richard Potter
  ventriloquist

Richard Potter's letter reveals a man of words, not usually of letters—an emphatically phonetic speller: "cum" (rhymes with "rum") instead of "come"; "Cort" (rhymes with "port") instead of "Court"; "no" instead of "know"; "thair" (rhymes with "hair") instead of "there." It also evinces traces of the formal education that he received in his early youth or (more likely) the practical training that he received in the Dillaway business: he may misspell "write" as "wright," but then he has learned how to spell "wright" and has had occasion to write the word before this (Samuel Dillaway senior had begun as a housewright, and his business dealt with shipwrights and housewrights regularly). And we learn that he has a Boston accent, too: "I sor you" (i.e., "I saw you") makes this very clear, and "I shall be gorn" (i.e., "I shall be gone") strongly indicates it as well.

He is also, beneath his courteous demeanor, a man of some spirit, as his conclusion demonstrates. He has been wronged, he feels, but he is very ready to call that injury a wrong, and he does not regard that wrong as the inevitable or acceptable lot of a black man: "if posabil punish thos villings."

IV

The ominous financial threat of the Rhode Island suit that was hanging over Richard Potter from the moment he returned to New Hampshire in early 1824 was only one of several financial and personal burdens that now suddenly encumbered him. Perhaps, indeed, he could hope for a while that the Rhode Island case would just go away, since court term after court term passed only for the case to be deferred and deferred again (as we have seen, depositions in the case were not even taken until late April 1826). Perhaps, too, he hoped for some time (evidence suggests that he did) that other burdens—essentially, family problems—would, with attention and careful planning and management, go away or diminish as well. Over the course of the next two or three years, all those hopes increasingly proved untenable.

In the rural and agricultural communities of America at this time, cash could be a rare, seasonal commodity, and promissory notes were a familiar fact of life, whether they took the form of credit granted by a local storekeeper and recorded in a ledger or notes exchanged between individuals. Usually there would be no public or permanent record of these transactions; unless a mortgage were recorded in a county registry of deeds, or a contested debt ended up as the subject of a court case, or someone died intestate and the probate court appointed an executor to inventory the deceased's assets and liabilities, a promissory note was private business, and, once it had been honored, no record of it was likely to survive. It can be difficult, then, to assess an individual's financial status in this period very accurately from such records as do remain today. Even so, it seems valid to say that throughout 1824 and for most of 1825 Richard Potter tended to be a lender and a purchaser, to appearances a man with both cash and confidence. From late 1825 on, however, he tended to be a borrower and a defaulter, to appearances a man with chronic money problems.

It is no surprise that Richard Potter would have been flush in 1824; he had just returned from an extensive campaign that had been designed to give him security for life, and, even if he did his banking in Meredith or Concord, he would have been bringing money into the Andover economy. Evidence of his sense of financial security and flexibility appears now in a variety of ways. For example, early in 1824 he loaned $300—a very significant sum—to a Boston acquaintance, Peter Rix. In 1825 he would similarly lend another large sum ($150) to a Boston friend, Samson Moody (a fellow African Lodge Mason since 1812, Moody was at that time the Grand Master of the Lodge). Between these two outlays, he expanded his Andover estate by purchasing a small piece of adjacent land (half an acre); and in 1825, he also made significant improvements to his estate, contracting for a new barn, a new bridge, and a new shed on his property.

Beyond all these deals and developments, the Potters were also entering upon a much larger one that would dramatically change their lifestyle. At the end of May 1824, the Andover town selectmen issued a license to Potter to sell liquor by the drink and maintain a tavern for one year. Richard Potter did not own this tavern; rather, it stood on an adjacent tract of land, close by his own house. Upon his return to Andover in early 1824, he clearly decided that renting it gave promise of being a worthwhile investment. Richard and Sally seem then to have operated the tavern themselves for about a year, and Richard Potter continued to be responsible for its rent for another three years thereafter.

This was a family decision. Managing the tavern, which also functioned as an inn, would have been primarily Sally Potter's responsibility. Richard would now be limiting his tours to regional trips through northern and southeastern New England, but even so he would be away from Andover for weeks at a time, so the day-to-day operations of the tavern, and the supervision of whatever staff or occasional help they employed, would have fallen entirely to Sally.

In the long run, Richard Potter's tavern venture proved to be a big financial liability and a big personal mistake. Clearly he hadn't carefully thought through what he was getting into. By the end of the year, he was already trying to dispose of the operation. He did find someone else to take over the management of the place; nevertheless, he continued to be tied to the business at least through the end of 1827.

The financial liability of the tavern is difficult to assess, but signs of it lurk everywhere in Richard Potter's business dealings in 1824 and the years immediately following. The tavern business seems, in fact, to have entangled Potter in complicated ways with several other men and proves to be the common thread linking many or most of his difficulties at this time, even though there is no allusion to it in any of the lawsuits that provide a paper trail of his difficulties. To appreciate this, we need to learn something of this particular tavern's history.

The tavern was already well established when Richard Potter first moved to Andover. It had been built in 1799 by Col. John C. Gale, a resident of Salisbury, the next town to the southeast. The property eventually passed to his son, also John Gale, who lived in Andover and then in New Chester (now Hill), the next town to the north. After Richard Potter had made his original purchase of sixty acres of land in Andover from Benjamin Thompson in 1813, it was from John Gale that he bought, the following year, the adjacent eighty-acre tract of raw land that comprised the larger part of his new estate. Then in 1817 Gale sold an adjacent forty-acre tract, including the tavern (which was "nearly opposite" Potter's home), to Peter Rix, then an Andover resident. Rix quickly mortgaged the property to Roger E. Perkins of Hopkinton, New Hampshire (a prominent businessman who had extensive property holdings in the area), renewed the mortgage after two years, and eventually relinquished the property to Perkins in 1822; in the interim Rix himself had moved to Boston and left the innkeeping business entirely (but not permanently: he eventually became an innkeeper in Marblehead, Massachusetts, for more than twenty years).

This history sheds some light on that significant three-hundred-dollar promissory note that Richard Potter accepted from Peter Rix in Boston early in 1824—a loan to Rix that we know about only because it was never repaid, and Potter eventually was forced to sue to recover it. In 1824 Peter Rix was an obscure clerk working in Boston and living on Federal Street near the Boston Theatre. To Richard Potter, however, Rix was a former neighbor and acquaintance or even friend from Andover, and presumably someone whose work ethic gave Potter confidence that the loan would be repaid. Perhaps, indeed, the loan to Rix even brought Potter a strong recommendation from Rix to Perkins that Potter would be a worthy, safe successor as innkeeper of the tavern.

The tavern's history also illuminates another difficult and expensive lawsuit, this one brought against Potter, that otherwise would be completely baffling. In the fall of 1825 John Gale sued Richard Potter, alleging that on 1 September 1824, Gale had been possessed of certain items but had that day lost them and that later that same day they had come into Potter's possession "by finding": in other words, Gale had lost some things, Potter had found them, and now Potter was wrongfully keeping them and Gale wanted them back.

As a suit over a lost wallet or trunk or horse, this kind of accusation would be easy to grasp. But Richard Potter was not even in Andover on 1 September 1824; he was performing in Newburyport, Massachusetts, at the time. And the items Gale was claiming he had lost (he placed a value on them of almost five hundred dollars) and Potter had found were not so easily moveable—or, for that matter, misplaceable. They included a bureau, a secretary, five feather beds, three bedsteads, a trundle bed ("under bed"), twelve pillows, a brass clock, a brass kettle, and an assortment of bolsters, coverlets, quilts, blankets, sheets, and pillowcases. Clearly, they were among the furnishings of the inn that Rix had bought from Gale. Who rightly owned them now? Gale was arguing that he had never conveyed them to Rix; Potter seems to have understood that they came with the inn, which he was now renting, and thus that they belonged to Perkins. The disagreement was thoroughly complicated by Perkins's death in mid-April 1825: his will was subsequently adjudged invalid, and his estate went into probate for settlement, a process that took several years to complete.

Gale, who like Perkins (although perhaps rather less successfully) dealt extensively in real estate, was living in New Chester in the fall of 1824, but he traveled to nearby Andover in early October because he was holding a public auction of several tracts of land there on 2 October—holding it in Richard Potter's inn (formerly his own), in fact. Certainly he would have seen then that the furnishings in question were no longer in the inn, and probably would have questioned Potter about this at that time. At the beginning of April 1825, he came to Andover to confront Potter about the matter again. A witness at the tavern, where their meeting occurred, deposed that

John Gale made a demand of Richard Potter for some house hold furniture which said Gale claimed as his property and at the same time Mr. Gale offered Potter a paper which Gale said was a note against Potter but being at some distance from them I did not see any Name to it by their conversation I understood Potter that he had agreed to give them up that evening, but said he had not conversed with Mrs. Potter on the subject and it was late in the evening he was tired and he would not give them up that night for five hundred Dollars that he was going away the next Day & should be back the first of May & if he would wait till then he would give them up[.]

And here (along with a hint at Potter's likely culpability in this case) we come, perhaps, to the crux of the problem: Richard Potter had—for months, it would seem—delayed discussing the whole issue with Sally, and now would not be doing so for at least another month.

*Gale v. Potter* ultimately went against Richard Potter: a jury found for Gale and assessed damages of $218.60 against Potter. Potter immediately appealed the verdict and, with the litigants' approval, the appeals court (the Superior Court of Judicature) appointed a three-man committee to investigate the case. The committee held its hearing in late April 1826 and again found for Gale, although it reduced his damages to $154.35. (Gale's costs [$43.25], the referees' costs [$50.48], and the court's costs [$147.12] brought the total assessment against Potter to $395.20.)

In its everyday operations, Potter's tavern/inn business apparently paid for itself. Probate accounts relating to Roger E. Perkins's estate for the period from late 1825 to early 1828 indicate that Potter was probably paying a rent of about twenty-five to thirty dollars per month for the tavern stand. Potter had been able to find another man, John Sholes, from nearby Goshen, New Hampshire, to sublet and take over the operation of the tavern as of the spring of 1825, and Sholes would have been paying the rent—and pocketing most or all of the profits—of the business after that time. Sholes was a married man, with at least one child already; another, a son, would be born in Andover in 1827. He had previously had some experience in Goshen as a tavern keeper, and he certainly made a respectable showing, for he was "very tall, very dignified and very precise in speech and address."

So finally most of the tavern business was off of Potter's shoulders, although the records do show that he was responsible for some rent in 1827 and was also reimbursed for making significant repairs to the building then. Once we factor in the Gale lawsuit, however, the picture changes: another large legal obligation was now hanging over him during this period, in company with the one from Smithfield, Rhode Island, and the still-unpaid debt of Peter Rix.

But if the financial consequences of Potter's abortive tavern-keeping project were daunting, the personal consequences were probably more damaging still. For at least two reasons, it was surprising—a friend of Richard Potter's might have said, highly concerning—that Potter ever settled on the venture of operating a tavern in the first place, however convenient the business might be and whatever opportunities it might give Sally to bring some income to the family. The first reason was that Richard Potter himself had acquired in Andover a reputation as a strong temperance man; the second—more sobering still, if you will, and doubtless closely connected to the first—was that Sally Potter had acquired a reputation as a severe alcoholic.

Richard Potter's personal temperance was regularly mentioned in the early accounts of his history. Ketchum noted that Potter was "an early mover in the cause of temperance," and the *Boston Journal* reported that "in all his habits Potter was an example of industry and sobriety. Although liquors were then by custom dispensed freely in public and private houses, he was said to have been one of the strictest temperance men." But Sally, so fortunately matched with her husband in so many other respects, in this one was not. Some reports, as we have already seen, suggested that it was her tendency to intemperance that led Richard to move from Boston to New Hampshire in the first place; others, pointing to a later onset, speculated that the death of her daughter in 1831 or the shameful behavior of her children "drove her to seek 'some nepenthe to her soul' in the oblivion of continual inebriation." There is widespread agreement that in her later years—she died in 1836, one year after her husband, at the early age of forty-nine—she was severely alcoholic, and Ketchum concludes that "she died the victim of her own indulgence." The *Boston Journal* reporter indicates that Sally stopped performing with and assisting her husband because she "had become so intemperate that he would not allow her to travel with him any longer." (Sally last performed with her husband in 1823, near the end of their national tour.)

There are other indicators that Sally's alcoholism was already a significant problem by the time she became a tavern keeper for a while in 1824. Most dramatically, in the fall of 1825—this was some months after Richard had turned the tavern operation over to John Sholes, so Sally would no longer have had immediate access to alcohol outside of her own home—Richard felt compelled to the desperate measure of cutting off her credit. This sad legal notice, dated 31 October, appeared in the *New-Hampshire Patriot* in early November that year: "All persons are forbid trusting any person on my account, without a special order from me. RICHARD POTTER, of Andover, N.H." This could only have concerned his wife: his children were not even teenagers yet, and his nephew Cromwell had not yet moved to Andover. Whether she was purchasing liquor during his frequent exhibition trips away from home or was simply indulging in alcohol-fueled extravagances, Sally had already reached the point where he could no longer place any trust in her self-control.

Richard was forced again to post (and was mocked for) a similar legal notice late in his life, in 1834, and perhaps it was their awareness of that later *contretemps* that has led some historians to date Sally's disability to the time of her daughter's death. But clearly it was well established long before then. Whether Richard was still in deep denial about her addiction in 1824 or was simply hopeful that the responsibilities and opportunities of innkeeping would help her triumph over her weakness, he was taking an enormous risk by installing her in that position. They both paid an enormous price for it; and the payments were not done yet.

V

For the next few years, Richard Potter's professional life settled, for the first time, into a less arduous pattern of regional touring. He traveled as far south as Providence and as far northeast as Portland, but for the most part confined his tours to eastern Massachusetts (the Greater Boston area, of course, but also Salem, Newburyport, Haverhill, Concord) and southeastern New Hampshire (Portsmouth, Exeter, Dover). These were modest out-and-back circuits from Andover, New Hampshire, or from Boston, so that, while he was regularly on the road for weeks at a time, he was also frequently back home with his family.

His family, of course, needed his attention. He and Sally had been away from their two children for five years; Richard junior and Jeanette, roughly five and four years old when their parents left, were now, at ten and nine, almost strangers to them. And Sally, unfortunately, was increasingly incapable of fulfilling the responsibilities of day-to-day parenting.

For Richard junior, in particular, Richard Potter felt responsibilities and made plans. Like many fathers, he had a profession in which he could train his son and a business that he could hope to pass on to him. He could also expect to pass the farm on to his son eventually, of course; but the farm was primarily a homestead for him, and farming simply an avocation, not a profession. But now that he was home again, he could start to pass on his performing skills: he could begin to train young Richard in balancing, dancing, acrobatics, slack-wire dancing, and the general business of being his father's assistant, with the prospect of training him ultimately in sleight of hand and even ventriloquism as well. It was perhaps a bit late to be beginning on this kind of professional apprenticeship, but that couldn't be helped now, and anyway Richard Potter himself had begun his own training quite a bit later than this, in his late teens. So now young Richard's new course of studies began in earnest; now

Richard senior was not only rehearsing his own routines while he was at home but also teaching his son the fundamentals of balancing and acrobatics—the skills which the father had pursued at the beginning of his own career but which he now, in his forties, had mostly left off performing himself. Richard could thus expect eventually to be able to contribute real variety to his father's exhibitions; he would not simply be performing lesser versions of stunts that were already on the program.

Richard's training continued for four years before he performed with his father in his own right. Very possibly he began to travel at least occasionally with his father before this as an assistant, but he was never mentioned on a program until the last days of 1827. He would have needed every one of those years of preparation.

We catch one other tiny glimpse of an aspect of Richard Potter's involvement in his local community at this time only as he was ending it. In September 1825, he was recorded as among ten men who withdrew from the First Universal Society at that time. This was the Universalist Church in Andover. It had been organized only after Potter had left Andover, in 1819, so he could not have discovered and joined it until 1824, the year that the new church also raised and completed its meetinghouse The church had engaged Robert Bartlett, a circuit-riding Universalist minister in New Hampshire, as its first, part-time preacher, and Bartlett continued thereafter to maintain his connection with the church; in 1835 he would conduct the services and deliver the sermon at Richard Potter's own funeral. This is the only church affiliation that Richard Potter is ever known to have entered. He was raised in a conservative Anglican household on the Frankland estate; the household of Rev. Daniel Oliver, where he lived in 1809–10, had been rigidly puritanical, and the First Church of Roxbury, in which he had been married (presumably, because it was his bride's church), had been quite conservative, too. But Universalism, with its belief in a loving God and universal salvation for men and its strong associations with antislavery sentiment, was a good fit for his personal creed.

We also have good reason to believe that, in these first years back in New England, Richard Potter reestablished his connection with Henry K. Oliver. While the Potters had been traveling for years across the country, Oliver had completed his studies at Dartmouth College in 1818, and then in 1819 had moved from Boston to Salem to teach school there. Despite his youthfulness, his talents and dedication were such that he quickly made a name for himself in his new home, so much so that, at the age of twenty-three, he was selected as the orator of the day in Salem for the Fourth of July celebration in 1824, a signal honor and distinction. Whether Richard Potter had passed through Salem and met Oliver in late 1823 on his way north to New Hampshire, we do not know (as mentioned before, Oliver might have been the person who put Richard Potter in touch with Andrew Dunlap at this time). But in any event Richard Potter, who had exhibited a few times in Salem in earlier years, now visited and performed in the town again in late April 1824. This time he surely met Oliver and learned something of the latter's activities and developing prospects, because barely five weeks later—an otherwise almost inexplicably brief period, for an itinerant performer would usually try to space his visits to a particular town a year or more apart so as not to let novelty lapse into familiarity—Richard Potter returned to Salem once again. He returned to be present for the town's Fourth of July celebration, so that he could honor his friend with his presence and savor his friend's address; presumably Oliver also attended at least one of Richard's own performances either that April or that July.

Certainly Henry K. Oliver did not disappoint. His Fourth of July address, in fact, spoke directly to Richard Potter's own fondest hopes and most cherished beliefs. As Oliver's biographer records about this "oration [that] was long remembered and spoken of highly," he dwelt enthusiastically on the cause of Greek independence, and "'denounced the melancholy exception to the purity of our institutions, *the scourge and curse of negro slavery,*' and also 'the persecution of the Indians in Georgia.'" (Richard Potter had just had an opportunity to see that persecution of the Indians firsthand as he traveled across formerly Creek territories in Georgia in the late summer of 1822. And Henry Oliver, son of a missionary to the Indians of Maine and New York, would have been sensitive to Indian persecutions anywhere.) Surely Potter did not disappoint, either. And henceforth Salem became for a while one of his familiar stops; he returned there to perform twice more in 1825, and then it was the first place where he introduced his son, Master Richard, as a performer at the very end of 1827.

As he began reestablishing himself in his familiar New England territory, Richard Potter again, as he had sometimes done in the past, occasionally combined his exhibitions with those of another performer to produce a program of even greater variety and novelty. A passing instance of this occurred early after his return, during a long stand in Boston in the summer of 1824, when he performed at Concert Hall for almost eight full weeks (at this time he also began advertising his exhibitions occasionally with a new motto, "Be Merry and Wise," a practice that he continued for a few years). Toward the end of his run there, he announced a "Great Exhibition" for one evening:

"Mr. Potter, the Ventriloquist, has it in his power to announce to the Ladies and Gentlemen of Boston, and to the lovers of music in particular, that he has engaged Mrs. Bray, the celebrated vocalist, lately from the Theatre, Kingston, Jamaica, who will, in addition to his evening's entertainment, sing many popular Airs, and recite the Seven Ages of Woman." Mrs. Sarah Bray may have returned most recently from an engagement in Jamaica, but she was a familiar and popular presence in Boston: she was an established actress, singer, and dancer with the Boston Theatre company, where her late husband, John (1782–1822), had also performed as an actor and musical composer. They were originally from England and had come to Boston from the Philadelphia Theatre in 1815. Her husband had retired in 1822 because of ill health and died soon thereafter, so she was now supporting their six children alone; she would have been very glad for supplementary employment when the theater was not in season, and Potter would have been well aware of this. Her connection with Richard Potter at this point provides one more glimpse of his recurring interactions with the Boston theater community, and another hint of the generous impulses that so regularly motivated him.

This Boston stand was also noteworthy in that, toward its end, Potter resurrected his rarely performed "anti-combustible MAN SALAMANDER" demonstration—passing a red-hot iron bar over his tongue, drawing it through his hands, bending it with his bare feet, and immersing his hands and feet in molten lead. As we have seen, he tended to introduce this performance only toward the end of a long stand, as a way of attracting repeat customers. He was presenting it now, he said, "for the first time in this city." It was also probably the last time he ever performed it; henceforth it disappeared entirely from his advertisements.

A more sustained period of combined exhibitions came in 1826, when a new performer, a Monsieur Weiss, appeared on the Boston scene. Weiss presented himself as "an Austrian subject, pupil of the celebrated Olivre," and claimed to have "distinguished himself in the principal cities of Europe." Performing a wide variety of legerdemain deceptions, and also some hot-iron, molten-lead, and strong-man feats, he exhibited in Boston for a week and a half and then in Charlestown for another week. He was accompanied by a young apprentice who "will exhibit his skill in the gymnastic art and balancing by forming pyramids." When and where Richard Potter met Weiss we do not know (Potter was himself performing in Shrewsbury, some distance across the state, in the midst of Weiss's Boston performances, so he might not have seen them); but two months later, in Dover, New Hampshire, "Mr. Potter and Monsieur Weiss" were headlining together at the Court House. Potter and Weiss both did legerdemain—"curious but mysterious experiments, with Eggs, Money, Fruit, Birds, Boxes, Cards, &c."; Potter delivered his "Dissertation on Noses" (with songs) and displayed his powers of ventriloquism; and Weiss's pupil, now introduced as "The Kamtchatkan Boy, only 12 years of age," presented "wonderful feats of BALLANCING, &c. assisted by Mons. Weiss." Dover was a small town, so Potter and Weiss were testing and refining their exhibition on the road. They appeared together again less than four weeks later in Exeter, New Hampshire; they probably had been giving performances in other north-of-Boston towns and villages as well.

Potter and Weiss then continued to Boston itself. Weiss, of course, had been performing there only three months earlier and could not by himself have hoped for much renewed patronage now, but Potter, a favorite, had not performed there for a year (saving a one-night performance in Charlestown the previous December) and had confidence of a good reception. This time they booked one of Potter's preferred venues, the Concert Hall, and they exhibited there for a full month. They drew large audiences: in their first week the *Boston Evening Gazette* noted that "The Exhibitions of Messrs. Potter and Weiss, at Concert-Hall, have been well attended this week, and deserved all the patronage they received," and in their last they added an extra performance "In consequence of an overflow of Company last evening." Thereafter they went their separate ways. Weiss performed alone a few weeks later in Keene, New Hampshire. He had clearly learned and gained much from his brief association with Potter: his new exhibition title, "Be Merry and Wise," was one he had taken directly from Potter (although they had never used it in their joint newspaper advertisements), and almost all of his specifically featured acts—"The Mysterious Bag," "Games of the Tumerous Balls," "The Wonderful Factory"—were also Potter's.

On Richard Potter's side, the potential advantages of a collaboration with Monsieur Weiss may have been rather different. He probably did not profit from his share of their net proceeds more than or even as much as he would have on his own: indeed, soon after Weiss left town Potter resumed his exhibitions in Boston *solus* and continued performing at Concert Hall for an additional three weeks. He probably did enjoy and profit from learning new techniques from Weiss even as he shared his own, but there is no evidence that any of Weiss's tricks made their way into his own regular repertoire. But, more than these, he may have been taking lessons not as a performer but as a teacher. Weiss's pupil, the Kamtchatkan Boy, was training in the arts of gymnastics and balancing, just as Richard junior was; and the two boys were the same age. By working with Weiss, Richard Potter could see exactly how Weiss was teaching his pupil, and how that pupil's abilities and skills compared with his own son's.

Richard Potter must have been making good money throughout this year. In his Boston performances he could charge fifty cents for front seats (twenty-five cents for back seats); and Concert Hall was a large venue, appropriate only for a performer who could draw large crowds. But something was wrong. In January 1826 he had contracted another large debt, more than $125, which fell due in June; that was now long overdue and still unrepaid. In March of that year, he had again been caught performing without a license, this time in Shrewsbury (near Worcester, Massachusetts), and now he would be facing a certain fine for that offense, too. Worse, he had also failed to repay an even larger debt to his Andover neighbor Aaron Cilley for the many major improvements he had hired Cilley to build on his farm—a new barn, a new bridge, a new shed frame. Somehow, money was being spent even faster than Potter could earn it.

The tavern venture had already been a failure. Richard Potter now resolved to take more drastic measures. In late September 1826, he submitted the following advertisement to the *New-Hampshire Patriot:* "A Farm for sale or to let at the halves in Andover, N.H." Not two weeks earlier he had already mortgaged the farm to Samuel Butterfield, a local lawyer-businessman-farmer, for $306. Not finding a buyer or a renter, later that fall he moved to Boston. He left Sally, Richard junior, and Jeanette behind in Andover.


VI

Richard could never have left Sally and Jeanette (now only about eleven years old) alone on their own; even with hired help for the farm, Sally would no longer have been able to manage. So now he reached out to his extended family. When he left Andover and temporarily moved to Boston at the beginning of October 1826, he also arranged for his cousin Cromwell Potter and his sister Phebe Potter to move up to Andover; they would help hold his family and his farm together in his absence.

Phebe Potter was probably the second-oldest of Richard's sisters; like him, she was a mulatto. She was now about fifty years old, and she was a paragon of domestic competence: Eastman described her as "an invaluable member of the community"—"honest, industrious, an excellent cook and a competent nurse." Probably she was also literate and numerate (she had been raised with and was very close in age to her sister Julia, who had been taught to read and write by Mrs. Swain, and had probably received the same advantages). Thus she could run the home, and she was an appropriate mother-figure and care-taker for Sally and Jeanette Potter. Cromwell Potter, now about thirty-one years old, had farming skills, so he was capable of overseeing the farm. He was the elder son of another of Richard's sisters, Sidney. Sidney, like Richard and Phebe, was a mulatto; Cromwell's father was probably Reuben Titus, a black man. Cromwell and Phebe were both quite dark. However uncertain and intrigued their Andover neighbors might originally have been about the possibly exotic racial backgrounds of Richard and Sally Potter, then, the Potter place was now, very clearly, a black household.

Richard's own removal to Boston was part of a business plan. He had learned during the previous year that he could attract repeat audiences in Boston for significant stretches of time. Now he would try to reclaim those audiences, and win new ones, with some new strategies. This time, he was not simply relying on varying his programs, as he and his fellow performers would typically do to stretch out or reinvigorate a stand. Instead, he developed a novel approach. Rather than treat Boston as one big city, he would approach it now instead as a collection of distinct areas and neighborhoods, and he would bring his performances into many different neighborhoods, varying his venues and his schedule of exhibitions by the week and even by the night. If he were already resident in Boston, this would be practicable for him; he could easily travel the short distance from his centrally located residence to each evening's place of performance and would also be spared the usual touring expenses of room and board. It was important, too, that he put his plan into effect quickly: the major part of his mortgage payment to Butterfield fell due on 18 November, the entirety was then due on the following 19 January, and beyond that dire deadline he had all those other accumulated debts and pending court judgments still to satisfy.

Richard Potter began his new, multipronged Boston campaign early in October 1826. His logistical arrangements were so manifold as to be confusing, and indeed he himself occasionally became confused by them, to his own detriment. But the plan was basically as follows. First, he set up a regular schedule of appearances at a new, smaller and more locally oriented venue—"Mr. William Crombie's and Mansur's New Hall, in Cambridge st. sign of the Leopard." Second, he scheduled a few interspersed performances at much larger Boston venues—not only Concert Hall, where he had frequently performed in the past, but also at Pantheon Hall. Finally, he also made arrangements to perform in outlying areas of Greater Boston, first in Charlestown, just across the mouth of the Charles River, and then in Roxbury, just south of Boston across the Neck (Boston's peninsular connection to the rest of the mainland).

(He may well have done the same in Cambridge, just across the Charles River to the west, but no records of performances there are extant.)

William Crombie and Stephen Mansur were innkeepers; their new hall allowed them to supplement their business occasionally with exhibitions such as Richard Potter's. Cambridge Street, although a major thoroughfare, was nevertheless far from the center of Boston, and would not have been a desirable location for an itinerant performer hoping to draw large audiences quickly in the big city. But Crombie and Mansur's new hall would have been a very attractive location for its more immediate neighborhood. It was located on the north side of Beacon Hill; it was, in fact, very close to Richard Potter's new residence in Boston (Ridgeway Lane, where he was now living, terminated at Cambridge Street at its northern end; Cambridge Street's intersection with Blossom Street, where Crombie's Tavern stood, was only three short blocks west). For Potter, then, performing at the Sign of the Leopard was like performing in his hometown. And we can be confident that now, very possibly for the first time, many of his friends and neighbors in Boston's black community were in his audiences. Acquaintances who might not have felt comfortable going to Concert Hall to see his performances the previous year would have felt much less hesitation about catching his show at the local tavern.

Concert Hall, a major performance space and one of Potter's regular venues for his large Boston shows, was located in north central Boston, northeast of the Common. Pantheon Hall, a smaller but still sizable venue, was toward the southern end of the city, near the southeast corner of the Common, on Boylston Square. Thus these halls, too, would have drawn on audiences from very different regions of the city. Performances in Charlestown and in Roxbury, finally, would have been decidedly local events. In Charlestown, Potter usually performed at Whitney's Hotel, although at least once he exhibited instead in "Massachusetts Hall, adjoining Ramsey's Tavern." In Roxbury, he performed at the Roxbury Hotel.

Potter's travel arrangements to any of these places would have been fairly easy, and his trip to Crombie and Mansur's, of course, required only a walk of a few short blocks through his own neighborhood. But if the traveling was easy, the scheduling was not; and the strain of juggling so many venues back and forth (in the second week of October, for example, his advertisements put him variously at Crombie and Mansur's, Concert Hall, and Pantheon Hall all in the same week) took its toll. Potter's newspaper advertisements during this last quarter of 1826 were frequently quite brief, concluding "For particulars see bills" or "For particulars see small bills"; he would be posting his bills, with fuller details about his performances, in the neighborhoods that he was targeting. But even when brief, his newspaper advertisements sometimes became rather confused and confusing during this time. For example, he published this brief notice in the *Boston Daily Advertiser* on 7 October: "MR. POTTER, the Ventriloquist, will exhibit next week, on Monday and Friday evenings, 8th and 12th inst. And at Crombie and Mansur's new Hall, in Cambridge-street, on Wednesday evening, the 10th." If he would be performing at Crombie and Mansur's on Wednesday, where would he be performing on Monday and Friday? Only the small bills he was posting could have said. And, worse, he got the days all wrong: Monday, Wednesday, and Friday were actually 9, 11, and 13 October, not 8, 10, and 12. Eventually the general messiness of his arrangements seriously affected his trade: "Mr. Potter, the Ventriloquist, respectfully informs the public, that in consequence of a misapprehension of the proprietor of Pantheon Hall, several mistakes in the newspapers, and not wishing to mislead the public, that he will not exhibit in the city this week as previously intended; but he will probably be able to give exhibitions in this city next week—the time and place will be mentioned in the papers of the day. Mr. P. wishes to add that irregularity in the advertisements was not his blunder."

Potter performed in and around Boston on a demanding schedule for the entire last three months of 1826, steadily amassing the new funds he would need to salvage and reestablish his family's situation. In early December he finally brought suit against Peter Rix for the three-hundred-dollar debt that had gone unrepaid since early 1824. In January he returned for a while to his home in Andover, New Hampshire; he needed to pay off the mortgage on his farm. He repaid Butterfield three hundred dollars on 15 January, and Butterfield relinquished his claim on the property; Potter's homestead, at least, was again free and clear of debt. Despite all his recent earnings, however, his finances were still badly stretched and even chaotic. In March, he won his case against Peter Rix (Andrew Dunlap served as his attorney), which presumably the court then enforced; in April, on the other hand, he defaulted on Cilley's case against him, but at least now he would have had the money available to satisfy Cilley's claims. And then Parker Noyes, his former lawyer, sued him in June for twenty-five dollars in attorney's fees that Potter had not paid for the unsuccessful defense of the Gale case.

Potter is listed in Butterfield's mortgage quitclaim as "Richard Potter of Boston," who "formerly lived" on the farm, so we know that his return to Andover at this time was still temporary. But he could not keep limiting his performance territory to Greater Boston forever. He needed now to resume his training of Richard junior, and by the by he might also pursue some brief local tours as opportunity presented. (We know, for example, that he performed at least one evening in Amherst, New Hampshire, about halfway between Boston and Andover, New Hampshire, in May. He probably gave at least a few other exhibitions on the same short tour.)

In late May and then again in June 1827, he had to deal with some unpleasant legal obligations, and in both instances he made a virtue of necessity. At the end of May he needed to be in Providence, Rhode Island, for his jury trial on the charge of having performed without a license in Smithfield back in late 1823. (The decision, as we have seen, went against him, and the penalties were enormous, but he immediately appealed the verdict, thereby postponing the reckoning for the time being.) Directly after the trial, he gave at least three performances in Providence. Similarly, in mid-June he had to travel to Worcester, Massachusetts, to answer court charges of performing without a license in Shrewsbury in March 1826. (This time he pleaded guilty; he was fined ten dollars, plus court costs of more than eighteen dollars.) Immediately after this trial, he performed in Worcester for at least three evenings. Then he returned straight to Boston to exhibit for at least three evenings there, this time again in the prestigious Concert Hall.*

The court case in Providence became something of a career marker for Potter because it brought him a surprising amount of publicity. The combination of Potter's now nationwide fame, the gentle harmlessness of his entertainments, and the breathtaking size of the fine imposed upon him caught the attention of editors looking for interesting filler items. A careful, straightfor-

---

*Perhaps it is worth mentioning here a story that Goodwin reported in 1872:

> The intemperance of [Potter's] wife was a perpetual source of trouble to him. In his absence she would run up heavy bills against him and on one occasion he resisted payment. Sam'l Butterfield brought an action for its recovery and Parker Noyes and George W. Nesmith were employed by Potter, the defense being that his wife was intemperate, and that the goods were not necessaries. The amount was greatly curtailed, but the case went against Potter.

The circumstantial details in this anecdote point to a time in mid-1827, when Richard Potter was living in Boston but Sally Potter was still in Andover. (Alternatively, it might have dated back as far as late 1825, when Potter published that legal notice forbidding anyone from "trusting any person on my account.") But no such case was ever brought to trial in Merrimack County. Still, since Nesmith was one of Goodwin's sources, it is difficult to dismiss the incident entirely. Perhaps it unfolded as a legal dispute in which Potter engaged his lawyers and a settlement was reached before a suit was filed.

ward notice of the case and the arguments was published on 30 May by the *Providence Patriot* and eventually reprinted by a few other newspapers. But soon a more opinionated report was published by the *New York Statesman*: "Potter, the ventriloquist and juggler, has been mulcted in the small sum of $400, for practicing his craft of boiling eggs in his hat, making guineas of ha'pennies, and delivering lectures upon noses, in Providence, R. I. without the formality of a license from the Town Council. He should contrive, by some slight of his hand, to evade the collection of such an ungracious penalty."

This brief report was widely circulated, in whole or in part (without the second sentence), by newspaper editors not only across New England but from as far away as Philadelphia, Baltimore, Washington, Cincinnati, and Charleston—a strong suggestion that Richard Potter was still well remembered in most of those cities and that his reputation was well known in all of them. Perhaps "mulcted" had not acquired, by 1827, the undertone of "cheated" or "swindled" that it now carries (the *OED* gives no instance of such a usage before 1857); but it probably had (as the immediate context of "juggler" and "slight of hand" also imply), because a Providence newspaper (the *Literary Cadet*), reacting defensively to a brief notice of the verdict (merely the first sentence of the *New York Statesman*'s story) as reported in a Philadelphia newspaper, took umbrage at its "very sneering manner." In any event, the article, between its opening irony ("the small sum of $400") and its closing outspokenness ("such an ungracious penalty"), conveys a sense of sympathy for Potter.

This sympathy was not universal. One small Massachusetts newspaper, after reporting briefly that "Potter, the Ventriloquist, has been fined $400 at Providence, for exhibiting his feats of skill without a license," editorialized very briefly, "*Good.*" And the *Providence Literary Cadet,* provoked by the *New York Statesman*'s suggestion that Potter had been treated too harshly by the court, offered a strident defense of the authorities in terms that make very clear what was at stake: "As the proper authorities of the town were not disposed to be browbeaten and put down, by a mere wandering juggler, they prosecuted him, very justly, for his audacity, and at the last term of the Common Pleas, he was fined four hundred dollars, a very suitable punishment, for the impudence and insolence of a wandering juggler.—The application of this punishment will, we hope, teach the black *gentleman,* that when he comes among us, he must not set the laws at defiance." This is not simply anti-itinerancy or antitheatricalism. The sneering allusion to "the black *gentleman*" (guilty of browbeating, audacity, impudence, and insolence) makes very clear that the *Literary Cadet*'s editor's animosity is essentially racist.

Rhode Island, at least, once one of his most regular touring areas, was becoming a less hospitable territory for Richard Potter. While he continued to perform there in later years, he did so much less frequently than before. Henceforth he would instead devote much more of his time to other parts of New England, especially New Hampshire and Vermont (a state with particularly strong antislavery sentiments). In these regions, for the most part, his race did not become an issue: people generally cherished their by now widespread notion that he was of East Indian extraction, "the native place of many famous jugglers." (Potter's frequent demonstration of "his WONDERFUL DECEPTIONS with TUMOROUS BALLS, in which he will give an imitation of the HINDOO JUGGLERS" only encouraged the misunderstanding, as he would certainly have realized.) The poet John Godfrey Saxe, born (in 1816) and raised in far northern Vermont near the Canadian border, "once, when a lad" saw Potter perform there — "a foreign chap," he later called him when he celebrated Potter as "The Great Magician." "I ne'er shall see another show / To rank with the immortal 'Potter's'," he fondly recalled, noting that, some forty years later, "'Potter, the Great Magician' . . . is still vividly remembered by many people in New Hampshire and Vermont."

We know of one other trip that Richard Potter made this summer, and it was a fairly extensive one. In August, he traveled to Saratoga Springs, New York, already a highly fashionable summer resort and spa, and performed there for a week. This would have required a trip of some 200 miles from Boston, or at least 160 miles (but over much rougher terrain and through less settled territory) from Andover, New Hampshire. Presumably, then, he would have exhibited at other towns along his way, out and back, and may very well have spent some time again in Albany, for the first time in years; but we have no records of any such events. We can at least be confident that he found the stand in Saratoga Springs quite profitable, because he made the same long trip the following August, too. Presumably he also traveled extensively in Vermont on both occasions.

By fall, if not before, Potter was back in Boston. This time, again, he was careful not to seek his large, fashionable audiences too soon after his last visit; as he had also done late the preceding fall, he devoted his time instead to the outlying communities. He exhibited for a few weeks north of Boston in Charlestown, again at Whitney's Hotel, and also promised at least one performance south of Boston, at the Savin Hill Hotel in Dorchester. It was probably in December (but possibly a few months later, in early 1828) that he finally returned to Andover, putting a conclusion to his period of residence in Boston. It had been a profitable, difficult, arduous year.

## VII

We have already noted that, when Richard Potter moved to Boston in late 1826, he took up residence on Beacon Hill on the edge of one of Boston's most prominent black communities. It is time now to fill in what can be known of his relationships within that neighborhood—which was much more white than black—at this stage of his life. Potter had been part of Boston's black community in the years before his move to Andover in 1815, of course; but he had inevitably lost regular contact with it thereafter, although he could have renewed ties there during his occasional tours to Boston. When he returned to New England in late 1823, he had been away from the Boston area for five years, and nonresident there for more than eight. Now, in late 1826, he was returning, for a time, to a community in which he had last lived some twelve years before. Much had changed in the interim.

Ridgeway Lane, where Potter lived now, only a block directly north of the gold-domed State House, was a back alley that bisected what had originally been one large city block. Lying between and parallel to Hancock Street to its west and Temple Street to its east, it ran north-south the length of the block between its northern terminus on Cambridge Street and its southern on Derne Street. It had until recently simply been called Ridgeway's Alley, and Ridgeways and their heirs still owned a cluster of lots facing onto Hancock and others around the corner on Cambridge. Most of the residents whose lots abutted Ridgeway Lane lived in dwellings facing either Hancock or Temple; Ridgeway was primarily the alley that provided access to the stables, barns, and backyards of Hancock Street and Temple Street houses. So Ridgeway Lane itself was still relatively unpopulated at this time. The 1818 *Boston Directory* listed only five individuals or families living there, and the 1826 Boston Tax Records show only three residences on the street, one of which housed unidentified black tenants. But the area was ripe for development, and that development was now beginning to accelerate.

Typically there were a few blacks as well as a modest number of whites living on Ridgeway Lane. William Nell had lived there in 1816; Peter Howard, a black musician who was now becoming a close Masonic associate of Potter's, had lived there with his family for many years, until as recently as 1820. Richard Potter's own landlord, one William Johnson, who at the time lived in Plymouth, was probably the "Free Colored" William Johnson listed in the census as living in Boston in 1830. In 1827, there were three other blacks (some perhaps with their families) on the street in addition to Richard Potter (there were also twelve whites). One of them, a servant named Harry Green, lived in a dwelling that was owned by Gardiner Greene; the latter was a tremendously wealthy, socially prominent Bostonian (who had made his fortune, incidentally, from a plantation in Demerara, Guyana, so he was a significant slaveholder); presumably Green was in service to Gardiner Greene, and he may well have taken his surname from his master. The other two—James Howe, a hairdresser, and Peter Osborn, a seaman—shared a single dwelling (the same dwelling that had been let to black tenants the year before, so they may have been living there then as well). We can be quite sure that Richard Potter knew both Howe and Osborn well, since James Howe soon (midsummer 1828) petitioned the African Lodge to be considered for membership and became a member shortly thereafter. Potter, as his immediate neighbor, would definitely have figured in Howe's Masonic introductions and initiation.

While Richard Potter had black neighbors on Ridgeway Lane itself, however, the rest of his mini-neighborhood—the large original block, bounded by Hancock, Cambridge, Temple, and Derne, which Ridgeway bisected—was entirely white. And among these approximately 175 individuals and families in his new neighborhood was one old friend, Samuel Dillaway junior, who with his family (his wife, son, and two daughters) was living just around the corner on Derne Street, at the south end of Ridgeway. (Dillaway's son, Charles K. Dillaway, now twenty-three years old, a recent graduate of Harvard and already well launched on his profession as an educator and scholar, was listed at the address separately as an "Usher," a schoolteacher.) Dillaway may well have been instrumental in finding Potter's new lodging for him: since he was on the scene, he would have been well aware of any rental opportunities in the immediate vicinity. (Dillaway's residence here at this time also makes it all the easier for us to understand how William C. Nell came to learn about Potter's childhood connection with the Dillaway family in the first place.)

Another old acquaintance of Richard Potter's lived nearby as well: Nathaniel K. G. Oliver, now a schoolmaster, lived close by on Hancock Street. This was Henry K. Oliver's older brother: he was the very same person whose Harvard College commencement festivities, back in the summer of 1809, Richard Potter had helped prepare while he was working as a domestic for the Rev. Daniel Oliver's family. Since Richard Potter had remained close to Henry Oliver and had probably seen him again more than once in Salem during the preceding few years, it is reasonable to think, given this close neighborhood juxtaposition, that he and Nathaniel had reestablished at least a minimal relationship again now (and even that Henry Oliver might have looked in on Potter occasionally when visiting his brother there).

Like much of Boston, this was a neighborhood in which, save at the economic extremes (there were no mansions here, no hovels), people of all classes and professions mixed together. Potter's immediate neighbors included a great many skilled workmen—carpenters, masons, painters, bakers, mariners, a stair maker, a surveyor, a sailmaker, a machinist, a shoemaker, a chaise maker, a paper hanger, a slater, a butcher, a blacksmith. There were a great many merchants and shop owners—druggists, grocers, victuallers, hairdressers and barbers, dealers in West Indies goods or lumber or dry goods or hardware or crockery, a stationer, a jeweler, a broker. There were many professionals, too—schoolteachers and schoolmasters, lawyers, a physician, a clergyman—and many clerks. The high sheriff of Boston was one of Potter's neighbors; so were a bank president, the cashier (chief financial officer) of the largest bank in Boston, the president of an insurance company, and several men of means who could be listed simply as "Gentleman." And so were many gainfully employed individuals with lesser credentials—ordinary seamen, journeymen carpenters and masons and painters and printers, tenders (waiters), servants.

Although this particular block, apart from Ridgeway Lane itself, was in 1827 all white, it was very close to the center of the black community here on Beacon Hill. Belknap Street, where the African Baptist Church stood, effectively the very heart of black respectability and conscience in Boston, was only one very short block away, west of and parallel to Hancock Street; Myrtle Street, another center of black enterprise and residency in Boston, began at Hancock, intersected with Belknap, then continued west past South Russell, Butolph, and Garden Streets; May Street and Southack Street ran parallel to and just north of Myrtle; Pinkney Street, parallel and just south. All of this area was predominantly white and, in social and economic terms, thoroughly mixed. Here was where many of Richard Potter's closest black friends lived.

VIII

In the black community of Boston in the 1820s, there were several organizations that brought thoughtful and committed black leaders and activists together. The most venerable of these were the African Masonic Lodge, which, as we have already seen, had been chartered in 1784 (it had been organized eight years earlier), and the African Baptist Church, under the leadership of the Rev. Thomas Paul, which had been founded in 1805. There were other service-minded black organizations that might also attract black activists of one inclination or another: the African Humane Society, founded in 1819, was something of a spiritual successor or heir to the now-lapsed African Society that had been created as far back as 1796; a Massachusetts Coloured People Fund Society was in existence at least through 1821–24; and a group for several years organized an annual commemoration of the abolition of the slave trade (celebrated on 14 July). Eventually a few additional black churches formed on Beacon Hill as well: the Rev. Samuel Snowden's African Methodist Society opened its new building on May Street in 1824, and a new African Methodist Episcopalian Church building (with the Rev. James Lee) on Center Street was dedicated on Christmas Day in 1827. Beyond these established organizations, there were also occasional ad hoc celebrations for the black community, most notably a celebration of France's breakthrough recognition of Haiti's independence in 1825 (celebrated in Boston on 23 August that year) and a celebration of and banquet for "the African Prince," Abduhl Rahhaman, on 20 August 1828.

So far as we know, Richard Potter was involved with only one of these organizations, the African Masonic Lodge. He had joined it and participated actively in it, as we have seen, beginning in 1811, but within a few years he had moved away from Boston, and his association with it thereafter could have been only highly irregular and infrequent at best. In the interim, the poorly led and increasingly disengaged African Lodge had become moribund, its active membership dwindling to perhaps only a dozen individuals. But in the late 1820s, under new leadership, it revived and flourished; again it became one of the most prominent and respectable black organizations in Boston. Thus its records from this period give us a valuable window on the social network of an extremely important segment of Boston's black community.

Almost all of the Masons Richard Potter had known and associated with in 1811 and thereafter were now either dead or gone. One of the rare exceptions, Samson Moody, who after finally joining in November 1812 (his earlier petition to join in May 1812 had been rejected) had risen to become the long-time Master of the Lodge during much or all of the period 1817–25 (he had presided over the Lodge's dramatic decline), was certainly no attraction to Richard Potter, not after having borrowed $150 from him in early 1825 that, two years later, he had still not repaid (Potter would finally bring a suit against Moody for the debt in November 1827). It is very clear, however, that as of the fall of 1826, Richard Potter was, at least for that year-plus of his renewed Boston residence, very active, very prominent, and very distinguished in African Lodge affairs. The change in his degree of engagement clearly was due to the changes in the Lodge's membership and commitments, as it once again, in the spirit of Prince Hall, sought to make a difference in the living conditions and personal dignity of Boston's black community.

Early in this decade (January 1821), the Rev. Thomas Paul, pastor of the African Baptist Church and one of the most prominent blacks in Boston, had become a member of the Lodge and quickly was established in the position of chaplain. Several other increasingly prominent black Bostonians had also joined during Potter's absence from Boston. These included Peter Howard, a musician and barber, who had joined by 1817, when he showed up in the records as (Senior) Steward; Thomas Revaleon, who by 1817 was the Junior Steward; and Cornelius De Randamie, a hairdresser, who joined in late 1814 and by 1817 had ascended to the second-in-command position of Senior Warden. Another newcomer to Boston, John T. Hilton, a hairdresser, probably arrived in the early 1820s and, after his initiation into the Lodge, soon rose to positions of leadership: he was elected Junior Warden (1824), then Senior Warden (1825), then Master (1826), his position when Richard Potter rejoined the Lodge. He was probably more responsible than anyone else for the resurrection of the Lodge. The period of Hilton's ascendancy in the Lodge also saw a spate of new memberships: William Brown (a tender), Walker Lewis (a hairdresser), William Vassal (a tender), Thomas Dalton (a bootblack), and Lewis York (a tender), along with some others, were admitted to membership in 1825; David Walker (a clothes dealer) and James Barbadoes (a hairdresser), among others, in 1826. George R. Holmes, a barber, seems to have joined by 1828, as did Potter's new neighbor on Ridgeway Lane, James Howe. As Stephen Kantrowitz has noted of this period, Freemasonry's "combination of spiritual sustenance and practical experience proved irresistible to many of the men who led Boston's black activist community." These were the new members who now made the African Lodge attractive to Richard Potter; their fellowship, and their values and actions, now encouraged him to make the Lodge again a focus of his energies and attention.

In 1826–28, under the new leadership of John T. Hilton, the African Lodge was reforming itself in two significant ways. First, as a selective organization with explicit moral values and a long tradition of advocacy for the black community, it was renewing its emphasis on black rights and aspirations. Second, as a propertied institution with dues-paying members and ongoing financial obligations, it was emerging from a period of dereliction and beginning to put its financial and organizational affairs into order. The first emphasis, already strongly implicit in the activities of its current members, finds expression also in Hilton's "Address, Delivered before the African Grand Lodge of Boston,

No. 459, June 24th, 1828," published shortly thereafter in Boston. Here Hilton not only lamented the evils of slavery and its inconsistency with Christian, American, and universal values but, looking even beyond slavery, proclaimed forthrightly, "it is . . . our duty to advert to the causes which oppress our brethren, and endeavor to find out some means of redress for their grievances." The second was manifested in part by the Lodge's increasing attention to its formal status: it approached its chartering English Grand Lodge for the first time in decades to reaffirm its connection and expand its own authority as a lodge; it sought to reassert its own connections to and authority over sister and daughter African Lodges elsewhere in America; and finally it resolved all confusion about its status by declaring its independence from the English Grand Lodge and its authority as a Grand Lodge in its own right.

Richard Potter must have renewed his association with the African Lodge in July 1823, when he spent a month in Boston at the end of his great national tour, because his name figures prominently in an important letter sent by the African Lodge to the Grand Lodge of England at the beginning of 1824: he is listed as one of nine named higher-level members of the African Lodge—"Sampson H. Moody, Peter Howard, Abraham C. Derandamie, John T. Hilton, James Jackson, Zadock Lew, Samuel G. Gardner, Richard Potter, Lewis Walker"—who are petitioning for a resumption of communications and permission to confer additional, higher degrees of Masonry beyond the three degrees already permitted by their original warrant. Potter himself was not in Boston when this letter was drafted, on 5 January 1824, although he had passed through Boston and spent a few days there about two weeks earlier; he was now in the midst of his three-week stand in Concord, New Hampshire. But his place in this roll demonstrates that his Masonic brothers now regarded him as again an active member, indicating that his recommitment to the African Lodge the previous July had been strong.

After his return to New Hampshire, Potter had visited Boston only rarely and fleetingly in 1824, somewhat more often in 1825, and then for some two months in the summer of 1826 before finally reestablishing his residence in Boston at the beginning of October that year. Again he was received and welcomed as an important and valuable member; soon he was being given specific new responsibilities. Early this year a group of men from New York City had approached the African Lodge seeking a charter for their own new lodge, and a committee had been appointed to explore the possibility. Now, nine months later, "a Committee was then chosen, consisting of the W. [Worshipful] Master J. T. Hilton, Rd. Potter, C. DeRandamie to settle with the Committee which was sent on to New York to Establish there a Lodge which committee consisted of then M. W. [Most Worshipful] Master S. H. Moody[,] R. Bro. [Reverend Brother] Thos. Paul and Bro. John [?Hay]."

Meanwhile, the Lodge's most significant organizational initiative, its move toward regularizing its status and gaining greater authority, culminated in 1827, when, in June, the African Lodge "proceeded to and did declare themselves independent of any Lodge in the known World" and chose John T. Hilton "to write and publish the declaration of Independence," with whatever helpers he might choose, "and also to write the Independent Charter." Just as the (white) Grand Lodge of Massachusetts had done in 1782, the African Grand Lodge was now breaking free from its mother Grand Lodge.

The formal declaration of independence soon followed; it was published on the front page of the *Boston Daily Advertiser* on 29 June 1827. Noting that the Lodge, once languishing, was now flourishing but unable to proceed in its mission because the Grand Lodge of England continued to ignore it, "We have come to the conclusion that, with what knowledge we possess of masonry, and as people of colour by ourselves, we are and ought by rights to be, free and independent of other Lodges.—We do, therefore, with this belief, publicly declare ourselves free and independent of any Lodge from this day—and that we will not be tributary, or governed by any Lodge than that of our own."

It is impossible to overstate how deeply thrilling and significant this formal, public declaration would have been to the black men—Richard Potter among them—who put it forward. The very words and phrases of the closing paragraph of America's Declaration of Independence now were being used by "people of colour," not as a plea or moral assertion but as a performative claim. This statement, moreover, makes abundantly clear how the housekeeping side of the African Lodge's activities at this time, far from being compartmentalized away from the black advocacy side, was thoroughly consistent and continuous with it.

America's own Declaration of Independence was first drafted as a formal proclamation, then speedily published. The African Lodge's declaration of independence was published first; the preparation and signing of a formal document, the new charter, followed soon (but not immediately) thereafter. Written on parchment, the "Declaration of Independence. Proclaimed by the AFRICAN GRAND LODGE in the City of Boston, Commonwealth of Massachusetts and United States of America through her Officers" is not, however, a simple inscribing of the text already published in the *Boston Daily Advertiser;* and its tone is rather different. Although bearing the same date, 18 June 1827, this new document was as much a pledge of continued allegiance "to the most excellent principles and solemn ties of Ancient Free Masonry" as it was a declaration of independence from "our Mother, the Grand Lodge of England, . . . or any other Lodge or Lodges whatsoever." There is no longer any mention of grievances against or neglect by the parent institution. What this charter proclaims is the independence of a juvenile now attaining his majority, not the rebellion of a defiant subordinate.

There are several irregularities in this charter suggesting that the document itself was not, in fact, produced in 1827 but instead dates from somewhat later. (It definitely was created at least a few months later than its ostensible date, because a committee "to prepare an Independent Charter for the Grand African Lodge agreeable to the Declaration in the Newspaper" was not even formed until 26 August 1827.) The text itself, however, is not in dispute. Having already declared the African Grand Lodge's independence (now reaffirmed) from all other lodges, the charter takes care of three matters of business. First, in place of its now-rejected 1784 charter from the Grand Lodge of England, it now creates itself (we "do Create instead thereof this Charter"). Second, it provides for its own safekeeping. And finally, it enjoins upon the members ("brethren") of the African Grand Lodge "strict observance to ancient usages and customs that the same may be preserved unsullied and transmitted in its purity to succeeding generations, that they may under its happy influence enjoy peace, union, prosperity and safety forever."

What concerns us especially here is the second matter of business, the arrangement for the charter's safekeeping. The three Past Masters who signed the charter included the following instructions: "We do therefore agreeably to the power vested in us present this GRAND CHARTER to our most worthy brethren Richard Potter, C. A. De Randamie and Rev. Thomas Paul, Royal Arch Masons, and their successors to hold and to keep the same for the special benefit of Masonry and the good of our Brethren." Clearly this designation is a mark of honor and a vote of confidence: Richard Potter and his two Masonic brothers are being distinguished by the Past Masters as men especially worthy of an important trust.

Given all this evidence that Richard Potter's new commitment to the African Lodge was driven by his admiration for and companionability with the relatively new members who were now leading and driving it, and that he in turn was valued and highly esteemed by them, there can be no doubt but that he shared their interests and their values. Nor is there any doubt about what those interests and values were. As Stephen Kantrowitz has cogently argued of this period's black Masonic lodges in general: "That a powerful strain of diasporan racial collectivity and solidarity formed part of the meaning and appeal of early black Freemasonry seems beyond dispute. At the very least, it is clear that the people who most effectively and emphatically rejected white exclusion and derision became eager and early participants in black Freemasonry." This was especially true in 1826–30 of the African Lodge in Boston, whose leaders and members were notably prominent in their expressions of black pride and their advocacy for the black community. The list of Masons who were leaders of these advocacy organizations (notably the Massachusetts General Coloured Association and the earlier African Humane Society) or organizers of and featured speakers at the biggest ad hoc celebrations of black success (notably the committee celebrating France's recognition of Haiti's independence and the organizers of the banquet for Prince Abduhl Rahhaman) comprises a significant portion of the African Lodge: John T. Hilton, Thomas Dalton, Cornelius De Randamie, Rev. Thomas Paul, David Walker, Peter Howard, George R. Holmes, Porter Tidd, James Barbadoes, William Vassal, William Brown, Lewis York, James Howe. Several of the African Lodge brothers, moreover—John T. Hilton, David Walker, James Barbadoes, Peter Howard—would soon (in the early 1830s) become early and prominent leaders among the black Bostonians supporting William Lloyd Garrison's abolitionist initiatives.

These men could differ among themselves on political issues. The Reverend Paul, for example, had colonialist and separatist leanings (colonialism, advocated by many whites, proposed to repatriate blacks to Africa or resettle them in other black countries, notably Haiti), while David Walker was fiercely anticolonialist (the fourth and culminating Article of his *Appeal* was titled "Our Wretchedness in Consequence of the Colonizing Scheme"). But they all harked to and treasured the promises of their country's founding documents, insisted that their rights as Americans and as men were being wrongly denied, and sought to raise up their "afflicted brethren." David Walker may have been the most vehement and outspoken among them, but his voice was still theirs.

IX

This focus on Richard Potter's family problems, financial and legal difficulties, expanding social network, and Masonic involvements throughout 1824–29 has kept our attention on the private man. What of the public Mr. Potter during this while? What was it like to attend one of his exhibitions?

Like his mentor in magic and ventriloquism, James Rannie, Richard Potter had developed an extensive and extremely varied repertory of individual feats and numbers that he could with little notice work into his act. Within the field of legerdemain alone, he—like Rannie—often promised that he would offer "One Hundred Curious, but Mysterious Experiments" in an exhibition—and these would make but a part of that exhibition, and he was fully capable of varying the experiments from one evening to the next to the next. He performed "Experiments with Eggs, Money, Fruit, Birds, Boxes, &c."; he did card tricks; he broke raw eggs into a gentleman spectator's hat and soon produced cooked pancakes from it; he swallowed tow, spat out fire, and pulled yards and yards of colorful ribbons from his throat.

To all this, he could add many other kinds of wonders. Early in his career, for example, he acquired a set of shadow puppets, typically known as *ombres chinoises*—he himself usually advertised them as "Chinese Umbrose," sometimes instead as "Italian Shades"—and he could present various stories and display several different landscape scenes with these. Along with his legerdemain he often presented what he called the "Philosophical Paper, that changes to various shapes": this was a thick, pleated sheaf of paper that could be quickly and deftly spread and manipulated into a wide variety of unanticipated shapes—a shoe, a building, an animal—all connected by a narrative line. Then he did dances: sometimes it was an Automaton Dance, sometimes a blindfold hornpipe danced over a dozen or more eggs without breaking any of them, sometimes simply what he advertised as a "Fancy Dance." He even performed "Secret Arithmetical Tricks."

Then there were all the scenes he could present as dramatic set-pieces— "the Comic Scenes of the Clown," the excerpts from well-known plays such as *The Review* or *The Children in the Wood,* possibly several others—and the comic songs (there were several dozen he performed at one time or another, and doubtless he was adding to his stock regularly). If Sally were on the program with him, then this part of his program could be expanded easily to include her: some of her own specialties, such as the Lilliputian Dance, would now be on tap, as well as some songs they would sing as duets. And his humorous "Dissertation on Noses," in which he impersonated various characters and introduced a variety of appropriate dances and songs, was a medley of entertainments in its own right. This particular feature of his program had become so thoroughly identified with him that the *Boston Patriot,* humorously alluding to it in a comic article on state politics, suggested that Potter held "the copy right" on it.

Topping everything else was the ventriloquism. In this portion of his program Potter would typically include a variety of bird and animal imitations, but then he would start "throw[ing] his voice into many different parts of the

Room, into Gentlemen's hats, trunks, &c."—into ladies' pockets, too. Soon a gentleman might hear a bee buzzing in his hat, or a lady, a chicken peeping in her reticule; and soon "invisible crying babies and Peters and Jacks were heard under the table and platform, in boxes and corners, and even outside the building, begging to be taken in at the window." Sometimes the importuning child might even be visible. James Rannie had sometimes worked his ventriloquism with a small doll, "Tommy," and Potter probably did this occasionally as well. Early in his career, he sometimes worked with "A Small Figure, in the character of Tom Thumb," who would "dance a hornpipe on a table, and put his body in many different forms" (see fig. 3): we cannot be certain that Potter then included this "Tom Thumb" in his ventriloquism routine, but the temptation to do so, especially given his training with Rannie, must have been irresistible. Later, an editor in Connecticut reported that Potter would throw a voice into "a wooden doll, with which we have seen him hold spirited conversations." Here as with his legerdemain, the potential variety of the scenarios he could create was immense.

In the earlier years of his career, Potter experimented continually with the contents and sequences of his exhibition programs. By the time he began pushing west in his great tour around the country in 1819, however, he had settled on a basic format to his liking, and he generally stayed with this for the remainder of his career. There were exceptions, of course: especially if he was going to present a major departure from his routine like his extensive Man Salamander act, other parts of his standard program would have to give way for that evening. Nevertheless, while the individual tricks and feats and songs and recitations and imitations of his program could vary enormously from one performance to another, drawn as they all were from so great a repertory, the overarching shape and format of his entertainment was consistent.

An evening with Richard Potter, which unfolded over a space of two hours or so, was divided into three parts. Part 1 was devoted entirely to legerdemain; it was an entire magic show in itself. Part 2 was devoted entirely to the "Dissertation on Noses," which, like his ventriloquism, became a Potter trademark. And part 3 was devoted entirely to ventriloquism. There would also be several comic songs, typically at the intermission points and at the conclusion.

Potter would often call for assistance from the audience for some of his tricks, "and his infinite humor, clear sense of propriety and quick wit would always enable him to pleasantly parry all remarks from the audience, and at the same time give no offence to those who volunteered to aid him." As this last reminiscence suggests, a Potter exhibition could easily involve casual repartee with his audience. But no one ever impeded the progress of his show, for everyone wanted to see what happened next. And indeed his exhibition had something for everyone. It is fascinating, in retrospect, to see how different spectators recalled such different and various tricks and performances from Potter's repertoire as especially memorable: the magic, the recitations, the songs and dancing, the comic skits, the ventriloquism, all had their enthusiastic fans. As one memorialist wrote less than twenty years after Richard Potter's death, "O, the wonder and delight which Potter caused to all the boys, both young and old."

X

Richard Potter moved back to Andover, New Hampshire, in very late 1827 or the spring of 1828, after having lived again in Boston for well over a year. With his new practice of frequent, more locally targeted exhibitions there and thereabouts, he had done much, during his year-plus of residence there, to repair and shore up his family's financial situation. While still embattled, he must have believed, or at least hoped, that he had now turned a corner; he could see a way out of the financial hole he was in. True, the large Rhode Island lawsuit was still hanging over him, and there were still unresolved consequences of the old Gale suit. But most of his other debts were now settled, he had been earning good money steadily from his performances, and early in March he won his own suit against Samson Moody ($177 plus costs). It was probably on the strength of that judgment that he was persuaded to lend another $50 to his nephew and employee, Cromwell Potter, in May, bringing Cromwell's debt to $105—unmanageably high for an ordinary farmhand with a drinking habit, but even so a loan that could have been understandable for family. (Meanwhile Moody, perhaps unsurprisingly, was very slow in paying anyway, even after the court judgment. Andrew Dunlap's records include three letters from him in June, July, and August, each offering excuses for his failure to pay earlier as arranged and promising to pay soon.)

In this year, as in the previous two, Potter restricted his travels to New Hampshire and Massachusetts for the most part. There were two exceptions: he made another trip to Saratoga Springs in August, and in December, since he had to be in Providence for his court appeal then anyway, he performed in that city for several days. His exhibitions now were deliberately more intimate than they ever could have been in large performance halls, his venues smaller, his audiences closer. These characteristics all made both his close-up sleight-of-hand demonstrations and his ventriloquism more challenging and their successes all the more astounding. He continued to please in these smaller venues even as he always had in larger ones. When he was performing in Roxbury early in 1829, for example, a Boston newspaper noted that "our neighbors of Roxbury" who usually had to travel to Boston for special entertainments "are now to be treated to something curious at home": "Potter, the ventriloquist, whom every body acknowledges as being one of the most wonderful conjurers of the present age, is to open his budget tomorrow evening, at Wise's Hotel; where will be manufactured, in the twinkling of an eye, money, fruit, birds, boxes, &c." The editor is sporting wittily with Potter's act here: a budget was a bag or pouch, and Potter would indeed mystifyingly produce objects (including money, fruit, and birds) from what he called his "Mysterious Bag" that had only moments before been demonstrably empty. But "open one's budget" had also come to mean "speak one's mind," so the description also held true of such acts as the "Dissertation on Noses," which the editor went on to describe as "the very *ne plus ultra* of satirical humor." "Those who intend to be present," he concluded, "had better take the precaution first to get their sides insured"—because they were likely to split their sides with their laughing.

But Richard Potter's exhibitions were now more intimate in a very important personal respect as well. One of his major ambitions for his family was now finding its first outward expression: his son, Richard junior, after several years of training, was now beginning to perform with him. Young Richard seems to have made his debut in Salem on Christmas Day, 1827—this, at least, is the first time he appears in any advertisements, and Salem, what with Richard's long-standing affiliation with Henry K. Oliver (now the prominent principal of the English High School there), had always been a welcoming venue for Potter, so it would have suited admirably as a friendly first stage for his son. The notice, included in Potter's own advertisement, was brief: "In the course of the evening, BALANCING, by Master Richard, son of Mr. Potter, who will go through many wonderful equilibriums, quite astonishing for a boy of his age." Later advertisements revealed an additional piece of the boy's new repertoire: "In the course of the Evening, will be introduced a PANTO-MIMIC DANCE, by Master and Mr. Potter."

Master Richard was now perhaps fourteen years old, just in his teens. This tour of exhibitions with his father encompassed a short loop of three significant Massachusetts towns where Richard Potter sometimes performed in sequence—Salem, Newburyport, Haverhill. Master Richard performed again with his father in Newburyport (only the balancing is mentioned this time). He is not mentioned in the very brief notices Potter published in Haverhill, but we may assume that he was still there and still appearing briefly. Then the

Potters returned to Andover. Potter did not perform often this year, and there is no further mention of his son in 1828; but Potter did exhibit for several days in Concord in June, and the final item on his program—"To conclude with BALANCING"—implies Master Richard's presence here, too, for the father had not made balancing feats part of his own program for many years. And in early 1829, the son is performing with his father again: Richard Potter's program in Roxbury is "To conclude with *Balancing by Mast. Richard, son of Mr. P.*" So the training and the rehearsals would have continued intensely throughout this period.

Here was the family's real hope for the future. Richard Potter could more than support his family and their farm with the earnings from his performances for the time being, but now he could also anticipate that his son would steadily improve and rise in the performing profession, too. The estate he could hope to pass on to his son someday was already impressive, but the value of the unique education, mentoring, and goodwill he could convey was incalculably greater. Richard Potter's greatest ambition from now on would be for his son.

# 7

# A New England Icon, a Broken Family, 1829–1835

## I

As 1829 began to unfold, Richard Potter seemed to be managing his professional life much as he had done during the preceding year. He was still performing exclusively in New England, usually making shorter stands and returning home more frequently and regularly: we know that he performed in Roxbury in early March and Medford shortly thereafter, Concord in mid-April, Portsmouth in early June, Newport in September. In June and July he moved to Boston and performed there for four weeks. He continued to bring his son into his exhibitions for brief performances, at least in smaller venues: Master Richard appeared briefly in Roxbury (and so must have been present in Medford, too) and even in Newport. It was probably at this time, too, that Potter "was assisted in his performance by his son Richard" in Richmond, New Hampshire, a small town in the southwest corner of the state. This tour, about which we would know nothing had it not been mentioned in a town history more than a half century later, doubtless also took in such larger nearby towns as Keene (New Hampshire), Brattleboro (Vermont), and possibly Greenfield (Massachusetts). Such tours through the hinterlands were precisely the kind of apprenticeship that young Richard would need to undergo, not only to put his developing skills to the test of public performance but to learn all the essential logistics of traveling, maintaining their professional kit, renting performance spaces, advertising, selling and collecting tickets, dealing with innkeepers, and where necessary obtaining licenses to perform (or not: in Medford, Potter was again prosecuted for performing without a license; ultimately he paid a fine of ten dollars and costs).

The long stand in Boston, where he was now regarded by many amusement-seekers as a treasure, was doubtless Potter's big moneymaker of the year. He again performed in Concert Hall, a prestigious venue in the center of the city. He was facing increased competition now, for his own sustained success had ensured that ventriloquists were no longer so rare as they once had been. Mr. Nichols was again touring in New England—he would be appearing for a short while in Boston in October this year, and again the following March—and now another young performer, Jonathan Harrington, a native of Boston and not yet nineteen years old, had begun performing in New England as well (he would exhibit in Boston in late December 1829). Nichols was still claiming to be the only American ventriloquist, while Harrington began advertising himself as "the celebrated and *only American Ventriloquist* in the United States" (when he thought Nichols had departed for Europe), then as "the Second American Ventriloquist," then as "the celebrated American Ventriloquist." But while these others were making only relatively short stands in Boston, Potter could successfully continue there at length. As a *Boston American Traveller* editor wrote in welcoming him back to Boston in June, "The celebrated *Potter* is among us again, and will figure at Concert Hall this evening, in his own comical and mysterious way. This fellow is the wonder of all antiquated maidens and children in the country; is deemed a prodigy by many *wise* people in town, and will undoubtedly amaze and gratify all who may favor him with their company at the appointed time."

Moneymaking was still important, even urgent, for Richard Potter at this time: the big Rhode Island court judgment of $200 plus significant costs fell due on 1 February. Meanwhile, the farm would have been requiring expenditures for repairs, stock, and spring planting and could not be expected to provide significant income again until summer and fall. It is unsurprising, then, to find Potter borrowing sums from many acquaintances in the first seven months of this year, and concerning to find these debts mostly still unrepaid by the fall. Before the Rhode Island settlement date, he borrowed $14 from Thomas Gilbert (a prominent Lyme, New Hampshire, sheep farmer) in early January, and $25 from Herbert Vose (the brother-in-law and one-time store partner of Samuel Butterfield of Andover, whom Potter had retained as a lawyer in 1826 and 1827) a few days later. After the settlement, he gave his note for $30.55 to Butterfield in early April, his note for $100 to John Sholes (the tavern keeper who was running the tavern stand close to Potter's home that Potter had rented from Roger E. Perkins in 1825 only to discover that his wife could not handle the responsibility of running it herself) in late July, and another note to Butterfield, this time for $16.97, just a few days later. On this latter occasion he also repaid almost $74 of his debt to Sholes, just two days after incurring it; even so, he had gone this year almost $100 deeper into debt.

Some of this borrowing might have been driven by simple liquidity needs in a cash-poor economy, of course. Potter's bank was in Meredith, and he might have found himself unexpectedly in need of some additional cash in Concord when he borrowed money from Butterfield and Sholes there (his stash of ready cash, meanwhile, would have been at his home in Andover), and might even have chosen to borrow from fellow Andover residents because it would be more convenient to repay them later. It is very clear that, at this point, he had no inkling of the family crises that lay just ahead. He had not yet discovered that John Sholes and Samuel Butterfield were two of the last people he would ever want to have involved in his life.

II

When Moses Goodwin began making inquiries in Andover about Richard Potter's background and history in 1872, he turned up one particularly memorable and disturbing story that had made a great stir at the time and had continued to simmer in the region's collective memory for decades afterward. The story, as Goodwin pieced it out, was a strange amalgam of carefully remembered detail (including names of most of the key participants), impossibly garbled dating, and provocatively misinterpreted implications and consequences. In certain ways, it becomes a parable of Richard Potter's life. More largely, it may be seen instead as a kind of oppositional counterpart—a tale of Potter uncelebrity.

What Goodwin learned about in 1872 was a "case in connection with the family, after the death of Potter, of a unique character in the history of New Hampshire justice trials." The occasion for the case was a family crisis: as Goodwin reported, "Potter had one daughter only, and she, not very bright, was found to be in a condition becoming only a married woman."

This was Jeanette Potter—Anganet, Richard Potter's Hindu-derived name for his beautiful, dusky daughter. Goodwin's brief phrase "not very bright" is the only contemporaneous (if long-belated) characterization of her that we have. We know nothing else about her. And even this fragment— what does it tell us? Goodwin was occasionally given to dry understatement; in his very next sentence, for example, he notes that the man accused of the crime in this case "kept tavern not a thousand miles from the girl's home" (the tavern was in fact almost directly across the road from her home). Was "not very bright" a similarly dry understatement, or not? Was Anganet foolish and clueless, or developmentally compromised (by fetal alcohol syndrome, perhaps?), or something in between? We simply do not know.

The Rev. Silas Ketchum (a practicing Congregational minister), the New Hampshire Antiquarian Society president who commissioned Goodwin to do further research on Potter in Andover in the winter of 1875–76, was clearly uncomfortable with this story of immoral behavior. There is no evidence that he ever learned anything more about it than what Goodwin had initially reported in 1872, but in Ketchum's hands the implicit narrative suddenly took a very different turn and acquired a distinctive new emphasis. Potter's daughter, Ketchum declared, was "a half-idiot, given to uncontrollable lewdness." "The lewdness of the half-idiot daughter," moreover, "occasioned litigation, after Potter's death, . . . out of which grew a curious decision in law in relation to adultery, that obtained considerable notoriety in New Hampshire."

So what did happen in this case involving Anganet? And why, if it was so memorable, controversial, and (as we shall soon see) well-attended, was her story so quickly forgotten?

Here is the complete story as Goodwin recounted it in 1872:

There was another case in connection with the family, after the death of Potter, of a unique character in the history of New Hampshire justice trials. Potter had one daughter only, and she, not very bright, was found to be in a condition becoming only a married woman. In this emergency, Stephen C. Badger, Esq., then of New London, issued a complaint and warrant returnable before Esquire Sam Brown, of Andover, against John S_____, a married man, who kept tavern not a thousand miles from the girl's home. Butterfield and Nesmith were employed by the tavern keeper. The case was so novel in its character that the distinguished justices came from all the region to the trial, and Esquire Brown, impressed with a sense of the responsibility, and inspired by professional courtesy, invited his distinguished brethren to the number of twelve to sit on the case with him, Jonathan Harvey, Sam'l C. Bartlett, Israel W. Kelly, Rob't Barbour, Dr. Tilton Elkins and Ephraim Eastman being of the extraordinary jury. Butterfield and Nesmith took the ground that as the woman was not married there was no commingling of blood upon which the action of adultery could stand, under the Levitical or the common law, and on this ground the landlord went clear under the New Hampshire Statutes as they then existed. Butterfield produced his Bible in the court, and expounded the Law of the great Israelite in so powerful a manner that a good many of the church going people in the uncommon multitude from all the surrounding region at the trial took occasion to say that the case did good service in causing the lawyers to shake the dust and cobwebs from their old neglected Bibles. The leading point in the case—as to commingling of blood—was one that was in controversy among lawyers and jurists in the state at the time, having been made prominent in the noted Amherst case, and was decided by the Andover jury, five to seven, that there was no commingling, that it was not adultery. The statutes have since made it otherwise.

This brief account is remarkable for its detailed list of jurors and its synopsis of (one side of) the main legal debate in play. But such attention to these particular jurisprudential details is not surprising. One of Goodwin's main sources—probably his primary source for this story—was George W. Nesmith, one of the most prominent lawyers in the region; and Nesmith not only had played a direct role in the trial but had also, on other occasions, served sometimes as Potter's lawyer, sometimes again as his opponent's. Another of Goodwin's sources was Potter's Andover neighbor Herod Thompson, a brother of Potter's longtime assistant Benjamin Thompson junior; one of the other Thompson brothers, Joseph C. Thompson, was a justice of the peace in Andover at this time and so would have been highly attuned to and almost certainly present at the proceedings. Butterfield himself, significantly, was also an Andover JP.

Despite all this detail, however, the dating of this scandal reported by Goodwin and repeated by Ketchum—"after Potter's death" (late 1835)—is badly wrong. It is needless to demonstrate this the hard way—by establishing, for example, that Stephen Badger had left New London in 1834. The simple, blinding fact—blinding, because how else could an entire community have suppressed it?—is that Anganet Potter did not survive her father but predeceased him, and by several years. She died, in fact, in March 1831; the first obituary announcing her death appeared on 28 March.

When, then, did this scandal break and this judicial hearing occur? It is possible to give a fairly specific answer to both questions. Tilton Elkins, one of the Andover justices of the peace included on Esquire Brown's special jury, did not begin his initial appointment until 29 June 1830; so the hearing could not have begun until after that date. And Anganet, as we will see, apparently gave birth to a child, a son, no later than May 1830; so her pregnancy must have begun showing by early 1830, and Stephen Badger would have issued his warrant against her seducer between then and the end of May 1830.

We do not know exactly when Anganet was born, but her obituary reported that she was "aged 16 years" at the time of her death, and she almost certainly had been born before the Potters took up residence in Andover in the spring of 1815. So she was about fourteen and a half years old at the time that she was impregnated by her neighbor, a thirty-something married man with children of his own. In that era, the average age of menarche for American girls was probably more than fourteen.

So much, then, for Ketchum's supposition that Anganet was "given to uncontrollable lewdness." Her pregnancy was scandalous, but it was her seducer's behavior, not her own, that was the root of the scandal.


### III

The scandal in Andover was only compounded and exacerbated by the trial of the accused. This "John S_____, a married man, who kept tavern not a thousand miles from the girl's home" was certainly John Sholes, who kept the tavern right across the road from Potter's estate: he was, in fact, the very man whom Potter had engaged back in 1825 to take the operation of the tavern off of his hands after Sally Potter had proved unable to manage it. He had been married since 1819, and now also had two children, the younger of whom had been born in Andover in 1827, not long after he moved there.

Confronted with the seduction and impregnation of a young minor by a married townsman, resulting in the birth of a bastard child, Esquire Brown's duty, once a complaint was lodged with him (since Stephen Badger was a JP in New London, not in Andover, it was necessary for him to refer the matter to an Andover JP), might well not have seemed entirely clear to him, however clear the wrong. There was a law on the books regarding "the maintenance of bastard children" (designed to protect the town as much as the mother), but this would have required Anganet herself to identify the father directly to a justice of the peace (ideally, she would also have made the same declaration to her midwife or some other attendant during her travail), and the case would then have been referred to the Court of Common Pleas.

There was, however, another New Hampshire law concerning "punishment of lewdness, adultery and polygamy" that would certainly apply: it dealt with situations in which "any man be found in bed with another man's wife" or "any man and woman, either or both of whom are married, and not to each other, shall lewdly and lasciviously associate and cohabitate together" or "any man or woman married or unmarried, shall be guilty of open gross lewdness and lascivious behavior." This kind of case needed to be referred directly to the Superior Court of Judicature. Presumably that is what Samuel Brown should have done now. But would someone else do it if the girl's own father would not? And apparently Richard Potter—whether due to his concern for his young daughter's vulnerability, shame for the scandal, mistrust of the court system after his fairly extensive experience with it, or guidance from a trusted lawyer or friend—would not press charges.

Finally, there was also a quite unrelated state law, newly amended (in June 1829), that might let an aggrieved citizen go public with at least a gesture of community disapproval against this particular villain. New Hampshire's act concerning "regulated licensed houses"—that is, taverns and inns—included one clause declaring that no taverner should "suffer any person at any time to drink to drunkenness or excess in his house, or suffer any minor or servant to sit drinking there, without the leave of their parent, guardian or master, on penalty of forfeiting twenty shillings for every such offence, on conviction of any justice of the peace in the county where the offence is committed." A recent amendment to this law empowered the justice of the peace to arrest and examine anyone thus complained against and, if he deemed that person to be guilty, obligated the justice to refer the matter to the next session of the Superior Court of Judicature. If it wasn't possible to get the culprit on a morals charge, in other words, then try to get him on a liquor violation. Perhaps this is what Badger had anticipated when he referred the matter to Brown.

Whatever the occasion for the justice of the peace hearing (it was not, strictly speaking, a trial at all), the result was a horrible community spectacle and a legal travesty, corrosive rather than cathartic. Esquire Brown clearly erred badly in impaneling a great number of his fellow justices of the peace with him in the first place (and obviously none of his colleagues called him on this point of law). "Professional courtesy" in this situation was a red herring, as was any suggestion that "the leading point in the case—as to commingling of blood—was one that was in controversy among lawyers and jurists in the state at the time"; for in fact the leading point of the case was the violation and impregnation of an unmarried girl in her early teens, and the New Hampshire law in question did not depend particularly upon the precise definition of adultery. The Levitical law may have been debated from pulpits at the time, but the legal statute was unambiguous: whether the individuals involved in the case were either of them married or not, whether the crime they or one of them committed were termed adultery or instead termed lewdness, the prescribed punishment was the same, although the court was granted great discretion in setting it: "The person or persons so offending, being thereof convicted before the justices of the superior court of judicature, shall be whipped, not exceeding thirty stripes, imprisoned not exceeding six months, fined not exceeding fifty pounds, bound to good behavior for a term not exceeding three years; all or any of the foregoing punishments at the discretion of the court before whom the conviction shall be."

It is true that this statute went on to prescribe an even harsher set of potential punishments (an hour's display upon the gallows with a rope around his or her neck, public whipping up to thirty-nine stripes, imprisonment up to one year, a fine up to one hundred pounds, binding to good behavior for up to five years—again, any or all of these at the discretion of the court) for anyone specifically found guilty of adultery, and true also that the statute did not define adultery (a genuine legal flaw). But there was no need to insist that John Sholes had behaved adulterously: he was being examined as a violator of the state statute "for the punishment of lewdness, adultery and polygamy," and the charge of lewdness alone was quite sufficient to catch him up. What had occurred was a crime, by New Hampshire law, whether it were considered adultery or not.

In any event, seven (out of twelve) local justices of the peace, drawn from the towns of Andover, Salisbury, Sutton, and probably a few other nearby towns such as Wilmot, New London, and Franklin, impressed and persuaded by Samuel Butterfield's and George W. Nesmith's Levitical argument that John Sholes had not committed adultery, somehow failed to remember or to care that a young teenage girl had been violated and impregnated by a married man and that she and her father deserved justice. John Sholes "went clear." He had already moved away from Andover in 1829 and was now living in Durham, across the state, again employed as an innkeeper. A few years later he had moved to Fishersfield (now Newbury), New Hampshire, still as an innkeeper. Andover had no more claims on him.

IV

For Anganet, on the other hand, leaving Andover was not a viable option. At fifteen, she was still legally her father's property. Now with an infant child, she was utterly dependent upon her family for their support. Andover was the only home that she had ever known, and in Andover she would necessarily stay.

For Richard Potter, the family history was playing itself out again. Once again a young black Potter woman had been used by an older, married white man; once again a mixed-race—and therefore, in America, black—baby boy was left behind for the mother and her family to raise as they might. In Hopkinton, however, that young mother had been but a servant on a once-grand family's estate. In Andover, Potter was one of the most prominent men in town and certainly the most famous man, and had created his own estate. Was his daughter's status still to be no better than his mother's had been?

New England in 1830 was still, despite the slow, gradual move away from the puritanism of its founding families, a religiously conservative society. Certain situations were literally unspeakable in this society: they were not spoken of. Whole towns simply understood, by common, silent consent, that the matter was not to be discussed or even acknowledged. This was now the fate of Anganet Potter. Thanks to the scandalous occasion for Esquire Brown's judicial hearing, the crowd-pleasing, Bible-shaking oratory that characterized it, and the "uncommon multitude from all the surrounding regions" who attended it, absolutely everyone in Andover and its environs now knew about Anganet Potter's situation and condition. It was all most uncomfortable. Anganet was now unspeakable; so she simply became invisible.

But for a short while, she was still there.

The 1830 national census shows four "Free White Persons," all males, living at Richard Potter's home in Andover as of 1 June: one male aged 40–49, one aged 30–39, one aged 20–29, and one aged 15–19. The first and last of these would be Richard Potter (now about 47) and Richard junior (now about 16), respectively. The other two would presumably have been farmhands.

But Potter's family lived not in one house, but in two, immediately adjacent. In the other house, where Cromwell Potter was the head of the household, the census listed two "Free White Persons," both males aged 20–29, and four "Free Colored Persons": one male and one female aged 36–54, one female aged 10–23, and one male aged under 10. The two white young men, again, would have been farmworkers. The two people aged 36–54 were Cromwell, the head of household, and almost certainly Phebe. (He was now actually 34 years old, while she was about twenty years older than he. But ever since they moved to Andover and set up house together to all appearances as man and wife, they had consistently fudged their ages to present themselves as being much closer in age—ten years—than they actually were.) The young female was—could only have been—Anganet; she was now about 15 years old. And the young male under the age of 10 was Richard Potter's only known grandchild, an infant boy whose name was never recorded by anyone. He was now perhaps one to four months old.

We do not know why Sally Potter was absent from this census (although such absences were not at all unusual during this era, when often even whole families were missed). But it seems highly probable that Sally, not Phebe, was the missing woman in this tally. Phebe was the reliable, competent woman in the household now, and her skills would have been particularly important for the care and nurturing of Anganet's infant. Indeed, it was probably her skillful care for the new Potter baby that marked the beginning of what became her enduring reputation in Andover over the next few decades. As Eastman reported in his town history in 1910, she "was an invaluable member of the community. . . . Twenty-five years ago there were many men and women living whose first toilets were made by the deft hands of Mrs. Potter." Childless herself, Phebe had at least grown up in a large family on the Frankland estate where the nurturing of younger siblings—including the baby Richard Potter—had been a family matter. Now she had an infant grand-nephew who needed that same care.

For Richard Potter, another sad echo from his own life (although he may not have known it) was also sounding here. It is impossible not to recall the description of his own mother in her late-life dementia: "She was free to go where she pleased, receiving a welcome even in the room where the new baby lay; and being allowed to take it in her arms and clasp it to her bosom, forgetting she was not a young mother herself, and the wee white child her own little one." Phebe, freshly trained by her experience of nurturing Richard's infant grandson, was soon doing for the white Andover community what his own poor, demented mother was even now also trying to do in her helpless later years in Hopkinton and Westborough.

v

Today we would regard the assault on Anganet Potter as statutory rape, and a crime against her; but this is an ahistorical response and was not a contemporaneous attitude in 1830, long before the very notion of an "age of consent" had ever arisen in New Hampshire law. As Susan B. Anthony and Ida Husted Harper noted in their magisterial *History of Woman Suffrage:* "The 'age of consent or protection' for girls, i.e., the age when they are declared to have sufficient understanding to consent to intercourse, and above which they can claim no legal protection, was fixed at ten years by the Common Law. No action was taken by any State to advance the age up to which they might be protected until 1864, when Oregon raised it to fourteen years." The injured party here was Richard Potter, because by law his daughter was his property. After the numerous justices of the peace of Andover and environs had ignored the injury to Richard Potter while swerving to the defense of the knockabout tavern keeper who had impregnated Potter's young daughter, Potter could no longer regard Andover as a congenial place to live. He still had some good friends and good neighbors there, but the larger community, perhaps paralyzed by the unspeakableness of their own shame, did not know how to include him.

He needed to resume his professional campaigning, too. The recent unhappy events had kept him home for most of 1830, although he had gone on the road for several weeks at midyear, after Anganet gave birth but probably before Squire Brown convened his judicial hearing, performing in Haverhill, Portsmouth, and Portland (and doubtless several other towns along his route) for about a month from early June to early July. Now he needed to get back to work, and, for the first time since he had returned to New Hampshire in 1823, he decided to seek out completely new audiences.

Richard Potter had continued to be a star in Boston and an icon throughout northern and eastern New England. But the competition for audiences was intensifying, and this was particularly true for ventriloquism. The European practitioners who had come to and thrived in America in the 1820s—notably Charles and Mathews—had long since returned to the Old World. But William Nichols, still only in his late twenties, had thrived and matured as an artist, and now a new American performer from Boston, Jonathan Harrington, twenty years old, was beginning to emerge. (Harrington's act and even the phrasings of his advertisements, unlike Nichols's, were for the most part slavishly patterned on Potter's, featuring a mix of sleight-of-hand tricks [a great many of which Potter also performed], balancing, and comic songs in addition to the featured ventriloquism. But in 1830 he also introduced an automaton band, and in later years he added other automata, although there is no indication he ever incorporated them into his ventriloquism routines.) Both men were campaigning widely and intensively up and down the East Coast and sometimes beyond. Lesser competitors were beginning to appear, too, as more and more entertainers learned that ventriloquism could be "got up" to some degree by a disciplined practitioner just like any other dramatic entertainment.

So Richard Potter now set his sights elsewhere. For this campaign, he would take his performances someplace quite new: he would tour through the British Maritime provinces of eastern Canada.

It is possible, although quite uncertain, that he had traveled and performed there before. Certainly his mentor James Rannie had done so; thus Richard would at the very least have had the benefit of Rannie's recollections and advice. Rannie had gone there, moreover, just after Richard Potter's marriage in 1808. Might the newlyweds Richard and Sally Potter have accompanied him then as his assistants? On the one hand, it would have been odd for them to have separated themselves from their supportive Boston community so soon after marrying. On the other hand, the travel to new cities and even a new country might have seemed an adventure to Sally, her grace and beauty would have made her a fetching stage assistant, the steady employment at the outset of their marriage would have been welcome, and Richard, now beginning to plan for his own, independent career, might well have valued a last, sustained chance to perfect his skills by working once more with a master. We know that by April 1809 James Rannie was back in Boston, by May 1809 Richard Potter was performing together with Benjamin Thompson, and by the summer of 1809 Richard Potter was working for and living with the Olivers in Boston. There is no evidence to show that he had not been away from Boston throughout the period from October 1808 through January 1809.

Rannie had spent at least four months in the Maritimes then, much of it in the vicinity of Halifax, Nova Scotia, and some in the Saint John and Fredericton area of New Brunswick. Richard Potter now spent several months there over the winter of 1831–32, too. Probably he traveled alone; there is no evidence whatever that his son accompanied him. By late December he had traveled the length of eastern Maine and was performing for a week or so in Eastport, at the Canadian border. He must have thought of James Rannie as he traveled up the Maine coast, for Rannie had made his home in Portland, and this area had been Rannie's home territory. If he and Sally had indeed traveled here with Rannie then, he must also have thought frequently of his newlywed days with her, too, as he visited again the same towns and villages at which they would have assisted at Rannie's performances then. A month later he was performing in Saint John. The distance between the two towns was only about one hundred miles by road; the slow pace of Potter's progress strongly suggests that he had regularly attracted large audiences and repeat customers at the smaller towns and little villages along his way. His decision to seek out fresh fields and new audiences was paying off.

Potter performed about two weeks in Saint John itself, appearing at the Masonic Hall there. (Whether they respected his own Masonic credentials is not known. But it is noteworthy that, on one night of his performance—Tuesday, 8 February 1831—one of the lodges that met regularly in this hall, Union Lodge No. 38, scheduled its own meeting there earlier the same evening. Presumably the brother Masons concluded their own business in time to attend Potter's exhibition immediately afterward.) Then, two weeks later, he began appearing in Fredericton, at Mr. Sloat's Long Room, where he performed for perhaps another two weeks. He continued touring in the Maritime provinces through the winter. By April he was in Halifax, where he engaged the theater for his exhibitions. Finally heading back to America in the late spring, he stopped again in the border town of Eastport, again at the Commercial Coffee House, to perform there for a while in late May, planning to continue thence to Calais. He had been in the Maritime provinces for a full five months and would probably still be campaigning through Maine for one month more before he reached home.

While we cannot be sure of Potter's itinerary back and forth across New Brunswick and Nova Scotia this winter, we can take the itinerary followed just a few years later, in 1837, by a Boston-based circus—the very circus that Potter's son joined and traveled with then, in fact—as a very reasonable proxy. Like Potter, that circus spent approximately five months touring through these two provinces; and like Potter, the circus followed the general Saint John to Fredericton to Halifax circuit. The circus's itinerary in Canada, so far as Stuart Thayer has been able to reconstruct it, was as follows: Saint John, Gagetown, and Fredericton, New Brunswick; Pictou, New Glasgow, West River, Truro, Stewiacke, Gay's River, and Halifax, Nova Scotia; and finally back to perform again in Saint John before returning to New England. Potter almost certainly followed a route much like this.

## VI

Potter returned home, alas, to a family even more devastated than when he had left it. During his long absence, his daughter, Anganet, had died. She was still only sixteen years old. He had been somewhere in the province of New Brunswick at the time. Probably he did not even learn of her death until he returned to Andover some three months later.

The Rev. Josiah Badcock, Andover's first settled minister and still, after his retirement from the pulpit, a prominent figure in town, recorded Anganet's death in his records in the last year of his own life. Uncertain of the date (although he knew it was after 3 March and before 29 April, the bordering death-dates of two other Andover residents), he recorded the blank month and day and identified the deceased according to his usual fashion very simply: "_____ __, Mr. Potter lost a daughter."

In her death, Anganet remained as invisible in Andover as she had been in the last years of her life. We do not know the cause of her death; we do not even know on what day in March it occurred. We do not know who submitted her obituary notice to the Concord and Boston newspapers. (It is difficult to imagine that Sally, Phebe, or Cromwell would have been able to do this. Had one of them reached out to someone like Samuel Dillaway or Henry K. Oliver for help? Perhaps someone in the Andover area such as their neighbor Herod Thompson, Benjamin Thompson junior's brother, is the most likely possibility here.) There is no record in Andover apart from Badcock's brief memorandum that acknowledges her life, no stone that marks her grave. Decades later Goodwin reported, and Ketchum soon echoed, that "the daughter's remains are said to have been buried by the side of the parents, though no stone nor indications of another grave are visible." Of course they were not visible: the daughter had been buried years before either of her parents died, not beside them years after, and then some years later Richard's and Sally's bodies and gravestones had been carefully moved a short distance to a new spot when the new Northern Railroad right-of-way came through Andover in 1847. Had a third grave been next to theirs, it would assuredly have been found and moved then, too.

Later still, new local tales began to circulate about Anganet's final resting place, and William Thyng picked these up when he made inquiries in 1895: "The girl, Julia [*sic*], died at the age of twenty [*sic*], casting despondency upon her mother, from which she never recovered. It is said that Mrs. Potter possessed valuable gems and curiously wrought articles of jewelry, brought from foreign lands; and that it was her custom, after her affliction, to visit the grave at night and place the gems upon the mound." This, of course, is the merest romantic-gothic claptrap, the imaginative speculation of local mythmakers (but still interesting for its new recognition that Anganet had died before her parents did, not after). It is quite consistent with the similarly exotic stories that were being fabricated about Richard Potter himself at the time but has no evidential basis whatever.

And as the people who had attended or at least known of Esquire Brown's hearing in 1830 died, even the suppressed memory of Anganet died with them. In the early years of the following century, when Eastman came to write his town history in 1910, all he could learn of her was this: "It is said that a daughter was born, but lived only a short time." (Was it perhaps Anganet's son who was born but lived only a short time?)

There is, however, a tilted stone fragment—possibly only a blank marker, possibly the base of a broken-off gravestone—standing beside the grave of Henry M. Potter in the Old Cemetery. If Anganet were buried in the cemetery (as was certainly the usual practice in Andover then) rather than on the Potter estate, she probably lies there. A stone that no longer holds up even an effaced inscription, a name not merely obscured but completely missing—it would be a fitting monument for the girl who became unspeakable and invisible in Andover.

VII

Richard Potter had been away from his Andover home for more than six months; now, grieving a young daughter who had died in his absence, he had to leave home again almost immediately. His next trip was, on its face, almost bizarre: he traveled to Philadelphia, some four hundred miles away; after performing there in a very limited way for merely two nights, he apparently returned as directly as he came. There is no indication that he gave any other exhibitions along the way in either direction.

In almost every respect, this trip was out of character for him. Unlike several of his major competitors—Charles, Mathews, Nichols, Harrington—who tended to concentrate on larger cities and to spend relatively less time on the road, Potter had always pursued a traditional itinerant's routine, pausing to entertain along his way in smaller venues between the big cities rather than hurrying past them. A quick-turnaround trip to a single city, particularly one so far away, was not his usual style. Moreover, why should he travel to Philadelphia without also exhibiting in New York, through which he would have to pass anyway?

But there was, after all, a straightforward explanation. Richard Potter had made a commitment to appear in Philadelphia. Now he was simply honoring his commitment. It was a difficult time for him to leave home to go on such a long trip, to be sure, which would explain why he traveled there and back so quickly. But perhaps there were compensations as well as obligations.

Brief though it was, Potter's rushed trip to Philadelphia provides another of those rare, wonderful glimpses into his connections with the larger entertainment world in which he worked. He appeared at the venerable Chestnut Street Theatre, offering entertainment during the interlude between the main drama and the afterpiece. Such entertainments were a regular feature of the contemporaneous theater; they might be a musical performance, a recitation of some sort, a dance, feats of balancing, or indeed almost any genre of entertainment. Richard Potter's first performance master, the great ropedancer Signior Manfredi, had frequently appeared in such interludes at theaters in New York, Newport, Charleston, and other cities. But the Rannies had never done it; and we have no record of Potter's having done so in his entire career apart from this occasion.

The Chestnut Street Theatre's entertainment on the evening of 14 July was a benefit for Mr. Roberts, an actor who had been performing there all that week. On that evening, as per contractual arrangement, the box office take, minus the theater's expenses, went to the actor or actors for whom the benefit was arranged; those proceeds comprised a major portion of the actor's income. It was to the actor's advantage, then, to drum up attendance for his or her benefit performance by enhancing its attractiveness and visibility in any way possible. Fellow actors, even from other companies, would often lend their services for the evening; beneficiaries would typically call particular attention to their benefit performances in their own supplementary newspaper advertisements. Roberts struck the typical note of solicitation in one of the personal advertisements he published immediately before his benefit performance: "Mr. Roberts, who, for the week past, has been delighting the lovers of the drama with his rich fund of merriment, takes a benefit this evening at the Chesnut street theatre, when, it is hoped, his Philadelphia friends will cheer him, as they have always heretofore done, with a bumper." In a separate advertisement, moreover, he also announced how he was arranging to boost the appeal of his benefit night: "Mr. Roberts has, at a considerable expense, engaged Mr. POTTER, the celebrated Juggler. Also, the celebrated SLACK ROPE VAULTER, who will appear for this night only in their wonderful performances." As this makes absolutely clear, Potter was in Philadelphia because Roberts had brought him there.

"Mr. Roberts" was James Roberts, a young man—he was now about thirty-three years old—who, despite his relative youth, had already become one of the most prominent and popular comic actors in America. He was a fixture in both New York and Philadelphia, and appeared occasionally on stage in Baltimore, Boston, and Charleston as well. Originally from Scotland (he had been born in Fife in 1798, according to a historian of Scot emigrants to America), he was advertised as "from the Edinburgh Theatre" upon his first appearance in Boston, in 1820; so perhaps he was a son or nephew of the Mr. Roberts who was performing in Edinburgh in 1819–22. He quickly became a favorite in New York, where he was associated particularly with the Bowery Theatre, and then also in Philadelphia, where he performed at all the theaters; since 1828 he had regularly traveled back and forth between these two cities, and by 1831 Philadelphia had become his base. He starred in "low comic" roles and was also a very popular singer and an adept mimic. He had even been a pioneer in blackface: his blackface performance (in full Continental soldier officer's uniform, complete with sword) of the patriotic negro-dialect song "Massa George Washington and Massa Lafayette" at the Chatham Garden Theatre in

New York in late 1824 and early 1825, after the conclusion of the ballad opera *The Saw Mill; or, A Yankee Trick,* had captivated audiences.

How had Richard Potter and James Roberts even met in the first place? It is at least possible that one encountered the other in New York City in June 1823: Roberts was making his first appearance (as of 31 May) there, singing comic songs at the Circus on Broadway, when Potter paused near the end of his great national tour to perform for a few days at Tammany Hall. Imaginably either one might have taken in the other's performance. This might well have been the best chance Roberts would ever have had to catch Potter's act. An alternative scenario has them meeting in Boston late the following December. Joseph Cowell, a popular English actor now living in America, had by then become the manager of the Circus and quickly converted it into a combination "equestrian and comedy company"; that company, including Roberts, was now appearing in Boston. Roberts himself had earlier performed in Boston in the 1820–21 season (the Brays were in the troupe with him then) and again in the summer of 1822, so by this time he knew the Boston acting community well. Now Cowell's company was performing in direct competition with the Boston Theatre (on a few occasions, including Christmas Day, both companies even staged the same play, *Tom and Jerry; or, Life in London,* opposite each other). Potter spent a week or so in Boston at just this time before pushing north finally to New Hampshire, so he could have met Roberts then, and mutual friends from the theater world could easily have introduced them.

It seems quite likely, incidentally, that Roberts now became the inspiration for a song that Potter soon began introducing into his own act. Roberts had revived the old popular comic song "Barney Leave the Girls Alone" at least as early as 1822 and made it a regular feature of his entertainments; the song seems, in fact, to have become strongly identified with him over the next few years. Potter had been including songs in his own entertainments since he first began performing on his own and was always on the lookout for good comic songs that would entertain his audiences. He picked up this song and began using it in his entertainments circa 1825. Given the timing, he probably picked it up from Roberts.

Whenever it was that they met, Roberts would surely already have known about Potter and probably would have been very curious about him. We can be fairly confident about this for several reasons beyond the basic one of Potter's national reputation. First, Roberts had worked with several performers who already knew Potter. There were the Brays from the Boston Theatre, of course, and possibly other Boston troupers as well, but also there was Miss Dupree, who performed on the slack wire: Potter had performed with her in

Albany and also in Philadelphia (and probably places in between) in 1816–17, and more recently Roberts had performed with her in the Circus at Baltimore in December 1822. And later there would be the Durangs, the Philadelphia theatrical family: Roberts would have known them all, because everyone in the Philadelphia theater world did. Young Charles Durang had joined John Rannie's big Philadelphia exhibition in late December 1803 just when Signior Manfredi did, and so had been present when young Richard Potter, Manfredi's assistant, first connected with a Rannie and a ventriloquist.

But Roberts's eventual interest in Potter greatly surpassed anything that these various two-degrees-of-separation connections (almost inevitable in the theatrical world anyway) might have predicted. For he also had a long-standing interest in and familiarity with ventriloquism, far exceeding what was usual at that time.

Roberts was an obvious admirer of Charles Mathews, the famous English comic actor and incidentally a ventriloquist, who had toured America with his "Mathews at Home" entertainment in 1822–23. Profiting from Mathews's example and closely imitating it, Roberts put together a "Roberts at Home" entertainment of his own, modeled on the "Stage Coach" sketches that Mathews had presented during his American tour; he regularly performed this solo act, a medley of comic lectures, dialogues, sketches, and songs, during periods when he was between theatrical engagements. Like Mathews, Roberts was a skilled mimic, well known particularly (again like Mathews) for his imitations of famous tragedians. So he had readily followed Mathews's example into some modest attempts at ventriloquism, which he included in his "At Home" just as Mathews had. A detailed program from one of his "At Home" performances shows that he featured this near the end of his program, just before the Finale: "LECTURE ON VENTRILOQUISM. Dialogue between a little boy in a box, and Mr. Roberts, as a Frenchman; Song in imitation of a child."

But beyond this, Roberts later for a short time worked directly with an expert ventriloquist. In 1829 he teamed up with Mr. Nichols, who by now was Richard Potter's primary competitor in ventriloquism, to produce a combined act called "Nichols and Roberts at Home." Their entertainment, which spliced together their two separate acts, had three parts. To begin, Roberts presented his stagecoach sketches, offered imitations of prominent personages, gave various comic sketches, and sang several songs. Part 2 belonged to Nichols, who gave several of his ventriloquial entertainments: for example: "He will hold a tete-a-tete with an old gentleman named Count Piper, and his little son, representing himself and uncle Ben, and two servants, Peter and Jack, in the kitchen below, and an amusing old lady singing under the floor, together with the crying of three children, apparently in great distress. In this scene there are eight voices, besides the three children"; "He will also throw his voice into the body of any gentleman present, and seemingly hold a conversation with him," and "will give some imitations, to show the difference between the art of imitating sounds and the power of ventriloquism." Finally, Roberts returned to give a variety of mostly theater-inspired sketches ("Wormwood turned waiter," for example, certainly took off from the starring role in which Roberts himself had won great acclaim, in Beazley's *The Lottery Ticket*) and a concluding song.

It is worth noting, too, that Roberts's professional life in New York and Philadelphia would frequently have brought him together with Mrs. Hackett and Mrs. Sharpe, sister actresses from England who were about his own age (Mrs. Sharpe was younger than the other two by about two years) and who had their own connection with ventriloquism. For several years he and they had all performed simultaneously in New York but at different theaters (he was usually at the Bowery Theatre; the sisters, usually at the Park Theatre), but by 1829–30 they were at least occasionally performing together as members of the same company. Catherine Hackett and Eliza Sharpe, both *née* Le Sugg or Lee Sugg, had been brought up as performers from a very early age; their father, Christopher Lee Sugg, was an archetypal stage parent, himself a failed actor, who had relentlessly trained and marketed his first two daughters — especially Catherine, his firstborn — as infant prodigies, making them the primary source of income for his very large family from the time that Catherine was only five years old. Apparently picking up immediately on news about the first sensational successes in Ireland of the original "Infant Roscius," a soon to be famous child-actor prodigy known as Master Betty, Sugg actually had his five-year-old Catherine making appearances with him in London as the "Infant Billington" (Elizabeth Billington, a noted opera singer and actress, was then at the height of her fame in London) or "Infant Roscius" (her father would later change that to "Infant Roscia") long before Master Betty himself even arrived there, putting her at the very forefront of the wave of would-be theater prodigies inspired by Master Betty's success.

But Sugg's own primary profession, apart from his managing of his daughters' careers, was as a ventriloquist. He was an inferior practitioner, but (as he was also on behalf of his daughters) a relentlessly self-promoting one, and he was a tireless campaigner to boot: he had done more than anyone to publicize and popularize ventriloquism throughout England during the period 1801–3, just after it had started gaining widespread attention there. Moreover, Sugg had been a colleague of Mathews for a while early in their respective careers. After Mathews became famous, Sugg began trading on Mathews's reputation by advertising himself—shamelessly, and quite falsely—as Mathews's original tutor in the art of ventriloquism. All of which is to say that Mrs. Hackett and Mrs. Sharpe, who had grown up parented by a ventriloquist and had doubtless heard claims from their father in later years about his fostering of Mathews, would have had a lively, ongoing interest in ventriloquism's subsequent American incarnations. Their own relation to "Lee Sugg, the Ventriloquist" was widely and generally known. (Indeed, when Roberts appeared with both of them in a benefit for Mrs. Sharpe at the Chestnut Street Theatre in December 1830, Mrs. Hackett was particularly advertised as "formerly the celebrated Miss Lee Sugg.") Roberts would surely have discussed ventriloquism with them, probably many times.

So while Roberts may not have known much about Richard Potter when they first met, he had learned a lot about ventriloquism by the time he engaged Potter for his benefit performance. Probably, as he observed Mathews and then Nichol, he became all the more curious about the skills of the acquaintance who had singlehandedly maintained a tradition of ventriloquism in America for so many years. He may have engaged Potter for his final benefit as early as the fall of 1830, knowing that he was contracted in Philadelphia on and off through the following July. Alternatively and more likely, he might have reached out to Potter as late as the spring of 1831.

The trip to Philadelphia might have seemed worthwhile to Potter in several ways. We should not discount the possibility, to begin with, that the two men had already developed something of a warm personal relationship. By all accounts, Roberts was one of the genuinely good, well-liked people in the theater world, a fundamentally decent, kindly man, and Potter had the same kind of reputation. Too, they may have felt a certain bond of mutual sympathy now from the domestic sufferings that both men were currently enduring. Roberts himself was probably already ill and failing, and his wife (an actress) was, too. He had had to cancel his run at the Chestnut Street Theatre that spring because of "circumstances beyond his control," and those probably involved not only his own health but hers as well. (She died the following year, after "long suffering" and "a lingering illness," at the age of thirty. Roberts himself, his health broken, died only a few months later; he was thirty-four.) They had four young children. So Roberts was all too able to appreciate and empathize with the domestic griefs and anxieties that Richard Potter was now enduring, and Potter, likewise, could appreciate all too keenly the burdens that Roberts was now bearing. Both of them, meanwhile, were in the business of "sweeping away care" for others. The lament expressed by one of Roberts's admirers after his death — "Shall all his untiring exertions under physical and mental impediments, to cheer many a passing hour, be forgotten?" — could have applied to both men.

There would have been professional inducements for Potter's appearance with Roberts in Philadelphia, too. In terms of public visibility and sheer name recognition, Potter was actually by a wide margin the more widely known man. But just as Mathews, as a celebrated English actor, brought a cachet of respectability and highbrow approval to ventriloquism by including it in his entertainments, Potter could now hope to gain a bit more of that same cachet for himself as well as for his art by appearing with a prominent American actor on the stage of one of America's most famous and venerable theaters.

## VIII

After returning to Andover, Richard Potter settled again into the pattern of relatively localized touring that he had adopted earlier from 1828 through 1830. No longer do we see signs of financial stress. He traveled to Nashua, New Hampshire, in mid-August 1831, exhibiting there for at least a few days; we can assume that he performed at various villages along his way, too, but there is no record of his having performed in the larger towns *en route,* such as Concord and Manchester. It was probably this summer, too, that he was performing in small towns in the vicinity of Lake Winnipesaukee when Nathan Hale encountered and interviewed him there. (One old man's boyhood memory of Potter also dates from this time: in 1895 Capt. William Gordon, then seventy-four, recalled "that Potter gave an entertainment in a vacant room in the paper mill of his father, Simeon L. Gordon, at Holderness. The room was filled to overflowing; a part of the audience coming from a long distance.") We have had occasion to consider Hale's account of Potter's conversation with him before; only now, from the perspective of Potter's personal situation in 1831 — alcoholic wife, increasingly disaffected son, dead daughter, illegitimate grandson, unsupportive town — can we begin to appreciate both the bittersweet undertones coloring Potter's discussion of his wife's "congenial occupation" of country homemaking and the proud reserve with which he shielded his privacy from the inquisitive editor.

In October Potter went to Boston for another long stand there. This time he opened at Concert Hall but, apparently after only a single night, moved immediately to Julien Hall, where he exhibited for three and a half weeks. At the end of his Boston stand, Potter once again indulged in his practice of teaming up with a fellow practitioner. Just as he had in the past shared the stage with Signor Cassania, Sieur Breslaw, and Monsieur Weiss, now he partnered very briefly with a Mr. Burge.

"Mr. H. Burge, Late from Europe," had recently appeared on the scene in Boston while Potter was performing in Nashua. He was probably a young man; he had appeared on the entertainment scene without warning and then disappeared from it without a trace soon after his time in Boston. Presenting himself as "Professor of Mechanical Experiments and Legerdemain," he had exhibited for just over a week, presenting an assortment of magic tricks that were highly reminiscent of and in many instances identical to Potter's; he also included additional diversions—interpolated comic songs, and "a Hornpipe, blindfolded, among a quantity of Eggs"—that could have come straight from Potter's act. He apparently did these capably: a Boston newspaper soon reported that "Those who have seen his performance of the feats of legerdemain, think them exceedingly skilful and amusing." Still, he clearly had nothing to bring to Potter's entertainments that Potter was not already providing. But soon the two men met (surely Burge attended one of Potter's shows in Boston that fall), and, at the very end of his stand, Potter announced that his farewell performance would be "assisted by Mr. Burge." (The weather that evening being inclement, and Potter "being requested by several ladies and gentlemen of this city to repeat his performance," they then performed together again the following Monday evening.)

This was almost certainly a gesture of support and mentorship. Potter was giving Burge some paydays, a bit of publicity, and a chance to work closely with a master. Burge was clearly the assistant, but he would take the stage for a few tricks himself. It is all remarkably, and sadly, reflective of the role that Richard Potter junior might have been playing now, but was not.

We catch a final, informal glimpse of Potter before he left Boston to return home when he popped into a newspaper office at the very end of his stand. The upshot was a little news item in the next day's paper:

*Unseasonable Fruit.*—Mr. Potter, the ventriloquist, has laid on our table a small branch of an apple tree, loaded with fresh, green leaves and the second growth of fruit. The apples are of the size of walnuts, and one is larger. Though this man is an acknowledged adept in matters of illusion, we are assured that this production is beyond his powers of conjuration. He plucked the branch from a tree belonging to Mr. E. Ford, of the Neponset House, Dorchester, where still remain other evidences of the same verdure and fertility. The tree blossomed the second time, Sept. 21.

To appearances this is utterly trivial, of course, although it is pleasant to be reminded again that Potter, child of the bountiful Frankland estate and now master of his own showplace and "passionately fond" of its plantings and flowers, still retained a horticulturalist's enthusiasm for fruiting anomalies such as this. But there is much more of significance here: the anecdote provides an importantly revealing glimpse into the ways Potter negotiated his relationships with white Boston.

The newspaper office to which Potter brought his fruited branch was that of the *Boston American Traveller,* and the longtime editor to whom he offered it (the newspaper's founder and publisher, too) was Nathan Hale—the very man who, taking advantage of a chance encounter near Lake Winnipesaukee, had interviewed Potter only a few months earlier. Potter had begun advertising in the *Boston American Traveller* only in 1829, as it happened; during his current stand in the city, after his meeting with Hale, he had sent more advertising business the *Traveller's* way. And now he was making a reader's and fellow citizen's personal visit to offer the editor a tidbit of a news story, the kind of local curiosity that readers love and editors therefore welcome. (The story was in fact soon picked up and republished by several other newspapers, including one as far away as New York.) Now that he and Hale had properly met, Potter was paying a follow-up social call and offering a favor. It was a gentlemanly gesture, and of course a politic one as well. Hale certainly knew full well that Potter was black ("a man of color" was practically the first thing he said about Potter in his *Notes Made during an Excursion to the Highlands of New-Hampshire*). But Potter was now, as he had done before, dealing with him as and like a gentleman, and Hale met him respectfully and affably on those terms.

IX

Throughout 1832 and 1833, and indeed for the rest of his life, Potter limited his touring to regional circuits and shorter stretches on the road. He was done, finally, with fortnight- or month-long stands in individual cities, even Boston. He still traveled regularly, but not as frequently as before, and he remained within the New England world where he had become a tradition and a legend—New Hampshire, Massachusetts, Rhode Island, southern Maine, eastern Vermont. So we find him during this period in a handful of familiar places—Boston and Roxbury and Newburyport and Springfield, Providence and Pawtucket, Nashua and Portsmouth; and we can be sure that he was performing, as he typically did, in many small towns and villages along the way.

His tours were shorter now, and he was spending more time at home between them. By now he likely had also engaged Stephen Fellows as his assistant, so again he had more help on the road.

It was probably at this time, during his trip to or from Roxbury in January 1833, that Potter stopped over in Woburn, Massachusetts, and won a local reputation as a ghost-exorciser, creating "quite a sensation among superstitious persons at the time." The old Fowle's Tavern, in the center of town, was said to be haunted. The tavern had one special guest room designed for "finer guests" who could be "lodged in statelier shape" than the usual (and usually communal) accommodations afforded. But this room could never be used, because it seemed to be "ghost-haunted": it was often filled with sounds of "rattling chains, and ghostly groans," and those "clanking sounds, with sobs and groans" not only made sleep there impossible but utterly terrified the villagers. The landlord had tried for months to resolve or at least diagnose the problem, to no avail. Then Potter, the famous ventriloquist and magician, showed up one wintry day, looking for lodging, to find the inn already full— "all but the ghost-haunted room." He was warned about its terrifying noises, but he accepted the lodging, hopeful that he could discover their source.

That evening, a blustery night, when he retired to go to bed (and there must have been many people watching him as he went), "the moans and groans pervaded all the room." He soon realized that, among the mixture of sounds now assailing his ears, the volume of the most fearsome groans correlated with the strength of the wind's gusts. Searching for the instrument that connected these, he finally found a thin splinter of wood, split out from a beam or sill by a driven nail, that was acting like the string of an aeolian harp or a blade of grass held taut and blown upon by a child: when the wind blew across it with sufficient force, it began to "g[i]ve out long drawn groans," and the stronger and more protracted the gust of wind, the louder and longer the groan. By removing the splinter, he was able to silence the horrible groaning.

There were still those other disturbing noises to trace, but he was able to identify and remedy these as well. The story above his room was given over to a long, unfinished loft, its windows but loosely boarded up, a place where doves roosted; and close by his room—immediately above his window, presumably—Potter located "a poor asthmatic dove": its "wheezy breath" immediately explained "the sobs at night" that had provided a softer, continuing undertone to the splinter's intermittent, louder groans. And finally, in one of the loft openings through which the doves flew in and out, he found a length of chain that had been left hanging. The passing doves would occasionally disturb it with their wings, giving rise to the occasional rattlings and clankings.

Thus it was that Potter "found out the ghost, and drove him from the house." As the local historian noted, "after the discovery of the ghosts by him, he was looked upon by ignorant people as having supernatural power, and his performances were even more patronized than before, although it was observed that some folks then seemed to be afraid of him."

X

While Richard Potter was now spending more time at home with his family on his rural estate, however, his home was still a troubled place. The emotional stressors of Sally's alcoholism, Squire Brown's disgraceful hearing, Anganet's death, and the community's passive failure of justice or support—and very possibly of the parents' long absences from home throughout the children's lives, to be sure—had taken a heavy toll. The saddest new evidence of this comes in a brief, legally formal sentence published in the summer of 1832— for three consecutive weeks, as legal notices typically were—in Concord's *New-Hampshire Patriot:*

### NOTICE.

I Hereby relinquish to my son RICHARD POTTER, Jr. his time, and declare him free to act and trade for himself—and will not claim any of his earnings nor pay any debts of his contracting after this date.

RICHARD POTTER.

Andover, N.H. July 3, 1832

Richard Potter was formally emancipating his minor son (young Richard was probably about eighteen years old at the time). Implicitly, his son was also now leaving home.

These formal emancipation notices—giving an under-twenty-one-year-old son his time (the remaining months or years until he turned twenty-one) and his independence—were not common, but they were not exactly rare, either. Sometimes they were mutually agreeable arrangements of necessity or convenience and acknowledgments of the son's maturity, as when young John Valentine's father in Hopkinton, Massachusetts, "gave him his time" when he, too, was about eighteen so that John could go off to Boston and set up in a business partnership there with his older Hopkinton friend Luther Bixby: John could not have conducted business on his own account in Boston were he still legally the ward of his father. But sometimes, and probably more often, an emancipation notice was an outward symptom of a previously private family conflict: a son was rebelling or carousing or slacking, and the father was finally drawing a line or even giving over the effort of parenting and mentoring. At this end of the spectrum, an emancipation notice had something in common with that which an aggrieved husband would post when his wife—or, rarely, a daughter—ran away from home: in those instances, the legal notice was a way of forswearing obligation for all "debts of her contracting hereafter" and incidentally of perhaps forcing her to return as well. A son who could earn his own income could not be brought back thusly so easily as a wife or daughter might be, but in the case of a son that was not usually the objective, and he would at least now be free to demonstrate that he could indeed now pay his own way.

In the Potters' case, both impulses—to give the son his freedom so he could go off and do business on his own, and to protect the father from the son's debts—probably obtained. Young Richard clearly did not want to work for or with his father: despite all the training he had received ever since his parents returned home in 1824, he had apparently stopped performing with and assisting his father back in September 1829, almost three years before this. Yet he seems to have ended up in the years soon after his father's death in 1835 as an acrobat and balancing master, skills he could never have relied upon professionally had he not been honing them throughout the intervening years. So he may well have decided to leave home and continue his training as an employee of some circus—the archetypal American boy-rebel fantasy, except that with all the training he had already received from his father he actually had quite a head start on it. At the same time, however, young Dick (as he was now known in Andover) was doubtless also beginning to display the excessive enthusiasm for drink that had already ruined his mother, and by the time he was twenty-five he would also prove himself a wastrel. His father, after coping so arduously for so long with the fiscal consequences of his wife's irresponsibilities, might well have been vigilant against incurring any such additional burdens from their son now.


XI

By 1834, Richard Potter had cut back on his professional traveling significantly and was finally spending much more time at home. There is much evidence that he now was increasingly directing his attention to the improvement of his Andover estate. In 1829, for example, he began keeping a second team of oxen; in 1831, he began raising sheep, gradually increasing the size of his flock over the next few years from fifteen to twice that number. We know that he "gave great attention to the raising of swine," too, "sought for choice breeds, [and] had a first-rate cellar for them, made at great expense under his sheds," and probably that avocation dates from this period as well. Early in 1834, moreover, he purchased a half acre of land that was located across the turnpike almost directly opposite his house. A year later, he bought a separate thirty-acre tract of land to the southwest of his estate—good land, to judge from the price; it must have been cleared for pasturage or mowing and may have been for the sheep—and then sold off an eleven-and-a-half-acre parcel of unimproved back land from his estate. These are the actions of a man settling in for a long term as the lord of his own manor.

Disturbing this picture of Georgic occupation, however, a jarring reminder of his old and continuing domestic troubles once more breached Richard Potter's privacy and surfaced into public view. Once again, he was trying to control Sally's profligacy, and probably her drinking. And once again, he found himself entangled with Samuel Butterfield—the same Samuel Butterfield who had thumped his Bible and distracted his fellow JPs from the facts and laws before them in Esquire Brown's shameful hearing, when Anganet Potter's seducer went unindicted.

Samuel Butterfield was a lawyer by profession and a litigious sharper by nature. He had moved to Andover in 1823, the year before Potter returned there after his long North American tour. He was the only lawyer in town, and accordingly Potter had retained him in a few legal cases over the next few years and had also turned to him for a mortgage on his estate when he was struggling financially back in 1826; but by 1828 Potter was instead using other lawyers, and then Butterfield had sued Potter for a thirty-dollar debt in April 1830 just as Anganet's unhappy situation came into public view, had pursued the case assiduously for the next year, and had finally won it.

Potter was clearly at fault in this case, and we can only speculate that his dismay over Butterfield's behavior *re* Anganet had provoked him to withhold payment of his debt. But this business of a lawyer's himself taking other people to court was a decided pattern in Butterfield's practice. He was in truth only a part-time lawyer. An energetic and enterprising man, he turned his hand to whatever promising business opportunities presented themselves, and he was soon a great mover and shaker in Andover. He built and owned the main tavern in Andover Center; he owned the main store there; he was also the postmaster. He also owned a cooper shop and several farms and held an interest in a stage line. He regularly gave mortgages and lent money. As a fellow lawyer noted of him, "He never lost an opportunity to add to his resources, in traffic or speculation." All of his many enterprises and speculations, of course, gave him opportunities to insist upon his legal rights, and he was clearly most eager to do this. As a consequence, by far his most lucrative and faithful legal client was himself. An index of Merrimack County court actions reveals that Samuel Butterfield was the plaintiff in at least 117 suits—a truly remarkable number—between 1825 and 1853 (he was also a defendant in two). He was a lawyer who sued on his own behalf early and often, and his reputation for doing so would soon have become well established.

It was in his role of store owner that Butterfield again became an irritant to Richard Potter now. As before, Sally had been spending irresponsibly despite Potter's best efforts to manage her. She was making purchases in Butterfield's store on credit, and he could not put an end to her practice—or to Butterfield's allowing her credit. (Almost certainly he had been trying to avoid patronizing Butterfield's store at all ever since the Sholes hearing, when Butterfield had been so largely responsible for denying justice to Anganet and thus to Richard Potter.) He certainly would have discussed this matter with Butterfield (who had, in fact, been present as a witness on 25 February when Potter purchased that half acre of land across from his house), but Butterfield had clearly insisted on the technical legality of his practice: Potter was responsible for his wife's debts unless he took legal action to prevent them.

Accordingly, Richard Potter soon published a straightforward legal notice in the *New-Hampshire Patriot:*

> NOTICE. Having found it very difficult by payment or otherwise to prevent charges upon the books of Samuel Butterfield, trader, of Andover, appearing against my name, and wishing that no occurrence of the kind may again happen either by the addition of new items, or the revival of old, I hereby give notice that I am now in no way indebted to the said Butterfield by book account or otherwise, and that I shall not myself, nor will I permit any other person on my account, to ask or receive any credit, or in any manner trade with said Butterfield so as to give any pretext to him for placing my name on his books.
>
> RICHARD POTTER.
>
> Andover, March 18th, 1834.

Once again, Potter was careful not to point to his wife in any way. Nevertheless, as anyone in Andover would immediately recognize, the Potter laundry was again being washed in public.

Although Potter dated his legal notice 18 March, he did not manage to submit it to the *Patriot* in time for its next number on Monday, 24 March. Concord was a significant distance away, and probably he waited to travel there until he had other business to transact there as well. Thus his notice began appearing (for three consecutive weeks, the standard practice for legal notices) on 31 March. By the following month, Butterfield was ready with what he clearly took to be a smart comeback—which, again, he ran for three consecutive weeks:

ANSWER TO RICHARD POTTER'S MAD NOTICE.

> OH, Dick! You were a silly fool,
> Or when you'r young you'd gone to school,
> And learned to read, and write, and cipher,
> With a spice of human nature.
> Now Richard, I have oft been told,
> Your malice is a grudge of old—
> Renewed again (I'm loth to say,)
> Because I called on you for pay.
> You say that charges often came
> Against Poor Richard's worthy name,
> And even undertake to say,
> You hope, again they never may.
> And now my books must be denied,
> And published both far and wide,
> Because poor Richard was unwilling,
> To pay a charge of 'bout a shilling.
> You say that you will never trade,
> Or suffer any charges made.
> Before your ink was scarcely dried,
> Your own words were quick belied,
> And if you can your meanness hide,
> No doubt the charge will be denied.
> I pledge myself that I'll prove true,
> Every charge I've made of you,
> I therefore pitty, and despise
> The author of your foolish lies.
>                          S. BUTTERFIELD
> Andover, April 10. 1834. [*sic* throughout]

So this was now the situation: Richard's notice, although drafted on 18 March, had not been published until 31 March. In the interim, without her husband's knowing, Sally had again run up a small charge at Butterfield's store. The debt had been incurred before Richard's notice appeared, so Richard was still legally liable for it. Butterfield was now calling him—very publicly—to account.

It would be hard not to wince at so mean and pathetic a triumph, hard not to feel the ill will behind it, even did we not know the context in which this exchange occurred. But to know that context—not merely the immediate, chronic one of Sally Potter's alcoholism and irresponsibility, but the acute, still painfully recent one of Anganet's communal victimization (in which Butterfield had played no unimportant role—cause for "a grudge of old" indeed!) and terribly early death—is to gasp in absolute astonishment at the gratuitous insults and sheer nastiness of Butterfield's jibes. This man was out for his pound of flesh, or at least a shilling of it. There was no quality of mercy in him.

Did the Andover community wince? Whether many of them did or no, it is again easy to see why Richard Potter now guarded his privacy so closely there.

And did Richard Potter, reading Butterfield's doggerel attack in the *New-Hampshire Patriot,* pause to reflect for a moment how different this was from being celebrated in verse by the fashionable, witty Croaker in the pages of the *New York Evening Post*?

Potter's response (for he did respond), dated "April 31"—clearly a mistake for 1 May—first appeared (it, too, ran for three weeks) in the *Patriot* on 5 May, along with the third and final appearance of Butterfield's "Answer," and was a model of dry and decorous restraint:

> THE accomplished piece of poetry that has lately appeared in this paper in answer to "Richard Potter's mad notice," I wish the public to understand, was written by Sam. Butterfield, the lawyer that formerly resided in Goffstown, and practiced in Epping in this state.
>
> RICHARD POTTER.
>
> Andover, April 31, 1834

Everyone in Andover already knew this, of course, but not everyone in the wider New Hampshire readership of the *Patriot* did. Potter had published his first notice about Butterfield the trader; now he was identifying his antagonist as Butterfield the lawyer. And, as was always his public practice, he was behaving like the gentleman that he was. Just as he could deal on gentlemanly terms with another gentleman (think of his interactions with Nathan Hale), so he understood how to deal as a gentleman with one who was not, and in a way that made the difference between them clear.

XII

This sad, almost farcical episode with Samuel Butterfield is almost the last we see of Richard Potter. He toured again through parts of New Hampshire in the late spring and early summer of 1835, appearing for a few days in early June in Concord and then for another day, perhaps more, in Nashua in early July. As the advertisement for his Concord appearances shows, he was still performing his entire, familiar program—the sleight-of-hand tricks, the Automaton Dance, the "Wonderful Factory," the "Dissertation on Noses" (with comic songs adapted to each character), all culminating with his display of ventriloquism. It was to be his last tour, although probably neither he nor his audiences had any inkling of this. After all, he had been acquiring real estate as recently as April; that is not the behavior of a man who is expecting to die soon.

But he did. Richard Potter died on 20 September 1835 at his home. His obituary mentioned no cause of death, but we can be sure that he had lain ill for some time, probably at least several weeks, because four different doctors from the area were brought in to attend or consult on him at one point or another during his "Last sickness," and the fees of his primary physician, Dr. Tilton Elkins of Andover, amounted to twenty-one dollars, indicating a great many days of attendance and care (fifty cents for a home visit would have been a steep price at this time).

His funeral, "attended by a large concourse of people," was a major event in this little village. The Rev. Robert Bartlett of Hopkinton, a Universalist circuit-rider, something of an institution himself, who had been preaching occasionally in Andover for some fifteen years, delivered "a highly appropriate sermon"; whether it was appropriate simply to a funeral or to the memory of a "celebrated ventriloquist and necromancer," no records say.

Had he been living in Boston when he died, Richard Potter would have received a Masonic funeral, honored by his African Lodge brethren—a "public presentation of black respectability." In remote Andover, New Hampshire, that was not going to happen, even though the (white) Masonic presence was fairly strong there: Masonic lodges had been established in two nearby towns, Salisbury and New London, and many prominent local residents were members (including several of the JPs who had participated in Esquire

Brown's hearing on Anganet's seducer—Brown himself, Samuel Bartlett, and Israel Kelly—as well as Potter's neighbor and the father of his onetime assistant Benjamin Thompson, and his doctor, Tilton Elkins). Still, the Reverend Bartlett's presiding presence and the large turnout betoken a decorous and respectful event, in the truest sense: many people wished to pay their respects.

Richard Potter was buried, not in the Old Cemetery in Andover Center, where his firstborn child, Henry M. (and possibly also his infant grandson), lay, but at the foot of the yard fronting his estate, very near the Fourth New Hampshire Turnpike; the following year his wife, Sally, was buried there beside him. Their graves are marked by large marble tombstones, his characterizing him simply as "The Celebrated VENTRILOQUIST" (see fig. 10). It was his final gesture of showmanship: given the little graveyard's prominent front-yard, roadside placement, it seems highly likely that its location was of Potter's own choosing. The old life-sized carved wooden statues that Potter had long ago acquired from "Lord" Timothy Dexter's Newburyport estate and mounted on pillars at the front of his own house would have been badly deteriorated by now and were probably already long gone. Now, in their stead, the Potter Place had even more prominent and durable advertising. Richard Potter was a showman to the end.

XIII

For this life story about celebrity and its contradictory attributes, attractiveness and vulnerability or stigma, we have seen, in his final years, a kind of bifurcating of the sense of what Richard Potter's vulnerability was. For the public, it was always his uncertain, ambiguous racial background. For his neighbors, however, his vulnerability was his family. How much the one vulnerability bled into the other—how much questions of race or effects of racism tinged the failings of his wife, the shaming of and communal blindness to his daughter, the shiftlessness of his son, the complete disappearance of his grandson—is very difficult to say.

In any case, Richard Potter's immediate family were soon gone. His wife, as we have seen, outlived him by barely a year, dying at the age of forty-nine. His young grandson, nameless to history, exists only in the anonymous record of that 1830 census registry. He was not living with Cromwell and Phebe Potter by 1840, and there is no known record of his life or death, in Andover or elsewhere.

Richard Potter junior, "Dick," the son and heir and one-time apprentice, never was able to make much of his patrimony, either the estate that he inherited or the professional skills that he had acquired. Goodwin reported this discouraging account of him, as learned years later in Andover: "He followed the business of his father, and had some of his father's abilities in the vocation, but he was not possessed of his father's nobility of character. He was not a good husbandman, and soon scattered the estate that fell to him. He finally mortgaged his professional apparatus and fit-out, and when it was taken from him under the mortgage, he broke into the premises and gobbled it up, and on this account left the country. He was in Lansingburg, New York, when last heard from." Ketchum soon provided some additional details (and some additional judgments: "He was dissolute and unprincipled"): "Taking his father's apparatus he traveled, in company with Stephen Fellows, for a time, giving exhibitions, but was not successful." And Eastman was later able to add that Dick Potter, after selling his father's estate (this happened in 1837), boarded at Jonathan Stewart's tavern nearby for some time, then later "lived in Lansingburg and near Troy, N.Y." So far as Andover knew, that was the extent of his story.

The broad outline of these accounts is generally accurate. Dick Potter quickly went through and gave up on the farm. Before the end of 1835, while his father's estate was still in probate, he had sold off the thirty-acre plot of land that his father had so recently bought, for the same price his father had paid for it (two hundred dollars). The next spring he mortgaged the farm to Samuel Butterfield; then, soon after his mother's death that fall, he paid off that mortgage by giving a larger one to another man, going ever deeper into debt. Realizing soon enough that he would never be able to make his debts good while still holding on to the estate, he then sold it in May 1837 but continued to live in Andover until 1840.

Throughout this period, he was, however, putting rather more effort into his belated career than the Andover gossip allowed, and that career was more variegated than his townspeople generally realized. In the summer and fall of 1835, Dick Potter had been performing in New York City at the American Museum, a locus for variety acts and exhibitions, presenting "Grecian & Chinese Exercises," which he described in his advertising as involving "Cups, Balls, Daggers, Knives, Bowls, Plates, &c., with Balancing, exhibiting extraordinary feats of dexterity." (He shared the museum with a collection of miniature automatons, a "Grand Cosmorama," and a living sloth.) Toward the end of his stand he was joined by a new attraction, "the Canadian Dwarfs," two young women "weighing but 30 pounds, and in height only 30 and 32 inches" ("What is more extraordinary, their limbs have a double set of joints"), and then also by a child performer, "Miss Honey, (aged ten years)," who sang songs.

After these three weeks at the American Museum in August, Dick Potter returned there in late October together with Mr. Blanc, a young magician who had himself begun performing (interestingly, in tandem with Mr. Sutton, a new ventriloquist on the American scene) in New York a few weeks earlier. (Richard Potter had died in the interim, on 20 September. Possibly Dick had received the news—Richard Potter's obituary notice had been picked up by at least two New York newspapers—and had returned to Andover soon after the funeral, but it is also quite possible that he did not learn of his father's death until he returned to Andover at the end of the year.) They performed together through 5 December, again sharing the museum with other acts and exhibitions; then Potter left the act, while Mr. Blanc continued on his own for another six weeks. It was during this time that Dick Potter garnered what was possibly his only published critical review—favorable, but very brief: in a long survey of the amusements currently on display in the city, the editor finally noted, at the American Museum (besides all the curiosities on display there), "two skilful young necromancers, who nightly amuse crowded audiences. Potter with his Grecian and Chinese exercises of cups and balls, &c., and a Mr. Blanc, who from his dexterity and rapidity in all the various transformations of the black art, we should judge to be a disciple of those celebrated masters Adrien and Blitz." The review went on to single out Mr. Blanc as "a young American, of Baltimore, with, however, a very amusing Irish accent, which keeps the audience in a continued roar."

But Dick Potter, unlike his famous father, never developed a special rapport with his audiences. He had acquired skills as a performer but not so much as an entertainer. He tried, belatedly, to master some of the other skills his father had so assiduously refined: by late 1836, shortly after he had paid off one mortgage on his estate only to assume a larger one, he advertised in New Haven that he would be performing feats of legerdemain as well as of gymnastics (he had already successfully performed in Philadelphia and Boston as well as in New York, he said). But he was not thriving as a solo act. He then gave the expanded routine one more try in Boston, where in late March 1837 he advertised the "RE-ENGAGEMENT OF MR. POTTER, The Celebrated Performer," for five more nights at the National Gallery. But this was a venture without commitment, for by now he had already decided to begin pursuing a different course: he returned to his strengths—juggling, gymnastics, balancing—and he joined a circus.

A new "equestrian and comedy company," with separate but overlapping equestrian and dramatic departments, had formed in Boston in early 1836, based at the new Lion Theatre. The troupe had performed successfully there that spring, and some of them had then toured regionally in the summer and fall before returning to reopen at Boston in November 1836. While Dick Potter was performing in Boston in late March 1837, the Lion Theatre company, or at least a large portion of it, was preparing to go on the road again as a traveling circus; and Dick Potter now joined this company as an acrobat and juggler, appearing with them in Boston ("perform[ing] his Chinese Exercises") as early as 1 April. (Thomas D. Rice had now started the "Jim Crow" craze, and George Dixon had expanded it, so the circus's program carefully included "Comic and Negro songs.") The troupe soon left Boston for a brief shakedown exhibition in nearby Tewksbury, Massachusetts, in late April, and then headed north. At this point Dick Potter departed from the company briefly, just long enough to return to Andover and finalize the sale of his estate (4 May), then rejoined the circus in Portland, its next stop (10–11 May; Potter was now presenting his "Grecian Exercises, and feats of balancing"). From Portland the circus traveled into the Canadian Maritime provinces, where it spent the entire summer, tracing a large, clockwise arc through the cities and towns of New Brunswick and Nova Scotia. Finally returning to the United States, it performed one last time in Newburyport and then disbanded.

During this 1836–37 period, while Dick Potter had often been working, he had still fallen further and further into debt, evidence that the "wastrel" label he had acquired in Andover had some validity. Through the summer of 1836, even though he had already mortgaged his estate for the first time and should have had plenty of cash on hand, he was steadily running up a tab at Lewis Bean's inn and tavern nearby; many of the charges were for "Sundries," but by mid-August most of them were for "Liquor." In September 1837, back from his stint with Fuller's circus, he was seeking a quick loan of ten dollars for a week or two and pawned his gold watch and chain to his landlord to get it; he never repaid the debt or claimed the watch. He had only recently sold his patrimonial estate for a net of $1,650; for him to have become already so destitute that he needed to find some ready cash in this way bespeaks an almost breathtaking degree of prodigality.

When Dick Potter returned to Andover at the end of this season, he would have been boarding at taverns in town, either Jonathan Stewart's tavern or others. (Daniel W. Hoyt, who claimed to have been his landlord circa September 1837, reported in 1838 that "Potter is said to be destitute of property.") There is almost no record of his performances for the next two years, but apparently he was now again working on a varied one-man act, including leg-erdemain, that he could take on the road much as his father had done. By now he had engaged Stephen Fellows (who had worked for his father) as his own assistant; and, to judge from Fellows's later re-creation of "Old Potter's" (but surely also "Young Potter's") exhibition, his show featured, in addition to bal-ancing and juggling, some legerdemain (he still had that magic kit, after all) and also a comic song or two and probably a "yankee story." He was advertis-ing only with locally distributed handbills, not in newspapers, so his passage was generally unrecorded, but a newspaper editor in Salem (always a friendly town for his father, and Henry K. Oliver was still a prominent citizen there) gave him a kind notice *gratis* in late 1838 — "Mr. POTTER, a gentleman who is distinguished in his line, is to exhibit 'Magical' exploits at the Academy Hall, in Marblehead, this evening" — and a receipt for printing a batch of handbills for him places him in Nashua, New Hampshire, the following spring. He left a trail of unpaid debts in Andover through 1838 and 1839 but remained on the tax rolls of the town into 1840, so his theft of his father's old magician's kit that he had previously mortgaged (this, of course, signaled his anticipation that he could continue to make a living with it as a showman) and his immediate disappearance from Andover would have happened in that year.

But while he disappeared from Andover, he did not disappear so quickly from the entertainment world. Once he had left the immediate vicinity of Andover, he needed have no fear of the law; and his father's great reputation was still a valuable asset for him, so the Potter name was very much worth keeping and using. Perhaps he went first to the Lansingburgh area, but he did not stay there. In 1841 he traveled with Noah Ludlow and Sol Smith's eques-trian theater company as an acrobat, touring through Alabama, Louisiana, Tennessee, Missouri; just possibly he then became part of the small "Magic Theatre" company — "six Missouri Songsters" — who entertained in the Boston–Portsmouth area in late 1842 and early 1843 (the act included "Gre-cian Exercises," "Plate Balancing," and legerdemain in addition to "Comic Songs, Negro Songs and break-downs," and a comic pantomime); and later in 1843 he was probably the Potter on the rolls of the company (part of the Welch and Mann circus troupe) that appeared in Boston in September.

And we get one last, oddly touching glimpse of Dick Potter in 1844, when he appeared among an assortment of entertainers who joined to present a "Grand Concert" at the Temperance Hall in Philadelphia. Clearly serving as an interlude and counterpoint to the musical performances of the evening, he was billed there as "Mr. Potter, the celebrated Hindoo juggler."

So it was that, as his performing career faded toward invisibility, even while

American society lurched into ever more strident racial profilings, Richard Potter's last child and heir, now a man of about thirty, reached desperately back to his teens for one of his racially ambiguous father's last tricks: he played the East Indian—"Hindoo"—card. Not only the juggling, but the man himself, would be exotic, and he would that way finesse, or at least confuse and confound, the racist categorizations of his society. The misdirection was Richard Potter's last family legacy.

# Afterword

## Hiding in Plain Sight

Richard Potter was indeed very, very good at what he did. This characterization, moreover, held far beyond his skills as a ventriloquist, magician, and dramatic performer on stage. It was equally true of his life performance—his fashioning of a persona and an identity. All his adult life, he was doing "Richard Potter, the celebrated ventriloquist and necromancer," and he knew exactly what he was about.

As a public figure and a showman, Richard Potter was always, in effect, on stage. It is quite clear that he realized this very early and took it very seriously. His genteel programs, his dress and bearing, his speech and decorum, his advertising, his habitual forbearance in the face of slights and insults, his consistent courtesy and lack of affectation, even the showmanship of his domestic estate—all were calculated to establish and maintain an image, whether on stage or off, not merely of professional expertise and success but of gentlemanly graciousness and virtue. On this image he staked his entire career, and indeed his life.

In an age before photography or even the still-developing technique of lithography could put mass-produced images into wide circulation, "image" in this sense was a highly metaphorical commodity: rarely did the public image of a national figure involve an actual perception of the person. Visual images of presidents, major political figures, and sometimes even famous actors and actresses did circulate around the country, of course (as life-sized waxwork figures exhibited widely by itinerant showmen, Peter Benes aptly reminds us, no less than in printed engravings and woodcuts), but these were few, and their distribution was limited. And even these could tell you nothing about a person's voice or speech or bearing or movements: such characteristics you would have to "imagine."

After the advent of portrait photography, however—effectively, that is to say, after 1841, when a portrait lens was developed for the new (1839) daguerreotype camera—all this changed. Not only could visual images be widely distributed, but they came with a kind of guarantee of veracity: the image purportedly showed what the camera, and the photographer, actually saw. (This was particularly true in the earlier days of photography: the long exposure times required by early photographic processes and the larger-format photographic plates used by them produced images with impressively fine detail and great depth of field.)

And in 1841, a mere six years after Richard Potter's death, Frederick Douglass began sitting regularly for formal photographic portraits to further his work in the campaign for the abolition of slavery. (From 1841 to 1895, he would pose for 160 portraits and would become "the most photographed American of the nineteenth century," more photographed even than Abraham Lincoln.) The portraits consistently presented Douglass as respectable, formal, well-dressed, dignified, genuinely impressive; they thus constituted powerful counters to the degraded caricatures and stereotypes of subhuman blacks that were flooding American culture. They were powerful precisely because they were photographs: they showed what actually was, not the distortions that racist artists might want to convey. Douglass himself "believed that photography highlighted the essential humanity of its subjects" and was the "great *democratic* art" that would finally assert and help demonstrate the humanity of blacks. His portrait-photographs bore out his judgment, for they proved to be strong arguments for the humanity of one prominent, representative black American, and thus of all blacks. As James Russell Lowell observed, "The very look and bearing of Douglass are eloquent, and are full of an irresistible logic against the oppression of his race."

Now think back in time just a few years, back to that era just before the advent of photography, and consider this: the American who, over the quarter-century period from 1810 to 1835, had appeared in person before vastly more of his compatriots than had any other—appeared, moreover, as the center of attention in hundreds and even thousands of assemblages large and small, gathered expressly for the purpose of attending to his performances—was also a black man. And that black man was notable not merely for his professional expertise but also for his gentlemanly carriage, his quick wit and repartee, his courtesy, his good humor, and his irreproachable decorum. Richard Potter was the one public figure of this period whom vast numbers of Americans did not need to "imagine"; they had seen him and heard him for themselves.

How have we managed to remain so ignorant of this immensely significant fact? Simon During's argument clearly applies here: Potter's situation in the apparently trivial, seemingly ephemeral world of "entertainment magic" has blinded historians not only to his significance but even to his presence. For almost two hundred years, Richard Potter, master of misdirection, has been hiding in plain sight.

It is true, certainly, that many of Richard Potter's patrons did not realize that he was black. But a great many did, and a great many more learned it eventually or at least came to suspect it. The uncertainty of his obviously mixed background, whether its mixing was racial or ethnic, allowed both him and his audiences a good deal of procedural latitude, and it would seem that those audiences took advantage of this every bit as much as he himself did. He did not advertise himself as black because he did not have to, and thus he had nothing to gain and much to lose by doing so. His audiences, intriguingly, appear to have felt much the same way. As the gentleman at the fine New Haven–area hotel said to the ashen landlord who had denied Potter a seat at his establishment's dinner table only to discover that the roasted pig he was just beginning to carve for his guests first grunted and then piercingly squealed under the strokes of his carving knife ("My goodness, this pig ain't dead!"), "I think if you should ask that gentleman there to dine with us, you could carve your pig."

What a remarkable conspiracy this was! On the one hand, a genteel, well-spoken, highly respectable black man was receiving the applause and favor of (almost entirely white) audiences throughout the country. On the other, those audiences were tacitly agreeing not to make an issue of the performer's race, instead patronizing and celebrating him in ways they could not possibly have allowed themselves to do had they acknowledged his blackness. Such a precarious balance would not have been possible in the late 1830s or the 1840s, when the Jim Crow craze and then the advent of minstrel shows reflected the hardening of racial politics all across America. But it was still just possible during Richard Potter's lifetime, given just the right artist suspended at that tipping point—and given, too (we must not forget this), a very significant majority among those audiences happier to see that artist succeed than to see him fail.

So, now that we can finally begin to see him ourselves, we need to reconsider the superficially accurate claim about Richard Potter advanced in the introduction to this work—that "he was not a participant or an instrument in a grand societal argument." For, his apolitical persona notwithstanding, of course this is exactly what he was: for an entire antebellum generation, to many tens of thousands of Americans nationwide, he bore unmediated witness that a black man, no less than a white man, could exemplify the best qualities of humanity. It is here, remarkably—not as an early exemplar for some future showman or trend in entertainment, but as the unrecognized precursor to a Frederick Douglass—that Richard Potter leaves to America his greatest legacy.

# Appendix A
## Richard Potter's Exhibitions: A Chronology

This chronology represents only a very small fraction of Richard Potter's touring appearances but even so can provide a fair sense of the range, rhythm, and duration of his travels.

Most of our knowledge of Potter's tours comes from his newspaper advertising. Most of the towns and villages where he performed did not, however, have newspapers; and most newspapers of the era published only once a week in any event, and their days of publication might not have jibed with his travel schedule. Often, moreover, he chose not to advertise in the local newspaper even if he might have done so, preferring to rely simply on his own broadsides or handbills, almost all of which have been lost to time.

In the absence of newspaper advertisements or stories, dated broadsides, or diary entries, I have included appearances in particular towns only when they can be confidently dated to within a particular year or so. Thus I include Potter's 1831 appearance in Holderness, New Hampshire, and his 1833 appearance in Plymouth, Massachusetts, because William Gordon's and William Davis's recollections give good reason for accepting those dates. On the other hand, I have not included Potter's many appearances throughout New England and Upstate New York that are attested to by many sources—in Hopkinton and Westborough, Massachusetts; Andover, New London, Salisbury, Boscawen, Contoocook, Lebanon, and Warren, New Hampshire; Barre, Guilford, and Highgate, Vermont; Catskill, New York, and many other towns—when they cannot be thus dated.

Unless otherwise indicated in the "Performers" column, Potter was the only performer featured in any particular stand.

This listing does not attempt to record all sources for information about Potter's exhibitions. The dates given are conservative; often Potter would also have been exhibiting before and/or after these dates. When advertisements in multiple newspapers are available (as they often are for stands in larger cities), I cite only a few representative advertisements. Many newspaper titles are abbreviated, especially by omission of the city name (for example, *Gazette* instead of *Boston Gazette*).

| DATE | LOCATION | PERFORMERS; VENUE NOTES | SOURCE |
|---|---|---|---|
| 7 Feb. 1809 | Westford, MA | Potter and Smith | Broadside (fig. 3) |
| 20–25 May 1809 | Portsmouth, NH | Potter and Thompson; The Assembly Room | *Portsmouth Intelligencer,* 20 and 25 May; *Oracle,* 20 May |
| 5–14 May 1810 | York, Upper Canada (now Toronto, Canada) | Potter and Thompson; Mr. Miller's Assembly Room | *York Gazette,* 5 and 12 May |
| 30–31 July 1810 | Utica, NY | Potter and Thompson; Maj. Bellinger's | *Columbian Gazette,* 31 July |
| 25–28 Sept. 1810 | Boston, MA | Potter and Thompson; Exchange Coffee House | *Gazette,* 24 and 27 Sept.; *Repertory,* 28 Sept. |
| 29 Jan.–15 Feb. 1811 | Providence, RI | Mr. and Mrs. Potter; E. Carey's Hall | *RI American,* 29 Jan.– 15 Feb. |
| 24–25 April 1811 | Northampton, MA | Mr. Copland's Hall | *Democrat,* 23 April |
| 7 June 1811 | Albany, NY | w/ Mr. Graham; The Theatre | *Albany Register,* 7 June |
| 2 July 1811 | Goshen, NY | Mrs. M'Intosh's Hall | *Orange County Patriot,* 2 July |
| 11 July 1811 | New Brunswick, NJ | Col. P. Keenon's Assembly Room | *Guardian,* 11 July |
| 23 July–1 Aug. 1811 | Philadelphia, PA | Mr. Quesnet's Assembly Room; then the Long Room of the Black Bear Tavern | *Aurora,* 20–25 July; *Relf's,* 20, 22, and 31 July; 1 Aug. |
| 2–28 Nov. 1811 | Boston, MA | Columbian Museum | *Gazette,* 7, 14, 25, and 28 Nov.; *Columbian Centinel,* 2 and 13 Nov.; *Independent Chronicle,* 4–28 Nov. |
| ca. 29 Jan.–10 Feb. 1812 | Portland, MA (now ME) | Union Hall | *Eastern Argus,* 6 Feb.; *Portland Gazette,* 10 Feb. |
| 4 March 1812 | Providence, RI | Sons of Tammany building | *RI American,* 6 March |
| 12–17 March 1812 | Boston, MA | w/ Mr. Reynolds, on the Irish pipes; Columbian Museum | *Patriot,* 11–14 March; *Repertory,* 17 March |
| 11 July 1812 | Charlestown, MA | Mr. Pierce's Hotel | Broadside (fig. 4) |
| 27 July 1812 | Albany, NY | Mr. and Mrs. Potter; Thespian Hotel | *Albany Gazette,* 27 July |
| 8ff. Sept. 1812 | Portland, MA (now ME) | Mr. and Mrs. Potter; Union Hall | *Portland Gazette,* 7 Sept. |

| DATE | LOCATION | PERFORMERS; VENUE NOTES | SOURCE |
|---|---|---|---|
| 7 Jan. 1813 | Albany, NY | Mr. Ingraham's Assembly Room | *Albany Gazette,* 7 Jan. |
| 1 April 1813 | Geneva, NY | (letter for RP in post office) | *Geneva Gazette,* 14 April |
| 26 May–4 June 1813 | Boston, MA | Mr. and Mrs. Potter; Mr. Durang's Dancing Hall | *Daily Advertiser,* 25 May–3 June; *Repertory,* 25 May–3 June |
| 30 Dec. 1813 | Albany, NY | Thespian Hotel | *Albany Gazette,* 31 Dec. |
| 29? Nov.–8? Dec. 1814 | Albany, NY | Thespian Hotel | *Albany Register,* 2 Dec. |
| 31 Dec. 1814 | Bennington, VT | (letter for RP in post office) | *Green Mtn. Farmer,* 16 Jan. 1815 |
| 5 April 1815 | Albany, NY | A song by Master Ried; Washington Hall | *Albany Gazette,* 3 April |
| 12 Aug. 1815 | Salem, MA | Upper Hall in the Hamilton Building | *Essex Register,* 12 Aug. |
| 12 Sept. 1815 | Greenfield, MA | Mr. and Mrs. Potter; Mr. Tucker's Hall | Broadside |
| 6–26 Oct. 1815 | Boston, MA | Columbian Museum | *Daily Advertiser,* 10–26 Oct.; *Gazette,* 5–26 Oct. |
| 27 Dec. 1815 | Salem, MA | Mr. and Mrs. Potter; Upper Hall in the Hamilton Building | *Essex Register,* 27 Dec.; *Salem Gazette,* 26 Dec. |
| 14 Nov.–1 Dec. 1816 | Albany, NY | w/ Signor Cassania, Miss Dupree; also infant Miss Flint, dance; also engages Caledonian boys band; The Theatre | *Albany Advertiser,* 14–29 Nov. |
| 10 Dec. 1816 and before | Hudson, NY | w/ Signor Cassania, Miss Dupree; Mr. Reed's Ball Room | *Northern Whig,* 10 Dec. |
| 17 Jan.–1 Feb. 1817 | Philadelphia, PA | Potter and Sieur Breslaw; also Miss Dupree; Washington Hall | *Aurora,* 16 Jan.–1 Feb.; *Relf's,* 14–16 Jan.; *US Gazette,* 14 Jan.–1 Feb. |
| 22 Feb.–1 March 1817 | Baltimore, MD | Mr. Bulet's Ball Room | *American,* 22 Feb.–1 March |
| 4 March 1817 or 11 March 1817 or 18 March 1817 | Georgetown, DC | Crawford's Hotel | Broadside, Christopher Collection; repr. Moulton, after 8 |
| 10–14 March 1817 | Alexandria, VA | City Hotel | *Gazette,* 12 March; *Herald,* 12 and 14 March |

| DATE | LOCATION | PERFORMERS; VENUE NOTES | SOURCE |
|---|---|---|---|
| 11 March 1817 or 18 March 1817 | Georgetown, DC | City Hotel | *Messenger,* 10 March |
| 24–26 March 1817 | Baltimore, MD | Mr. Hulett's Assembly Room | *American Commercial Daily Advertiser,* 22–26 March |
| 28 July–1 Aug. 1817 | Albany, NY | Mr. and Mrs. Potter; Mr. S. Sanford's large room | *Albany Gazette,* 28–31 July |
| 22ff. Sept. 1817 | Charlestown, MA | Mr. Chandler's Coffee House | *Yankee,* 19 Sept. |
| 23–30 Sept. 1817 | Salem, MA | Mr. and Mrs. Potter; Hamilton Hall; then the Salem Hotel | *Essex Register,* 20–27 Sept; *Salem Gazette,* 23–30 Sept. |
| 4–5 Nov. 1817 | Providence, RI | Mr. Aldrich's Assembly Room | *RI American,* 4 Nov. |
| 22–26 Nov. 1817 | Boston, MA | Dancing Hall in the Exchange Coffee House | *Daily Advertiser,* 25–26 Nov.; *Columbian Centinel,* 22–26 Nov. |
| 29 Dec. 1817 | Newport, RI | | *Newport Mercury,* 27 Dec. |
| 5–7 Jan. 1818 | Providence, RI | Mr. Blake's Hotel | *Providence Patriot,* 3 Jan. |
| 1817–18 | Taunton, MA | | G. E. Hill, *Scenes,* 27–28 |
| 1 July 1818 | Hanover, NH | (letter for RP in post office) | *Dartmouth Gazette,* 8 July |
| 9 July–24 Aug. 1818 | Boston, MA | Occasionally Mrs. Potter, too; Association Hall; then Columbian Museum | *Gazette,* 10–20; *Repertory,* 7 and 9 July; *Independent Chronicle,* 15 July–22 Aug. |
| ca. 15–17 Sept. 1818 | Northampton, MA | Mr. and Mrs. Potter; The Hall in the new Brick Building, directly over the Printing Office | *Hampshire Gazette,* 15 Sept.; broadside (fig. 5) |
| 2 Feb.–10 April 1819 | New York, NY | Washington Hall; then the Columbian Picture Gallery | *Evening Post,* 2 Feb.–10 April; *National Advocate,* 12 Feb.–16 March |
| 26 April–22 May 1819 | Philadelphia, PA | Washington Hall | *American Centinel,* 26 April–18 May; *Franklin Gazette,* 21 April–12 May; *Union,* 22 April–22 May |
| ca. 8 June 1819 | New Haven, CT | Two evenings | *Connecticut Herald,* 15 June |

| DATE | LOCATION | PERFORMERS; VENUE NOTES | SOURCE |
|---|---|---|---|
| 20–23 July 1819 | Quebec, Lower Canada | Malhiot's Hotel | Broadside, Christopher Collection |
| ca. 30 July–6 Aug. 1819 | Montreal, Lower Canada | The Theatre | *Canadian Courant,* 31 July; 4 Aug. |
| 24 Nov. 1819 | Pittsburgh, PA | Mrs. Irwin's Long Room | *Statesman,* 24 Nov. |
| ca. 2 Feb. 1820 | Zanesville, OH | Mr. and Mrs. Potter; Mr. Dugan's Hotel | *Zanesville Express,* 2 Feb. |
| ca. 25–26 Feb. 1820 | Chillicothe, OH | Mr. and Mrs. Potter; Mr. Watson's Hotel | *Scioto Gazette,* 17 Feb. |
| 1 April 1820 | Lexington, KY | (letter for RP in post office) | *Kentucky Gazette,* 7 April |
| ca. 20–27 April 1820 | Hamilton, OH | Mr. and Mrs. Potter; Mr. Latham's | *Hamilton Gazette,* 24 April |
| ca. 14ff. May 1820 | Louisville, KY | | *Louisville Public Advertiser,* 13 May |
| 13–20 June 1820 | Lexington, KY | Mr. and Mrs. Potter; Mr. Darrac's Assembly Room | *Western Monitor,* 6, 13, and 20 June |
| 30ff. June 1820 | Danville, KY | The Theatre | *Olive Branch,* 30 June |
| 30 Sept. 1820 | Shawneetown, IL | (letter for RP in post office) | *Illinois Gazette,* 7 Oct. |
| 7–14 Dec. 1820 | St. Louis, MO | Mr. and Mrs. Potter; "the house lately occupied by the St. Louis Thespian Company" | *Missouri Gazette,* 6 and 13 Dec. |
| 14ff. May 1821 | Natchez, MS | Mr. Kennedy's Room | *Mississippi Republican,* 15 May |
| 1–2 June 1821 | Port Gibson, MS | Mr. and Mrs. Potter; Mr. Smith's large Room | *Port Gibson Correspondent,* 1 June |
| 4–8ff. Aug. 1821 | New Orleans, LA | Théâtre St. Philippe (St. Philip Street Theatre) | *Louisiana Gazette,* 2–8 Aug. |
| 1822 | Mobile, AL | (letter for RP in post office, 1 July 1822) | *Comm. Register,* 4 July |
| 1 June 1822 | Pensacola, West Florida | Jacksonian Commonwealth Theatre | *Floridian,* 1 June |
| 1 Sept. 1822 | Augusta, GA | (letter for RP in post office) | *Augusta Chronicle,* 3 Sept. |
| 27ff. Sept. 1822 | Raleigh, NC | The Theatre | *Raleigh Register,* 27 Sept. |
| 13 Dec. 1822–13 Feb. 1823 | Norfolk, Portsmouth, and Smithfield, VA | Mr. and Mrs. Potter; Long Room in Mr. Metcalf's building, formerly the Museum; or the Long Room over Mr. Mitchel's Confectionary Store (Norfolk); Capt. Reynold's Hotel (Portsmouth) | *American Commercial Beacon,* 13 Dec. 1822–12 Feb. 1823; *Herald,* 13–20 Dec. |

| DATE | LOCATION | PERFORMERS; VENUE NOTES | SOURCE |
| --- | --- | --- | --- |
| 1 April 1823 | Washington, DC | (letter for RP in post office) | *Daily National Intelligencer,* 7 April |
| ca. 5 June 1823 | New York, NY | 3 nights only; Tammany Hall | *National Advocate,* 5 June; *Evening Post,* 4 June |
| 10 June 1823 | New Haven, CT | Columbian Hotel | *Connecticut Journal,* 10 June |
| 22–29 July 1823 | Boston, MA | Columbian Museum | *Commercial Gazette,* 21–24 July; *Intelligencer,* 19 July; *Columbian Centinel,* 23 and 26 July |
| 29 Nov.–1 Dec. 1823 | Smithfield, RI | David Farnum's Tavern | Providence Co. CCP records |
| 13 Dec. 1823 | Woonsocket, RI | Potter barred from performing at Nathan Mowry's Inn | *RI American,* 30 Dec. |
| 31 Dec. 1823–17 Jan. 1824 | Concord, NH | The Masonic Hall; then moves elsewhere | *NH Patriot,* 29 Dec. 1823; 3 and 10 Jan. |
| 11 Feb. 1824 | Brattleboro, VT | | Potter, letter to Dunlap (fig. 8) |
| mid-Feb. 1824 | Greenfield, MA | | Potter, letter to Dunlap (fig. 8) |
| ca. 6–12 April 1824 | Haverhill, MA | Golden Ball Hotel | *Haverhill Gazette,* 10 April |
| 19–23 April 1824 | Newburyport, MA | Washington Hall | *Newburyport Herald,* 13, 20, 21, and 23 April |
| 26–27 April 1824 | Salem, MA | Essex Coffee House | *Salem Gazette,* 20 and 27 April |
| 30 April 1824 | Charlestown, MA | Massachusetts Hall | *Daily Advertiser,* 30 April |
| 5–9 July 1824 | Salem, MA | Concert Hall; then Essex Coffee House | *Salem Gazette,* 2–9 July |
| July 12–30 Aug. 1824 | Boston, MA | Once w/ Mrs. Bray. Extended his planned stand due to arrival of Lafayette. Concert Hall | *Commercial Gazette,* 12 July–30 Aug.; *Courier,* 10 July–30 Aug. |
| 23–28 Aug. 1824 | Portsmouth, NH | In consequence of arrival of Lafayette in Boston, Potter *canceled* this trip and continued in Boston. | *Portsmouth Journal,* 21 Aug. |
| 1 Sept. 1824 | Newburyport, MA | Phoenix Hall | *Newburyport Herald,* 31 Aug. |
| 11 Nov. 1824 | Roxbury, MA | Mrs. Mayo's | *Daily Advertiser,* 11 Nov. |

| DATE | LOCATION | PERFORMERS; VENUE NOTES | SOURCE |
| --- | --- | --- | --- |
| 12 Nov. 1824 | Cambridge, MA | Mr. Porter's Hall | *Daily Advertiser,* 11 Nov. |
| 15–16 Nov. 1824 | Charlestown, MA | Charlestown Hotel | *Daily Advertiser,* 11 Nov. |
| 22 Nov.–3 Dec. 1824 | Charlestown, MA | Charlestown Hotel | *Daily Advertiser,* 20 and 26 Nov.; *Evening Gazette,* 20 Nov. |
| 19–21 Jan. 1825 | Providence, RI | Minard's Hall | *Patriot,* 19 Jan.; *RI American,* 18 and 21 Jan. |
| 28 Feb.–9 March 1825 | Salem, MA | Lafayette Coffee House | *Essex Register,* 28 Feb., 3, 7, and 10 March; *Salem Gazette,* 1–8 March |
| ca. 15–22 March 1825 | Newburyport, MA | Phoenix Hall | *Newburyport Herald,* 15–22 March |
| 11–12 April 1825 | Haverhill, MA | Golden Ball Hotel | *Haverhill Gazette,* 9 April |
| 15 April 1825 | Exeter, NH | Col. J. Burley's Hall | *Rockingham Gazette,* 12 April |
| March–May 1825 | Concord, MA | Two visits within past two months | *Concord Gazette,* 14 May |
| 28 April–6 May 1825 | Portland, ME | Union Hall | *Eastern Argus,* 28 April, 2 May; *Portland Advertiser,* 30 April; *Portland Gazette,* 3 May |
| 23 June 1825 | Boston, MA | Concert Hall | *Commercial Gazette,* 6 and 13 June; *Courier,* 4–23 June; *Columbian Centinel,* 15 June |
| 6–12 Dec. 1825 and before | Charlestown, MA | Massachusetts Hall | *Daily American Statesman,* 6, 9, and 12 Dec. |
| 19–23 Dec. 1825 and before | Salem, MA | Concert Hall | *Salem Gazette,* 20 and 23 Dec. |
| 17–19 May 1826 | Dover, NH | w/ Mons. Weiss and the "Kamtchatkan Boy"; The Court House | *NH Republican,* 16 May |
| 13–14 June 1826 | Exeter, NH | w/ Mons. Weiss; Col. Burley's Hall | *Rockingham Gazette,* 13 June |
| 21 June–21 July 1826 | Boston, MA | w/ Mons. Weiss; Concert Hall | *Daily American Statesman,* 22 June–21 July; *Evening Gazette,* 24 June–15 July |

| DATE | LOCATION | PERFORMERS; VENUE NOTES | SOURCE |
|------|----------|------------------------|--------|
| 7–25 Aug. 1826 | Boston, MA | Concert Hall | *Courier,* 7–18 Aug.; *Daily American Statesman,* 5–25 Aug. |
| 14–12 Oct. 1826 | Boston, MA | Crombie & Mancer's new hall; also Concert Hall | *Commercial Gazette,* 3 and 9 Oct.; *Courier,* 3–12 Oct. |
| 20 Oct.–30 Nov. 1826 | Charlestown, MA | Whitney's Hotel (i.e., Charlestown Hotel) | *Commercial Gazette,* 26 Nov.; *Daily American Statesman,* 20 Oct. |
| 11 Dec. 1826–2 Jan. 1827 | Roxbury, MA | Roxbury Hotel | *Daily Advertiser,* 11 Dec.; *Courier,* 1–2 Jan. |
| 6 March 1827 | Shrewsbury, MA | Potter tries to perform without a license | Worcester Co. CCP records |
| 21 May 1827 | Amherst, NH | Mr. S. Nutt's Hall | *Farmer's Cabinet,* 19 May |
| 31 May–2 June 1827 | Providence, RI | Aldrich's Hotel; then Arnold's Washington Hall | *Patriot,* 30 May, 2 June; *RI American,* 1 June |
| 20–22 June 1827 | Worcester, MA | Worcester Hotel | *National Aegis,* 20 June |
| 26–29 June 1827 | Boston, MA | Concert Hall | *Commercial Gazette,* 28 June; *Daily Advertiser,* 26 June; *Intelligencer,* 23 June |
| 7–11 Aug. 1827 | Saratoga Springs, NY | The Large Room in Walton's Row | *Saratoga Sentinel,* 7 Aug. |
| ca. 11–13 Oct. 1827 | Andover, NH | | Town Clerk Ledger 1823–30, 75 |
| 22 Nov.–3 Dec. 1827 | Charlestown, MA | Charlestown Hotel | *Commercial Gazette,* 22 Nov., 3 Dec.; *Intelligencer,* 24 Nov.; *Daily Advertiser,* 27 Nov. |
| 25 Dec. 1827–1 Jan. 1828 | Salem, MA | w/ his son; Concert Hall | *Essex Register,* 27 and 31 Dec.; *Salem Gazette,* 25 and 28 Dec., 1 Jan. 1828 |
| 9–16 Jan. 1828 | Newburyport, MA | w/ his son; Washington Hall | *Newburyport Herald,* 8, 11, and 15 Jan. |
| 21ff. Jan. 1828 | Haverhill, MA | Mr. S. Prime's Hall | *Essex Gazette,* 19 Jan. |
| 3–4 June 1828 | Concord, NH | The Hall in Hill's Building | *NH Patriot,* 2 June |
| 1? July 1828 | Worcester, MA | (letter for RP in post office) | *National Aegis,* 9 July |
| 12ff. Aug. 1828 | Saratoga Springs, NY | The Large Room in Walton's Row | *Saratoga Sentinel,* 12 Aug. |

| DATE | LOCATION | PERFORMERS; VENUE NOTES | SOURCE |
|---|---|---|---|
| 26–28 Nov. 1828 | Springfield, MA | The hall in Carew's building | *Hampden Journal,* 26 Nov. |
| 25ff. Dec. 1828 | Providence, RI | The Theatre | *RI American,* 19, 23, and 28 Dec.; *Patriot,* 24 Dec. |
| 2–3 March 1829 | Medford, MA | Performs w/o license? | *Portsmouth Journal,* 20 June |
| 4 March 1829 | Roxbury, MA | w/ his son; Mr. Wise's Roxbury Hotel | *American Traveller,* 3 March |
| 13–14 April 1829 | Concord, NH | Eagle Coffee House | *NH Patriot,* 13 April |
| 3–5 June 1829 | Portsmouth, NH | Assembly Room | *NH Gazette,* 2 June |
| 15 June–11 July 1829 | Boston, MA | Concert Hall | *Courier,* 17 June–10 July; *American Traveller,* 16 June |
| 10ff. Sept. 1829 | Newport, RI | w/ his son; The Theatre | *RI Republican,* 10 Sept. |
| ca. 11–15 June 1830 | Haverhill, MA | Golden Ball Hotel | *Essex Gazette,* 12 June; "Diaries of Isaac W. Merrill," 15 June |
| 22–23 June 1830 | Portsmouth, NH | Franklin Hall | *NH Gazette,* 22 June; *Portsmouth Journal,* 19 June |
| 5–9 July 1830 | Portland, ME | Union Hall | *Eastern Argus,* 5 July; *Portland Advertiser,* 9 July |
| ca. 1830 | Richmond, NH | w/ his son; Power's Tavern | Bassett, *History of the Town of Richmond,* 207 |
| ca. 20–23 Dec. 1830 | Eastport, ME | Commercial Coffee House | *Eastport Sentinel,* 22 Dec. |
| 29 Jan.–8 Feb. 1831 | Saint John, NB | Masonic Hall | *NB Courier,* 29 Jan., 5 Feb. |
| 23 Feb.–4 March 1831 | Fredericton, NB | Mr. Sloat's Long Room | *Royal Gazette,* 23 Feb., 2 March |
| 2 May 1831 and before and after | Halifax, NS | The Theatre | *Halifax Journal,* 2 May |
| ca. 23–25 May 1831 | Eastport, ME | Commercial Coffee House | *Eastport Sentinel,* 25 May |
| ca. 28 May 1831 | Calais, ME | | *Eastport Sentinel,* 25 May |
| 14–16 July 1831 | Philadelphia, PA | w/ Mr. Hess, ropedancer; benefit for James Roberts, Chestnut Street Theatre | *Inquirer,* 13 July; James, *Old Drury of Philadelphia,* 476, 488 |

| DATE | LOCATION | PERFORMERS; VENUE NOTES | SOURCE |
|---|---|---|---|
| Early August 1831 | Holderness, NH | Simeon L. Gordon's paper mill | Capt. William Gordon, in Thyng, "Reminiscences" |
| 12–15 Aug. 1831 | Nashua, NH | Mr. Tyler's Hall | *Nashua Gazette,* 12 Aug. |
| 1 Oct. 1831 | Lowell, MA | (letter for RP in post office) | *Lowell Mercury,* 14 Oct. |
| 19 Oct.–14 Nov. 1831 | Boston, MA | Concert Hall; then Julien Hall | *Patriot,* 22 Oct.–8 Nov.; *American Traveller,* 25 Oct.–11 Nov. |
| 19–23 April 1832 | Boston | Julien Hall | *Commercial Gazette,* 19 April; *Daily Advertiser,* 21 April; *American Traveller,* 17 April |
| 4 May 1832 | Pawtucket, RI | Geo. W. Blake's Dolly Sabin Hotel | *Pawtucket Chronicle,* 4 May |
| 17–18 Sept. 1832 | Nashua, NH | Mr. Tyler's Hall | *Nashua Gazette,* 14 Sept. |
| 13–23 Nov. 1832 | Providence, RI | Mechanic's Hall | *Providence Patriot,* 17 Nov.; RI *American,* 20 and 23 Nov. |
| 21 Jan. 1833 | Roxbury, MA | Mr. Fisher's Hotel | *Daily Advertiser,* 17 and 19 Jan.; *American Traveller,* 18 Jan. |
| 1833 | Plymouth, MA | Pilgrim Hall | William T. Davis, *Plymouth Memories,* 25, 457 |
| ca. 7–11 April 1833 | Lowell, MA | Masonic Hall | *Lowell Journal,* 10 April |
| 5–15 May 1833 | Portsmouth, NH | Franklin Hall | *NH Gazette,* 6 and 14 May; *Portsmouth Journal,* 3 May |
| ca. 20–24 May 1833 | Newburyport, MA | Phoenix Hall | *Newburyport Herald,* 21 May |
| 15 Jan. 1834 | Springfield, MA | Franklin Hall | *Hampden Whig,* 15 Jan. |
| 5–6 May 1834 | Portsmouth, NH | Jefferson Hall | *Portsmouth Journal,* 3 May |
| 3–4 June 1835 | Concord, NH | Eagle Coffee House | *NH Patriot,* 1 June |
| 2–6 July 1835 | Nashua, NH | Washington Hall | *Nashua Gazette,* 3 July |

# Appendix B
## Notes on the Illustrated Broadsides and the Stereoview

### FIGURE 1. MANFREDI BROADSIDE, PORTSMOUTH, 1803 (AMERICAN ANTIQUARIAN SOCIETY COLLECTION)

"Signior Manfredi" (he was probably Pietro; he eventually Americanized his name to Peter Manfredi or Manfredy), an Italian tightrope artist, came to America for a year-plus in 1803, then returned in 1805 with his performing family (his wife and his two daughters, Catherine and Louisa, were all skilled ropedancers).

Manfredi was probably young Richard Potter's early mentor and master in Europe in the arts of ropedancing and balancing. After they came to America, whether together or separately, they seem to have reunited at this Portsmouth exhibition; Potter would then have accompanied Manfredi as he continued his tour from Portsmouth on to Newburyport, Salem, Boston, and Philadelphia. Potter lived for a while in Portsmouth and was probably advertised on this broadside as the "person of This Town [who] will perform a number of feats on the rope, with the ballance pole."

The woodcuts on this broadside, illustrating some of Manfredi's feats, would have been commissioned and owned by him. They were almost certainly the work of a New York City artist.

### FIGURE 2. RANNIE BROADSIDE, 1810 (OLD DARTMOUTH HISTORICAL SOCIETY—NEW BEDFORD WHALING MUSEUM COLLECTION)

Like Signior Manfredi's illustrated broadside (fig. 1), this one from James Rannie illustrates a variety of the performer's feats: cutting off and restoring the head of a rooster (*upper left*); balancing in various ways (*upper middle and lower right;* in the upper-middle woodcut, Rannie balances two clay pipes vertically on his nose and chin while beating a tambourine, all the while standing, with a table and two lighted candles, on a platform that is itself suspended from slack ropes); imitating birds (*upper right;* Rannie has attracted a tree full of birds to himself by means of his imitations); and ventriloquism (*lower left*).

The large woodcuts at the top, twice the width of the two smaller ones below, did not adapt well to use in newspapers (they were two columns wide), although Rannie nevertheless did occasionally use a few of them in such advertisements. They were better suited for use in broadsides, where their size could attract attention from a distance.

Although Rannie used this particular copy of his broadside in 1811, the woodcuts themselves all date from 1804, when he acquired them while performing in New York; he used all of them in his advertising, either in newspapers or on broadsides, at that time. The broadside itself was probably printed in late 1810, for Rannie, who varied his advertising with some frequency throughout his career, did not until then begin advertising that with his ventriloquism he could cause a codfish "to make a noise like that of a Hog" or "cause an OYSTER to imitate a number of BIRDS."

FIGURE 3. POTTER & SMITH BROADSIDE
(J. V. FLETCHER LIBRARY COLLECTION,
WESTFORD, MASSACHUSETTS)

This broadside demonstrates how an entertainer's advertising could be repurposed and reused in changed circumstances. The original broadside, an advertisement for "Potter and Smith," was later cut into three pieces, and the pieces were then overlapped to hide a few lines of text that pertained to Smith only. Originally, directly under the line "SLIGHT OF HAND," the line "Slack Wire Dancing" appeared (it is now hidden by the overlapping top piece of the broadside); then directly after "Part 3d." appeared the information, "Mr. Smith will perform a great variety of feats on the slack wire in full swing. He will balance pipes, swords, keys, plates &c. &c." (this is now hidden by the overlapping middle piece of the broadside). Thus an advertisement for "Potter and Smith" was converted into one for Potter alone. (He could not, however, eliminate his one-time associate's name from the line "By Messrs. POTTER & SMITH" near the top of the broadside.)

The phrasing and even the formatting of the opening of this broadside, apart from the now-hidden line referring to Smith's contribution, is, *mutatis mutandis,* identical to that of Potter's first-known newspaper advertisement, which dates to May 1809:

EXHIBITION.
Monday Evening, May 22.
At the Assembly Room.
A genteel Entertainment of
Slight of Hand,
Theatrical Performances, &
Ventriloquism,
By Messrs. POTTER and THOMPSON,
Who have performed in the most capital
Cities in Europe and America.

[*Portsmouth Oracle*, 20 May 1809, 3]

Potter thereafter abandoned this particular introduction, never to revive it, strongly suggesting that this broadside dates from approximately the time of that advertisement. Various other details of the program reinforce this impression. "He will swallow a case of knives and forks" recalls one of James Rannie's feats; Potter quickly dropped this act from his own program. The "Tom Thumb" and "Magic Wonders" also never appeared in his subsequent advertising. And while a few "Italian Shades" (shadow puppet) shows did remain in his repertory for a while, from July 1810 on he consistently referred to them instead as "Chinese Umbrose" (his version of the traditional *ombres chinoises*). Moreover, this particular "Broken Bridge" show never appeared in his advertising apart from this one broadside.

Potter might have seen a "Broken Bridge" Italian Shades show in Boston when a touring puppeteer, Peter Blancan, presented it in his "Picturesque and Mechanical Exhibition" there for a few days in late September 1808, soon after Richard and Sally Potter were married. (We know that Blancan's show included "the Broken Bridge" because he specifically listed it on his program in a New York advertisement a few months later.) "The Broken Bridge" had long (since 1786) been popular in America; if Potter wanted to include it in his own program, he would not have found it difficult to acquire or make his own shadow puppets for the purpose.

The inscribed information on this broadside reads, "Mr. T C [or I ?] Wilkns [*sic*] taven [*sic*] Westford" "Tuesday" "Feb the 7." The only possible Tuesday, 7 February in the period 1805–14 is 7 February 1809; that is almost certainly the date of the performance advertised here. The broadside itself, advertising a "Potter and Smith" performance, surely dates from late 1808 or early 1809. This broadside is thus the earliest-known record of a Richard Potter professional exhibition and provides the best available marker for the very beginning of his independent career.

### FIGURE 4. POTTER BROADSIDE, WITH DETAIL OF MASONIC EMBLEM (ROBERT A. OLSON COLLECTION)

This broadside is a remarkable artifact on several levels. First, simply as a material object it beautifully illustrates the essential ephemerality of showmen's broadsides. This one was repurposed to serve as the lining for the lid of a small trunk or document chest: it was carefully cut and fitted and then pasted into place. It survived two hundred years to the present time only because the chest itself did. Even within the chest, it was at risk: at various times it was damaged by both moisture and insects (possibly mud daubers).

Second, the text of Potter's advertisement and the supplementary information inserted into it give us important information about his early exhibitions. The inserted details include the venue (the town is "Charlestown," the exhibition room, "Mr. Pierce's") and the date ("Saturday," the "11th"). The text so closely tracks the language and arrangement of some of Potter's early newspaper advertisements that we can confidently date this broadside to 1811. One of the deceptions he promises to perform, "the [ ] Bushel; Or, a New Way of Measuring Seed," is not, I think, mentioned anywhere else in his advertising and probably was dropped from his repertory early in his career. Although the broadside itself dates to about 1811, its use to advertise an exhibition at Mr. Pierce's in Charlestown occurred perhaps a year—perhaps even several years—later. Capt. Abraham Pierce kept the Neponset Hotel in Charlestown, Massachusetts, from April 1812 until October 1815, when he left to become manager of Concert Hall in Boston; a few months later, he returned to Charlestown and managed the Charlestown Hotel from March 1816 to October 1819. During his time at the Neponset Hotel, Saturday the 11th could have been 11 July 1812; 11 September or 11 December 1813; 11 June 1814; or 11 February or 11 March 1815. The earlier dates are the more likely, for Potter was already using new, revised and updated broadsides by 1812–13. (I have tentatively accepted the date of 11 July 1812 in the Chronology, appendix A.)

Finally, the small woodcut illustration between "Mr." and "POTTER" graphically demonstrates that Potter relied on his Masonic affiliation as a token of his respectability and thought that quietly but openly advertising it was good business (see also fig. 5). The woodcut shows a collection of iconic Masonic items—a compass, a square, a mallet, a trowel, a book (implicitly the Bible)—assembled on a planar surface beneath the all-seeing gaze of the sun and the moon.

FIGURE 5. POTTER BROADSIDE, 1818 (HISTORIC NORTHAMPTON MUSEUM COLLECTION)

Here again we see Potter using a Masonic emblem in his advertising, even more prominently than before.

The woodcut of the bird imitator is one of those that had belonged to James Rannie in 1804 and had been used by him as late as April 1811 (fig. 2). While the figure of the bird imitator would naturally be taken here as a representation of Potter, then, it actually represents, if anyone, James Rannie.

Potter acquired the woodcut from Rannie in 1811 or 1812, and used it for the printing of this broadside soon after. (The Boston printing firm responsible for this broadside, the partnership of True and Rowe, was in existence only during 1812–13 and dissolved on the last day of 1813.) Comparison of the 1810 Rannie broadside with this one reveals that cracks have begun developing across the woodcut. Those cracks do not appear in the Bostonian Society copy of this same broadside, used in Greenfield, Massachusetts, on 12 September 1815, or in other extant reproductions of this woodcut in different Potter broadsides. One of these, formerly in the Christopher Collection—but not there, or at least not shown to me, when I viewed that collection in 1998— is reproduced in Christopher, *Magic,* 43. The other, obviously by the same printer but with a few variations of line spacing and without the Masonic compass symbol immediately before "POTTER" near the top, is reproduced in Vox, *I Can See Your Lips Moving,* 61 (Vox, by way of acknowledgment, cites only "Dover Publications" [213]). Probably this woodcut did not survive long if at all after it was used by True and Rowe to print broadsides for Potter in 1812 or 1813.

The handwritten text entered onto this broadside identifies the town ("Northampton"), the venue ("the brick Ball Room over the Printing Office"), the day ("Wednes"), and the date ("Sept 16th 1818"). This is consistent with Potter's corresponding newspaper advertisement in the *Northampton Hampshire Gazette,* which identifies the venue as "the HALL in the new Brick Building, directly over the Printing Office," and the dates of performance as "Tuesday, Wednesday, and Thursday evenings next" (that is, 15, 16, and 17 September). Insertions at the bottom of the broadside also specify the price of admission as "25" (cents) and inform that tickets might also be obtained "at

Mr. Lyman's Inn." The text whited out and overwritten by "and at Mr. Lyman's Inn" presumably said, "Children under twelve years of age, half price"; cf. the Bostonian Society copy of the broadside.

FIGURE 6. STEREOVIEW OF POTTER ESTATE, ANDOVER, NEW HAMPSHIRE, CIRCA 1869 (PRIVATE COLLECTION)

This stereoview photograph was probably taken by the professional photographer John Bachelder circa 1869. It is inscribed on the reverse in a contemporaneous hand, "Home of Richard Potter the celebrated ventriloquist Potter Place NH." The original blind arches with carved drapery panels above the front windows were still present at this time; both the blind arch above the front door and the upstairs dormer centered above the front door may also be glimpsed here. In Potter's time the front lawn extended much farther downhill than it did at the time of this photograph. The picket fence and granite pillar were later additions to the grounds; the wing visible at the rear left was similarly a later addition to the house.

# Appendix C
## The Potter Mythography

I have already addressed the various wild stories about Richard Potter's and Sally Potter's origins, the confused claim of his having been picked up by a sea captain and taken to London and abandoned there at the age of ten, and the equally unfounded romantic-gothic tales about Sally's supposed behavior at her daughter's grave, and I will not revisit them now. But so many other bogus or improbable anecdotes about Potter continue to circulate that it might be useful to note and annotate a few of the main ones here.

### I. POTTER PERFORMED THE INDIAN ROPE TRICK (AND SUNDRY OTHER INCREDIBLE FEATS)

This claim came from Dana Taylor, in a letter published in the *Conjurer's Monthly Magazine* (vol. 1, no. 4 [15 Dec. 1906]), a new publication by Harry Houdini. Houdini was greatly interested in the history of magic and had advertised requesting information about old-time magicians. (He later commissioned a researcher to assemble an extensive documentation of the "History of Magic in Boston 1792–1915.") Taylor, a young (he had just turned twenty), still-amateur magician who lived in Andover, New Hampshire, in the home that had once been Benjamin Thompson senior's tavern, wrote to Houdini to "give some account of a certain man named Richard Potter, who was known as a wonderful magician" and also—this was something new in Potter lore!—"a hypnotist." Among the stories he passed along was this one: "Before a score of people and in the open air, free from trees, houses or mechanism, he threw up a ball of yarn and he and his wife climbed up on it and vanished in the air. A person coming up the road asked what the people were gazing at, and being told, he said he met them going down the road." But this deception, the famous Indian rope trick, was a hoax, perpetrated in 1890 by a *Chicago Tribune* newspaperman, John Elbert Wilkie (writing under the byline Fred S. Ellmore), as a circulation-boosting stunt ("It Is Only Hypnotism," *Chicago Daily Tribune,* 9 Aug. 1890, 1). The paper came clean about the matter some four months later, professing astonishment that anyone had believed so far-fetched a tale: "The principal character was Mr. F. S. Ellmore (sell-more), and the writer considered that the name would suggest to a careful reader that it was a 'sell'" ("Queries and Answers," 6 Dec. 1890). Nevertheless, a credulous public had already seized upon the story and made it into an enduring urban myth. Taylor's allusion to Potter as a hypnotist points clearly to the source of his imaginative anecdote.

Taylor was eager to ingratiate himself with the great Houdini ("P. S. I am about to make my profession publicly known and shall throw a mist before their eyes as is supposed to have been done by Potter") and retailed a few other howlers, similarly explicable only by recourse to wild notions about hypnotism: "Potter crawled through a solid log. One day he happened to be passing a farm, where several men were trying to start a load of hay, which was to be pulled up the hill into a barn. Potter laughed at them and unhitching the horses, he produced a rooster from his pocket and hitching him on with a string he pulled the load up into the barn. The next morning when they went to pitch off the hay, they found it at the foot of the hill."

These, too, have subsequently crept into the Potter mythography. (Thyng had already reported a different version of the "rooster pulling a heavily laden cart" story in 1895—in that version, Potter first fashioned the rooster from a wad of tow—noting simply that "This incredible story goes to show to what an extent the popular mind of his time was influenced by his powers of ocular deception.") They are equally impossible.

### 2. POTTER USED VENTRILOQUISM TO TRICK A FARMER INTO UNLOADING A WAGONLOAD OF HAY

In contrast to the claims put forth by Taylor, this one is far from improbable as an incident. What is dubious is the insistence that Potter did this in Andover.

Certainly the claim had currency in Andover: it was picked up there by Goodwin in 1872 and again by Thyng in 1895, then reaffirmed by the anonymous respondent to Thyng's article, mentioned again in the 1906 *Boston Herald* article, and collected by Hilton in her annotations to Eastman's town history. Here is the anecdote as Goodwin recounted it: "He did many amusing things with his ventriloquism in Andover, an instance of which was when he met a sour old fellow with a load of hay who would not give him a chance to get by him with his carriage. A child began suddenly to cry in his load of hay, and the old sinner went at with desperation and pitched it nearly all off, seeking, in vain, for the source of the screaming which was in fact in the road before him." (The other Andover sources say this occurred during the winter and that Potter was in a sleigh, not a carriage.)

But in fact this anecdote was one of the archetypal stories of ventriloquism and had wide circulation both after and before Potter's career. The trick was particularly associated with and attributed to the great ventriloquist Alexandre Vattemare, the preeminent European ventriloquist of the 1820s, who was said to have demonstrated it in London and also in Scotland. James Hogg, in his 1833 story "Scottish Haymakers," recounted Alexandre's performance of the jest in what his editor calls "a slightly fictionalized account of an episode in his own past, which occurred sometime during the 1820's." John Rannie also claimed in 1805 to have done it on the way from Boston to Roxbury, "in order to create a little sport to some Gentlemen that had been bearing him company." In 1805 W. F. Pinchbeck recounted the episode as having happened sometime before near London. James Rannie also laid claim to it as early as December 1801: "He has many times caused men to unload carts of hay, suspecting they heard the voice of a person smothering within." Kirby reported that Lee Sugg had done it near the Isle of Ely, in England, in November 1799, and Sugg himself planted a story claiming credit for another such stunt (the cartload this time was dung, not hay or oats) in the summer of 1801. But the story seemingly originates with England's ur-ventriloquist, James Burns: Kirby dates the episode to August 1792, and it had already been reported and attributed to Burns as early as 1796.

Richard Potter himself, moreover, sometimes included a reenactment of such a scene in his act. As a Montreal newspaper editor reported of Potter's performance in 1819, "By the aid of ventriloquism, even loads of hay become social." And Potter himself sometimes advertised that he would "give an imitation of a child, whose voice will be heard at different parts of the room, and a dialogue between the child and Mr. Potter, after the manner in which he obliged the man to unload his hay in Portsmouth."

In Portsmouth? Based on Potter's own assertion, then, he pulled off this trick there, if anywhere. But such a trick, which victimizes and greatly inconveniences another, while entirely characteristic of performers like Sugg, the Rannies, and Charles, would have been quite uncharacteristic of Potter, who assiduously strove to be inoffensive and unprovocative. Perhaps, after all, he did do it once in Andover. It is much more likely, however, that he enacted, or reenacted, the incident in some of his exhibitions, and that the story itself, thus associated with him, was eventually adopted and claimed by his neighbors and their descendants as a local memory.

## 3. POTTER OPERATED A STATION ON THE
### UNDERGROUND RAILROAD

Mary Grant Charles floated this supposition in an article published in the *Negro History Bulletin* in October 1942 ("Richard Potter," 6:22–23) and then elaborated on it in a note in the *Franklin (NH) Journal Transcript* on 3 February 1944. (Interestingly, she made no mention of it in her longer essay on Potter, "America's First Negro Magician," published in the *Negro Digest* in 1949 [8:74–79].) Although she claimed vaguely that "It is said that [Potter Place] was an Underground station in Potter's day," she adduced only a single piece of evidence: "The frontispiece map of the 'New England Underground Railroad,' in Henrietta Buckmaster's *Let My People Go,* shows a line that appears to end in the immediate vicinity of the Potter Place."

The map in question, which is not a frontispiece, is less than an inch and a half high (imagine a map of New England inscribed on a commemorative postage stamp), and the lines on it simply trace the main thoroughfares north to Canada or seaward to port towns. It is true that the Fourth New Hampshire Turnpike (on which Potter's home stood) passed through Andover, New Hampshire, toward Lebanon, New Hampshire, where it crossed into Vermont and connected with the main road north to Montreal. But this is very far from identifying any Andover resident, much less one specific resident, as an Underground Railroad operator.

While Potter was a close friend of many men who were involved in antislavery efforts, any attempt to associate him with the Underground Railroad *per se* verges on the anachronistic, simply because the Underground Railroad—at least overland to Canada—could hardly be said to exist before the end of 1833, when slavery in Canada was abolished, and was not a significant movement until circa 1840. Given that Potter died in 1835, and that no stories associating him with any such activity ever arose in Andover either during his lifetime or for the next one hundred years, the claim that he served as an operator for the Underground Railroad must be judged to have no standing.

## 4. POTTER WAS BURIED IN AN UPRIGHT POSITION

This bizarre story sprang up apparently out of nowhere in 1895 and disappeared as quickly as it had arisen. But nothing, it seems, ever dies completely on the Internet; the story has recently been dredged up and circulated again. Like many skillful folk myths, it strives for verisimilitude by including a handful of very specific details and claims.

In 1895 a handful of newspapers across the country included the following brief note as "filler," an anecdote that would engage and amuse readers:

Buried in a Standing Position.

"Notes from the Curious" has been made a repository for many accounts of curious and eccentric burials, but one of the most remarkable on record still remains to be told. Potter, the magician, was a most eccentric living character, and it was not at all out of keeping with his every day life that he should make a dying request that his remains should be interred in a standing position. He died at Potter Place, N.H., and was buried on the following day in a grave 21 × 30 inches and 9 feet deep. The coffin was lowered small end first, and to this day "as upright as Potter's corpse" is one of the proverbs of New Hampshire.

"Notes for the Curious" was a column of curiosities published in the Saturday and daily editions of the *St. Louis Republic* from 1888 until the very beginning of 1899. It was widely reprinted, but there is no evidence that this anecdote ever appeared there. I have been able to locate it in only three small newspapers, all based in towns quite remote from New Hampshire: the *Spokane (WA) Weekly Spokesman Review* (30 May 1895, 2), the *Anderson (SC) Intelligencer* (12 June 1895, 4), and the *Omaha (NE) Daily Bee* (12 June 1895, 4). Whether these picked it up from some earlier, still unidentified source is not known.

Richard Potter was not, in fact, an eccentric person, and such a request would most definitely not have been in keeping with his everyday life. In any event, there is no trace of such a rumor anywhere in all the New Hampshire lore about Richard Potter, nor any trace of the supposed regional "proverb" invoking his corpse. Moreover, the coffins of both Potter and his wife were exhumed, moved a few yards, and reburied at a new site circa 1847, when the new Northern Railroad came through Andover. Had Potter's original interment been so unusual, it would have attracted attention and prompted comment at this time, no less than it would have at his funeral in 1835; it did not. Finally, Potter's grave is marked not only by a headstone but by a footstone as well. Had his coffin been interred vertically, there would have been no call for a footstone, and indeed in those circumstances a footstone would probably have provoked comment. All evidence suggests, then, that the "Buried in a Standing Position" story is completely bogus.

# Notes

## Introduction

2    *"Last evening, Mr. Potter"*: *Mississippi Republican* (Natchez), 15 May 1821, 3.

5    *"Among the ignorant the magician"*: *Boston Journal,* 31 July 1874, 1.

6    *"that Potter told him . . . ten years of age"*: Ketchum, "Richard Potter," 57.

7    the *"increasing forgetfulness . . . instead of Frankland Street"*: Stimson, "Sir Harry Frankland."

7    *Ketchum speculates that . . . happy to mislead him:* Ketchum, "Richard Potter," 57, 60, 58.

7    *"the general understanding . . . West India Islands"*: Ibid., 57.

8    *"a black silk robe"*: "Hocus-Pocus Potter," *Portsmouth (NH) Journal,* 19 June 1852, 1.

8    *"When definitely questioned . . . the popular belief"*: Eastman, *History of the Town of Andover, New Hampshire,* 1:425.

9    *One survey:* Hinks, *To Awaken My Afflicted Brethren,* 267–68.

9    *For a slightly different perspective:* "Massachusetts, Boston Tax Records, 1822–1918."

11    *"celebrated in their own day . . . shadowy figures now"*: Burke, *Popular Culture in Early Modern Europe,* 87. The quotations come from the conclusion of a chapter characterizing popular culture and its transmitters as "An Elusive Quarry."

11    *As Simon During:* During, *Modern Enchantments.* The quotations are from 1, 2, 60.

12    *Joseph Roach, writing:* Roach, *It,* 8, 3, 235n24.

12    *unless your name . . . Webster or Lafayette:* Even in this context, it is worth harkening to Ketchum's apt reminder that Richard Potter "was almost as well known in his day as Daniel Webster" (Ketchum, *The Original Sources of Historical Knowledge,* 13). Ketchum's pamphlet reprises his address to the New Hampshire Historical Society's annual meeting, 13 June 1877.

12    *Roach proposes:* Roach, *It,* 36–37.

## 1. The Hopkinton Years, 1783–1795

15    *"Black Dinah, stolen"*: Holmes, "Agnes," pt. 3, lines 9–10, in *The Complete Poetical Works of Oliver Wendell Holmes,* 92.

15 *Frankland owned . . . sixteen other slaves:* Nason, *Sir Charles Henry Frankland,* 112. See also Bauer, *Marblehead's Pygmalion,* a revisionist examination of Agnes Surriage's story that effectively refutes or questions many of the more sentimental aspects of the traditional tale.

15 *at least six children:* Nason, in *Sir Charles Henry Frankland,* names six children (114–15). In his manuscript "Notes for a History of Hopkinton, MA," however, he indicates that there were seven—"Villot, Phebe, Julia, Sidney, Robert and Richard and one more" (304).

15 *probably her last:* The 1850 census indicates that Phebe was born circa 1785; the 1860 census, circa 1783. In both of these, Cromwell was listed as ten years younger than she. But after they both died, as paupers in the town's care, later in 1860, her age at death was recorded as eighty-four; his, as sixty-four (which was correct). So Phebe was born circa 1776; she was probably Dinah's second child and second daughter, after Julia (b. 1775) ("Andover Selectmen Reports and Accounts, 1860–1882": "County Paupers": 20 Feb. 1861 entry, "Names and ages of those [paupers] who have died within the year").

16 *"gave her a crown . . . wear to meeting":* Nason, *Sir Charles Henry Frankland,* 24–25.

16 *"a few aged persons":* Ibid., 36.

16 *"even this and . . . to their knowledge":* Foote, *Annals of King's Chapel,* 2:156.

16 *"retirement from the . . . tongues of Boston":* Nason, *Sir Charles Henry Frankland,* 39.

17 *Agnes set out to find him:* Ibid., 64.

17 *As an English nun in Lisbon:* Sister Catherine Witham, letter of 27 Jan. 1755/6; qtd. in Bauer, *Marblehead's Pygmalion,* 99, who cites (136n98) the Archives of Syon Abbey, Marley Head, South Brent, Devon.

17 *In any event, Sir Harry:* Nason, *Sir Charles Henry Frankland,* 67, quoting Frankland's journal.

17 *"from which arose . . . ease and safety":* Ibid., 73.

18 *"the show place of the country":* The quotation is from page 12 of a manuscript in the possession of the Hopkinton, Massachusetts, public library—apparently notes made by Nason toward his biography of Frankland, "Thrown away by Mrs. Pulver" but salvaged by someone else.

18 *"large and strongly built . . . anterooms and chambers":* Nason, *Sir Charles Henry Frankland,* 41–42.

18 *Jacques Joseph Villiers:* Nason, from notes "Thrown away by Mrs. Pulver," 11–12.
We find mention of Villiers in a diary entry by the Rev. Ebenezer Parkman, the first minister of the adjacent town of Westborough:

> I proceeded to Sir Harry Frankland's seat kept now by Mr. Jacques Joseph Villiers de Rohan marié avec Mademoiselle Frances de Turenne, he gave me such slips, branches, cions, and seeds, as I desired, and lent me Du Moulin's book of ye Accomplishment of ye Prophecies, or Third Book of ye Defense of ye Catholique Faith. . . . It being in French, I presume not to read much of it. [19 April 1759]

> My brother assists me in graffing [*sic*] apricocks and apples wc [which] I brought from Sr Henry Frankland's last week. [27 April 1759]

"Visit to Sir Charles Henry Frankland, Hopkinton, Mass. Rev. C. [*sic*] Parkman's Diary."

Nason seems to have viewed Parkman's diary independently, and I have followed his transcription (*Sir Charles Henry Frankland,* 84) of the first passage here (except that Nason's date of April 9 is probably wrong; on this point I have accepted the alternative "April 19" transcription published in "Visit to Sir Charles Henry Frankland").

18    *"many of which she cultivated":* Nason, from notes "Thrown away by Mrs. Pulver," 10.

19    *"Dinah was . . . reason out of her":* Nason, *Sir Charles Henry Frankland,* 113. Nason's description of Dinah's marks in his "Notes for a History of Hopkinton, MA" includes some additional details: "She had 3 marks on each cheek and 3 on her forhead [*sic*] as branded with iron" (304).

19    *As Daniel Littlefield summarizes:* Littlefield, *Rice and Slaves,* 175, 117.

19    *"She went to . . . with Lady Agnes":* Forbes, *The Hundredth Town,* 188.

19    *The brands on her face:* See Dunn, "'Dreadful Idlers' in the Cane Fields," 801.

19    *"She is remembered":* Forbes, *The Hundredth Town,* 188.

19    *Dinah, it is important to recall:* Nason, *Sir Charles Henry Frankland,* 43, 105. Holmes's poetic license puts Dinah in the Frankland household when Agnes Surriage is first introduced there, which happened in 1752. This is surely incorrect.

20    *Agnes's older sister . . . stayed with them in Bath:* Frankland's journal records their departing Bath for Bristol and a passage back to America in early April 1765 (Nason, *Sir Charles Henry Frankland,* 95).

20    *theirs was a small household:* Ibid., 96.

20    *An essay in the "Universal Museum":* Universal Museum 2 (December 1763): 623.

21    *Nason states quite firmly:* Nason, *Sir Charles Henry Frankland,* 113. See also his "Notes for a History of Hopkinton, MA": Julia "was baptized in infancy and was born in the Frankland house" (305); "All [Dinah's] children were baptized while living with Mrs. Swain" (304); "Richard was b. at Mrs. Swain's" (304; Mrs. Swain was Lady Agnes's sister, who continued living on the estate until 1793); "Dick Potter was b. on the Frankland place in the house of Frankland" (303).

21    *Those records were destroyed:* Personal communication from Rev. Michael Billingsley, rector of St. Paul's Episcopal Church, 17 June 2012.

21    *Nason reports, for example:* Nason, "Notes for a History of Hopkinton, MA," 305, 304. When Julia died in 1861, the register of her death indicates that her unnamed father was born in England. So Butler had not only gone to England with Frankland, but he had also originally come from there (*Ashland [MA] Record of Deaths,* 8 May 1861, "Massachusetts Deaths, 1841–1915," database with images, *FamilySearch* [https://familysearch.org/ark:/61903/1:1:N7R6-WLN: 10 December 2014], Julia Bullard Titus, 8 May 1861; citing Ashland, Middlesex, Massachusetts, vol. 148, p. 40, State Archives, Boston).

21    *a story about Potter's surname:* Nason, "Notes for a History of Hopkinton, MA," 303.

21    *"all mulattoes and very bright":* Nason, *Sir Charles Henry Frankland,* 115.

21  *this further to tell:* Nason, "Notes for a History of Hopkinton, MA," 304, 303, 287.

22  *he lived on the Framingham side:* Temple, *History of Framingham, Massachusetts,* 706.

22  *His parents moved . . . to Hopkinton in 1738:* George senior's "dismission" (transfer) from the Chebacco church in Ipswich to the Hopkinton church is recorded in 1738 (see Felt, *History of Ipswich, Essex, and Hamilton,* 81). The birth of his seventh child, Alice, is recorded in Hopkinton after 5 November 1738 (Foster, *Vital Records of Hopkinton, Massachusetts, to the Year 1850,* 172); he and his wife were formally received into membership of the First Congregational Church in Hopkinton on 4 February 1739 (*Manual of the First Congregational Church in Hopkinton, Massachusetts,* 44).

22  *In 1755, he served:* Hurd, *History of Middlesex County, Massachusetts,* 3:788; Nason, "Hopkinton," 1:489.

22  *one very dramatic anecdote:* Prout, "Old Times in Windham, 17," *Windham (NY) Journal,* 17 June 1869, www.rootsweb.ancestry.com/~nygreen2/prout_17.htm.

22  *he was an early enlistee:* There is a record of Stimson's presence in the army at the beginning of June 1776, when he and other soldiers in Capt. Jesse Emes's company (Fifth Middlesex Company) signed a petition to their regimental commander, Col. Samuel Bullard, asking that the company be divided into two companies (*Massachusetts Soldiers and Sailors of the Revolutionary War,* 15:33).

22  *Stimson was recorded again:* Ibid.

22  *"We have advice . . . a moment's warning":* "Providence, July 26," *Boston Gazette,* 31 July 1780, 3.

22  *"The alertness of . . . advance towards Kingsbridge":* Boston *Independent Chronicle,* 10 Aug. 1780, 3.

23  *"grant liberty to . . . flour equivalent thereto":* Hoadley, *The Public Records of the State of Connecticut, from May, 1778, to April, 1780, Inclusive,* 328 (May 1779).

23  *diary of the Rev. Ebenezer Parkman:* Parkman, *The Diary of Rev. Ebenezer Parkman,* 126–28.

23  *"the Congregational Church's particular opprobrium":* "Congregational Church Records 1724–1838," Hopkinton (MA) Public Library, microfilm reel 79–1: "Early Records 1724–1791," entries for 5–8 Oct., 16 Oct., 23 Nov., 4 Dec., and 15 Dec. 1777, and 16 April 1778. A former Hopkinton librarian, Rose Leveille, noted and transcribed these entries some years ago, and I found them in the church records with the help of her memoranda, which are also on file in the library. My quotations are from the church records and differ in minor ways from her transcription.

24  *he went to court quite frequently:* Case files of the Middlesex County (Massachusetts) Court of Common Pleas: Nehemiah Mason v. George Stimpson Junr., March Term 1752; Jonathan Foster v. George Stimson Junr., March Term 1752; John Turing v. George Stimson Junr., March Term 1752; Daniel Fairbank v. George Stimson Junr., May Term 1756; William Brown v. George Stimpson Junr., Sept. Term 1762; Abraham Whitney v. George Stimson Junr., May Term 1765; George Stimson Junr. v. James Mellen, Sept. Term 1765; Joseph Wood v. George Stimson Junr., Sept. Term 1765; Ephraim Ware v. George Stimson Junr.,

Sept. Term 1768; David Cutler v. George Stimson, Nov. Term 1773, case 2 (presumably Stimson's father died between 1768 and 1773, after which the son was no longer "Junior"); Convene Richardson v. George Stimson, Nov. Term 1781, case 77; Samuel Haven v. George Stimson, March Term 1784, case 40; Jephtha Richard v. George Stimson, March Term 1781, case 18; Richard Everett v. George Stimson, Nov. Term 1781, case 48; George Stimson v. Enoch Fisk, March Term 1784, case 11; Boston Marine Society v. George Stimson, Nov. Term 1784, cases 42 and 43. Massachusetts State Archives. These represent but a fraction of Stimson's court entanglements. In addition to his suits against fellow Congregationalists, for example, he was a defendant in a case brought by Isaiah Lealand in 1786 (neither party appeared in court, so the case was dropped), and he was published in the *Massachusetts Gazette* in 1765 as "now absconding or concealing himself" from his creditors, a case that I have not been able to identify further (see *The Acts and Resolves, Public and Private, of the Province of the Massachusetts Bay,* vol. 4 [Boston, 1890], 795–96; and *Boston News-Letter,* 21 Nov. 1765, 4).

25    *In late 1771:* Case files of the Middlesex County (Massachusetts) Court of Common Pleas: Gilbert Dench v. George Stimson, May Term 1772, case 41; George Stimson v. Gilbert Dench, May Term 1772, case 58.

25    *Dench now brought three suits:* Case files of the Middlesex County (Massachusetts) Court of Common Pleas: Gilbert Dench v. George Stimson, Sept. Term 1782, case 3; Gilbert Dench v. George Stimson, Sept. Term 1782, case 19; Gilbert Dench and Lawson Buckminster v. George Stimson, Sept. Term 1782, case 8; George Stimson v. Gilbert Dench and Lawson Buckminster, Sept. Term 1782, case 20. Massachusetts Superior Court of Judicature, Suffolk County: Gilbert Dench and Lawson Buckminster v. George Stimson, April Term 1785, 79.

26    *Stimson refused to . . . of Stimson's debt:* Middlesex County (MA) Land Records: Deeds 1785–1788, vol. 89, 273–75.

26    *two other sons . . . were schoolmasters:* Barry, *A History of Framingham, Massachusetts,* 79n., reports that George and Ephraim Stimson were reputedly schoolmasters in Framingham, probably in the 1780s.

27    *"he would not live where justice could not be done him":* Diman, *Leaves from a Family Tree,* 19. Diman gives no source for this quotation.

27    *Stimson in 1786 moved to the eastern Catskills:* Vedder, *History of Greene County,* 121, 127.

27    *Local history recounts . . . rejoin his young son:* Ibid., 127; Dodd, "Centennial of the Old First Congregational Church, Windham, New York 1803–1903," www.rootsweb.ancestry.com/~nygreen2/1st_congregational_church_windham.htm.

27    *In a single season . . . villages in New York:* For records of Stimson and his family in Windham and Ashland, New York, see Vedder, *History of Greene County,* 15, 121, 127; see also Woodworth, comp., "Men of Greene County in the American Revolution," www.rootsweb.ancestry.com/~nygreen2/rw_-_men_of_greene_county.htm.

28    *In support of that scheme: Proceedings of the Commissioners of Indian Affairs, appointed by law for the Extinguishment of Indian Titles in the State of New York,* 119–26n; Stimson's presence is noted on 122n and 125n.

28   *As Lewis Cass Aldrich summarizes:* Aldrich, comp., *History of Ontario County, New York,* 80–85; the quotation is from 82.

28   *she was almost certainly George Stimson's sister:* Nason guessed that Daniel Mc-Clester's wife was the Sarah Stimson who was George Stimson's daughter (see his "Notes for the History of Hopkinton," 267, 302). But this is certainly wrong. We know that a Sarah Stimson married Increase Claflin in Framingham in April 1782 (Baldwin, comp., *Vital Records of Framingham, Massachusetts to the Year 1850,* 377; she was twenty-one years old at the time; he was twenty-three); and we also know that, when George Stimson took his entire family (save son Jeremy) with him to the Catskills in 1787 or so, one of his sons-in-law accompanying him there was Increase Claflin. Increase and Sarah had several children (two in Hopkinton, then six more in Windham, New York); she finally died in Ohio in 1843. So Stimson's daughter was certainly not the Sarah Stimson who married Daniel McClester. Moreover, Daniel McClester's wife died of smallpox in January 1793 at the age of fifty, indicating a birth year of 1742. George Stimson's sister Sarah was born in 1740 (his daughter Sarah was born in 1759). Daniel McClester was born in about 1738 or 1739, making him an agemate for George Stimson's sister. Further, another genealogical tradition records that "his son, Jeremy Stimson, M.D., wedded Col. Jones' daughter, and his sister, Sarah, a nephew of Lady Henry Frankland" (*The National Cyclopaedia of American Biography,* 10:361). It was George Stimson's sister Sarah, not his daughter Sarah, who married Daniel McClester.

29   *house was adjacent to the Frankland estate:* Nason reports that Sarah Stimson Mc-Clester, who died of smallpox at the Frankland estate in January 1793, was buried "in the woods between that house [the Frankland house] & Dr. Stimpsons" ("Notes for a History of Hopkinton, MA," 333).

29   *"in the year 1800 . . . a buggy bought instead":* Frederic J. Stimson (great-grandson of the first Dr. Jeremy Stimson), "Views of Readers: Sir Harry Frankland," *New York Times,* 3 Dec. 1910, BR12.

29   *when Potter's estate was inventoried:* Merrimack County (NH) Office of Probate, Richard Potter 1835, Case No. 1233.

30   *"last heard of at Lansingburg, N.Y.":* Ketchum, "Richard Potter," 61.

30   *living usually in Westborough:* Forbes, *The Hundredth Town,* 191, reports that Julia returned to the town in 1820 "and lived in Mr. Wesson's family."

30   *she lived with a succession of local families:* In the 1850 census, she is living in the household of Hannah Fairbanks, recently widowed, and her six children; in the 1855 Massachusetts census, she is living with the family of Samuel and Sally Frail (Samuel was Hannah Fairbanks's older brother) and their seven children; in the 1860 census, she is living in a mixed household headed by Joel T. Pratt.

30   *Violet, too, remained on the Frankland estate:* Nason, *Sir Charles Henry Frankland,* 115n.

30   *Sidney . . . town of Westborough:* Forbes, *The Hundredth Town,* 191. Forbes reports that she was "Mrs. Gibson" in her first marriage.

30   *the intention of Reuben Titus . . . she gave birth to two sons:* Foster, ed., *Vital Records of Hopkinton, Massachusetts, to the Year 1850,* 159, 348. I have confirmed these records from the originals in the town clerk's office at the Hopkinton Town Hall.

Nason, "Notes for the History of Hopkinton, MA," 304, reports some of the gossip about another of Sidney's children decades afterward: "Sidney, [Dinah's] daughter, lived at Abel Smith's and had a son Robert who was said to be son of Abel." A later entry adds, "Aaron Smith says Jno. Barret was the father."

30  *Reuben was a known slacker:* Reuben Titus, described as "a negro man and idler," later became a ward of the nearby town of Holliston after the selectmen petitioned to have a guardian appointed for him, "for that said Reuben by excessive idleness and debauchery so expends wasts [wastes] and lessens his estate as thereby to expose himself to want and sufferring [*sic*] circumstances and also to endanger and expose the said town of Holliston to a charge and expense for his support and maintenance." At this time he "had not any property which could be inventoried." He remained a ward for decades, probably for the rest of his life: an account rendered by his guardian in October 1830, well over twenty-three years later, showed that he had been a ward all that time. Reuben signed the account with his mark, *X:* he was illiterate (Middlesex County [MA] Probate File 22622: Reuben Titus, Massachusetts State Archives).

30  *Robert Potter:* There were two different men—both named Robert Potter, both black, both married to black women—who were members of the First Church of Charlestown circa 1815, and probably one of these was Richard Potter's brother. (Membership in a predominantly white, Congregational church would have been consistent with his upbringing in Dr. Jeremy Stimson's household.) The records of the First Church of Charlestown show that Robert Potter's wife, a black, died at the age of thirty-three on 26 November 1815. But then another Congregationalist, also described as Robert Potter's wife, a black, died at the age of thirty-four on 27 April 1816. Then a Robert Potter, also black, died at the age of thirty-five on 17 September 1816. This indicates he had been born in 1781, which would be an excellent fit for Richard Potter's brother (First Church [Charlestown, Boston, MA] Records, "Vital Statistics 1797–1894," Box 3, Folder 9: "The Deaths from Jany 1st 1815 to the 1st Jany. 1816," "Deaths in the year, 1816," collection of the Massachusetts Historical Society).

The records of Charlestown show a "Mr. Robert Potter of Charlestown and Miss Jane Perkins of Cambridge" publishing their marriage intention at the beginning of September 1805 ("Blacks" is recorded in the margin of the entry) and then marrying on 17 October of that year. Six years later, this Robert (described as a "laborer") purchased from Prince Jones, a black mariner, a half part of a lot with buildings in Charlestown. Jane signed off on the accompanying mortgage (Robert was spreading his payments for the lot over a three-year period), relinquishing her right of dower. Robert, however, signed only with his mark; he was illiterate (see Joslyn, *Vital Records of Charlestown, Massachusetts to the Year 1850,* 1:520; Wyman, *The Genealogies and Estates of Charlestown, Massachusetts 1629–1818,* 768, 1136; and Middlesex County [MA] Registry of Deeds, vol. 194, 488 [Prince Jones to Robert Potter] and 490 [Robert Potter to Prince Jones]). It is quite difficult to imagine that Richard's brother Robert could have been raised in Hopkinton in his half brother's highly educated family (Jeremy Stimson was a doctor, and his oldest son attended Harvard) and yet kept illiterate while his siblings, living next door on the Frankland estate, were being taught to read and sent to school, so this particular Robert Potter was probably not Richard Potter's brother.

30   *Cromwell himself had already spent some time living in Andover:* Case files of the Hillsborough County (NH) Court of Common Pleas, September Term 1816, Charles Thompson v. Richard Potter, case 1181; Cromwell Potter v. Richard Potter, case 1182, New Hampshire State Archives.

31   *"an invaluable member . . . solved the race question":* Eastman, *History of the Town of Andover, New Hampshire,* 1:427.

31   *while awaiting her departure:* Nason, *Sir Charles Henry Frankland,* 104.

31   *the local Committee of Safety:* Ibid., 109, 112.

32   *Lady Agnes Frankland . . . died at the age of fifty-seven:* Bauer, *Marblehead's Pygmalion,* 125–26.

32   *the grand Boston house was willed:* Nason, *Sir Charles Henry Frankland,* 106.

32   *trying to sell it:* In a 1786 letter to his old friend William Price (son of the former rector) in Hopkinton, Cromwell sought help in engaging "as Honest a Lawyer as you can find" to serve as agent in the sale, and was willing to subdivide it as necessary: "let it be Divided into as many Parts as you think it will sell to the best advantage" (Henry Cromwell to William Price, 24 July 1786; collection of the Massachusetts Historical Society).

32   *the couple had moved to Holliston:* Nason, *Sir Charles Henry Frankland,* 107. (Henry Frankland Dupee was erroneously recorded there in the 1790 census as "Henry Franklin Dupree.")

32   *Sarah Stimson McClester:* Ibid., 108; Foster, ed., *Vital Records of Hopkinton, Massachusetts,* 435.

32   *the Dupees and his mother:* Nason, *Sir Charles Henry Frankland,* 107.

32   *"a great favorite . . . her early days":* Ibid., 108.

33   *little more than two years old:* According to Chapman, comp., *Vital Records of Marblehead, Massachusetts to the End of the Year 1849,* 1:463 (citing the records of the town's Second Congregational [Unitarian] Church), she was baptized on 30 January 1774. Nason, in *Sir Charles Henry Frankland,* however, says her birthday was 27 January 1773 (108). Such intervals between birth and baptism were common. Nason was well aware of the baptismal date (see 24n) and presumably had some evidence for the actual birthdate.

33   *she and Jennie used to plague old Robert:* Nason, *Sir Charles Henry Frankland,* 113.

33   *"were set at liberty soon after" this decision:* Ibid., 112.

33   *Other legal decisions soon followed:* On the James v. Lechmere case, see Zobel, "Jonathan Sewall," 123–36. On the Quock Walker cases, see esp. Cushing, "The Cushing Court and the Abolition of Slavery in Massachusetts: More Notes on the 'Quock Walker Case,'" 118–44. For a general appraisal, see MacEacheren, "Emancipation of Slavery in Massachusetts: A Reexamination 1770–1790," 289–306.

34   *Potter "attended school" in Hopkinton:* Nason, *Sir Charles Henry Frankland,* 113. See also Nason, "Notes for a History of Hopkinton, MA," 303.

34   *according to a local historian:* Weston, "The Valentines of Boston and Hopkinton," 130.

34 *Samuel Valentine and his wife:* Ibid.

35 *the marriage intention of Dinah Franklin:* Foster, ed., *Vital Records of Hopkinton, Massachusetts,* 273.

35 *the marriage never actually took place:* In the 1790 census a Mr. Allen (no first name given), a freeman (that is, not white), is recorded living alone in Boston. In late November 1794 the marriage of "Pompe Allen resident of Stoughton & Annis Rings of Stoughton" was published in Stoughton, Massachusetts (Endicott, ed., *The Record of Births, Marriages and Deaths and Intentions of Marriage, in the Town of Stoughton from 1727 to 1800, and in the Town of Canton from 1797 to 1845,* 162; Baldwin, comp., *Vital Records of Sharon, Massachusetts, to the Year 1850,* 131). In the 1800 census, "Pompy Allen" is included in a short list of "Negro" residents appended at the end of the census for Needham, Massachusetts.

35 *"Undertook to sell some negros":* Nason, "Notes for a History of Hopkinton, MA," 302.

35 *Julia left Hopkinton . . . returned to Hopkinton:* Nason, *Sir Charles Henry Frankland,* indicates that Julia "was a servant of Mrs. J. Dupee until the age of 17" (114), but in his unpublished "Notes for a History of Hopkinton, MA," he further records that she "lived with Mrs. Swain and Dr. Dupee till she was 18 years old in H[opkinton] and in Dedham" (305). Nason also notes, from an entry in Dr. Shepherd's manuscript journal, that Julia and Vilot (Violet) were among Dr. Shepherd's servants as of July 1794 (*Sir Charles Henry Frankland,* 115n).

35 *"she used to live in a nail shop":* Nason, "Notes for a History of Hopkinton, MA," 304. Weston, "The Valentines of Boston and Hopkinton," 126, notes that Samuel Valentine, who owned a large farm adjacent to the Frankland estate, was part owner of "a nail-factory, near the 'Old Ford,' some distance from his farm" and also of "a wire-mill on the stream below the grist-mill" closer by (of which he was also a part owner).

35 *service with Isaac Surriage's family:* Nathan Hale, who met Potter in 1831 and was "curious to know a little of his history," recounted that "he was the favourite pet of a very respectable mistress, and of her whole family, whom I after visited at H*** about thirty miles from town [Boston]" (*Notes Made during an Excursion,* 92). This could only have been Jennie Surriage Bixby, who continued to live in Hopkinton until her death in 1839.

## 2. The Boston Years and Europe, 1795–1803

37 *a close neighbor . . . associate of Nell's father:* "Nell Sr. was a tailor who ran a shop just a few doors down from David Walker's used clothing store in Boston. Both Nell Sr. and Walker were members of the General Colored Association of Massachusetts, an anti-slavery association founded in 1826" (*Encyclopedia of African American History,* 488).

37 *Nell is the first historian:* Nell, *The Colored Patriots of the American Revolution,* 93.

38 *Richard Potter lived for a year or so only a few blocks away from the Nells:* The Boston Tax Records for 1827 show that Nell was then living on May Street just off

of South Russell Street, while Potter and Pitts were both living on Ridgeway Alley, three streets east of South Russell (see Tax Books, 1827, Ward 7, 51; Transfer Books, 1827, Ward 7, 51; Valuation Books, 1827, Ward 7, 45).

38 *Peletiah Bixby Jr.:* Foster, ed., *Vital Records of Hopkinton, Massachusetts,* 226. Nason reports that Peletiah "once lived with Mrs. Swain & Col. [?] Jno Jones—and thus made acquaintance with Jane S" ("Notes for a History of Hopkinton, MA," 311).

38 *how the Dillaways and the Bixbys intersected:* Nason, *Sir Charles Henry Frankland,* 106, mentions that the Boston mansion, while still in possession of the Frankland family, was rented to (among others) a Mr. Bixby.

39 *"he remained with his father a few years":* Weston, "The Valentines of Boston and Hopkinton," 132.

39 *"ignorant, haughty, and ill-tempered":* Nason, "Notes for a History of Hopkinton, MA," 283.

40 *the brig Neptune:* The *Neptune* was captured in the Caribbean by a French privateer in April 1797 while en route from Martinique back to Boston, then retaken by a British armed ship (see Williams, *The French Assault on American Shipping, 1793–1813,* 261).

40 *He also traded in other merchandise:* See, for example, advertisements in the Boston papers *Federal Orrery* (17 Sept. 1795), *Massachusetts Mercury* (13 Oct. 1795, 5 April 1796, 12 Oct. 1802), *Boston Columbian Centinel* (2 and 12 Nov. 1796, 15 June 1803, 20 March 1805), *Boston Commercial Gazette* (22 Dec. 1800, 4 May 1801, 18 Feb. 1802), *New-England Palladium* (18 Aug. 1807, 13 May 1809).

We get a glimpse of Dillaway's business from a newspaper story about the major fire that incinerated much of the Boston waterfront on 30 July 1794: the long list of losses included "Mr. Samuel Dillaway's Compting house and new barn, containing a quantity of fish, together with his lumber wharf, containing near 200,000 feet boards, 100.000 shingles, timber, etc." (*Concord [NH] Mirror,* 11 Aug. 1794, 3; see also *Boston Apollo,* 31 July 1794, 3; *Newburyport [MA] Morning Star,* 5 Aug. 1794).

40 *an infant son, who most probably came to live with his mother's family:* The 1800 census shows Samuel Dillaway—this was Samuel junior—living in Roxbury in a household that included two free white males under the age of ten. He himself had one son at the time (Charles Knapp Dillaway, born circa 1798); the other boy was probably John Somes.

41 *she was recorded as relinquishing her right of dower:* See Suffolk County (MA) Deeds, vol. 177, 161v. She had done the same on earlier sales of property in 1780 and 1790; see vol. 132, 55; and vol. 168, 154v.

41 *born in November 1747: Boston Births from A.D. 1700 to A.D. 1800,* 264: "Mary Daughter of William Lambert and Judeth his Wife, 22 November 1747."

41 *"to my Son Samuel Dillaway . . . anything more of my estate":* Suffolk County (MA) Probate Records, "Samuel Dillaway," 1822, No. 26720, Massachusetts State Archives. It should be noted that Dillaway, having provided for a generous lifetime annuity for his daughter Eliza (still a "Singlewoman" at that time), directed that, after her death, his estate should pass in equal shares to his grandchildren

who were the children of his son Samuel Dillaway and of his late daughter Mary Skinner. His other grandchild, John Somes, is not mentioned. (This may be because John Somes was already a notorious "spendthrift"; in 1818, when he turned twenty-four, a guardian was appointed for him by the court for that reason, he having demonstrated over the course of the three preceding years that he could not responsibly manage his own affairs.) (Suffolk County [MA]: Reports of Cases Argued and Determined in the Supreme Judicial Court, "Somes v. Brewer," March Term 1824, vol. 19, 184–85.) Nor did Dillaway think or choose to make any provision for any future grandchildren by Eliza should she later marry (as in fact she did, in 1824, although she never had children).

42 *the captain of a ship . . . Boston from Martinique: Boston Columbian Centinel,* 11 April 1798, 3; *New York Price-Current,* 19 May 1798, 4. The latter paper mistakenly gives the name of the brig as *Brothers,* but the captain is the same, so this is clearly the same ship. After the Revolutionary War, American vessels were barred from direct trade with British Caribbean ports; young Samuel Dillaway was apparently confining his travels to French Caribbean islands.

42 *the younger Dillaway advertised: Boston Daily Advertiser,* 11 Sept. 1816, 2. After the Congress of Vienna, free trade had reopened British West Indies ports to American shipping.

42 *he told . . . he had been in the West Indies:* [Hale], *Notes Made during an Excursion,* 93.

42 *"finally went . . . to reside in England":* Nason, *Sir Charles Henry Frankland,* 113.

42 *referred to familiarly as part of Roxbury:* William Skinner's estate was on the Dorchester side of the road then marking the boundary between Roxbury and Dorchester. The property had earlier been the estate of Increase Sumner, the fifth governor of Massachusetts (1797–99), who was always called a resident of Roxbury (see Massachusetts Land Records, 1620–1986: Norfolk County [MA] Deeds, 1814–1816, vol. 50, 9).

42 *Some of the brothers traveled:* Court records indicate that William's brother Richard was doing business in Paris in 1795 or 1796 (there was some dispute about the date) (Child, "Review of a Report to the House of Representatives," "Appendix," 8). William himself sailed from Boston to London on the ship *Minerva,* Captain Turner, on 30 May 1796 (*Massachusetts Mercury,* 27 May 1796, 2; *New Hampshire Gazette* [Portsmouth], 28 May 1796, 3; *Alexandria [VA] Columbian Mirror,* 7 June 1796, 3). It arrived at Dover on 21 June.

43 *"was at ten years . . . magician and ventriloquist":* Ketchum, "Richard Potter," 57.

43 *This account was . . . by Stephen Fellows:* It is clear that Fellows misunderstood, misremembered, embellished, or even made up many of the stories about Potter that he later spread—the story, for example, that Potter was the child of Benjamin Franklin, who had established his mother and him in a home in a back street behind the statehouse in Boston, where Potter had lived until he was ten years old, or again the story that Potter's wife was "a full-blooded Penobscot-Indian Squaw" (she was a black or mulatto woman from Roxbury, Massachusetts). Even Ketchum, who was eager to fill in the outlines of Potter's life, recognized that Fellows was a gullible, fanciful, and often unreliable source. Moreover, once Fellows

came to realize that there was a growing desire for information about Potter's life, he tried to take advantage of the opportunity. In the Milbourne Christopher Collection (which has since been dispersed) there was a handwritten receipt from J. Currier made out to "Potter Jr." on 23 March 1839 for a one-dollar payment (this was possibly Joshua Currier, who had a business in Meredith, New Hampshire, Glover & Currier, at this time). Appended to this receipt, surely decades later, is the following handwritten note: "Any person wishing information of the history of Richard Potter, the ventriloquist I will freely give all the information in my power with pleasure. Stephen Fellows Grafton Center N.H." I am grateful to Maurine Christopher, Milbourne Christopher's widow, who generously gave me access to the collection in February 1998.

44 *very authoritative account of Potter's background:* Oliver, letter to the editor, *Boston Journal,* 7 Aug. 1874, 1. Oliver was responding to a story about Potter that had appeared in the paper a week earlier.

44 *Potter told Hale:* [Hale], *Notes Made during an Excursion,* 92.

45 *John Skinner & Sons and then Baker & Skinner had imported goods:* John Skinner & Sons advertisement, *Boston Independent Chronicle,* 23 May 1793, 3, lists goods "just received by the Minerva, Captain Prince, from France"; Baker & Skinner advertisement, *Massachusetts Mercury,* 11 Nov. 1800, 3, lists goods received by the ship *Diana;* Shipping News, *Boston Columbian Centinel,* 9 Aug. 1800, 3, reports that the *Diana,* Captain Thomas, had recently been at Leghorn; Shipping News, *Boston Columbian Centinel,* 29 Nov. 1800, 3, reports that the *Diana,* Captain Thomas, of Boston, had been captured by Corsican pirates in the Mediterranean, but he had been able to retake the ship (by the time this report appeared the ship had already returned to Boston); William S. Skinner advertisement, *Columbian Centinel,* 24 June 1801, 3, lists for sale (among other fancy goods) "One thousand dozen of Paris made Gloves, some extra long and fine"; William S. Skinner advertisement, *Boston Independent Chronicle,* 16 Nov. 1801, announces the public auction of "The Whole of his Stock of European Goods," including "Many French and Italian Goods."

45 *"the London Little Devil":* Relf's *Philadelphia Gazette,* 31 July 1811, 2.

45 *Highfill, Burnim, and Langhans:* Highfill, Burnim, and Langhans, *Biographical Dictionary of Actors, Actresses, Musicians, Dancers,* 12:289; cf. 14:144 ("Smith, George"), 14:339 ("Sully, Matthew"), 14:344 ("Sutton, Giles").

45 *In 1786 alone: Morning Chronicle (London),* 31 May 1786; *Morning Post* (London), 12 July 1786; *Morning Post* (London), 14 July 1786; *Morning Chronicle (London),* 20 July 1786.

46 *by the turn of the century . . . "Little Devils" every year:* For examples, see *Diary or Woodfall's Register,* 2 July 1793 (Sutton at Astley's Amphitheatre); *London Recorder,* 12 May 1793 (Smith with Hughes' Royal Circus); *Felix Farley's Bristol Journal,* 15 June 1799 (Smith); *Newcastle Advertiser,* 23 Feb. 1799, 3 (Saxoni).

46 *a Mr. Martin:* See, for example, the *New York Daily Advertiser,* 2, 7, and 8 Oct. 1793, where he mentions having "exhibited in the theatre here last year by the name of the Little Devil" as well.

46 *a Mr. Maginnis: New York Chronicle Express,* 26 April 1804, 3; *Morning Chronicle,*

28 April 1804. Maginnis had been performing in the United States since 1795, and in Canada the year before that.

46 *Signior Manfredi: Philadelphia True American,* 14 Jan. 1804.

46 *Redigé, the original "Little Devil":* For a review of Placide's and Redigé's careers, see Moore, "New York's First Ballet Season," 478–91.

47 *"He balances . . . goes to his knees":* Boston Gazette, 19 Nov. 1810; cf. *Boston Columbian Centinel,* 1 Dec. 1810.

47 *he "will go through . . . boy of his age":* Salem (MA) Gazette, 25 Dec. 1827. See also *Newburyport (MA) Herald,* 11 Jan. 1828, 3; *Rhode-Island Republican* (Newport), 10 Sept. 1829.

47 *"from London" . . . "from Sadler's Wells":* "from London": *York Gazette* (Toronto), 5 May 1810, 4; 12 May 1810, 4; "from Sadler's Wells (London)": *Orange County Patriot* (Goshen, NY), 2 July 1811, 3; "late from Sadler's Wells, London": *New Brunswick (NJ) Guardian,* 11 July 1811, 3.

48 *"as agile as a squirrel":* [Hale], *Notes Made during an Excursion,* 92.

48 *As A. H. Saxon has noted:* Saxon, *The Life and Art of Andrew Ducrow,* 39–40.

49 *"lately from Saddlers Wells":* See, for example, his advertisements in the *Philadelphia Aurora* on 31 Dec. 1803, 5 Jan. 1804, and 10 Jan. 1804.

49 *traveled to Paris . . . and performed there:* see the advertisements for "C[itoye]n Manfredy" in the *Journal de Paris,* 30 Jan.–4 Feb. 1803, 829, 837, 843, 849, 891 [*sic*; actually 853].

49 *sailed on the ship South Carolina:* Through typographers' errors as the news passed from one paper to another, Manfredi shows up on the published lists of passengers sometimes as "Maufredi" or Murfredi" or "Maufrede." (Since a print *u* is simply an inverted print *n* the *n/u* confusion is a common typesetter's error.) See the *New York Evening Post,* 16 May 1803, 3 ("Manfredi"); the *New York Gazette,* 16 May 1803, 3, and the *Fredericktown (MD) Political Intelligencer,* 27 May 1803, 3 ("Maufredi"); the *New York Chronicle Express,* 19 May 1803, 4 ("Maufrede"); the *Albany (NY) Register,* 20 May 1803, 3, and the *Troy (NY) Gazette,* 24 May 1803, 2 ("Murfredi").

49 *Manfredi quickly won wide attention:* New York American Citizen, 27 May 1803, 3; *New York Republican Watch-Tower,* 4 June 1803, 3; *New York Herald,* 4 June 1803, 2.

50 *Manfredi's repertoire:* "Signior Manfredi" broadside, Portsmouth, NH, 23 Sept. 1803; collection of American Antiquarian Society (fig. 1).

50 *Manfredi's announced destination now was Boston:* New York Daily Advertiser, 1 Aug. 1803; *New York American Citizen,* 1 Aug. 1803.

50 *his "astonishing feats . . . ever attempted":* Rhode-Island Republican, 20 Aug. 1803.

51 *"Our old citizens . . . fire of 1812":* Portsmouth (NH) Journal, 19 June 1852, 1. The Great Fire that destroyed so much of central Portsmouth actually occurred in December 1813 (Brewster wrote a column about that event, too); and the hotel was usually called the New Hampshire Hotel.

51 *"On the west . . . early life a servant":* Brewster, *Rambles about Portsmouth,* 2:209. This "Rambles about Portsmouth" column originally appeared in the *Portsmouth (NH) Journal* of 5 Jan. 1861, 2.

52 *what a broadside!:* "Signior Manfredi, artist of agility and rope dancer," 1803 broadside; collection of the American Antiquarian Society (fig. 1).

52 *a skilled artisan . . . in New York City:* This is highly likely because Manfredi had remained so long in New York, his first venue in the United States, before he headed north. It is further confirmed by another extant Manfredi broadside, this one dating from September 1805, when he exhibited in Albany. That broadside, printed on both sides of a sheet—text on one side, illustrative woodcuts on the other—includes eight woodcuts, among them three that Manfredi had used earlier in his 1803 Portsmouth broadside. Of the remaining five woodcuts, moreover, four show, not Manfredi, but Mrs. Manfredi (two woodcuts) and one or both of his young daughters (two more woodcuts). Manfredi had gone back to Europe to rejoin his family in 1804 and had just brought them back with him in June 1805; they had exhibited in New York City for more than two and a half months before moving directly on to Albany. Since four of these new woodcuts show Manfredi's wife and daughters, they could not date back to 1803; they must have been newly carved for his new, family tour in America, and thus carved in New York City. (It is unlikely that he brought them with him from Europe.) The highly distinctive near-circular frame and the consistent artistic style of all of the woodcuts, moreover, strongly suggest that they all are the work of the same artist (see broadside, "Exhibition, at the Thespian Hotel, Pearl-Street, Albany. A numerous company of rope dancers," 19 Sept. 1805, Early American Imprints, 2nd ser., no. 8414; the attribution of the wood engravings there to "famed woodengraver DR. ANDER-SON" is surely incorrect).

55 *The case was tried before the Circuit Court of Judiciary at Inverness:* Circuit Court of Judiciary case files, JC26–1800–58; held in the National Archives of Scotland, NAS02026. News of the court's judgment was published in the *Caledonian Mercury* (Edinburgh), 8 May 1800, the *Edinburgh Advertiser,* 6 May 1800, and the *Aberdeen Journal,* 12 May 1800.

55 *James was performing in Aberdeen: Aberdeen Journal,* 12 May 1800.

56 *"MR. RANNIE, The celebrated Ventriloquist": Philadelphia Gazette,* 5 May 1801, 2.

57 *during his week in Salem: Salem (MA) Gazette,* 21 Oct. 1803, 3; 28 Oct. 1803, 3.

57 *his first advertisement in Boston: Boston Columbian Centinel,* 9 Nov. 1803.

58 *no one in America . . . Rannies and Duff:* For the sake of completeness, I should acknowledge that a Mr. Shepherd advertised programs of legerdemain and balancing that included a few of Rannie's tricks in Philadelphia in December 1802 (in company with a Mr. Niel, who did most of the balancing feats) and again (solo, this time) in Lansingburgh, New York, in July 1804 (*Philadelphia Aurora,* 7, 10, 14, and 23 Dec. 1802; *Troy (NY) Farmer's Register,* 17 July 1804. His advertisements, too, seem derivative of Rannie's. Shepherd is not known ever to have performed again, apart from these two occasions.

58 *performances in Jamaica: St. Jago de la Vega Gazette,* 12–19 Nov. 1803, 395; Rannie's advertisement is dated 19 November.

58 *advertising his second performance in Boston: New-England Palladium,* 11 Nov. 1803.

58 *Manfredi . . . planning his own trip to Havana:* "Mr. Manfredi does not purpose

exhibiting any more than this week owing to his going to the Havanna. THIS EVENING will be his last appearance here" (*Philadelphia Aurora General Advertiser*, 7 Jan. 1804, 3).

59 *"Mr. G. Durang": Philadelphia Aurora, 31 Dec. 1803; Poulson's American Daily Advertiser* (Philadelphia), 4 Jan. 1804.

59 *Manfredi reunited with Durang: Baltimore American and Commercial Daily Advertiser,* 16 Aug. 1804.

59 *another Durang: Jacob junior: Boston Daily Advertiser,* 25 May 1813, 2. Brooks, in *John Durang,* notes that Jacob Durang junior apparently performed with John Durang's company in 1800 and again a few years later but can find no other trace of his stage or dancing career (129–30). But he was working in Boston as a dancing master at least in 1811–13 (see the *Boston Columbian Centinel,* 13 Nov. 1811, 4 ["Mr. Durang, jun."] and 11 March 1812, 4 ["J. P. Durang"]; and the 1813 *Boston Directory* ["Jacob Durang"]).

59 *There is perhaps a hint of him: Philadelphia Aurora,* 14 Jan. 1804; *Philadelphia True American,* 14 Jan. 1804.

60 *Manfredi himself... to a new young pupil:* See, for example, the *Petersburg (VA) Intelligencer,* 12 Sept. 1806, 3; the *Alexandria (VA) Daily Advertiser,* 30 Oct. 1806, 3; and the *Washington, DC, National Intelligencer,* 26 Nov. 1806, 2.

## 3. The Apprentice Years and Early Career, 1804–1815

61 *They traveled now... another month or so: Easton (MD) Republican Star,* 28 Feb. 1804, 3; 17 April 1804, 3; *Maryland Gazette* (Annapolis), 8 March 1804; *Bartgis's Republican Gazette* (Fredericktown, MD), 20 April 1804, 3; *Fredericktown (MD) Republican Advocate,* 20 April 1804, 3; 27 April 1804, 3.

62 *he and his brother were together in Newport: Rhode-Island Republican* (Newport), 29 Jan. 1803, 3; 20 Aug. 1803, 3; *Newport (RI) Mercury,* 16 Aug. 1803, 3.

63 *"Mr. Rannie, the younger... surprising imitations": Newport (RI) Mercury,* 2 June 1804, 3.

63 *"cause the voice... or gentleman present": St. Jago de la Vega Gazette,* 12–19 Nov. 1803, 395.

63 *"when the voice... from being bitten": New York American Citizen,* 27 April 1804, 3. Rannie suddenly began inserting these anecdotes in his advertising beginning on 27 April, so they probably occurred on 26 April.

64 *cutting off and then restoring a cock's head: Montreal Gazette,* 31 Dec. 1804, 3; *New York Daily Advertiser,* 24 April 1804.

64 *"carrying a table covered with glasses": New-England Palladium,* 13 July 1804, 3; *Quebec Mercury,* 23 Feb. 1805, 64.

64 *"a Richard Potter picture on display":* In fact there was no such "picture" (much less portrait) of Richard Potter in the Bostonian Society's collection. When the Bostonian Society refreshed and rearranged its exhibitions in the Old State House in 1888, a curator prominently mounted a recently acquired (in 1887) Potter broadside (another surviving copy of the broadside shown in figure 5) in one of the rooms there. A reporter for the *Boston Daily Journal,* writing a review of the new

exhibition, called attention to this broadside as "one of the most interesting articles in the collections": "It is a picture of Potter, the first black ventriloquist and necromancer on the continent of America" (9 April 1888, 4). The reporter, naturally enough, assumed that the figure illustrated on this broadside was a representation of Potter; actually, however, Potter had acquired this woodcut from James Rannie, and the figure was originally carved to represent Rannie (see appendix B, figure 5).

64 *"After one of . . . give his public exhibitions": Boston Journal,* 18 April 1888.

65 *the person who bought . . . none other than Samuel Dillaway:* Suffolk Co. (MA) Deeds, Vol. 203 (1802–1803), 181, Willett et al. to Dillaway, entered 2 Dec. 1802.

66 *the story of his first acquaintance with Potter:* [Goodwin], "The Potter Place," 2.

67 *"married and became a housekeeper":* Buckingham, *Personal Memoirs,* 1:53.

67 *we can date it . . . before that marriage:* Silas Ketchum assumed that, since Buckingham had left the *Greenfield Gazette* and moved to Boston in 1800, this anecdote surely belonged to 1800–1801 ("Richard Potter," 59). All later commentators have relied on this erroneous assumption.

67 *Joseph Bradley operated . . . took it over in June 1804: Boston Independent Chronicle,* 7 June 1804, 3; *New-England Palladium,* 17 Feb. 1804.

67 *the stage lines . . . all stopped there:* Concerning the stage line connections, see, for example, the *Boston Independent Chronicle,* 13 May 1805, 1; *Newburyport (MA) Herald,* 28 May 1805, 1, *Boston Directory,* 1806.

67 *Barely two years . . . on Marlborough Street: Boston Independent Chronicle,* 21 Aug. 1806, 4.

68 *In the spring of 1804 . . . his new marriage:* Buckingham, *Personal Memoirs,* 1:52–53.

69 *"tears gathered in Buckingham's eyes . . . printer and friend": Boston Journal,* 18 April 1888, 6. The writer, the Hon. John D. Lyman, of Exeter, said Nesmith had told him this story only "a few years since" (quite possible, since Nesmith lived until 1890). The anecdote also appeared in the *Merrimack Journal* (Franklin, NH), 20 April 1888.

69 *"just arrived from the West-Indies . . . a few evenings in this country": New York Daily Advertiser,* 3 April 1804, 2. See also the *New York American Citizen,* 2 April 1804, 3.

69 *a ventriloquial trick he had played in Paris:* See, for example, the *Boston Repertory,* 25 April 1809, 2 (Copenhagen); *Baltimore Federal Gazette,* 11 Dec. 1809, 3; *New York Columbian,* 3 March 1810, 3; and *Philadelphia Aurora,* 14 April 1810, 3 (Paris).

69 *"when in the Indies . . . 18 shillings each": New York American Citizen,* 30 March 1810, 3.

69 *"during the last twenty years . . . the United States":* [Hale], *Notes Made during an Excursion,* 93.

70 *"It is certain . . . not as a soldier":* Ketchum, "Richard Potter," 59.

70 *Potter "went to England and India . . . magician's arts":* [Thyng], *Manchester (NH) Union,* 8 March 1895, 5.

70 *"He went to England . . . to India as stated":* Letter to the editor, *Manchester (NH) Union,* ?/?/1895. This letter was prompted by Thyng's article in the *Union* of 8 March 1895. Charles Adams Bachelder later clipped it and pasted it into one of

his scrapbooks on Andover, New Hampshire, people and events, dating it only "Mon. 1895." The typeface and column width as well as the content indicate that it appeared in the *Union*, but I have not been able to locate it there.

70 *"Potter made two trips . . . practice of his profession":* Boston Herald, 11 Feb. 1906, 52.

70 *She was so identified . . . Andover town history:* Eastman, *History of the Town of Andover, New Hampshire,* 2:277.

71 *"In Andover, Miss Anganet Potter . . . aged 16 years":* New-Hampshire Patriot (Concord), 28 March 1831, 3.

71 *Anganet is adapted from Hindi . . . "a beautiful woman":* See, for example, Gandhi, *The Penguin Book of Hindu Names,* 23 (Angana), 24 (Anjana); and Dogra and Dogra, *A Dictionary of Hindu Names,* 13 (Angana, Anjana, Anjani).

72 *Rannie proceeded again . . . Salem and Newburyport:* See Rannie's advertisements in (among many other Boston newspapers) the *Boston Gazette,* 7, 11, 18, 21, and 28 Jan. 1808; and the *New-England Palladium,* 2 Feb. 1808, 3; also the *Norwich (CT) Courier,* 13 April 1808, 3; *Portsmouth (NH) Oracle,* 30 April 1808, 3; 7 May 1808, 1; *Essex Register* (Salem, MA), 4 and 7 May 1808; *Newburyport (MA) Herald,* 29 April–10 May 1808.

72 *closer to the offices of Thomas & Andrews:* Thomas and Andrews, "then supposed to be the largest printing establishment in America," according to Buckingham (*Personal Memoirs and Recollections,* 1:40), was headquartered at 45 Newbury Street (Newbury Street was a continuation of Marlboro Street to the south; the two met at Winter Street); Buckingham's office, at 15 Winter Street (sometimes given simply as "back of Winter Street"), around the corner from Newbury, probably backed up to the main buildings.

72 *The synopses of the Society . . . hint of his labors:* See "Discourse before the Society for Propagating the Gospel among the Indians and Others in North America" (which contains the annual reports of the Society) for the years 1805 (32–33), 1806 (33), 1807 (21), 1808 (49), 1810 (67), and 1811 (43).

74 *He and Reverend Oliver . . . Others in North America:* Porter was one of the original incorporators of the Society in 1787; and on 5 November 1807 he delivered the main address at the Society's annual meeting (see "A Discourse before the Society for Propagating the Gospel among the Indians and Others in North-America" [Boston: Munroe, Francis & Parker, 1808]).

74 *neither her baptism . . . the church's archives:* The Records of the First Church in Roxbury, 1733–1861, are archived in the library of the Andover-Harvard Theological Library. Richard and Sally's marriage on 15 September 1808 is recorded in the "Register of Marriages, 1782 to 1862" (Box 4[7]). The "Baptisms" records for 1779–1862 (Box 4[4][4], 4[4][5], and 4[4][6]) make no mention of Sally or any other relevant Harris; nor do the records of "Members who have owned the Baptismal covenant 1779 to 1829" (Box 4[3]) or of "Persons admitted to Church Fellowship 1779 to 1830" (Box 4[2]).

74 *"well acquainted . . . a congenial occupation":* [Hale], *Notes Made during an Excursion,* 94.

74 *when Potter, by then . . . painted that week:* [Greenwood], "A List of Portraits Painted by Ethan Allen Greenwood," 145.

74 *Dillaway and his family . . . Reverend Porter's congregation:* Samuel Dillaway junior shows up regularly in the First Church of Roxbury's records; see, for example, the "Church Record Book, 1733–1815" (Box 1[1], 371, 382, 494); "Burials from 1779 to 1862," no. 1 (Box 4[8]), record for burial of his son, Henry, 17 July 1805, and no. 2 (Box 4[9]), record for burial of Dillaway himself, 28 July 1862, Andover-Harvard Theological Library.

75 *The Olivers' younger son, Henry Kemble Oliver . . . dates quite certain:* Boston Journal, 7 Aug. 1874, 1.

76 *"many a winter's evening . . . tricks and pranks":* Boston American Traveller, 6 Nov. 1851.

76 *"While living with us . . . vastly amusing us afterward":* Oliver, letter to the editor, Boston Journal, 7 Aug. 1874, 1.

76 *"Richard Potter & Sally Harris of Roxbury, (blacks)":* McGlenen, comp., *Boston Marriages from 1700 to 1809,* 2:499.

77 *Potter "was a colored man . . . was his wife":* Boston American Traveller, 6 Nov. 1851. The editors of the *Boston American Traveller* at this time were the Rev. George Punchard and Ferdinand Andrews, and either could easily have learned about Potter from Oliver. Oliver and Andrews (formerly editor of the *Salem [MA] Gazette*) were well known to each other from their years together in Salem (they were both managers of the Salem Lyceum in 1836, for example). And Oliver had prepared George Punchard for Dartmouth College, Oliver's alma mater (Dexter, "Memoir of the Rev. George Punchard," 262).

77 *"a small-sized, sharp-eyed, dark-complexioned man":* Merrimack Journal (Franklin, NH), 8 Nov. 1872, 2.

78 *There was one fraternal . . . was significantly engaged:* There is one intriguing piece of evidence that Potter was also a member of another fraternal organization, the Sons of Tammany. On 4 March 1812, the Providence tribe of the organization held a large, festive rally, dinner, and entertainment at which "Mr. POTTER, one of the tribe, and the celebrated Ventriloquist, also displayed his wonderful powers, in the performance of many surprising Tammanial feats" (*Rhode-Island American* [Providence], 6 March 1812, 2). Potter was certainly not residing in Providence; but he regularly traveled there, and this notice and performance seem to indicate that he was regarded as a member of the Providence tribe, which dated to October 1809 (see Kilroe, *Saint Tammany and the Origin of the Society of Tammany or Columbian Order in the City of New York,* 211.) He and his wife had performed in Providence in early 1811, so he may have established his connection with the Providence Sons of St. Tammany then.

78 *Potter petitioned the Lodge . . . early December 1811:* Prince Hall Records, Minutes of African Lodge, Boston, 1807–1846, "Minutes of African Lodge, Boston, 1807–1826," entries for 5 Nov. 1811 ("at Close a special meeting was called for the purpose of attending a petition R. Potter"), 3 Dec. 1811 ("The Lodge met to instate R. Potter [? He was also?] Crafted.and Raised to the third degree of masonry"). Confirmed by personal correspondence from Raymond T. Coleman, Grand Historian, Prince Hall Grand Lodge, 22 Feb. 2000.

78 *"doing what we can . . . such a time as this"*: Letter to Absalom Jones, 16 Sept. 1789; qtd. in Hinks, *To Awaken My Afflicted Brethren*, 71.

79 *George Middleton:* On Middleton, see White, "The Black Leadership Class and Education in Antebellum Boston," 506–10.

79 *Prince Saunders:* On Saunders, see White, "Prince Saunders: An Instance of Social Mobility among Antebellum New England Blacks," 526–28; and "The Black Leadership Class and Education in Antebellum Boston," 510.

80 *Peter Lew:* For information on the Lew family, see Dorman, *Twenty Families of Color in Massachusetts 1742–1998*, 272–79.

80 *"The most prominent figures . . . members of their community"*: Hinks, *To Awaken My Afflicted Brethren*, 84.

81 *Like many contemporaneous . . . into his printed advertisements:* Masonic archives, as yet mostly unexplored by historians, may, I conjecture, prove to be important sources of information about itinerant performers in both England and the Americas. Masonic brotherhood could be a great boon to an itinerant arriving to perform in a town where he was a stranger: it could give him an instant connection and even fellowship with local men, otherwise unknown to him, who themselves tended to be well-established and even prominent members of their community. Masons belonging to a lodge in one place could, as guests, attend meetings of lodges elsewhere (lodge meetings typically occurred once a month, often on full-moon evenings that made nighttime traveling easier), and meet brother Masons that way. But even at other times of the month they could—for example, by their advertising—make their own Masonic affiliation clear, thereby inviting local fellow Masons to reach out to them on that ground. Too, the local Masonic lodge building often afforded one of the best performing venues in town, and many performers accordingly would seek it out as a venue. The hall would be rented, and one need not be a Mason to rent it, but it couldn't hurt.

John Rannie and Christopher Lee Sugg (an early English ventriloquist) both advertised themselves as Masons upon occasion, as did Ingleby (an English magician); so did many actors.

Little research has been done on the involvement of itinerant performers with Masonry, and most of that concerns actors (see, for example, Burger, *L'activité théâtrale au Québec [1765–1825]*, 158–64; and Porter, *The History of the Theatres of Brighton, from 1774 to 1886*, 202).

82 *"A genteel entertainment . . . Europe and America"*: *Portsmouth (NH) Oracle*, 20 May 1809, 3; *Portsmouth (NH) Intelligencer*, 25 May 1809, 3.

82 *"from London"*: *York Gazette* (Toronto), 5 May 1810, 4; 12 May 1810, 4.

82 *The first commentator . . . providing extensive testimonials:* "The Great Magician," *Boston Evening Journal*, 31 July 1874, 1; *New-Hampshire Patriot* (Concord), 11 May–27 July 1813; 3 May, 21 June, and 28 June 1814; *Concord (NH) Gazette*, 3 May–19 July 1814, 9 May–11 July 1815; *Amherst (NH) Farmer's Cabinet*, 17–24 June 1815.

83 *the Thomsonian system of medical practice:* For a careful review of this widespread phenomenon, see Haller, *The People's Doctors: Samuel Thomson and the American Botanical Movement, 1790–1860*.

83　*In Concord, he ... governor Isaac Hill:* Wilder, *History of Medicine,* 491. Hill was listed first among a number of prominent civic leaders and divines endorsing the "unrivaled" healthiness of situation and beauty of arrangement of Dr. Thompson's Botanic Infirmary in Concord and affirming the accuracy of his prospectus for it (*Thomsonian Recorder* 4 [1835–36]: 115).

83　*"He was a handsome ... no settled occupation":* Lyford, ed., "The Thompsonian Infirmary, Concord," 346.

83　*"my profession ... gambling, drinking, and idleness":* [Hale], *Notes Made during an Excursion,* 93.

84　*York, Upper Canada ... Utica, New York: York Gazette* (Toronto) 5 May 1810, 4; 12 May 1810, 4; *Utica (NY) Columbian Gazette,* 31 July 1810, 3.

84　*Boston (where they performed in late September): Boston Gazette,* 24 Sept. 1810, 3.

85　*"Dwarf Hornpipe" ... "Wonderful Little Giant":* "Dwarf Hornpipe": *Rhode-Island American* (Providence), 20 Jan. 1811, 3. "Wonderful Little Giant": Potter broadside, 1815. Durang's "Dwarf Dance": Brooks, *John Durang,* 35–36, including an illustration by Durang.

85　*William Bates:* On William Bates, see Highfill, Burnim, and Langhans, *Biographical Dictionary of Actors, Actresses, Musicians, Dancers,* 1:386–88.

86　*"POTTER, the West Indian": Boston Gazette,* 24 Sept. 1810, 3; *New Brunswick (NJ) Guardian,* 11 July 1811, 3; *Philadelphia Aurora,* 25 July 1811, 3; *Philadelphia Democratic Press,* 22 and 23 July 1811.

86　*a correspondent to the "New York Evening Post":* The lengthy letter is reprinted in the *Norfolk (MA) Gazette,* 2 Oct. 1813, 2; and the *Vermont Register* (Middlebury), 13 Oct. 1813, 1; both papers attribute it to the *New York Evening Post.* I have not been able to locate it there.

86　*Advertising in Portland ... Albany in late 1816: Portland (ME) Gazette,* 10 Feb. 1812, 3; *Boston Daily Advertiser,* 3 June 1813, 3; *Boston Repertory,* 3 June 1813, 3; *Albany (NY) Daily Advertiser,* 29 Nov. 1816, 3.

87　*"Laugh When You Can":* Frederick Reynolds, *Laugh When You Can* (Boston: Oliver C. Greenleaf, 1809). I quote from this, the first American edition, because it represents the play as it was staged in Boston in 1809, at or near the time when Potter would have encountered it, and was the text that the Boston Theatre used. It is essentially identical to the first English edition. Citations are to act and page.

89　*"Sambo the blackface buffoon ... an anti-slavery spokesman":* Gibbs, "Performing the Temple of Liberty: Slavery, Rights, and Revolution in Transatlantic Theatricality (1760s–1830s)," 299.

89　*"was ever very popular ... GENEROUS YANKO": Claypool's Daily Advertiser* (Philadelphia), 6 July 1792, 2.

90　*the Boston Theatre staged ... Providence in August 1811: Boston Gazette,* 20 March 1809, 3; 14 Oct. 1811, 3; *Boston Repertory,* 22 Sept. 1809, 3; 29 Dec. 1809, 3; 22 May 1810, 3; 19 Feb. 1811, 3; *Providence (RI) Columbian Phenix,* 24 Aug. 1811, 3.

90　*Early in the year ... the Columbian Museum in Boston:* See, for example, the *Rhode-Island American* (Providence), 29 Jan. 1811; 1 and 15 Feb. 1811; *Relf's Philadelphia Gazette,* 20 and 31 July 1811; *Philadelphia Aurora,* 20 and 25 July 1811;

*Boston Gazette,* 7, 14, and 25 Nov. 1811; and *Boston Columbian Centinel,* 13 Nov. 1811, 3.

90    *in late April . . . stand in Philadelphia:* See the *Northampton (MA) Democrat,* 23 April 1811, 3; *Albany (NY) Register,* 7 June 1811, 3; *Orange County Patriot* (Goshen, NY), 2 July 1811, 3; and *Guardian, or New Brunswick (NJ) Advertiser,* 11 July 1811, 3.

91    *In New Brunswick . . . had just run away: Guardian, or New Brunswick (NJ) Advertiser,* 11 July 1811, 3.

91    *he began advertising . . . he actually did this: New York Aurora,* 29 March 1810, 3; *Boston Columbian Gazette,* 2 April 1810, 2.

91    *"just on the point of retiring from public life":* Broadside, "For the Benefit of Youth," Salem, MA, 14 June 1810, collection of the James Duncan Phillips Library, Peabody and Essex Museum, Salem, MA.

91    *"by the Little Devil as he is called": Boston Columbian Centinel,* 26 Dec. 1810, 3; see also *Boston Gazette,* 19 and 26 Nov. 1810.

93    *He was in Portland in February 1812 . . . husband was or not: Portland (ME) Gazette,* 3 and 10 Feb. 1812; 7 Sept. 1812, 3.

93    *During these years Potter . . . that town then, too: Providence (RI) Phenix,* 18 Jan. 1812, 3; *Boston Columbian Centinel,* 11 and 14 March 1812; *New-England Palladium,* 6 March 1812, 3; *Boston Gazette,* 12 and 16 March 1812; *Albany (NY) Gazette,* 27 July 1812, 2; 7 Jan. 1813, 3; 30 Dec. 1813, 3; *Boston Daily Advertiser,* 25, 28, and 31 May 1813; 3 June 1813; *Albany (NY) Register,* 25 and 29 Nov. 1814; 2 Dec. 1814; *Green Mountain Farmer* (Bennington, VT), 16 Jan. 1815, 4.

94    *"The surest anchor . . . always set my course":* [Hale], *Notes Made during an Excursion,* 93–94.

94    *as Eastman summarized:* Eastman, *History of Andover, New Hampshire,* 1:426.

94    *Potter bought this first . . . April the following year:* Hillsborough County (NH) Deeds, Book 115, 730 (Thompson to Potter, 10 May 1813); Book 107, 2 (Gale to Potter, 23 April 1814).

94    *That year he also . . . of his own designing:* Eastman, *History of Andover, New Hampshire,* reported that "Potter made the plans and 'Esq. Graves' built the house. . . . Rev. E. B. Rollins, then a young man, just returned from the war of 1812–15, worked for Potter and carried the mortar for the house" (1:426). This was probably John Graves, of East Andover; see ibid., 2:174.

94    *as Potter told Hale in 1831:* [Hale], *Notes Made during an Excursion,* 94. Since the original New Hampshire statehouse, in Concord, was being built (of local granite) just after Potter's house was completed (a site was selected in 1815, and the cornerstone was laid in 1816; the building was completed in 1819), a joking comparison of the two Federalist structures was doubtless an easy conversation-starter at the time. There is no reason to take Potter's drily witty supposition seriously.

95    *The two-story . . . Boston and Salem:* The festooning over the front door was reported and sketched by a Manchester artist, J. Warren Thyng, circa 1894; the then-owner of the house had pointed it out to Thyng as one of the remaining original features of "the old magician's handiwork" ([Thyng], "Reminiscences in Life of Ventriloquist Potter"). The blind arches above the windows, no longer present

in 1894 due, presumably, to re-siding, are prominently visible in the circa 1869 stereoview of the house (fig. 6), probably by John Bachelder (private collection).

95  *A dormer centered . . . one single, large room*: Ketchum, "Richard Potter," 59.

95  *"two projecting wings"*: *Boston American Traveller*, 6 Nov. 1851.

95  *Goodwin and Ketchum both stated in the 1870s:* [Goodwin], "The Potter Place"; cf. Ketchum, "Richard Potter," 59. When Potter's estate went through probate after his death, the description of the property being set aside as his widow's dower alluded to "the door yard between the two dwelling-houses." The second house stood perhaps a hundred feet to the southwest, along what was then called the Wilmot Road, which ran along the southeast side of Potter's yard (Richard Potter account [1835], Merrimack County [NH] Probate Records, vol. 12, 63, file 1233). It was a true house, not a mere outbuilding: when the "Farm . . . formerly owned by Richard Potter" was put up for sale in 1837, only two years after his death, the advertisement listed "two good Dwelling Houses" first among its buildings (*New-Hampshire Patriot* [Concord], 23 Oct. 1837, 3).

95  *"The grounds about his house . . . were passionately fond"*: Ketchum, "Richard Potter," 60.

95  *"When I used to pass . . . mansion in Newburyport"*: Oliver, letter to the editor, *Boston Journal*, 7 Aug. 1874. The same report about these statues appears independently in the *Boston American Traveller* in 1851, an article that relied on information from Oliver.

96  *dozens of life-sized images:* On Dexter's statues, see esp. Knapp, *Life of Lord Timothy Dexter*, 18–21; Todd, *Timothy Dexter*, 5; Currier, *History of Newburyport, Massachusetts 1764–1905*, 2:422–24; and Little, "Carved Figures by Samuel McIntyre and His Contemporaries," 183–84.

96  *Dexter himself once claimed there were thirty-seven:* *Newburyport Herald*, 28 April 1807, 3.

96  *the images sold . . . at any price:* Knapp, *Life of Lord Timothy Dexter*, 21.

97  *"in order to withdraw . . . in city life"*: [Goodwin], "The Potter Place"; cf. Ketchum, "Richard Potter," 60.

97  *Andover itself had more than its share of taverns:* "The long list of innholders or tavern keepers in Andover seems remarkable, if one considers the size of the town" (Eastman, *History of Andover, New Hampshire*, 1:175).

97  *"there is the place . . . these close their doors"*: James Davis, qtd. in Davis and Rosseter, "A Brief Account of the Origin and Progress of the Boston Female Society for Missionary Purposes," 7–8.

## 4. Ascent to Fame, 1815–1819

98  *Albany . . . Salem . . . Greenfield . . . Boston:* *Albany (NY) Gazette*, 3 April 1815, 2; *Essex Register* (Salem, MA), 12 Aug. 1815, 3; Potter broadside, location filled in "Greenfield," date filled in 12 Sept. 1815; *Boston Gazette*, 5, 12, 19, and 26 Oct. 1815. The broadside is in the collection of the Bostonian Society; see "Ventriloquism. Mr. Potter," Early American Imprints, Second Series, 1801–1819, Shaw-Shoemaker no. 36431.

99 *Ethan Allen Greenwood:* [Greenwood], "A List of Portraits Painted by Ethan Allen Greenwood," 147.

99 *Day Francis . . . Mr. Handel:* For a sample of Francis's exotic appellations for his tricks, see the *New York Courier,* 7 Feb. 1816, 3. For the rupture and feud between Francis and Handel, see the *New York Columbian,* 15–25 May 1816.

100 *Francis had the misfortune . . . die soon thereafter:* Boston Gazette, 22 Jan. 1818, 2.

100 *"when advanced age . . . this temporary enjoyment":* [Hale], *Notes Made during an Excursion,* 93–94.

100 *"Mr. Francis will dance . . . injury to himself":* Boston Columbian Centinel, 24 July 1816, 3.

101 *Miss Dupre or Dupree . . . and Signor Cassania:* Albany (NY) Daily Advertiser, 14–29 Nov. 1816.

101 *"perform the part . . . Body of Fire":* Hudson (NY) Northern Whig, 10 Dec. 1816, 3.

101 *"since her performance . . . the astonished crowd":* Kirby, *Kirby's Wonderful and Eccentric Museum,* 6:23–25 (Kirby spells her name as "Giraldelli," which is how it was spelled in some of her advertisements in the London *Times*). See also Dawes, *The Great Illusionists,* 56–57; and Jay, *Learned Pigs and Fireproof Women,* 258–67.

102 *Potter's oldest child . . . in an accident:* Eastman, *History of Andover, New Hampshire,* 1:318, 426. Eastman does not cite his authority for the cause of death, but Henry M. Potter's gravestone documents the date.

102 *he gave a note . . . on 16 October:* Hillsborough County (NH) Court of Common Pleas, Gale v. Potter, Sept. Term 1817, case 1310.

102 *Potter's new tour:* See, for example, the *Philadelphia Aurora,* 16 Jan.–1 Feb. 1817; *Baltimore American,* 22 Feb.–1 March 1817; *Alexandria (VA) Gazette,* 12 March 1817, 2; *Georgetown (DC) Messenger,* 10 March 1817, 3.

102 *After this collaboration, Breslaw would once:* Norfolk (VA) American Beacon and Commercial Diary, 16 May 1818, 3.

103 *"The novelties were surprising . . . emperor of all conjurers!!":* Alexandria (VA) Herald, 12 March 1817, 3.

103 *Potter did present . . . his next performance:* See Alexandria (VA) Herald, 14 March 1817, 3.

103 *pausing again in Baltimore:* Baltimore American Commercial Daily Advertiser, 22 March 1817, 3.

103 *Albany . . . Charlestown and Salem:* Albany (NY) Gazette, 28–31 July 1817; *Essex Register* (Salem, MA), 20 and 27 Sept. 1817; *Boston Yankee,* 19 Sept. 1817, 3.
Exactly when Potter left Andover is not clear. He was a registered taxpayer and voter there as of 1817 but then disappears entirely from the town tax rolls until 1824. The tax rolls occasionally indicate when one person is paying taxes on another's property—the entry "Seavey for Gale" appears on the 1820 roll, for example—but the practice seems not to have been consistent. Potter remained the owner of his Andover property and resumed his residence in Andover in 1824.

103 *Potter concentrated . . . and in Rhode Island:* Rhode-Island American (Providence), 4 Nov. 1817, 3; *Boston Columbian Centinel,* 22 Nov. 1817, 3; *Newport (RI) Mercury,* 27 Dec. 1817, 3; *Providence (RI) Patriot,* 3 Jan. 1818, 3; *Boston Repertory,* 9 July 1818,

4; *Boston Gazette,* 10–20 Aug. 1818; *Hampshire Gazette* (Northampton), 15 Sept. 1818, 3.

Potter may also have returned to the Albany area at this time: a brief newspaper report in the spring of 1819 stated that he had been "prosecuted, last winter, by the good people of Catskill, for showing them his heterodox amusements." "Last winter" probably refers to 1818–19, but possibly to 1817–18. We know nothing else of such a visit (*Northern Whig* [Hudson], 23 March 1819, 4).

104  *"pretense of preparation . . . drinking, and idleness":* [Hale], *Notes Made during an Excursion,* 93.

104  *"He had several . . . before the public":* Oliver, letter to the editor, *Boston Journal,* 7 Aug. 1874, 1.

104  *"When 'Potter the ventriloquist' . . . unhallowed exhibition":* Holmes, *Over the Teacups,* 77.

105  *"personate the characters . . . adapted to each":* Essex Register (Salem, MA), 27 Sept. 1817, 3.

105  *"a Grand Display of Chinese Brilliancies" . . . "Chinese Umbrose":* Columbian Gazette (Boston), 31 July 1810, 3; see also *Rhode-Island American* (Providence), 1 Feb. 1811, 3, and *Orange County Patriot* (Goshen, NY), 2 July 1811, 3.

Bates apparently retained his other "brilliancies" and his "Transparent Painting, taken from the celebrated Engraving of The Apotheosis of Washington," when he removed to Albany for the 1810–11 theater season. He died in Albany in early March 1813, but in the spring of 1815—at a time, notably, when Potter was in town—the Albany Theatre presented several "Ombre Choinoise" [*sic*] and also the grand transparency of the apotheosis of Washington (see *Columbian Museum,* 13 Aug. 1810, 3; and *Albany [NY] Register,* 28 March 1815, 3).

106  *Potter had his pocket picked:* All information about this suit comes from Suffolk County, Massachusetts Court of Common Pleas, September Term 1818, case No. 548, Samuel Sampson v. Richard Potter, case files—a single document, with a drafted and then revised writ, on which the constable's note is also written; in pursuance of the writ, he arrested Potter on 14 April 1818, and Potter "gave Bail for want of goods or [?] Estat [?]." Potter was renting at the time, so his goods and estate were all in New Hampshire.

107  *a small house on South Russell Street:* Suffolk County (MA) Deeds, vol. 263, 265, "Cushing et al. to Sampson," 10 Sept. 1819. Sampson is specified as a "Coloured man."

107  *But he also . . . was a suicide:* See the *Boston Weekly Messenger,* 21 Nov. 1822, 3 (Samuel Sampson fined ten dollars for assault, ordered to recognize one hundred dollars to keep peace six months); the *Independent Chronicle and Boston Patriot,* 29 Jan. 1823, 3 (relocation from Congress Street to School Street); *Portland (ME) Eastern Argus,* 16 March 1824, 3; and *Boston Daily Advertiser,* 30 March 1824, 1 (death notices); the *Boston Columbian Centinel,* 18 Aug. 1824, 4 (description of his estate and debts). The initial Portland death notices all gave his age as twenty-seven, but most of the subsequent Boston death notices instead said thirty-two. Since Sampson was already listed in the *Boston Directory* in 1816 as a hairdresser at the Exchange Coffee House then, the age given in the Maine newspapers is

clearly an error that was subsequently corrected by Boston editors, with their local sources of information.

107 *James George Barbadoes . . . Sampson in March 1819:* James Barbadoes and Almira Long ("people of color") intention to marry: *Boston Marriage Publications,* vol. 9, 1817–1823. Samuel Sampson/Almira Long ("people of color") marriage notice (officiated by the Rev. Mr. Francis Parkman, minister of the New North Church, North Street): *Boston Daily Advertiser,* 17 March 1819, 2.

107 *"This celebrated Drama . . . Chorusses, &c.":* *Boston Patriot,* 29 Jan. 1818, 3.

108 *The play is set . . . in South America:* For a brief but shrewd analysis of the political and historical issues informing this play, see Swindells, "Abolitionist Theatre," 1:12–14.

108 *African slave "of giant strength":* Morton, *The Slave.* Citations are to act, scene, and page.

110 *"an appropriate panegyric . . . cause of Africa":* "Theatre," *Morning Post* (London), 13 Nov. 1816.

111 *"he may never . . . leaving the country":* *Boston Gazette,* 20 Aug. 1818, 3.

112 *"Washington Hall contained . . . for many years":* Barrett, *The Old Merchants of New York City,* 18–19.

112 *Mr. Potter, whose . . . of his visitors":* New York Daily Advertiser, 6 Feb. 1819, 2; *New York Columbian,* 8 Feb. 1819, 2; *New York Evening Post,* 8 Feb. 1819, 2; *New York Columbian,* 18 Feb. 1819, 2.

113 *"On Saturday (his . . . manner than heretofore."):* New York Columbian, 8 Feb. 1819, 2; *New York Evening Post,* 8 Feb. 1819, 2; *New York National Advocate,* 2 Feb. 1819, 2; 13 Feb. 1819, 2.

113 *"in consequence . . . admittance on Saturday evening":* New York National Advocate, 2 March 1819, 2.

113 *"he has received . . . one person to another":* New York Evening Post, 20 March 1819, 3. Potter later named this new apparatus "the beautiful MERCURY" instead.

114 *Other new mechanisms:* New York Evening Post, 27 March 1819, 3; 30 March 1819, 2.

114 *the magician Mr. Stanislas:* See Stanislas's advertisement in the *New York Mercantile Advertiser,* 18 Jan. 1818, 2; for an indication of the specific mechanisms in his repertory (which are not given in his New York advertisements), see, for example, his advertisement in *Relf's Philadelphia Gazette,* 7 May 1818, 3. They included "the Mysterious Orange" and "the Goddess Flora's garden."

114 *"where he will . . . ease and convenience":* New York Evening Post, 20 March 1819, 3.

114 *"To Mr. potter, the Ventriloquist":* The poem has been collected in Drake and Halleck, *The Croakers,* 10–11.

114 *socially conservative . . . introduce a bill:* The legislative threat was a real one and had models in many other states. As the *Albany (NY) Argus* reported in its "Legislature of New York in Assembly. Wednesday March 10" update under "Petitions, &c.," there was a new one "Of sundry persons of the western district, against the exhibitions of mountebanks and jugglers" (16 March 1819, 2).

115 *As one critic has noted:* Letter, "New York in 1819: Defining a Local Public in the 'Croaker' Poems of Joseph Rodman Drake and Fitz-Greene Halleck," 50–71. The quotations are from 50; a brief discussion of "To Mr. Potter" is on 63.

115 *article in the "Boston Independent Chronicle"*: Boston Independent Chronicle, 15 Feb. 1810, 2.

115 *"it was slang . . . kind of naysayer"*: Letter, "New York in 1819," 61.

116 *"the many applications . . . witnessing his exhibition"*: Poulson's American Daily Advertiser (Philadelphia), 20 May 1819, 3.

116 *review published in the Franklin Gazette*: Franklin Gazette (Philadelphia), 30 April 1819, 2.

116 *"Mr. POTTER, the Ventriloquist . . . who attended"*: "Blue Laws," Connecticut Herald (New Haven), 15 June 1819, 3.

117 *The anonymous poem to Potter in the "Connecticut Herald"*: Letter to the editor, Connecticut Herald (New Haven), 15 June 1819, 3.

118 *the song "Shelty the Piper"*: "Shelty the Piper" had also made part of Potter's and Thompson's program in 1810, when they were touring through Upper Canada (see York Gazette [Toronto], 12 May 1810).

## 5. The Grand North American Tour, 1819–1823

119 *"it is probable . . . leaving the country"*: Boston Gazette, 20 Aug. 1818, 3; Boston Columbian Centinel, 19 Aug. 1818, 3.

120 *"purchased a farm . . . pursuit of Agriculture, &c."*: James Rannie broadside, "For the Benefit of Youth," 14 June 1810. I have found two different versions of this broadside. One, printed by C. Hosmer, of Hartford, with spaces left open beneath the title and in the first line of text so that the time and place of performance could be entered by hand, is in the collection of the Connecticut Historical Society. Rannie had toured briefly through Connecticut in 1808, so this broadside probably dates from that time. The spaces are filled in "At Washington Hall" and "Thursday June 14 1810," so this broadside was actually used in Salem on that date. The second, with a specific place and time of performance printed on the broadside beneath the title—"AT WASHINGTON HALL—Thursday Evening, June 14, 1810"—is in the collection of the James Duncan Phillips Library of the Peabody Essex Museum, in Salem, Massachusetts. It must have been printed in Salem just in advance of the performance.

120 *he undertook . . . amassing a nest egg*: A Maine folklorist suggests that Rannie, although he had "made considerable money" (definitely true), had "lived recklessly" and was trying "to recoup his scattered fortunes by a tour" at the end of his life (quite probable, judging from the condition of Rannie's estate after his death) (Haynes, Casco Bay Yarns, 173).

121 *"Having a good . . . set my course"*: [Hale], Notes Made during an Excursion, 94.

121 *"When travelling about . . . Mrs. McKee's possession"*: "Man of Mystery World Famous," Boston Sunday Herald, 11 Feb. 1906, 52.

122 *And their house . . . south of Concord*: Aaron Colby moved back to Bow in 1867, and Harrison also moved back there no later than 1875, when his house and barns in Andover were destroyed by fire. So there were no Colbys in Andover for Moses Goodwin to interview in the winter of 1875–76, when he began making inquiries about Potter among the local residents.

122 *Aaron Colby, moreover ... estate finally passed:* Technically, the immediate purchaser of the Potter estate was a John Colby of Concord (according to the deed;
both Ketchum and Eastman say, of Bow), who apparently then sold it to Aaron
Colby (Merrimack County [NH] Deeds, Book 50, 365). This was probably a
straw-man, family transaction.

123 *"the two traveled together very pleasantly for many years":* Boston Journal, 31 July
1874, 1.

123 *"little Mr. Potter":* New-England Galaxy (Boston), 25 Sept. 1818, 2.

124 *"self-willed, proud ... several times separated":* Lyford, "The Thompsonian Infirmary, Concord," 347.

125 *"Ventriloquial, Philosophical and Theatrical Talents":* Potter broadside, formerly
in the Christopher Collection. I am grateful to Milbourne Christopher's widow,
Maurine Christopher, for granting me access to the Richard Potter items in this
collection in 2000.

125 *"Mr. POTTER":* Canadian Courant (Montreal), 31 July 1819, 3; 4 Aug. 1819, 3.

126 *his next known appearance was in Pittsburgh:* Pittsburgh Statesman, 24 Nov. 1819, 3.

126 *Zanesville, Chillicothe, Hamilton:* See the Zanesville (OH) Express, 2 Feb. 1820, 3;
*Scioto Gazette (Ohio),* 17 Feb. 1820, 3; *Hamilton (OH) Gazette and Miami Register,* 24 April 1820, 3.

127 *a state where slavery was still legal:* The distinction between "free states" and "slave
states" was in fact more complex and nuanced at this time than we tend to recognize now. Slavery had been not so much abolished as "grandfathered" in many
northern states in the early part of the nineteenth century; the final elimination
of slavery did not come until 1827 in New York, for example, and 1848 in Connecticut. In 1820 there were still some individuals legally bound in slavery in most
northern states.

128 *Louisville ... Lexington ... Danville:* See the Louisville (KY) Public Advertiser,
13 May 1820, 3; *Lexington (KY) Western Monitor,* 6 and 13 June 1820, 3; and *Danville (KY) Olive Branch and Western Union,* 30 June 1820, 7.

128 *Shawneetown, Illinois:* Illinois Gazette (Shawnee-Town), 7 Oct. 1820, 3.

128 *St. Louis, Missouri Territory:* Missouri Gazette and Public Advertiser, 6 and 13
[misdated 14] Dec. 1820, 3.

129 *There was a letter ... Natchez post office:* Mississippi State Gazette, 14 April 1821, 4.

129 *"Last evening, Mr. Potter ... pleasure to themselves":* Mississippi Republican (Natchez), 15 May 1821, 3.

130 *in Port Gibson he ... Sally frequently staged:* Port Gibson (MS) Correspondent,
1 June 1821, 3.

130 *both Mr. and Mrs. Bray ... roles that night:* The Boston Repertory, 7 Oct. 1815, 4,
gives the casts for that evening's performances. A highly favorable review of this
cast's presentation of *The Children in the Wood* appeared in the *New-England
Palladium* (Boston), 6 Feb. 1816, 1.

131 *"The Children in the Wood" ... early February 1821:* St. Louis Inquirer, 3 Feb.
1821, 3.

131 *Potter's first exhibition ... bilingual "Louisiana Gazette":* Louisiana Gazette,
7 Aug. 1821, 4.

131 *the wig he sometimes wore in his performances:* "The wig which Potter wore while performing," along with several other items, was donated by Stephen Fellows; years later a curator recorded, "Wig destroyed by moths" ("Historical Collections, V. 5, 1978–1958," 194, Collection of the New Hampshire Antiquarian Society).

132 *when he performed . . . seventy-five cents per ticket: Pensacola Floridian,* 1 June 1822; cited by W. G. Dodd, "Theatrical Entertainment in Early Florida," 132.

132 *In that case . . . South Carolina through Columbia:* There was a letter waiting for Richard Potter in the Augusta, Georgia, post office as of 1 September 1822, indicating that he had expected to be passing through that town in the not too distant future. This suggests that he had indeed planned to travel from Mobile up the old Federal Road, rather than east from Pensacola across the Floridas to St. Augustine (*Augusta [GA] Chronicle,* 3 Sept. 1822, 3).

132 *He was once . . . the opposite direction:* Ketchum, "Richard Potter," 60. Ketchum's source for these anecdotes was probably Herod Thompson (one of Benjamin's younger brothers), who had been a close neighbor of Potter's for many years.

134 *"It is said . . . plunder of the city":* New York Gazette; reprinted in *Alexandria Herald,* 24 July 1822, 2.

134 *"the Negro Plot":* Governor Bennett's letter has been reprinted in Rose, ed., *A Documentary History of Slavery in America,* 116–21. The quoted passages appear on 117, 119, and 120.

134 *Gullah Jack, was very dangerous:* the following quotations are taken from the "Account of the Intended Insurrection" as it appeared in the *Augusta [GA] Chronicle,* 3 Sept. 1822, 2—the publication from which Potter probably learned about the Vesey conspiracy.

135 *he finally paused in Raleigh, North Carolina, to exhibit: Raleigh [NC] Register,* 27 Sept. 1822, 3.

135 *a sustained set of newspaper advertisements:* See the *Norfolk and Portsmouth (VA) Herald,* 13–20 Dec. 1822; *American Commercial Beacon,* 13 Dec. 1822–12 Feb. 1823 (at Portsmouth, 20, 28, and 30 Dec. 1822; 3, 6, 11, 13, and 15 Jan. 1823; 10 Feb. 1823; at Smithfield, 21 Jan. 1823).

136 *A "letter remaining in Post Office" notice: Washington, DC, Daily National Intelligencer,* 7 April 1823, 4.

136 *"after an absence . . . three nights only": New York National Advocate,* 5 June 1823, 2.

137 *he sometimes presented himself as "Mr. L. Charles":* See, for example, the *Morning Chronicle* (London), 15 Nov. 1813; the *New York Mercantile Advertiser,* 8 Sept. 1819, 2; *New York Evening Post,* 18 Sept. 1819, 3.

137 *He was probably French:* See the allusion to "the ventriloquism of the Sieur Charles" in *The Repository of Arts, Literature, Commerce, Manufactures, Fashions, and Politics* 11 (April 1814): 224; undated handbill from a London exhibition, reproduced in Houdini, *The Unmasking of Robert-Houndin,* 128 (Houdini dates this to 1829, but that cannot be right, since the exhibition room was no longer Wigley's after about 1825; it probably dates instead from late 1813 or early 1814, when Charles was indeed exhibiting in this very venue); *New York Evening Post,* 5 Nov. 1819, 2.

137 *"Paris, Vienna, Warsaw . . . Edinburgh, and London": Leeds Mirror,* 1 Nov. 1817.

137 *"recommendations from the . . . perform before him"*: *Boston Intelligencer,* 9 Oct. 1819, 2.

138 *"He did not know . . . perfectly successful"*: The story is attributed to the *Albany (NY) Daily Advertiser,* but I have taken it from a reprint in the *New York Evening Post,* 5 Sept. 1821, 2.

139 *"1. Mr. Nichols will converse . . . Power of Ventriloquism"*: *Poulson's American Daily Advertiser* (Philadelphia), 11 Feb. 1823.

140 *"Albany, Oct. 3d . . . Charles, the celebrated ventriloquist"*: *New York National Advocate,* 7 Oct. 1819, 2. A slightly different version of this letter to the editor was also addressed to the *New York Evening Post* and appeared there on 8 Oct. 1819, 2. Both versions were soon picked up and reprinted by other editors and were summarized by still more.

140 *"Sir, The following . . . this laughable merriment"*: *Philadelphia Democratic Press,* 20 June 1820, 2.

141 *Slightly different versions of this anecdote:* See the *Franklin Gazette* (Philadelphia), 20 June 1820, 2; *Relf's Philadelphia Gazette,* as reprinted by the *Carolina Centinel* (New Bern, NC), 8 July 1820, 2.

141 *Ira Aldridge would . . . role of Mungo:* See Lindfors, *Ira Aldridge: The Early Years, 1807–1833,* 105.

142 *a new strain of humor, condescending and racist:* Shane White, noting the surge of demeaning parodies and burlesques of blacks in the northern states in the 1820s, suggests: "It was as though the now-free blacks were more visible than they had ever been as slaves, and their activities were attracting the eye of 'witty' whites. Yet the humor had an edge. 'Black dialect' and the various 'humorous' stories that were told about blacks were designed to separate blacks from whites, to ensure that although all were now free, the two groups could not be confused" (*Stories of Freedom in Black New York,* 198–99).

142 *"the American Ventriloquist"*: *New York National Advocate,* 5 June 1823, 2.

143 *"On his arrival . . . carve your pig'"*: Hilton, "History of the Town of Andover, NH: Additions and Corrections," n.d., typescript in the collection of the Andover Historical Society. The story also appears in the *New London (NH) Highlander,* 4 Dec. 1928, 1–2.

143 *"The squeal of . . . reached its climax"*: *Providence (RI) Evening Press,* 1 Aug. 1874, 2.

144 *"My profession . . . short of total destruction"*: [Hale], *Notes Made during an Excursion,* 93.

## 6. Return to New England, 1824–1829

146 *"A mulatto juggler . . . left the State"*: *Rhode-Island American* (Providence), 30 Dec. 1823, 3.

146 *"as [it] shall . . . all disorderly behavior"*: *The Public Laws of the State of Rhode-Island and Providence Plantation,* 440.

147 *"It seems that . . . kind of exhibitions?"*: *New-Hampshire Repository,* 5 Jan. 1824, 2.

148 *"Mr. POTTER . . . this place, this evening"*: *New-Hampshire Patriot* (Concord), 19 Jan. 1824, 2.

148 *"MR. POTTER AGAIN . . . with other accommodations"*: New-Hampshire Repository, 19 Jan. 1824, 3.

149 *"Notice that the Agent . . . notify him accordingly"*: Entry for January 13, 1824, Records of the Blazing Star Lodge 5810 [Concord, NH]: December 1809–March 1847. Fourteen members were present (as well as four visitors and six petitioners), so a minimum of ten votes would have been needed to pass the amendment.

149 *"Mr. Editor, I fear . . . HOMESPUN"*: New Hampshire Statesman, 19 Jan. 1824, 1.

151 *"not less than ten . . . costs of prosecution"*: The Laws of the State of New-Hampshire, Enacted since June 1, 1815, 2:114.

152 *"Tavernkeepers are reminded . . . Town-Council therefor"*: Rhode-Island American (Providence), 30 Dec. 1823, 3.

152 *the Superior Court's agreement:* Providence County (Rhode Island), Superior Court Record Book 10, September Term 1828, 327–29.

153 *The Providence County case file:* Providence County [Rhode Island] Court of Common Pleas, May Term 1827, cases 12 and 13, "Wilkinson vs. Potter," case files, deposition of David Farnum.

154 *he reached Boston in mid-December:* A letter from Richard Potter dated in Boston on 23 Dec. 1823 confirms that he was in Boston and making immediate plans to continue north to New Hampshire at that time (ALS letter, Richard Potter to Mr. Colby, Esq., New London (NH) Town Archives [see fig. 7]).

154 *"Could the voice . . . can be reared"*: Dunlap, An Oration, Delivered at the Request of the Republicans of Boston, at Faneuil Hall, on the Fourth of July, 1822, 20–21.

155 *Dunlap had won an important court case:* Crocker, The Magic of the Many: Josiah Quincy and the Rise of Mass Politics in Boston, 1800–1830, 127.

155 *he had studied . . . under John Pitman:* Loring, The Hundred Boston Orators Appointed by the Municipal Societies and Other Public Bodies, from 1770 to 1852, 504.

156 *"Brattleborough Vt . . . Richard Potter ventriloquist"*: Peabody Essex Museum, Andrew Dunlap Papers, Box 4, folder 2, Correspondence Sept. 1823–1824 (fig. 8).

158 *he did his banking in Meredith or Concord:* Nathen Hale quoted Potter as telling him about his home in New Hampshire, "Here, as I returned periodically from my excursions, I found a bank established, which gave good interest for my deposits" (*Notes Made during an Excursion,* 94). Historians have always assumed that "Here" meant "Andover, New Hampshire." Not so; there was no bank in Andover then. "Here" must refer more largely to "New Hampshire" (Potter and Hale were in New Hampshire when this discussion occurred). Later in his life Potter seems to have done his banking at the Winnipisiogee Bank (incorporated in December 1824), located in Meredith Bridge, in what is now Laconia, New Hampshire. Before that, he presumably banked in Concord.

158 *Peter Rix:* Richard Potter v. Peter Rix, Suffolk County (MA) Court of Common Pleas, January Term 1827, case 416.

158 *Samson Moody:* Richard Potter v. Samson Moody, Suffolk County (MA) Court of Common Pleas, January Term 1828, case 181.

158 *expanded his Andover estate:* Merrimack County (NH) Registry of Deeds, Book 5, 159.

158  *significant improvements to his estate:* Aaron Cilley v. Richard Potter, Merrimack County (NH) Court of Common Pleas, April Term 1827, case 76.

158  *issued a license to Potter:* Andover Town Records, 1:464, New Hampshire State Library.

159  *"nearly opposite":* New-Hampshire Patriot (Concord), 2 Oct. 1826, 3.

160  *John Gale sued Richard Potter:* Merrimack County (NH) Court of Common Pleas, October Term 1825, Gale v. Potter, case 255; New Hampshire State Archives.

160  *he would have seen . . . in the inn:* Potter had probably moved the items to his own home. When a deputy sheriff, in the process of serving Gale's writ, attached some of Potter's property in October 1825, he took care to attach in particular several of the items that had been specified in Gale's claim (including the secretary, feather beds, bedsteads, under bed, bolsters, and pillows) (Endorsement of Amos Pressey, Deputy Sheriff, 8 Oct. 1825 to the 28 Sept. 1825 writ. Merrimack County [NH] Court of Common Pleas, October Term 1825, Gale v. Potter, case 55; New Hampshire State Archives). When another attachment was made in the process of serving a writ for a separate case in September 1826, a brass clock and a bureau were specified among the attached items (Endorsement of Saml. George, D. Sheriff, 8 Sept. 1826, to the 7 Sept. 1826 writ, Cilley v. Potter, Merrimack County Court of Common Pleas, April Term 1827, case 76).

It is worth noting that when Potter advertised the tavern for lease in December 1824, he specified that the house "will be leased with the standing furniture or unfurnished, as may best suit the person who may wish to take the same" (New-Hampshire Patriot, 20 Dec. 1824, 3). So it is possible that some or much of the furniture later specified in Gale's suit was still in the inn at this time, if not later.

161  *"John Gale made . . . give them up":* Deposition of Edmund Buswell [this is probably Edmund Buzzell], Gale vs. Potter, Merrimack County (NH) Court of Common Pleas, October Term 1825, case 255.

161  *paying a rent . . . thirty dollars per month:* The trustee for Perkins's estate squared accounts with Potter on 13 July 1827, and then received a final payment of $179.44 for the balance of Potter's rent on 9 Feb. 1828, implying a monthly rent of approximately twenty-five dollars (if the rental continued until this date) or—more likely—approximately thirty dollars (assuming Potter's rental ended at the end of 1827) (Probate File of Roger E. Perkins, Merrimack County [NH], file 177).

161  *John Sholes:* Sholes was given a tavern license by the Andover selectmen in April 1825—he must have been a recent arrival in town then, because he was not on the 1825 tax roll but shows up on the roll in 1826 through 1829—and again in late March and early September 1827 (Andover Town Records, 1:817, 822, 824).

161  *experience in Goshen as a tavern keeper:* The Goshen, New Hampshire, town records show that John Sholes was licensed by the selectmen to "exercise the business of a taverner" for one day in November 1819 (he was barely twenty-one at the time), and again to sell spirits for one day in March 1824 and again in March 1825 (these were probably election days); so it would seem that he was already working in a tavern then (Goshen Town Records, 1:205, 207, 238).

161  *another, a son . . . in Andover in 1827:* Re the birth year (1827) and birthplace (Potter Place, New Hampshire) of his son, Charles H. Sholes, see "Massachusetts

Deaths, 1841–1915," database with images, *FamilySearch* (https://familysearch .org/ark:/61903/1:1:N4Q4-GWB), Charles H. Sholes, 24 Feb 1912; citing Boston, Massachusetts, 481, State Archives, Boston; FHL microfilm 2,396,251.

161   *"very tall, very . . . speech and address"*: Nelson, *History of Goshen New Hampshire,* 375, 439.

162   *"an early mover . . . cause of temperance"*: Ketchum, "Richard Potter," 60.

162   *"in all his habits . . . strictest temperance men"*: *Boston Journal,* 31 July 1874, 1.

162   *her tendency to intemperance . . . New Hampshire: Merrimack Journal* (Franklin, NH), 8 Nov. 1872, 2.

162   *"drove her to . . . continual inebriation"*: Ketchum, "Richard Potter," 60.

162   *she "had become . . . him any longer"*: *Boston Journal,* 31 July 1874, 1.

162   *"All persons are forbid"*: *New-Hampshire Patriot* (Concord), 7 Nov. 1825, 3.

164   *the First Universal Society:* "Andover (N.H.) First Universalist Church Records, 1819–1832," New Hampshire Historical Society archives. Bartlett compensated for preaching, 29 Oct. 1821; hired to preach regularly, 3 March 1829; Potter and nine others "notify that they withdraw from this Society," 2 Sept. 1825.

165   *visited and performed . . . late April 1824: Salem (MA) Gazette,* 20 and 27 April 1824.

165   *Richard Potter returned to Salem once again:* Ibid., 2 and 9 July 1824.

165   *His Fourth of July address:* Jones, "Henry Kemble Oliver," 8.

165   *he returned there . . . more in 1825: Essex Register* (Salem, MA), 28 Feb 1825; 3, 7, and 10 March 1825; *Salem (MA) Gazette,* 1, 4, and 8 March 1825; 13–23 Dec. 1825; *Salem (MA) Observer,* 26 Feb. 1825; 5 March 1825.

165   *"Be Merry and Wise"*: Potter seems to have begun using the phrase in his advertising in the *Boston Commercial Gazette,* 23 Aug. 1824, 3.

166   *"Mr. Potter, the Ventriloquist . . . Seven Ages of Woman"*: *Boston Columbian Centinel,* 11 Aug. 1824, 3. The "Seven Ages of Woman" is a mystery. A popular poem with this title was published by Agnes Strickland in 1827 and became a favorite text for theater recitations soon thereafter; but I cannot find that the poem ever appeared anywhere before 1827.

166   *probably the last time . . . from his advertisements: Boston Commercial Gazette,* 26 Aug. 1824, 3.

Robert A. Olson, who has made a distinguished career from his reenactments of Richard Potter's magic exhibitions (including twenty-five years as the resident magician at Old Sturbridge Village, Massachusetts), was motivated by Potter's "Man Salamander" example to introduce those feats, too, into his program. After successfully learning the techniques and performing fire magic for a few years, he discontinued the practice. "As most magicians will tell you, it was just too dangerous," he says (personal communication, 29 April 2011).

166   *Monsieur Weiss . . . the Boston scene: Boston Evening Gazette,* 25 Feb. 1826, 3; 4 March 1826, 7; 11 March 1826, 7.

166   *"Mr. Potter and Monsieur Weiss"*: *New Hampshire Republican* (Dover), 16 May 1826, 3; *Rockingham Gazette* (Exeter, NH), 13 June 1826, 3.

167   *Potter and Weiss then continued to Boston: Boston Evening Gazette,* 24 June 1826, 2; *Boston Daily American Statesman,* 21 July 1826, 3.

167 *Weiss performed . . . Keene, New Hampshire:* New Hampshire Sentinel (Keene), 4 Aug. 1826, 3.

167 *Potter resumed his . . . additional three weeks:* see, for example, the *Boston Daily American Statesman,* 7–24 Aug. 1826.

168 *In January 1826 . . . new shed frame:* William Bailey v. Richard Potter, Merrimack County (NH) Court of Common Pleas, October Term 1827, case 189; Commonwealth v. Richard Potter, Worcester County (MA) Court of Common Pleas, January Term 1827, docket book 549; Aaron Cilley v. Richard Potter, Merrimack County (NH) Court of Common Pleas, April Term 1827, case 76, New Hampshire State Archives.

168 *"A Farm for sale . . . Andover, N.H.":* New-Hampshire Patriot (Concord), 2 Oct. 1826, 3.

168 *mortgaged the farm to Samuel Butterfield:* Merrimack County (NH) Registry of Deeds, Book 5, 159.

168 *"an invaluable member . . . a competent nurse":* Eastman, *History of Andover, New Hampshire,* 1:427.

169 *the Potter place . . . a black household:* We have already noted Eastman's awareness of "the colored blood in [Phebe Potter's] veins, and it was very dark" (*History of Andover, New Hampshire,* 1:427). An anecdote about Cromwell Potter, dating probably from the late 1850s or early 1860s, demonstrates how evident his blackness (no less than his alcoholism) was to his fellow townspeople, too. The following recollection came from the scrapbook of Mrs. Walter Scott Starr, an Andover resident:

> Dr. Weymouth told me that at one time he was called to attend Cromwell Potter. When the doctor entered, Mr. Potter was sitting by the fireplace throwing ashes into the fire. The doctor inquired the nature of his illness, and Mr. Potter said, "Doctor, God's called and this nigger ain't ready, but the devil is here in this fireplace waiting for me and I'm going to burn him up." The doctor noticed a great commotion in the ashes and in a short time there emerged a very sorry looking cat, which Mr. Potter in his delirium had mistaken for the devil and driven into the ashes.

Dr. Henry Weymouth was (since 1843) Andover's preeminent doctor and a leading town father (see Eastman, *History of the Town of Andover, New Hampshire,* 1:369–70). Town records establish that he was the doctor attending on both Phebe and Cromwell Potter at the times of their deaths in 1860 and 1861 ("Andover Selectmen's Reports and Accounts, 1860–1882," "County Paupers," entries for 12 Oct. 1860 and 21 Jan. 1861). Mrs. Carr was Maria E. Thompson Carr; she was a daughter of George Washington Thompson, the youngest brother of Richard Potter's one-time partner and traveling companion—hence, perhaps, her interest in Richard Potter, about whom she also collected various anecdotes. This recollection appeared in the *New London (NH) Highlander,* 4 Dec. 1928, 2.

169 *he would bring . . . many different neighborhoods:* Potter had other new motivations for this new practice as well. He had already noted in an advertisement in December 1825 that he would be extending his current stand in Charlestown

rather than, "as previously contemplated," appearing in Boston itself, "in consequence of the extravagant tax imposed on him by the Mayor and City council of Boston." By exhibiting in Charlestown, Roxbury, or Cambridge, he could still attract many Boston patrons while avoiding the heavy fees that Boston was now imposing (*Boston Daily American Statesman,* 9 Dec. 1825, 3).

169 *"Mr. William Crombie's . . . sign of the Leopard":* Boston Daily Advertiser, 3 Oct. 1826, 3.

170 *William Crombie and Stephen Mansur:* Their full names and occupation are given in the City of Boston Tax Records; see the Valuation Books, 1826, Ward 6, 5.

170 *Cambridge Street's intersection . . . Crombie's Tavern stood:* The tavern's location at the intersection of Cambridge and Blossom Streets is specified in a *Boston Columbian Centinel* advertisement for another establishment (12 Nov. 1825, 3).

170 *Concert Hall . . . Pantheon Hall:* For brief descriptions of these venues, see Bowen, *Bowen's Picture of Boston,* 76, 78.

170 *Performances in Charlestown and in Roxbury:* See, for example, the *Boston Daily American Statesman,* 20 Oct. 1826, 3 ("at Whitney's Hotel, in Charlestown"); *Boston Courier,* 30 Nov. 1826 ("at Massachusetts Hall, adjoining Ramsey's Tavern"); and *Boston Daily American Statesman,* 1 Jan. 1827, 3 ("at the Roxbury Hotel").

170 *the strain of juggling . . . took its toll:* Potter's advertisement in the *Boston Courier* on 7 Oct. 1826, for example, announces that he will be appearing at Pantheon Hall on Monday and Friday, 8 and 12 Oct. (he was actually appearing on 9 and 13 Oct.) and at Crombie and Mansur's on the intervening Wednesday, but his advertisement in the *Boston Commercial Gazette* on 9 Oct. 1826 announces instead that he will be appearing at Concert Hall on that Monday and Friday (this advertisement got the dates of the month right), and at Crombie and Mansur's on Wednesday.

171 *"Mr. Potter, the Ventriloquist . . . not his blunder":* Boston Courier, 11 Oct. 1826, 3.

171 *Parker Noyes, his former lawyer, sued him:* Merrimack County (NH) Court of Common Pleas, October Term 1827, Parker Noyes v. Richard Potter, case 540.

171 *"Richard Potter of Boston":* Merrimack County (NH) Deeds, Book 11, 4.

172 *Amherst, New Hampshire:* Amherst (NH) Farmer's Cabinet, 19 May 1827, 3.

172 *three performances in Providence:* Providence Patriot, 30 May 1827, 3; 2 June 1827, 2, 3.

172 *performed in Worcester:* Worcester (MA) National Aegis, 20 June 1827, 3.

172 *to Boston to . . . prestigious Concert Hall:* Boston Intelligencer, 23 June 1827, 3.

172 *published on May 30 by the "Providence Patriot":* Providence (RI) Patriot, 30 May 1827, 2.

173 *"Potter, the ventriloquist . . . an ungracious penalty":* I quote the notice as it was reprinted in the *Essex Register* (Salem, MA), 18 June 1827, 1. The attribution to the *New York Statesman* was confirmed by the editor of the *Charleston Courier,* 22 June 1827, 2.

173 *This brief report . . . Cincinnati, and Charleston:* see, for example, the *Baltimore Gazette,* 15 June 1827, 2; *United States Telegraph* (Washington, DC), 18 June 1827, 2; *Cincinnati Chronicle,* 30 June 1827, 3; and *Charleston Courier,* 22 June 1827, 2.

173   *a Providence newspaper . . . "very sneering manner": Providence (RI) Literary Cadet and Rhode Island Statesman,* 20 June 1827, 2, responding to the brief notice given in the *United States Gazette* (Philadelphia), 15 June 1827, n.p.

      The *Literary Cadet* editor's response is additionally interesting because it inadvertently demonstrates how widespread was Potter's renown, even among those who affected to condescend to him. While the article to which he took umbrage had described such details of Potter's act as "boiling eggs in his hat, making guineas of ha'pennies, and delivering lectures upon noses," this editor instead scoffingly alluded to Potter's "displaying the art of eating fire, and frying pan cakes." These, too, were part of Potter's act, but no newspaper article of the time ever mentioned them in reporting on Potter's Rhode Island court case. This editor's awareness of them shows that he was familiar with Potter's exhibitions and had probably attended them himself.

173   *One small Massachusetts newspaper: Dedham (MA) Village Register,* 21 June 1827, 2.

173   *"As the proper . . . laws at defiance": Providence (RI) Literary Cadet and Rhode Island Statesman,* 20 June 1827, 2.

174   *"the native place of many famous jugglers":* "Potter the Wizard," *Boston Journal,* 18 April 1888, 6.

174   *"his WONDERFUL DECEPTIONS . . . the HINDOO JUGGLERS":* broadside, "Ventriloquism. MR. POTTER," in Moulton, *Houdini's History of Magic in Boston,* after 8.

174   *"The Great Magician":* Saxe, *The Poems of John Godfrey Saxe,* 182–83, 461n.

174   *Saratoga Springs: Saratoga (NY) Sentinel,* 7 Aug. 1827, 3; 12 Aug. 1828, 3.

174   *He exhibited for . . . Hotel in Dorchester: Boston Commercial Gazette,* 22 Nov. 1827, 3; *Boston Intelligencer,* 24 Nov. 1827, 2; *Boston Daily Advertiser,* 27 Nov. 1827, 1; *Boston Commercial Gazette,* 3 Dec. 1827, 3.

176   *James Howe soon . . . introductions and initiation:* James H. Howe petitioned for membership in the African Lodge on 7[?] July 1828 and was accepted soon thereafter. He shows up with some frequency and regularity thereafter in the Lodge's scanty minutes of meetings and events in 1828, 1829, 1832, and 1835. On 7[?] Aug. 1829 he and another brother of the Lodge, William Brown (who had recently been fined by the Lodge for disorderly conduct), "had Maid friends with each other and settled the matter on amicable terms"—an instance of the Lodge's stress on civility, brotherhood, and reconciliation (Prince Hall Records, Minutes of African Lodge, Boston, 1807–1846).

176   *Charles K. Dillaway:* There is good reason to think that Charles K. Dillaway was later an agent for the Underground Railroad, the network of antislavery workers who hid and transported escaped slaves to freedom in the 1840s and 1850s (see Curtis, *Black Heritage Sites,* 311–12 ["Roxbury: Dillaway Thomas House"]).

177   *this was a neighborhood . . . professions mixed together:* All the data about the residents of Potter's Boston neighborhood are gleaned from the Boston Tax Records, especially those for 1827 ("Massachusetts, Boston Tax Records, 1822–1918," Images, *FamilySearch.* http://FamilySearch.org, City of Boston Archives, West Roxbury).

177 *The high sheriff . . . one of Potter's neighbors:* The sheriff was Charles Sumner, father of the Charles Sumner who became a prominent, fiercely antislavery senator from Massachusetts and one of the country's foremost abolitionists. At this time young Charles, now sixteen, was about to enter Harvard. The Charles Sumner House on Hancock Street is now a National Historic Landmark.

178 *Abduhl Rahhaman:* Prince Rahhaman, from the Guinea coast, had been captured in battle in his youth, sold into slavery, and transported to America, where he lived as a slave near Natchez and then in New Orleans for forty years. After a chance encounter in New Orleans with an old acquaintance, a surgeon on an English ship who had stayed with his family in his boyhood, persistent efforts were made to free him; he was finally freed through the agency of President John Quincy Adams. He then went on a tour through several eastern states, seeking to raise funds to free his slave children, before sailing to Africa with his wife in 1829 (see Alford, *Prince among Slaves*).

179 *Early in this decade . . . James Howe:* Prince Hall Records, Minutes of African Lodge, Boston, 1807–1846.

179 *Stephen Kantrowitz has noted:* Kantrowitz, *More Than Freedom: Fighting for Black Citizenship in a White Republic, 1829–1889,* 23.

180 *"it is . . . redress for their grievances":* Hilton, "Address, Delivered before the African Grand Lodge of Boston, No. 459, June 24th, 1828," 14.

180 *"Sampson H. Moody . . . Lewis Walker":* Wesley, *Prince Hall,* 6–7. "Lewis Walker" is an obvious error for "Walker Lewis."

180 *"a Committee was . . . Bro. John [?Hay]":* Prince Hall Records, Minutes of African Lodge, Boston, 1807–1846. The entry is dated 23 Oct. 1826.

181 *"proceeded to and . . . the Independent Charter":* Prince Hall Records. The entry is dated [?] June 1827.

181 *The very words . . . a performative claim:* The African Lodge notice's closing invocation of the Declaration of Independence anticipates the rhetorical strategy that David Walker would soon utilize in his *Appeal to the Coloured Citizens of the World* and may well have influenced him.

181 *the new charter:* The charter is reproduced in Wesley, *Prince Hall,* 157. Wesley's own transcription of the charter (156–57) is riddled with errors; I have quoted directly from the charter, not from the transcription.

182 *several irregularities in . . . from somewhat later:* As Henry Wilson Coil and others have noted, the charter is signed by three men who explicitly present themselves as "Past Masters"—John T. Hilton, Walker Lewis, and Thomas Dalton. But none of these men was a Past Master at this time. Hilton first became Master in 1826 and was still Master at this time in 1827 (and so signed himself on the declaration dated 18 June 1827 and published in the *Boston Daily Advertiser* on 29 June 1827), Lewis first became Master in 1829, and Dalton in 1831 (Coil, "A Documentary Account of Prince Hall and Other Black Fraternal Orders," 92–94). It is also noteworthy (although I believe it has never been noted before) that the charter errs in claiming that the African Grand Lodge had published its declaration of independence "in a paper called the Columbian Sentinel printed in this City"; it appeared in the *Boston Daily Advertiser* but never appeared in the *Columbian Centinel.*

This, too, hints at a gap of some time between the ostensible date and the actual penning of this charter.

182 *a committee . . . 26 August 1827*: Coil, "A Documentary Account of Prince Hall," 90.

182 *"That a powerful . . . in black Freemasonry"*: Kantrowitz, "Intended for the Better Government of Man," 1005.

184 *Potter held "the copy right"*: Boston Patriot, "Nosology," 26 April 1828, 2.

185 *"invisible crying babies . . . at the window"*: "The Great Magician," *Boston Journal,* 31 July 1874, 1.

185 *"a wooden doll . . . spirited conversations"*: *Connecticut Mirror* (Hartford), 1 Nov. 1819, 2.

185 *In the earlier . . . remainder of his career:* We can see Potter working toward this program arrangement through 1817 and 1818, but he does not seem to have settled on it until early 1819. This specific three-part structure first appears in New York in February (with the "Man Salamander" performances inserted into part 1) and then in Philadelphia in April. See, for example, the *New York National Advocate,* 26 Feb. 1819, 3; and the *Franklin Gazette* (Philadelphia), 21 April 1819, 3.

185 *"and his infinite . . . to aid him"*: Boston Journal, 31 July 1874, 1.

186 *"O, the wonder . . . young and old"*: "Hocus-Pocus Potter," *Boston American Traveller,* 6 Nov. 1851, 4.

186 *bringing Cromwell's debt to $105:* Merrimack Co. (NH) Court of Common Pleas, October Term 1828, Richard Potter v. Cromwell Potter, case no. 532, case files.

186 *Moody . . . slow in paying:* Andrew Dunlap Papers, Box 4, folder 5, "Correspondence Oct. 1827–1828," letters from Moody dated 18 June 1828, 26 July 1828, 4 Aug. 1828, Peabody Essex Museum.

187 *"Potter, the ventriloquist . . . get their sides insured"*: "Ventriloquism," *Boston American Traveller,* 3 March 1829, 3. For Potter's "Mysterious Bag," see, for example, *New-Hampshire Patriot* (Concord), 2 June 1828, 3.

187 *"In the course . . . boy of his age"*: Salem (MA) Gazette, 25 Dec. 1827; *Essex Register* (Salem, MA), 24 Dec. 1827.

187 *"In the course . . . Master and Mr. Potter"*: Salem (MA) Gazette, 28 Dec. 1827, 1 Jan. 1828; *Essex Register* (Salem, MA), 27 and 31 Dec. 1827.

188 *"To conclude with BALANCING"*: New-Hampshire Patriot (Concord), 2 June 1828, 3.

188 *"To conclude with . . . son of Mr. P"*: Boston American Traveller, 3 March 1829, 3.

## 7. A New England Icon, a Broken Family, 1829–1835

189 *performed in Roxbury . . . moved to Boston:* See the *Boston American Traveller,* 3 March 1829, 16 and 26 June 1829; *New-Hampshire Patriot* (Concord), 13 April 1829, 3; *New Hampshire Gazette* (Portsmouth), 2 June 1829, 3; *Columbian Centinel,* 17 and 24 June 1829; 8 July 1829; and *Rhode-Island Republican* (Newport), 10 Sept. 1829, 3.

189 *"was assisted in . . . his son Richard"*: Bassett, *History of the Town of Richmond, Cheshire County, New Hampshire,* 207. Bassett places the appearance at "about 1830."

190 *in Medford, Potter was again prosecuted:* See the *Portsmouth (NH) Journal of Literature and Politics,* 20 June 1829; *Rhode-Island American* (Providence), 16 June 1829.

190 *"The celebrated Potter . . . the appointed time":* Boston *American Traveller,* 16 June 1829, 2. The reference to "antiquated maidens" apparently alludes to a comic incident that Potter sometimes worked into his routine: via ventriloquism, as a Montreal newspaper had reported of Potter's act in 1819, "old maiden aunts have heard masculine voices in the chambers of their nieces—and even loads of hay become vocal."

190 *he borrowed $14 . . . after incurring it:* Merrimack Co. (NH) Court of Common Pleas, October Term 1829, Thomas Gilbert v. Richard Potter, case 360; April Term 1831, Herbert Vose v. Richard Potter, case 32; Moses Whitney v. Richard Potter, case 72 (Sholes had transferred the note to Whitney, and Butterfield had also transferred his second note to Whitney); Samuel Butterfield v. Richard Potter, case 79.

Another vestige of the Rhode Island court case was also still hanging over Potter at this time: he still owed his Providence lawyer fifty-five dollars for legal fees incurred (he had earlier paid the ten-dollar fees for 1825 services, but not the 1826–28 fees that had since accrued). The lawyer, John Whipple, brought suit and had a writ served (Potter posted bail) when Potter was performing in Boston at Concert Hall in July 1829; he won the case when Potter defaulted (Suffolk County [MA] Court of Common Pleas, October Term 1829, John Whipple v. Richard Potter, case 227). One feature sets this lawsuit apart: all its court papers consistently describe Potter's occupation as "laborer." Given his fame, this characterization must have been intended by the exasperated Whipple as an insult.

191 *"case in connection . . . a married woman":* [Goodwin], "The Potter Place," 2.

192 *"a half-idiot . . . notoriety in New Hampshire":* Ketchum, "Richard Potter," 60, 61.

193 *the first obituary . . . on 28 March:* New-Hampshire *Patriot* (Concord), 28 March 1831, 3.

193 *Tilton Elkins, one . . . 29 June 1830:* Merrimack County (NH) Court Records, Roster of Officers 1780–1840, "Justices of the Peace of the County of Merrimack," Box 701011, Roster No. 3 (1820–1830), 184, and Roster No. 4 (1830–1840), 65, New Hampshire State Archives.

194 *the average age . . . more than fourteen:* See, for example, Wyshak and Frisch, "Evidence for a Secular Trend in Age of Menarche," 1033–35.

194 *There was a law . . . "offence is committed":* Constitution and Laws of the State of New Hampshire, 307–8, 278–79, 337. These laws had been enacted in 1792.

195 *A recent amendment:* "Amendment to 'An Act Regulating Licensed Houses,'" *Laws of New Hampshire,* 10:28–29.

196 *What had occurred . . . adultery or not:* Goodwin's assertion that "The statutes have since made it otherwise" is also misleading. The statute in question (along with most of New Hampshire's laws) was significantly revised in 1842. But the main thrust of the revision was to change the penalties, chiefly by limiting them to imprisonment and fines—there would be no more whippings or stints on the gallows. It is true, however, that the revised statute did put to rest the argument

about adultery. After setting out the punishment for adultery in section 1 of the new law, the next section said as follows: "If any married man or woman shall commit an act, or have a connection with an unmarried person, which would constitute adultery, if both were married, such married woman or the man so offending, shall be guilty of adultery and punished accordingly" (*Revised Statutes of the State of New Hampshire,* Chapter 219, sections 1 and 2; 444).

196   *He had already moved . . . as an innkeeper:* 1829: See New Hampshire Town Records; Andover Town Records, 1751–1845, Taxes for 1829; also Samuel Kimball is licensed as Taverner "at the house recently occupied by John Sholes," 23 Nov. 1829 (p. 829), 1829–31: see John Sholes, Durham, NH, 1830 census; *Boston Daily Advertiser,* 11 Nov. 1830, 2 (John Sholes occupies the Durham Hotel, a public house); Durham Town Records, vol. 2, 540, 548, 571, 577 (entries cite or allude to John Sholes as an innkeeper in Durham, Dec. 1829–March 1831). 1833–34: A suit in the Merrimack County (NH) Court of Common Pleas, Samuel Cochran, Jr., v. John Sholes, places Sholes in Fisherfield and identifies him as an innkeeper in 1833 (Sept. Term 1833, case 440). An advertisement in the *New-Hampshire Patriot* also places him as an innkeeper in Fisherfield (13 Jan. 1834, 3).

198   *"was an invaluable . . . hands of Mrs. Potter":* Eastman, *History of Andover, New Hampshire,* 1:427.

198   *"She was free . . . own little one":* Forbes, *The Hundredth Town,* 188.

198   *"The 'age of consent' . . . to fourteen years":* Anthony and Harper, eds., *History of Woman Suffrage,* 4:460.

199   *performing in Haverhill . . . to early July:* See the *Essex Gazette* (Haverhill, MA), 12 June 1830, 3; *Portsmouth (NH) Journal,* 19 June 1830, 3; *New Hampshire Gazette* (Portsmouth), 22 June 1830, 3; *Portland (ME) Eastern Argus,* 5 July 1830, 3; *Portland (ME) Advertiser,* 9 July 1830, 3.

199   (*Harrington's act and . . . his ventriloquism routines*): For sample Harrington programs that feature a great many of Richard Potter's tricks, acts, and phrases, see, for example, the *Portland (ME) Eastern Argus,* 3 July 1829, 3; and the *New York Commercial Advertiser,* 24 March 1833, 3. For a description of his automaton band, see the *Nantucket Inquirer,* 8 Aug. 1829, 2.

200   *Probably he traveled alone:* We can also be certain that Stephen Fellows, who according to Ketchum "was Potter's assistant during the last years of his travels" ("Richard Potter," 57), was not with him now: Fellows was married in Grafton, New Hampshire, on 23 December 1830, when Potter was already at the Canadian border (Ancestry,com. *New Hampshire, Marriage and Divorce Records, 1659–1947* [database online]. Provo, UT, USA: Ancestry.com Operations, Inc., 2013; citing New Hampshire Bureau of Vital Records, Concord).

200   *performing for a week or so in Eastport:* Eastport (ME) Sentinel, 22 Dec. 1830, 3.

200   *Potter performed about . . . thence to Calais:* See *New Brunswick Courier,* 29 Jan. 1831; and 5 Feb. 1831, 3; *Royal Gazette* (Fredericton), 23–25 Feb 1831; 2–4 March 1831; *Halifax Journal* (Nova Scotia), 2 May 1831; and *Eastport (ME) Sentinel,* 25 May 1831, 3.

201   *The circus's itinerary . . . to New England:* For the route of this circus, see Thayer, *Annals of the American Circus,* 2:218.

201 "_____ _____, Mr. Potter lost a daughter": Eastman, *History of Andover, New Hampshire*, 1:311.

202 "*the daughter's remains . . . grave are visible*": [Goodwin], "The Potter Place"; cf. Ketchum, "Richard Potter," 61.

202 "*The girl, Julia . . . upon the mound*": [Thyng], "Reminiscences in Life of Ventriloquist Potter," *Manchester (NH) Union*, 8 March 1895, 5.

202 "*It is said . . . a short time*": Eastman, *History of Andover, New Hampshire*, 1:426.

204 "*Mr. Roberts, who . . . their wonderful performances*": *Philadelphia Inquirer*, 14 July 1831, 3. As Reese James's examination of the Chestnut Street Theatre records makes clear, the ropedancer who also appeared with Potter in Roberts's benefit was a Mr. Hess (*Old Drury of Philadelphia*, 476, 488).

204 (*he had been . . . emigrants to America*): Ross, *The Scot in America*, 343.

204 *he was advertised . . . Edinburgh in 1819–22*: *Boston Repertory*, 3 Oct. 1820, 3. See Highfill, Burnim, and Langhans, *Biographical Dictionary of Actors, Actresses, Musicians, Dancers*, 13:7; and Dibdin, *The Annals of the Edinburgh Stage*, 298–301.

204 *his blackface performance . . . had captivated audiences*: For an interesting argument that "New York street English in 1824, like New York street performance, was already a creole dialect" and that the "dialogue characteristics" of *The Saw Mill*, "far from being the racist caricature that superficial examination of blackface texts has sometimes presumed, may well represent attempts to capture a creole dialect shared across ethnic groups, in sometimes unexpected ways," see Smith, *The Creolization of American Culture*, 107–17; the quotations are from 111.

For a contemporaneous illustration of Roberts performing the song in blackface and in full Continental uniform, see Hutton, "The Negro on the Stage," 138. The image has been widely digitalized.

205 "*equestrian and comedy company*": The descriptive phrase is from Clapp, *A Record of the Boston Stage*, 216.

205 (*on a few . . . opposite each other*): *Boston Commercial Gazette*, 25 Dec. 1823, 3; *Boston Intelligencer*, 27 Dec. 1823, 7.

205 *He picked up . . . entertainments circa 1825*: He first advertises this song in the *Boston Commercial Gazette*, 13 June 1825, 3.

206 *Roberts had performed . . . in December 1822*: See, for example, *Baltimore American and Commercial Daily Advertiser*, 5–7 Dec. 1822.

206 "LECTURE ON VENTRILOQUISM . . . *of a child*": *Philadelphia Inquirer*, 25 March 1831, 3. Roberts describes his entertainment as "partly original and partly compiled from Matthews' [*sic*] Stage Coach Adventures."

206 "*Nichols and Roberts at Home*": *New York Daily Advertiser*, 17 Dec. 1829, 3.

208 "*formerly the celebrated Miss Lee Sugg*": *Philadelphia Inquirer*, 16 Dec. 1830, 3.

208 *He had had to cancel . . . applied to both men*: See *Philadelphia Inquirer*, 25 March 1831, 3; 16 May 1833, 2, 5 (benefit for the Roberts children); *Poulson's American Daily Advertiser* (Philadelphia), 5 Dec. 1832, 3 (Mrs. Roberts's death notice); *Charleston Southern Patriot*, 1 May 1833, 2 (Roberts's obituary).

209 *He traveled to Nashua . . . a few days*: *Nashua (NH) Gazette*, 12 Aug. 1831, 3.

209 *It was probably . . . interviewed him there*: [Hale], *Notes Made during an Excursion*, 92, reports that "a lecturer on astronomy" was also competing for perfor-

mance space when he met Potter. The lecturer was most probably a Mr. Wilbur, from Boston, who was lecturing in upper New England in the summer of 1831. We pick him up (doubtless on his way back to Boston) in Amherst, New Hampshire, in early August, then in Lowell, Massachusetts, two weeks later, then in Salem ten days later still. He traveled with two orreries and a variety of illuminated diagrams and was prepared to deliver a course of up to five or even more lectures on astronomy (see, for example, the *New Hampshire Sentinel* (Keene), 17 Jan. 1833, 3; *Dedham (MA) Patriot,* 18 Feb. 1831, 3; *Amherst (NH) Farmer's Cabinet,* 6 Aug. 1831, 3; *Lowell (MA) Mercury,* 20 Aug. 1831, 3; *Salem (MA) Gazette,* 30 Aug. 1831, 6; and 9 Sept. 1831.

209   *"Potter gave an entertainment . . . a long distance":* [Thyng], "Reminiscences in Life of Ventriloquist Potter," *Manchester (NH) Union,* 8 March 1895, 5.

209   *This time he opened . . . a half weeks:* Boston Patriot, 19 Oct. 1831, 3 (at Concert Hall); 22 Oct.–8 Nov. 1831 (at Julien Hall).

210   *now he partnered . . . a Mr. Burge:* Burge advertised in the *Boston Patriot,* 16 Aug. 1831. The notice of him also appeared in that newspaper (24 Aug. 1831, 7). Potter noted Burge's assistance in his advertisements in the same newspaper (10 Nov. 1831, 2) and in the *Boston Commercial Gazette,* 14 Nov. 1831, 3.

210   *disappeared from it . . . time in Boston:* Mr. Burge made at least one other appearance in America: in mid-January 1832, he appeared briefly in Lowell, Massachusetts, assisted by a Mr. Hovey—probably the same Mr. Hovey who had appeared briefly with Smith's equestrian theater troupe in Boston the preceding February (see *Lowell [MA] Journal,* 18 Jan. 1832, 3; and *Boston Patriot,* 4 Feb. 1831, 7).

210   *"Unseasonable Fruit.–Mr. Potter . . . time, Sept. 21":* Boston American Traveller, 15 Nov. 1831.

211   *(The story was . . . as New York):* The story in the *Boston American Traveller* was picked up by, among others, the *Nantucket Inquirer,* 26 Nov. 1831, 2; the *New York Mercury* 4, no. 12 (23 Nov. 1831): 74; and the *Boston Patriot,* 16 Nov. 1831, 2 (without mention of Potter).

211   *"a man of color":* [Hale], *Notes Made during an Excursion,* 92.

212   *Potter stopped over . . . a ghost-exorciser:* The story is told by Converse, *Legends of Woburn, 1642–1892,* 86–89.

213   NOTICE. *I Hereby . . . July 3, 1832:* New-Hampshire Patriot (Concord), 9, 16, and 23 July 1832.

214   *In 1829 . . . twice that number:* Yearly inventories of some livestock were recorded in the Andover Town Records as part of the "State and Town Taxes" for each year; see "Andover Town Records, 1751–1845," New Hampshire State Library.

215   *"gave great attention . . . under his sheds":* [Goodwin], "The Potter Place," 2.

215   *Early in 1834 . . . from his estate:* The real estate transactions are recorded in the Merrimack County (NH) Registry of Deeds: Book 35, 339; Book 41, 434; Book 45, 71.

215   *Butterfield had sued . . . finally won it:* Butterfield v. Potter wended through the Merrimack County (NH) Court of Common Pleas for several sessions. See April Term 1831, case 73.

216   *"He never lost . . . traffic or speculation":* Bell, *The Bench and Bar of New Hampshire,* 234.

216 *index of Merrimack County court actions:* The index was prepared as a finding aid by the New Hampshire State Archives, and may be consulted there. It probably misses cases in which Butterfield was involved as the second plaintiff or second defendant.

216 NOTICE. *Having found . . . March 18th, 1834:* New-Hampshire Patriot (Concord), 31 March 1834; 7 and 14 April 1834.

217 ANSWER TO RICHARD . . . *April 10. 1834:* New-Hampshire Patriot (Concord), 31 and 28 April 1834; 5 May 1834.

218 *Butterfield was now calling him . . . to account:* Butterfield's allusion to "a grudge of old" not only hints at the 1830 lawsuit for recovery of a debt and the 1831 John Sholes hearing but also evokes a story similar to this one, dating probably to 1827, that Goodwin reported in 1872: see above, 172n.

218 "THE *accomplished piece . . . April 31, 1834":* New-Hampshire Patriot (Concord), 5 May 1834, 3.

219 *in Concord and then . . . in Nashua:* Ibid., 1 June 1835, 3. Potter's advertisement for his Nashua performance appears in the *Nashua (NH) Gazette,* 3 July 1835, 3.

219 *four different doctors . . . amounted to twenty-one dollars:* Inventory, Richard Potter probate file, 1233, Merrimack Co. (NH) Registry of Deeds, Concord, NH.

219 *fifty cents for . . . at this time:* For a sampling of contemporaneous doctors' fees, see Dearborn, collator, *History of Salisbury, New Hampshire,* 402.

219 "*attended by a . . . highly appropriate sermon":* New-Hampshire Patriot (Concord), 28 Sept. 1835, 3.

219 "*public presentation of black respectability":* Sesay writes interestingly about the significance of public funerals for black Masons in "Emancipation and the Social Origins of Black Freemasonry, 1775–1800," 21–39; the quotation is from 35.

219 *Masonic lodges had . . . doctor, Tilton Elkins:* Eastman, *History of Andover, New Hampshire,* 1:348–49; Dearborn, collator, *History of Salisbury, New Hampshire,* 353–57.

221 "*He followed the . . . last heard from":* [Goodwin], "The Potter Place," 2.

221 *Ketchum soon provided some additional details:* Ketchum, "Richard Potter," 61.

221 *Eastman was later able to add:* Eastman, *History of Andover, New Hampshire,* 2:277.

221 *he had sold . . . in May 1837:* Merrimack County (NH) Registry of Deeds. Deed Books, 43:282, 45:346, 48:105, 48:225, 50:365.

221 *Dick Potter had . . . the American Museum:* Dick Potter advertisements: see, for example, the *New York Evening Star,* 10, 26, and 31 Aug. 1835.

222 *Dick Potter returned . . . few weeks earlier:* Blanc and Potter: see the *New York Evening Star,* 26 Oct.–12 Nov. 1835 (review, 29 Oct.); *New York Commercial Advertiser,* 27 Oct.–5 Dec. 1835. Blanc and Sutton: *New York Herald,* 5–24 Oct. 1835.

222 *Richard Potter's obituary . . . New York newspapers:* Richard Potter obituary notices appeared in the *New York Commercial Advertiser,* 30 Sept. 1835, 2; *New York Spectator,* 1 Oct. 1835, 3.

222 "*two skilful young . . . a continued roar":* New York Evening Star, 29 Oct. 1835, 2.

222 *he advertised in New Haven . . . as of gymnastics:* New Haven Daily Herald, 7 Dec.

1836, 4. The advertisement mistakenly advertises "Mr. I. POTTER, the celebrated Gymnastic Performer," but this must certainly be Potter junior.

222 *"RE-ENGAGEMENT OF MR. POTTER, The Celebrated Performer"*: Boston American Traveller, 24 March 1837, 3.

223 *Dick Potter now joined . . . as 1 April:* Boston Columbian Centinel, 1 April 1837, 3.

223 *The troupe soon . . . and then disbanded:* Portland (ME) Advertiser, 9 May 1837, 3; Thayer, *Annals of the American Circus,* 2:218.

223 *Through the summer . . . claimed the watch:* Merrimack County (NH) Court of Common Pleas, Feb. Term 1837, Lewis D. Bean v. Richard Potter, case no. 639; Sept. Term 1839, Enoch W. Eastman v. Richard Potter, case 096, affidavit from Daniel W. Hoyt.

224 *to judge from . . . a "yankee story":* Fellows's re-creation of "Old Potter's" act occurred on a ship bound from Boston to San Francisco during the California gold rush, in 1849. Fellows twice put on exhibitions for his fellow passengers. Moses Pearson Cogswell, a fellow passenger, kept a journal of the voyage, which lasted from 1 March 1 to 3 August. For Fellows's performances, see especially the entries of 8 May 1849 and 22 June 1849. Fellows's sleight of hand was well received; his attempts at comic songs and a Yankee dialogue were disasters. Cogwell's *Journal* is in the collection of the New Hampshire Historical Society.

224 *"Mr. POTTER, a . . . Marblehead, this evening":* Salem Gazette (MA), 9 Nov. 1838, 3.

224 *a receipt for . . . the following spring:* A receipt to "Messrs. Potter & Co." from Morrill and Densmore, publishers of the *Nashua (NH) Gazette,* acknowledging payment for "Printing 300 large handbills" puts Dick Potter in Nashua on 25 March 1839. The receipt, and one other, were saved by Stephen Fellows, who therefore must have been traveling with Dick Potter then (Milbourne Christopher Collection; viewed by courtesy of Maurine Christopher, 25 Feb. 1998).

224 *He left a . . . 1838 and 1839:* Merrimack County (NH) Court of Common Pleas, September Term 1838, Enoch W. Eastman v. Richard Potter, case 341 (Potter gave his promissory note for eighteen dollars on 9 Jan. 1838; March Term 1841, Asa Lowe v. Richard Potter, case 294 (Potter gave his promissory note for twenty dollars on 14 Oct. 1830 to Joseph C. Thompson, who then turned it over to Lowe).

224 *In 1841 he . . . Boston in September:* Mr. Potter, acrobat, with Ludlow and Smith's circus, 1841: Thayer, *Annals of the American Circus,* 2:274. With Welch and Mann's Circus: ibid., 2:119. The "Missouri Songsters": *Newburyport (MA) Herald,* 19–26 Dec. 1842; *New Hampshire Gazette* (Portsmouth), 20 Dec. 1842, 3; *Boston Daily Atlas,* 11 April 1843, 3.

224 *"Mr. Potter, the celebrated Hindoo juggler":* Philadelphia Public Ledger, 24 Feb. 1844, 2.

## Afterword

227 *Peter Benes aptly reminds us:* Benes, *For a Short Time Only,* 271–87.

228 *the long exposure . . . depth of field:* see Gates, "Epilogue: Frederick Douglass's Camera Obscura," 199.

As Stauffer, Trodd, and Bernier argue, Douglass was typical of his age in accepting the objectivity of photographs: "Photographers recognized that their medium lied—many self-consciously manipulated the image, solarizing it, airbrushing out unwanted subjects, or distorting it in other ways. But Douglass and most patrons of the art believed that the camera told the truth" (*Picturing Frederick Douglass,* xii).

228 *"the most photographed . . . the nineteenth century":* Stauffer, Trodd, and Bernier, *Picturing Frederick Douglass,* ix.

228 *"believed that photography . . . great democratic art":* Ibid., xii, x.

228 *"The very look . . . of his race":* James Russell Lowell, "The Prejudice of Color," qtd. ibid., xiii.

229 *Simon During's argument:* During, *Modern Enchantments,* 60.

229 *came to suspect it:* In the Boston area, as we have seen, Potter was always widely recognized as a black man (or "a man of color," in Hale's words). A recollection from many decades after his death suggests that, even in Boston, this recognition sometimes came with a racist sneer. An 1893 newspaper article on the history of Boston's grand old Concert Hall detoured to discuss Potter as one of the most memorable entertainers to have performed there (particularly referencing his exhibitions of 1825 and 1831). The author closely paraphrases Nason's brief account of Potter but introduces one particularly striking change. Where Nason had said, "Many persons still living can well remember his marvelous exploits," the *Boston Herald* writer instead said, "There are many still living in this city who remember 'nigger' Potter and his marvellous tricks" (*Boston Herald,* 11 April 1893, 4). This rare application of the racist epithet to Potter may simply reflect its author's 1893 sensibilities; but it may also reflect an increasing coarsening of racial attitudes infecting even Boston ca. 1825–31.

## Appendix B

243 *Potter might have . . . Italian Shades show in Boston: Boston Democrat,* 28 Sept. 1808, 3.

243 *Blancan's show included "the Broken Bridge": New York Daily Advertiser,* 2 Jan. 1809, 3.

243 *"The Broken Bridge" . . . popular in America:* on the popularity of the "Broken Bridge" in America, see Benes, *For a Short Time Only,* 164–66.

## Appendix C

249 *one of the archetypal stories of ventriloquism:* On Vattemare, see Jennings, *Theatrical and Circus Life,* 452. On "Scottish Haymakers," see Hogg, *Tales of Love and Mystery,* 27. For John Rannie's claim, see the *Tennessee Gazette* (Nashville), 9 Nov. 1805, 3. For Pinchbeck, see *The Expositor,* 56–57. For James Rannie, see his broadside "VENTRILOQUISM. The Ladies and Gentlemen of Boston," 1801. For Lee Sugg, see *Kirby's Wonderful and Eccentric Museum,* 3:388–89 (the anecdote also appeared in the *Manchester Mercury* [England], 17 June 1800, 4; and *Observer*

[London], 26 July 1801, 3). For Burns, see Kirby, *Kirby's Wonderful and Eccentric Museum,* 2:371–72; a briefer version also appears in Burns's obituary notice in the *Gentleman's Magazine,* 1 Jan. 1796, 84.

249 *"By the aid . . . hay become social":* Canadian Courant, 31 July 1819, 3.

249 *"give an imitation . . . hay in Portsmouth":* New York National Advocate, 26 Feb. 1819, 3.

# Bibliography

## Archival Sources

American Antiquarian Society, Worcester, Massachusetts
  Broadside: "Signior Manfredi, artist of agility, and rope dancer." 1803 (fig. 1).
Andover Historical Society, Andover, New Hampshire
  Andover Town Clerk Ledger, 1823–1830
  Charles Adams Bachelder scrapbooks
  Hilton, Marcia Frances. "History of the Town of Andover, NH: Additions and Corrections." Typescript, n.d.
Andover-Harvard Theology Library, Cambridge, Massachusetts
  Records of the First Church in Roxbury, 1733–1861
Blazing Star Lodge, Concord, New Hampshire
  Records of the Blazing Star Lodge 5810: December 1809–March 1847
Boston Public Library
  City of Boston tax records [1780–1821]. Microfilm.
Milbourne Christopher Collection, New York City
  Richard Potter broadsides
  Richard Potter, jr. receipts
City of Boston Archives, West Roxbury, Massachusetts
  Boston Tax Records, 1822–1918. City of Boston Archives, West Roxbury. Microfilm accessible online at:
  "Massachusetts, Boston Tax Records, 1822–1918." Images. FamilySearch. http://Family Search.org.
Connecticut Historical Society, Hartford
  James Rannie broadside (1810), "For the Benefit of Youth"
Dartmouth College, Rauner Special Collections Library
  Benton, C. C. "The Lafayette Hotel with Memories of Earlier Days." In A. B. Downs, comp., "Historical Material Relating to Lebanon, N.H.," 2:189. Typescript.
Faith Community Church (successor to First Church), Hopkinton, Massachusetts
  "Congregational Church Records 1724–1838." Original records.
General Register Office for Scotland, Edinburgh, Scotland
  Old Parish Registers of Scotland: Elgin
Grafton County (NH) Registry of Deeds, North Haverhill
Grand Masonic Lodge of Massachusetts, Boston

Hillsborough Co. (NH) Registry of Deeds, Nashua

Hopkinton Public Library, Hopkinton, Massachusetts

"Congregational Church Records 1724–1838." Microfilm.

Nason, Elias. "Notes for a History of Hopkinton, MA." Manuscript notes. Microfilm.

———. "Thrown away by Mrs. Pulver." Manuscript notes apparently toward Nason's biography of Charles Henry Frankland.

Massachusetts Historical Society, Boston

First Church (Charlestown, Boston, MA) Records, 1631–1980. "Vital Statistics 1797–1894," Box 3, Folder 9: "The Deaths from Jany 1ˢᵗ 1815 to the 1ˢᵗ Jany. 1816," "Deaths in the year, 1816."

Henry Cromwell, letter to William Price, 24 July 1786.

James Rannie broadside (1801), "VENTRILOQUISM. The Ladies and Gentlemen of Boston."

Massachusetts Land Records, 1620–1986

Microfilm accessible online at "Massachusetts Land Records, 1620–1986." Images. *FamilySearch*. http://FamilySearch.org: accessed 14 June 2016. County courthouses and offices, Massachusetts.

Massachusetts State Archives, Judicial Archives, Boston

Court records, Suffolk and Worcester Counties

Massachusetts Deaths, 1841–1915

Probate records, Middlesex County

Merrimack Co. (NH) Office of Probate, Concord

Merrimack Co. (NH) Registry of Deeds, Concord

Middlesex County (MA) Registry of Deeds, Cambridge

National Archives of Scotland, Edinburgh, Scotland

Circuit Court of Judiciary records

New Hampshire Antiquarian Society, Hopkinton

Ketchum, Silas. Manuscript draft (with variants) by his wife, Georgia C. Ketchum, of the essay he later published as "Richard Potter." "Historical Collections, Vol. 5, 1878–1958," pp. 169–84.

Richard Potter dancing shoe, donated by Stephen Fellows. 1983.1629.

Portrait of Hannah Colby Thompson, by Ruth Whittier Shute.

New Hampshire Historical Society, Concord

"Andover (N.H.) First Universalist Church Records, 1819–1832."

Cogswell, Moses Pearson. "Journal." Voyage on the ship Sweden from Boston to San Francisco, 1 March–3 Aug. 1849; journal continued through 26 Aug. 1849. 1933–1 Mss Diaries Cogswell.

New Hampshire State Archives, Concord

"Andover [NH] Selectmen Reports and Accounts, 1860–1882"

Court records, Hillsborough and Merrimack Counties

Roster of Officers, 1780–1840. No. 3, "Justices of the Peace in the County of Merrimack, 1820–1830"; No. 4, "Justices of the Peace in the County of Merrimack, 1830–1840."

New Hampshire State Library, Concord
    New Hampshire Town Records. Microfilm.
New London (NH) Town Archives, New London
    Richard Potter letter, 1823 (fig. 7)
New York County City Register's Office, New York
    Mayor's Court Records
Norfolk County (MA) Registry of Deeds, Dedham
Peabody Essex Museum, James Duncan Phillips Library, Salem, Massachusetts
    Andrew Dunlap (1794–1835) Papers
    James Rannie broadside (1810), "For the Benefit of Youth"
Prince Hall Records, Minutes of African Lodge, Boston, 1807–1846
Rhode Island Judicial Archives, Pawtucket
    Providence County Court Records

## Other Sources

*The Acts and Resolves, Public and Private, of the Province of the Massachusetts Bay.* Vol. 4. Boston: Wright and Potter, 1890.

Aldrich, Lewis Cass, comp. *History of Ontario County, New York.* Edited by George S. Conover. Syracuse, NY: D. Mason & Co., 1893.

Alford, Terry. *Prince among Slaves.* New York: Harcourt Brace Jovanovich, 1977.

Anthony, Susan B., and Ida Husted Harper, eds. *History of Woman Suffrage.* Vol. 4: 1883–1900. Rochester, NY, 1902.

Baldwin, Thomas W., comp. *Vital Records of Framingham, Massachusetts to the Year 1850.* Boston: Wright and Potter, 1911.

———, comp. *Vital Records of Sharon, Massachusetts, to the Year 1850.* Boston: Stanhope, 1909.

Barrett, Walter [Joseph Alfred Scoville]. *The Old Merchants of New York City.* 3rd ser. New York: Carleton, 1865.

Barry, William. *A History of Framingham, Massachusetts.* Boston: Heritage, 1847.

Bassett, William. *History of the Town of Richmond, Cheshire County, New Hampshire.* Boston: C. W. Calkins & Co., 1884.

Bauer, F. Marshall. *Marblehead's Pygmalion: Finding the Real Agnes Surriage.* Charleston, SC: History Press, 2010.

Bell, Charles H. *The Bench and Bar of New Hampshire.* Boston: Houghton, Mifflin, 1894.

Benes, Peter. *For a Short Time Only: Itinerants and the Resurgence of Popular Culture in Early America.* Amherst: University of Massachusetts Press, 2016.

*Boston Births from A.D. 1700 to A.D. 1800.* Report of the Record Commissioners of the City of Boston. Vol. 24. Boston: Rockwell and Churchill, 1894.

*Boston Directory.* Boston: publisher varies (John Norman, 1789; John West, 1796–1803; Edward Cotton, 1805–18; John H. A. Frost and Charles Stimpson Jr., 1820–26; Stimpson and Clapp, 1832). 1789, 1796, 1798, 1800, 1803, 1805, 1807, 1809, 1810, 1813, 1816, 1818, 1823, 1832.

Bowen, Abel. *Bowen's Picture of Boston: or The citizen's and stranger's guide to the metropolis of Massachusetts, and its environs.* Boston: Otis, Broaders, and Co., 1838.

Brewster, Charles Warren. *Rambles about Portsmouth.* 2 vols. Portsmouth, NH, 1859–69.

Brooks, Lynn Matluck. *John Durang: Man of the American Stage.* Amherst, NY: Cambria, 2011.

Buckingham, Joseph T. *Personal Memoirs and Recollections of Editorial Life.* 2 vols. Boston: Ticknor and Fields, 1852.

Burger, Baudouin. *L'activité théâtrale au Québec (1765–1825).* Ottawa: Les Editions Parti Pris, 1974.

Burke, Peter. *Popular Culture in Early Modern Europe.* Cambridge University Press, 1978. Rev. reprint. Aldershot, England: Scolar Press, 1994.

Chapman, Joseph Warren, comp. *Vital Records of Marblehead, Massachusetts to the End of the Year 1849.* Salem, MA: Essex Institute, 1903.

Child, David L. *Review of a Report to the House of Representatives of the Commonwealth of Massachusetts, on the Case of William Vans.* Boston, 1833.

Christopher, Milbourne. *Magic: A Picture History.* New York: Dover, 1991. (Originally published as *Panorama of Magic,* 1962.)

Clapp, William Wieland. *A Record of the Boston Stage.* Boston: John Munroe and Co., 1853.

Coil, Henry Wilson. "A Documentary Account of Prince Hall and Other Black Fraternal Orders." St. Louis: Missouri Lodge of Research, 1982.

*Constitution and Laws of the State of New Hampshire.* Dover, 1805.

Converse, Parker Lindall. *Legends of Woburn, 1642–1892.* Woburn, MA, 1892.

Crocker, Matthew H. *The Magic of the Many: Josiah Quincy and the Rise of Mass Politics in Boston, 1800–1830.* Amherst: University of Massachusetts Press, 1999.

Currier, John J. *History of Newburyport, Massachusetts 1764–1905.* Newburyport, MA: Damrell and Upham, 1909.

Curtis, Nancy C. *Black Heritage Sites: An African American Odyssey and Finder's Guide.* Chicago: American Library Association, 1996.

Cushing, John D. "The Cushing Court and the Abolition of Slavery in Massachusetts: More Notes on the 'Quock Walker Case.'" *American Journal of Legal History* 5 (1961): 118–44.

Davis, James, and Dudley B. Rosseter. "A Brief Account of the Origin and Progress of the Boston Female Society for Missionary Purposes." Boston: Lincoln and Edmands, 1818.

Davis, William T. *Plymouth Memories of an Octogenarian.* Plymouth, MA: Memorial, 1906.

Dawes, Edwin A. *The Great Illusionists.* Secaucus, NJ: Chartwell, 1979.

Dearborn, John J., collator. *History of Salisbury, New Hampshire.* Manchester, NH: William E. Moore, 1890.

Dexter, Henry M. "Memoir of the Rev. George Punchard." *Proceedings of the Massachusetts Historical Society* 19 (1881–82): 262–64.

Dibdin, James C. *The Annals of the Edinburgh Stage.* Edinburgh: Richard Cameron, 1888.

Diman, Louise. *Leaves from a Family Tree: being random records, letters, and traditions of the Jones, Stimson, and Clarke families of Hopkinton, Medfield, Norton, and Boston, Massachusetts and Rhode Island.* Providence: Roger Williams Press, 1941.

"Discourse before the Society for Propagating the Gospel among the Indians and Others in North America." (Author varies. Boston: publisher varies.) Reports for 1805 (published in 1806), 1806 (1806), 1807 (1808), 1808 (1808), 1810 (1810), 1811 (1812). (The reports for 1810 and 1811 were included in volumes titled "Signs of the Times. A Sermon, Preached before the Society . . ." and "A Sermon, Delivered before the Society . . ."), respectively.

Dodd, Henry Martyn. "Centennial of the Old First Congregational Church, Windham, New York 1803–1903." www.rootsweb.ancestry.com/~nygreen2/1st_congregational_church_windham.htm.

Dodd, William G. "Theatrical Entertainment in Early Florida." *Florida Historical Quarterly* 25 (1946): 121–74.

Dogra, Ramesh C., and Urmila Dogra. *A Dictionary of Hindu Names.* New Delhi: Aditya Prakashan, 1992.

Dorman, Franklin A. *Twenty Families of Color in Massachusetts 1742–1998.* Boston: New England Historical Genealogical Society, 1998.

Drake, Joseph Rodman, and Fitz Greene Halleck. *The Croakers.* New York: Bradford Club, 1860.

Dunlap, Andrew. *An Oration, Delivered at the Request of the Republicans of Boston, at Faneuil Hall, on the Fourth of July, 1822.* Boston: True and Greene, 1822.

Dunn, Richard S. "'Dreadful Idlers' in the Cane Fields: The Slave Labor Pattern on a Jamaican Sugar Estate, 1762–1831." *Journal of Interdisciplinary History* 17 (1987): 801.

During, Simon. *Modern Enchantments: The Cultural Power of Secular Magic.* Cambridge: Harvard University Press, 2002.

Earman, Cynthia D. "A Census of Early Boardinghouses." *Washington History* 12 (2000): 118–21.

Eastman, John R. *History of the Town of Andover, New Hampshire 1751–1906.* Concord, NH: Rumford Printing Co., 1910.

*Encyclopedia of African American History.* Edited by Leslie M. Alexander and Walter C. Rucker. 3 vols. paginated as one. Santa Barbara, CA: ABC-CLIO, 2010.

Endicott, Frederic, ed. *The Record of Births, Marriages and Deaths and Intentions of Marriage, in the Town of Stoughton from 1727 to 1800, and in the Town of Canton from 1797 to 1845.* Canton, MA: William Bense, 1896.

Felt, Joseph Barlow. *History of Ipswich, Essex, and Hamilton.* Cambridge, MA: Charles Folsom, 1834.

Foote, Henry Wilder. *Annals of King's Chapel from the Puritan Age of New England to the Present Day.* 2 vols. Boston: Little, Brown, 1896.

Forbes, Harriette Merrifield. *The Hundredth Town: Glimpses of Life in Westborough, 1717–1817.* Boston: Rockwell and Churchill, 1889.

Foster, F. Apthorp, ed. *Vital Records of Hopkinton, Massachusetts, to the year 1850.* Boston: New England Historical Genealogical Society, 1911.

Gandhi, Maneka. *The Penguin Book of Hindu Names.* New Delhi: Viking, 1989.

Gates, Henry Louis, Jr. "Epilogue: Frederick Douglass's Camera Obscura: Representing the Anti-Slave 'Clothed and in Their Own Form." In Stauffer, Trodd, and Bernier, *Picturing Frederick Douglass,* 197–216.

Gibbs, Jenna Marie. *"Performing the Temple of Liberty: Slavery, Rights, and Revolution in Transatlantic Theatricality (1760s–1830s)."* Ph.D. diss., University of California, Los Angeles, 2008.

[Goodwin, Moses B.]. "The Potter Place." *Merrimack Journal (Franklin, NH),* 8 Nov. 1872, 2.

"The Great Magician." *Boston Journal,* 31 July 1874, 1.

[Greenwood, Ethan Allen.] "A List of Portraits Painted by Ethan Allen Greenwood, 1801–1824." *Proceedings of the American Antiquarian Society,* n.s., 56 (1947): 129–53.

[Hale, Nathan.] *Notes Made during an Excursion to the Highlands of New-Hampshire and Lake Winnipiseogee.* Andover, MA: Flagg, Gould, and Newman, 1833.

Haller, John S., Jr. *The People's Doctors: Samuel Thomson and the American Botanical Movement, 1790–1860.* Carbondale: Southern Illinois University Press, 2000.

Haynes, William. *Casco Bay Yarns.* New York: D. O. Haynes, 1916.

Highfill, Philip H., Kalman A. Burnim, and Edward A. Langhans. *A Biographical Dictionary of Actors, Actresses, Musicians, Dancers, Managers and Other Stage Personnel in London, 1660–1800.* 16 vols. Carbondale: Southern Illinois University Press, 1973–93.

Hill, George Handel. *Scenes from the Life of an Actor. Compiled from the Journals, Letters, and Memoranda of the Late Yankee Hill.* New York: Garrett, 1853.

Hilton, John, T. "Address, Delivered before the African Grand Lodge of Boston, No. 459, June 24th, 1828." Boston: David Hooton, 1828.

Hinks, Peter P. *To Awaken My Afflicted Brethren: David Walker and the Problem of Antebellum Slave Resistance.* University Park: Pennsylvania State University Press, 1997.

"An Historical Account of the Most Celebrated English Beauties." *Universal Museum* 2 (December 1763): 623.

Hoadley, Charles J. *The Public Records of the State of Connecticut, from May, 1778, to April, 1780, Inclusive.* Hartford, 1895.

"Hocus-Pocus Potter." *Boston American Traveller,* 6 Nov. 1851, 4.

Hogg, James. *Tales of Love and Mystery.* Edited by David Groves. Edinburgh: Canongate, 1985.

Holmes, Oliver Wendell. *The Complete Poetical Works of Oliver Wendell Holmes.* Boston: Houghton, Mifflin, 1910.

———. *Over the Teacups.* Boston: Houghton, Mifflin, 1891.

Houdini, Harry. *The Unmasking of Robert-Houdin.* New York: Publishers Printing, 1908.

Hurd, D[uane] Hamilton, comp. *History of Middlesex County, Massachusetts.* Philadelphia: J. W. Lewis, 1890.

Hutton, Laurence. "The Negro on the Stage." *Harper's New Monthly Magazine* 79 (June 1889): 131–47.

James, Reese D. *Old Drury of Philadelphia: A History of the Philadelphia Stage, 1800–1835.* Philadelphia: University of Pennsylvania Press, 1932.

Jay, Ricky. *Learned Pigs and Fireproof Women.* New York: Villard, 1987.

Jennings, John J. *Theatrical and Circus Life; or, Secrets of the Stage, Green-Room and Sawdust Arena.* St. Louis: Sun, 1883.

Jones, Jesse H. "Henry Kemble Oliver." In *Seventeenth Annual Report of the [Massachusetts] Bureau of Statistics of Labor,* 1–48. Boston: Wright and Potter, 1886.

Joslyn, Roger D. *Vital Records of Charlestown, Massachusetts to the Year 1850.* Vol. 1. Boston: New England Historic Genealogical Society, 1984.

Kantrowitz, Stephen. "'Intended for the Better Government of Man': The Political History of African American Freemasonry in the Era of Emancipation." *Journal of American History* 96 (2010): 1001–26.

———. *More Than Freedom: Fighting for Black Citizenship in a White Republic, 1829–1889.* New York: Penguin, 2012.

Ketchum, Silas. *The Original Sources of Historical Knowledge. A Plea for Their Preservation.* Pamphlet. Windsor, CT: George Crowell Ketchum, 1879.

———. "Richard Potter." *Granite Monthly* 2 (1878): 56–61.

Kilroe, Edwin Patrick. "*Saint Tammany and the Origin of the Society of Tammany or Columbian Order in the City of New York.*" Ph.D. diss., Columbia University, 1913.

Kirby, R. S. *Kirby's Wonderful and Eccentric Museum; or, Magazine of Remarkable Characters.* 6 vols. London: R. S. Kirby, 1820.

Knapp, Samuel L. *Life of Lord Timothy Dexter.* 1838. Reprint, Boston: J. E. Tilton and Co., 1852.

Lambert, David Allen, comp. *Vital Records of Stoughton, Massachusetts to the End of the Year 1850.* Braintree: Massachusetts Society of Mayflower Descendants, 2008.

*Laws of New Hampshire. Volume Ten, Second Constitutional Period, 1829–1835.* Concord, NH: Evans, 1922.

*The Laws of the State of New-Hampshire, Enacted since June 1, 1815.* Vol. 2. Concord, NH: Isaac Hill, 1824.

Letter, Joseph J. "New York in 1819: Defining a Local Public in the 'Croaker' Poems of Joseph Rodman Drake and Fitz-Greene Halleck." *American Periodicals* 21 (2011): 50–71.

Lindfors, Bernth. *Ira Aldridge: The Early Years, 1807–1833.* Rochester, NY: University of Rochester Press, 2011.

Little, Nina Fletcher. "Carved Figures by Samuel McIntyre and His Contemporaries." *Essex Institute Historical Collections* 93 (1957): 179–99.

Littlefield, Daniel C. *Rice and Slaves: Ethnicity and the Slave Trade in Colonial South Carolina.* Baton Rouge: Louisiana State University Press, 1981.

Loring, James Spear. *The Hundred Boston Orators Appointed by the Municipal Societies and Other Public Bodies, from 1770 to 1852.* Boston: John P. Jewett, 1852.

Lyford, James O., ed. "The Thompsonian Infirmary, Concord." *Granite State Monthly* 23 (1897): 345–51.

Lyman, John D. "Andover." Letter to the editor. *Merrimack Journal* (Franklin, NH), 20 April 1888, page unknown. From the Charles Adams Bachelder scrapbooks, "Clippings from Merrimack Journal for 1886, 1887, 1888 (remnants) and Local Personal and Missellaneous [sic] Scraps," pp. 45–46. Andover Historical Society.

MacEacheren, Elaine. "Emancipation of Slavery in Massachusetts: A Reexamination 1770–1790." *Journal of Negro History* 55 (1970): 289–306.

"Man of Mystery World Famous." *Boston Sunday Herald,* 11 Feb. 1906, 52.

[Manfredi, Peter.] "Exhibition, at the Thespian Hotel, Pearl-Street, Albany. A numerous company of rope dancers," 19 Sept. 1805. Broadside. Early American Imprints, 2nd ser., no. 8414.

*Manual of the First Congregational Church in Hopkinton, Massachusetts.* Boston: Alfred Mudge and Son, 1881.

*Massachusetts Soldiers and Sailors of the Revolutionary War.* Vol. 15. Boston: Wright and Potter, 1906.

McGlenen, Edward W., comp. *Boston Marriages from 1700 to 1809.* Vol. 2: 1752–1809. *A Volume of Records Relating to the Early History of Boston.* Vol. 30. Boston: Municipal Printing Office, 1903.

Moore, Lillian. "New York's First Ballet Season." *Bulletin of the New York Public Library* 64 (1960): 478–91.

Morton, Thomas. *The Slave; A Musical Drama, in Three Acts.* 2nd ed. London: John Miller, 1818.

Moulton, H. J. *Houdini's History of Magic in Boston, 1792–1915.* Glenwood, IL: Meyerbooks, 1983.

Nason, Elias. "Hopkinton." In *History of Middlesex County, Massachusetts,* ed. Samuel Adams Drake. Vol. 1. Boston, 1880.

———. *Sir Charles Henry Frankland, Baronet: or Boston in the Colonial Times.* Albany, NY: J. Munsell, 1865.

*The National Cyclopaedia of American Biography.* Vol. 10. New York: J. T. White, 1900.

Nell, W[illiam] C[ooper]. *The Colored Patriots of the American Revolution, with Sketches of Several Distinguished Colored Persons.* Boston: R. F. Wallcut, 1855.

Nelson, Walter Ralph. *History of Goshen, New Hampshire.* Concord, NH: Evans Printing Co., 1957.

Oliver, Henry Kemble. "Richard Potter, the Magician and Ventriloquist." Letter to the editor. *Boston Journal,* 7 Aug. 1874, 1.

[Parkman, Ebenezer.] *The Diary of Rev. Ebenezer Parkman, of Westborough, Mass.* Edited by Harriette M. Forbes. Worcester, MA: Westborough Historical Society, 1899.

———. "Visit to Sir Charles Henry Frankland, Hopkinton, Mass. Rev. C. [*sic*] Parkman's Diary." *New England Historical and Genealogical Register* 16 (1862): 220.

Pinchbeck, W. F. *The Expositor; or, Many Mysteries Unravelled.* Boston: printed for the author, 1805.

Porter, Eliphalet. "A Discourse before the Society for Propagating the Gospel among the Indians and Others in North-America." Boston: Munroe, Francis, and Parker, 1808.

Porter, Henry C. *The History of the Theatres of Brighton, from 1774 to 1886.* Brighton: King and Thorne, 1886.

*Proceedings of the Commissioners of Indian Affairs, appointed by law for the Extinguishment of Indian Titles in the State of New York.* Intro. and notes by Franklin B. Hough. Albany: Joel Munsell, 1861.

Prout, Henry Hedges. "Old Times in Windham, 17." *Windham (NY) Journal,* 17 June 1869. www.rootsweb.ancestry.com/~nygreen2/prout_17.htm.

*The Public Laws of the State of Rhode-Island and Providence Plantation.* Providence: Miller and Hutchens, 1822.

*Revised Statutes of the State of New Hampshire.* Passed 23 December 1842. Concord, NH: John F. Brown, 1851.

Reynolds, Frederick. *Laugh When You Can.* Boston: Oliver C. Greenleaf, 1809.

Roach, Joseph. *It.* Ann Arbor: University of Michigan Press, 2007.

Rose, Willie Lee, ed. *A Documentary History of Slavery in America.* Athens: University of Georgia Press, 1999.

Ross, Peter. *The Scot in America.* New York: Raeburn, 1896.

Saxe, John Godfrey. *The Poems of John Godfrey Saxe.* Boston: Ticknor and Fields, 1868.

Saxon, A. H. *The Life and Art of Andrew Ducrow and the Romantic Age of the English Circus.* Hamden, CT: Archon, 1978.

Sesay, Chernoh M. "Emancipation and the Social Origins of Black Freemasonry, 1775–1800." In *All Men Free and Brethren: Essays on the History of African American Freemasonry,* edited by Peter P. Hinks and Stephen Kantrowitz, 21–39. Ithaca: Cornell University Press, 2013.

Smith, Christopher J. *The Creolization of American Culture: William Sidney Mount and the Roots of Blackface Minstrelsy.* Urbana: University of Illinois Press, 2013.

Stauffer, John, Zoe Trodd, and Celeste-Marie Bernier. *Picturing Frederick Douglass: An Illustrated Biography of the Nineteenth Century's Most Photographed American.* New York: Liveright, 2015.

Stimson, Frederic J. "Sir Harry Frankland." *New York Times,* 3 Dec. 1910, BR12.

Swindells, Julia. "Abolitionist Theatre." In *The Encyclopedia of Romantic Literature,* edited by Frederick Burwick. 3 vols. Chichester, England: Wiley-Blackwell, 2012.

Temple, J. H. *History of Framingham, Massachusetts.* Town of Framingham, 1887.

Thayer, Stuart. *Annals of the American Circus.* Vol. 2: 1830–1847. Seattle, WA: Peanut Butter, 1986.

[Thyng, J. Warren]. "Reminiscences in Life of Ventriloquist Potter." *Manchester (NH) Union,* 8 March 1895, 5.

Todd, William Cleaves. *Timothy Dexter.* Boston: David Clapp and Son, 1886.

Vedder, Jessie Van Vechten. *History of Greene County.* Catskill, NY, 1927.

Vox, Valentine. *I Can See Your Lips Moving: The History and Art of Ventriloquism.* Studio City, CA: Players, 1993.

Wesley, Charles H. *Prince Hall: Life and Legacy.* 2nd ed. United Supreme Council, Southern Jurisdiction, Prince Hall Affiliation, 1983.

Weston, Mrs. F. E. "The Valentines of Boston and Hopkinton." Chapter 15 of T. W. Valentine, *The Valentines in America 1644–1874.* New York: Clark and Maynard, 1874.

White, Arthur O. "The Black Leadership Class and Education in Antebellum Boston." *Journal of Negro Education* 42 (1973): 504–15.

———. "Prince Saunders: An Instance of Social Mobility among Antebellum New England Blacks." *Journal of Negro History* 60 (1975): 526–35.

White, Shane. *Stories of Freedom in Black New York.* Cambridge: Harvard University Press, 2002.

Wilder, Alexander. *History of Medicine.* New Sharon, ME: New England Eclectic, 1901.

Williams, Greg H. *The French Assault on American Shipping, 1793–1813: A History and Comprehensive Record of Merchant Marine Losses.* Jefferson, NC: McFarland 2009.

Woodworth, Olive N., comp. "Men of Greene County in the American Revolution," www.rootsweb.ancestry.com/~nygreen2/rw_-_men_of_greene_county.htm.

Wyman, Thomas Bellows. *The Genealogies and Estates of Charlestown, Massachusetts 1629–1818.* 1879; repr., Somersworth, NH: New England History Press, 1982.

Wyshak, Grace, and Rose E. Frisch. "Evidence for a Secular Trend in Age of Menarche." *New England Journal of Medicine* 306 (1982): 1033–35.

Zobel, Hiller B. "Jonathan Sewall: A Lawyer in Conflict." *Proceedings of the Cambridge Historical Society* 40 (1964–66): 123–36.

# Index

Woonsocket, Rhode Island, 146–47, 236
Worcester, Massachusetts, 26, 104, 168, 172, 238

Yellow Banks (now Owensboro), Kentucky, 128

York (now Toronto), Upper Canada, 84, 95, 119, 126, 232
York, Lewis, 179, 183

Zaneville, Ohio, 126, 235
Zebere, Silva (fortune teller), 140–41